THE CONTRIBUTIONS OF INFRASTRUCTURE AND HUMAN DEVELOPMENT TO ECONOMIC GROWTH IN GUJARAT

An Empirical Evidence

Dr Gargi Ghosh

KALPAZ

ISBN: 978-93-5128-158-0
Price : ₹ 1250

First Published, 2016

Published by

Kalpaz Publications
C-30, Satyawati Nagar,
Delhi-110052
Ph. : 9212142040
E-mail: kalpaz@hotmail.com

Laser Typesetting : Abhishek Mandal, Delhi
Printed at : G. Print Process, Delhi

Cataloging in Publication Data—DK
Courtesy: D.K. Agencies (P) Ltd. <docinfo@dkagencies.com>

Ghosh, Gargi, author.
The contributions of infrastructure and human development to economic growth in Gujarat : an empirical evidence / Dr. (Ms) Gargi Ghosh.
pages cm
Includes bibliographical references (pages) and index.
ISBN 9789351281580

1. Infrastructure (Economics)—India—Gujarat. 2. Economic indicators—India—Gujarat. 3. Social indicators—India—Gujarat. 4. Economic development—India—Gujarat. I. Title.

DDC 338.95475 23

Contents

List of Tables

List of Figures

List of Appendices

List of Abbreviations and Acronyms

AIFE	Adjusted Intensity of Formal Education
BMI	Body Mass Index
BPL	Below Poverty Line
CAG	Comptroller and Auditor General
CAGR	Compound Annual Growth Rate
CHC	Community Health Centre
EG	Economic Growth
GER	Gross Enrolment Ratio
HD	Human Development
HDI	Human Development Index
IFE	Intensity of Formal Education
IMR	Infant Mortality Rate
LEB	Life Expectancy at Birth
MMR	Maternal Mortality Rate
MPCE	Monthly Per Capita Consumption Expenditure
NHDR	National Human Development Report
NSDP	Net State Domestic Product
PBD	Per Capita Bank Deposit
PCA	Principal Component Analysis
PHC	Primary Health Centre
SDP	State Domestic Product
TFR	Total Fertility Rate
U5MR	Under-Five Mortality Rate
VECM	Vector Error Correction Model
WAEII	Weighted Aggregate Economic Infrastructure Index
WASII	Weighted Aggregate Social Infrastructure Index
WAII	Weighted Aggregate Infrastructure Index
WAIEG	Weighted Aggregate Index of Economic Growth

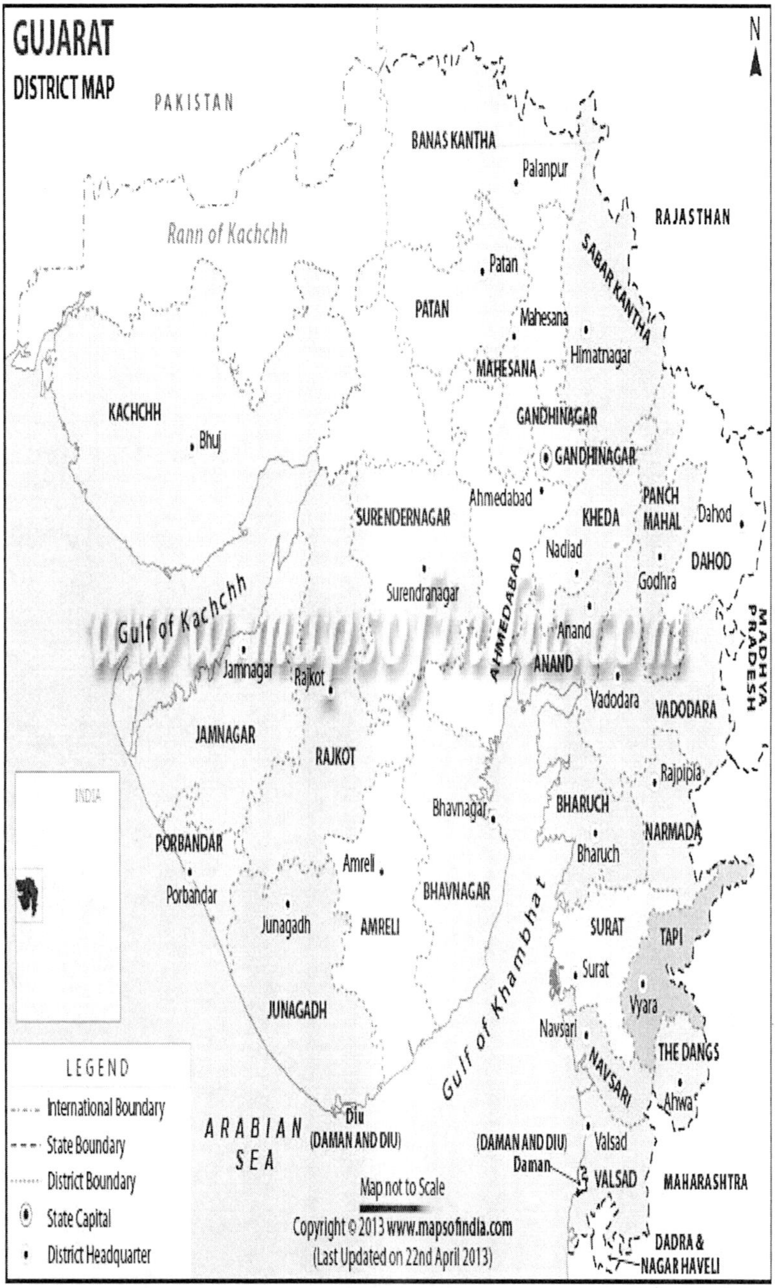

Source: Downloaded from http://www.mapsofindia.com/maps/gujarat/gujarat-district-map.jpg

Acknowledgements

At the outset I express my gratitude to the Almighty for giving me an opportunity and ability to be a small part within the large plethora of research. I would like to express my most heartfelt gratitude to all the gifted people who have provided me their unprecedented and valuable help towards the completion of my book.

My thanks are due to the Library Staff of Department of Economics, Panjab University, Chandigarh for their whole hearted co-operation. I appreciate the help of Directorate of Economics and Statistics, Government of Gujarat, Gandhinagar for supplying me required data.

I must express my profound appreciation and owe very much to my husband, Mr Rupak Mukherjee, for his tremendous patience, inspiration and for the endurance he had put up with me during the entire period of my study.

Dr Gargi Ghosh

Preface

Infrastructure facilities and Human resources both are essential ingredients which promote economic growth. Availability of adequate infrastructural facilities is not only a precondition, but also a fundamental ingredient in shaping the pace of economic growth. Again, Human Development essentially means, the expansion of opportunities for people through improvement in their capabilities which promotes economic growth as well as promoted by it.

Gujarat is a fast growing state with high economic growth on one hand and comparatively low human development on the other. Though, Gujarat's economy has shown a consistently increasing rate of growth-Compound Annual Growth Rate (CAGR) of per capita Net State Domestic Product (NSDP) at factor cost and constant prices (1999-2000) has gone up from 3.045 per cent (in the time period 1980-81 to 1985-86) to 7.573 per cent (in the time period 1990-91 to 1995-96) and became 8.763 per cent (in the time period 2005-06 to 2009-10), yet the state was unable to improve its rank in HDI and sustained its rank in sixth position among 15 major Indian states [as per National Human Development Report (NHDR) 2001 and India Human Development Report 2011].

It is in this background that the present study is set to analyse the relationship between infrastructure, economic growth and human development in Gujarat using sophisticated econometric techniques. Overall, the study concludes that Gujarat is a state with high economic growth but comparatively low human development. The conclusions and policy implications derived and suggestions given may be useful for policy makers.

Dr Gargi Ghosh

1

Introduction

1.1 Introduction

Modern Gujarat has one of the fastest growing economies in India. It is one of the main trade and commerce centers of India. Gujarat accounts for six per cent of India's geographical area and five per cent of population according to 2011 census and contributed 7.48 per cent of India's GDP in 2010-11 (at constant prices). Gujarat's economy has shown a consistently increasing rate of growth, Compound Annual Growth Rate (CAGR) of per capita Net State Domestic Product (NSDP) at factor cost and constant prices (1999-2000) has gone up from 3.045 per cent (in the time period 1980-81 to 1985-86) to 7.573 per cent (in the time period 1990-91 to 1995-96) and became 8.763 per cent (in the time period 2005-06 to 2009-10). Gujarat's GSDP at factor cost and current prices increased from Rs 109861 crore in 1999-00 to Rs189118 crore in 2004-05 and became Rs 427555 crore in 2009-10. Gujarat obtained 3rd rank with per capita NSDP Rs 48511 among 15 major states, after Maharashtra (achieved first rank with Rs 57458 per capita NSDP) and Haryana (achieved second rank with Rs 54884 per capita NSDP) in 2009-10. Gujarat improved its economic performance remarkably in almost all constituents of secondary and tertiary sectors Gujarat is accelerating towards the process of urbanisation and modernisation due to fast growing economy of the state.

The State emerged stronger and a beacon of hope for the rest of the country in terms of economic development. But when the focus is shifted toward education or health condition of the state, the picture becomes different and not comparable with rapid economic prosperity of the state. There are some crucial problems like- disparities between the social and economic infrastructure development, comparatively low Human

Development Index (HDI) etc. in the state Gujarat. As per National Human Development Report (NHDR) 2001 and India Human Development Report 2011 the state was unable to improve its rank in HDI and sustained its rank in sixth position among 15 major Indian states. Though, Gujarat obtained 79.31 per cent of literacy rate (as per Census 2011), yet there is strong discrimination between male (literacy rate 87.23 per cent as per Census 2011) and female (literacy rate 70.73 per cent as per Census 2011) literacy rates. As per 2007-08 data (ref: India Human Development Report, 2011, p. 371), there were 21.3 per cent out of school children (6-17 years) in Gujarat and obtained 11th rank among 15 major states of India (in ascending order). Gujarat's overall LEB was 69.1 in the time period 2006-10 and obtained fifth rank among 15 major states of India. Gujarat's Infant Mortality Rate (IMR) was 48 in 2009 and the state obtained seventh rank among 15 major states of India. So, Gujarat's performance of education and health sector was not as good as its economic performance. It experienced comparatively higher percentage of out of school children (6-17 years), low life expectancy at birth, high infant mortality rate etc.

Gujarat is a fast growing state with high economic growth on one hand and comparatively low human development on the other. Infrastructure and human development both are the crucial ingredients of economic growth. In this study the contribution of infrastructure and human development behind Gujarat's rapid economic growth and the causal relationship between them have been examined empirically.

Infrastructure is an essential ingredient for expansion, diversification and modernisation of the economy culminating in an improvement in living standard and to keep the economy moving forward. It is universally accepted that if the goals of development are to be achieved an efficient and adequate infrastructure is an important precondition. Infrastructure is the physical framework of a country that helps the country in its progress and prosperity. Inadequacy of Infrastructure is the major reason for the underdevelopment of a country.

Infrastructure contributes to economic growth both by increasing productivity and by providing amenities which enhance the quality of life. Infrastructure services act as intermediate inputs of production and any shortfall in these inputs hinders the expansion in output, income, employment and profitability of production. All constituents of infrastructure are complementary to each other and are essential and integral part of economic growth. Access to adequate infrastructure brings progress and prosperity to both individual and the economy. The importance of infrastructure for sustained economic growth is well recognised. High transaction costs arising from inadequate and inefficient infrastructure can prevent the economy from realising its full growth potential regardless of the progress on other fronts. A number of research studies have brought to the fore that infrastructure development always brings economic prosperity and adequate and efficient infrastructure is a pre-condition for achieving higher growth, which in turn paves way for welfare society.

According to World Development Report (1994) "Infrastructure for Development", it is argued that, "The adequacy of infrastructure helps to determine one country's success and another's failure-in diversifying production, expanding trade, coping with population growth, reducing poverty or improving environmental conditions — a one per cent increase in the stock of infrastructure is associated with a one per cent increase in GDP across all countries."

In this report it is also assessed that economic development and infrastructure facilities have direct positive relationship and significant level of infrastructure facilities are needed for overall development of a country. Infrastructure provisions must be fashioned as per the needs and circumstances of the country, which vary widely.

The term infrastructure has been used since 1927 to refer collectively to the roads, bridges, rail lines, and similar public works that are required for development of an economy.

Generally, infrastructure can be classified as:

1. **Social infrastructure**—water supply, sanitation, sewage disposal, education, health and such others.
2. **Economic infrastructure**—transportation, electricity, communication, irrigation, banking and such others.

In developed nations the meaning of 'infrastructure' has shifted from physical infrastructure (e.g. roads, airports, seaports, telecommunications, water distribution system, sanitation etc.) to notions of softer types of infrastructure such as information system and knowledge bases.

According to Planning Commission (Secretariat of Infrastructure) Report (2008), 'While Infrastructure is recognised as a crucial input for economic development, there is no clear definition of infrastructure according to the current usage of the term in India. For policy formulation, setting of sectoral targets and monitoring projects, a clear understanding of what is covered under the rubric of 'infrastructure' is necessary to ensure consistency and comparability in the data collected and reported by various agencies over time.'

Many studies attempt to link aggregate infrastructure development to growth of GDP. Whether, **Paul Roseinstein Rodan (1957)** in **'Big Push Theory'** and **Albert Hirschman (1961)** in **'Unbalanced Growth'** focused on the importance of infrastructure for development and give the concept of **'Social Overhead Capital (SOC)', Professor**

Gunnar Myrdal built his theory of economic development and underdevelopment due to inequalities in infrastructure stock between developed and under developed countries. **W.W. Rostow "The stages of economic growth", 1960** included social over head capital as one of the pre-conditions for accelerated growth of the economy. The economists' like- **John M. Antle "Infrastructure and Aggregate Agricultural Productivity: International Evidence", L.N. Bhagat "Interregional Disparities in Agricultural Infrastructure: A case study of Bihar", Fabrizio Felloni, Thomas Wahl, Philips Wandschneider "Evidence of the Effect of Infrastructure on Agricultural Production and Productivity:Implications for China"** proved strong positive relationship between infrastructure development and agricultural productivity in their studies. **Deepika Goel** in her study- **"Impact of Infrastructure on Productivity: Case of Indian Registered Manufacturing Sector in India",** proved the enhancement of productivity in manufacturing sector by infrastructure development. **Seetanath Boopen "Transport Infrastructure and Economic Growth: Evidence from Africa using Dynamic Panel Estimates", Randall Elberts "Understanding the Contribution of Highway Investment on National Economic Growth: Comments on Mamuneas's study" and Rudra Prakash Pradhan "Transport Infrastructure, Energy Consumption and Economic Growth Triangle in India: Cointegration and Causality Analysis",** proved that the contribution of transport infrastructure to economic progress is positive and significant in their studies. **Anjum Aqueel and Mohammad Sabihuddin Butt "The relationship between Energy Consumption and Economic Growth in Pakistan" and Kamal Raj Dhungel "A Causal Relationship between Energy Consumption and Economic Growth"** in their studies proved the strong positive causal relationship between energy consumption and economic growth. Whether **H. Prakash** in his study **"Evaluation of Institutional Base for Infrastructure in Industrial Development of Karnataka"** proved that the social and economic infrastructure development in Karnataka contributed 50.99 per cent of gross domestic product (GDP), **S.Surekha** in her study- **"Infrastructure and economic development with special reference to Transport and Communication in Karnataka"** established strong positive relationship between infrastructure development and gross national income (GNI).

Infrastructure development, such as improved transportation reduces worker's time-spent on non-productive activities and thus increases their productivity. Transport and communication as an input in the production process helps in transferring of goods and people between and within production and consumption centers. Increased level of transport and communication infrastructure in a particular region would lead to an expansion in investment in allied sectors, which can produce high value-added products. Adequacy of transport and communication facilities helps to improve the quality of life and reduces poverty.

Irrigation infrastructure development provides large benefits to the production activities in agriculture. The development of irrigation facilities contribute to increased productivity and raises long-term production and income levels. By providing access to irrigation water, the farmers are enabled to better manage risks caused by drought or other seasonal climatic fluctuations.

Telecommunications can increase the efficiency of economic, commercial and administrative activities, improve the effectiveness of social and emergency services and distribute the social, cultural and economic benefits of the process of development more equitably throughout the country.

While energy is a crucial input in the process of production, it is an important item of the consumption menu. Use of more energy not only facilitates life but also helps mankind, fight the vagaries of nature, and thereby make life more comfortable.

With the economic infrastructure, we also need the social infrastructure. Social infrastructure and Economic infrastructure are complementary to each other and both of them facilitate growth through their backward and forward linkages.

We need strong educational base, healthy life, sanitation, good quality water supply. An educated, healthy person can contribute in productivity positively. Better access of clean drinking water, sanitation facilities improve people's health status. Infrastructure increases the efficiency of educational institutions, health service centers, productivity of labour and capital. It is worth emphasising that all of the above contributions of infrastructure derive not from mere existence or creation of physical facilities but from their operation and the quality of the services generated. Infrastructure capital only increases the capacity and productivity of already existing resources of a nation. While economic infrastructure facilities help to increase productivity of physical capitals, social infrastructure helps to increase human capabilities through upgradation of skills, knowledge, health, education etc. and both of them act as the stimulant of economic growth.

Economic growth, which is the major concern of any State, is the increase in the market value of goods and services produced by an economy over time. It is conventionally measured as the percentage rate of increase in real gross domestic product. More importance is given to the growth of the ratio of GDP to population, which is also called per capita income. An increase in per capita income is referred to as intensive growth. GDP growth caused only by increase in population or territory is called extensive growth.

J.A. Schumpeter (1934) in his book "The Theory of Economic Development" defined economic growth as "a gradual and steady change in the long run which comes about by a gradual increase in the rate of saving and population".

C.P. Kindleberger in his book "Economic Development (1965)" pointed out "Economic growth may well involve not only more output, derived from greater amounts of input but also greater efficiency, i.e., an increase in output per unit of input".

Simon Kuznets (1955) in his paper "Economic Growth and Income Inequality" defines economic growth as "a long term process in the substantial and sustained rise in real national income, total population and per capita income".

Therefore, economic growth is the process by which productive capacity of an economy increases over time to bring about rising levels of national output and income. It refers basically the rise in the value of the goods and services produced by an economy.

Human development is a crucial ingredient of economic growth. It stimulates as well as stimulated by economic growth. There are plenty of research studies which prove that human development is positively linked with economic growth. Human development and economic growth should move together. Human Development means to build human capabilities of the people. Though material capital is crucial for economic achievements, in the beginning of 1960's the emphasis was shifted from material capital to human capital.

According to **New Endogenous Growth Theory (**given by **Arrow, Romer and Lucas)**, growth rate should be determined endogenously and it focused on human development. Human beings are considered as human capital in modern economic literature. Improved skill, training, higher education, healthy life, new modern technologies, research and development, proper nutrition, food, sanitation are essential to achieve economic growth. The developing countries, like India, should concentrate in human capital formation to converge its economy with developed countries.

The New Endogenous Growth Theory which focused on human development criticised the pessimistic exogenous growth model for its constant returns to scale and exogenously determined economic growth. With 'Spill Over Effect' and concept of 'Human Development', endogenous growth model gives the increasing returns to scale of the economy.

The association between human development and economic growth is well recognised. According to Ranis, Stewart and Ramirez (2000), there is "strong connection between economic growth and human development. On the one hand, economic growth (EG) provides the resources to permit sustained improvement in human development (HD). On the other, improvements in the quality of the labour force are an important contributor to economic growth (EG)."

Ranis, Stewart and Ramirez (2000) in their study "Economic Growth and Human Development" categorised country performance into four categories:-

1. Virtual Cycle: High HD enhances growth, which in turn promotes HD and so on.
2. Vicious Cycle: Poor performance of HD tends to lead to poor growth performance which in turn depresses HD achievements and so on.
3. EG Lopsided: It will occur when high EG does not bring about high HD because of weak linkages such as a low social expenditure ratio.
4. HD Lopsided: It will occur when high HD performance does not generate high EG, due to dearth of complementary resources arising from low investment rates.

Basically economic growth and human development has 'two chains', one from economic growth to human development and other from human development to economic growth. When resources from national income are allocated to activities contributing human development then the chain runs from economic growth to human development. When human development helps to increase national income the chain runs from human development to economic growth.

In 1990, the concept of human development was introduced in the first Human Development Report (HDR, 1990). Human Development is a wide concept. Human Development Index (a composite index), given by Nobel laureate Amartya Sen, is calculated by taking three indicators-

1. Longevity (life expected at birth)
2. Educational attainment combination of adult literacy (2/3 weight) and combined primary, secondary and tertiary Enrollment ratio (1/3 weight)
3. Decent Standard of living [measured by real GDP per capita based on purchasing power parity in terms of dollar ($)]

According to Amartya Sen "Human Development Index (HDI) is a crude index, attempting to catch in one simple number a complex reality about human development and deprivation."

Now human development is a very important agenda for developing countries and the sources of human development are education, health, skill development, clean drinking water, sanitation etc.

According to UNDP (1990), "The most critical ones are to lead a long and healthy life, to be educated and enjoy a decent standard of living. Additional choices include political freedom, guaranteed human right and self respect."

Further, as per UNDP (1990), human development has two sides. With one side the formation of human capabilities, such as improved health, knowledge, skill can be achieved and other side is related to the use people make of their acquired capabilities for leisure and for productive purposes of being active in cultural, social and political affairs.

According to Selim Jahan (2000) The concept of human development emphasised that-

1. Development is about enlarging people's choices by enhancing their functioning and capabilities.
2. Development is of the people, for the people and by the people. The first refers to human capital formation and human resources development through nutrition, health and education. Development for the people stresses that the benefits of economic growth must be translated into lives of people. Development by the people means that people must be able to influence the process, which affects their lives.
3. Development must be woven around people, and not people around development.

Many studies attempt to link **Human Development** with **Economic Growth.** Whether **P.R. Gopinath Nair, "Education and Economic Development in Kerala", Rudra Prakash Pradhan "Education and Economic Growth in India: Using Error Correction Modelling"** in their studies established strong positive relationship in their studies established strong positive relationship between education and economic growth, **P. Duriasamy and Ajay Mahal, "Health, Poverty and Economic Growth in India"** proved strong association between enhancement in health status and economic growth in their studies. **Parminder Kaur, "Education and Human Resource Development in Rural Punjab: A Study of Bathinda District" and Divya Singhal "Human Development in Rajasthan- The Education Challenge"** proved strong association between educational improvement and human development in their studies. **Swarnalekha Bihari, "Human Resources for Economic Development with reference to India", Madhusudan Ghosh, "Economic Growth and Human Development in Indian States", Sacchidananda Mukherjee and Debasis Chakraborty "Is**

there any relationship between Economic Growth and Human Development? Evidence from Indian States" established positive, significant relationship between human development and economic growth in their studies. **Vijayamohan N. Pillai** in his study **"Infrastructure, Growth and Human Development in Kerala"** proved the link between infrastructure, economic growth and human development in the state Kerala. In this study human development is represented by development in social infrastructure in the state Kerala.

So it is clear from the above discussion that in the modern era of Indian economy infrastructure (both social and economic) and human development both have been given a major focus and it is relevant to study the role of infrastructure and human development for accelerating the economic growth process. Economic growth is stimulated both by increasing provisions of infrastructure facilities as well as human development on one hand and infrastructure facilities as well as human development both are fuelled by economic growth on the other. Briefly it can be said that infrastructure increases economic growth, economic growth accelerates human development and human development leads to further economic growth. Therefore, infrastructure, economic growth and human development are interlinked with each other.

In this study the focus has been given on India's one of the most rapidly growing states Gujarat. Infrastructure, Economic Growth and Human Development of the state Gujarat as a whole as well as in its district level have been studied here.

1.2 Objectives of the study

The basic objectives of the study are:

1. To analyse the trend behaviour of infrastructure development and economic growth (per capita net state domestic product (NSDP) at factor cost and constant prices) in Gujarat and also Gujarat's relative performance in these two components with respect to India. To examine the long run as well as short run causal relationship between weighted aggregate infrastructure index and economic growth in Gujarat.
2. To examine the achievements of the state Gujarat with respect to different components related to human development and also the category and rank of the state with respect to human development index among fifteen major states of India.
3. To identify the category of the districts with respect to different components of infrastructure (under consideration) and economic growth as well as weighted aggregate infrastructure index and weighted aggregate index of economic growth in Gujarat. To examine the relationship between the variables weighted aggregate

infrastructure index and weighted aggregate index of economic growth at district level in Gujarat.

4. To identify the category of the districts with respect to their human development index. To examine the relationship between the variables human development index and weighted aggregate index of economic growth at district level in Gujarat.
5. To study the trend and pattern of public expenditure on social and economic services in the state Gujarat.
6. To suggest remedial measures to overcome the deficiencies related to infrastructure, economic growth and human development in the state Gujarat.

1.3 Preview of Chapter Scheme

The present study has been organised into eight chapters given below:

Chapter one- Introduction: It is exploratory in nature. It provides the introduction, research issues, objectives and preview of chapter scheme.

Chapter two- Data Source and Methodology: This chapter provides the data sources, research methodologies (which are used to analyse the time series data and the district-wise data of the state Gujarat) and limitations of the study.

Chapter three- Quantitative Analysis of Infrastructure and Economic Growth in Gujarat: This chapter discusses the trends of different infrastructural components (under consideration) and Per Capita Net State Domestic Product (NSDP) at factor cost and constant prices (represents Economic Growth) in Gujarat as well as the relative position of the state with respect to India on the basis of these indicators in tabular and graphical form. The long run and short run causal relationship between Weighted Aggregate Infrastructure Index and Economic Growth in Gujarat has also been examined here.

Chapter four- Human Development in Gujarat: This chapter examines the human development in Gujarat with the help of different indicators related to human development and also with respect to 'Human Development Index (HDI)'. The achievements of the state in the selected indicators related to human development have been discussed by comparing the state's performance with respect to India as well as among fifteen major states of India. Distribution of states (fifteen major states in India) according to four Categories of development (Virtuous Cycle, Lopsided Economic Growth, Lopsided Human Development and Vicious Cycle) with reference to Per capita NSDP at factor cost and constant prices and Human Development Index (HDI) has also been given in this chapter.

Chapter five- District-wise Quantitative Analysis of Infrastructure, Economic Growth and Human Development in Gujarat: It provides the district-wise analysis of infrastructure, economic growth and human development for 1991, 2000-01 and 2009-10. The categorisation of districts into high, medium and low developed districts has been done on the basis of different indicators of Infrastructure and Economic Growth separately as well as with respect to Weighted Aggregate Infrastructure Index and Weighted Aggregate Index of Economic Growth. The district-wise nature of association and relationship between the variables Weighted Aggregate Infrastructure Index and Weighted Aggregate Index of Economic Growth has also been examined here.

This chapter also provides the district-wise human development index (HDI). The categorisation and ranking of the districts has been done on the basis of different components of HDI as well as with respect to their HDI values. District-wise nature of association and relationship between the variables HDI and Weighted Aggregate Index of Economic Growth has also been examined.

Chapter six- Trend and Pattern of Public Expenditure on Social and Economic Services in Gujarat: It provides the trend and pattern of public expenditure on social and economic services in Gujarat for the time period 1991-92 to 2009-10. It also examines the rank of the Gujarat among 15 major states of India with respect to their percentage of total expenditure on different selected social and economic services.

Chapter seven- Summary and Policy Implications: In this chapter summary, major findings and policy implications are given.

2

Data Source and Methodology

This chapter deals with the data sources and research methodologies which are adopted to pursue the objectives of this study. To solve the research problem systematically and scientifically the most suitable research methodology needs to be adopted. Research methodology is a scientific tool, through which the researchers not only know how to develop certain indices or tests, but they also understand which of these methods or techniques are relevant and which are not and what would they mean and indicate and why and also the assumptions underlying various techniques.

2.1 Data Source and Description of Variables

In this section the data sources and description of variables both for data analysis of Gujarat state as well as its district-wise data analysis have been given.

2.1.1a Data Source of Variables related to Infrastructure, Economic Growth and Human Development in Gujarat

This part of the study deals with the data sources of time series variables- Infrastructure and Economic Growth for the period 1980-81 to 2009-10 in Gujarat (***though this study is between the time periods 1991-92 to 2009-10, in order to use time series analysis, we have used thirty years time series data for the time period 1980-81 to 2009-10***) and also the data sources regarding different components of Human Development (considered in this study) in Gujarat, all India as well as other fourteen major states of India. Secondary data for different Infrastructure components (considered in this study), Economic Growth

(Per Capita) Net State Domestic Product (NSDP) at factor cost and constant prices), Human Development Index (HDI) and variables relevant to discuss Human Development in Gujarat have been collected from some relevant sources, given below:

1. Censuses 1981, 1991, 2001 and 2011.
2. Central Electricity Authority, New Delhi.
3. Compendium of India's Fertility and Mortality Indicators, based on Sample Registration System, Register General India.
4. CSO, MOPSI, New Delhi.
5. Handbook of statistics on the Indian Economy, RBI.
6. India Human Development Report, 2011. Institute of Applied Manpower Research, Planning Commission, Government of India. Oxford University Press.
7. Infrastructure, CMIE, Mumbai.
8. Ministry of Surface Transport, Government of India, New Delhi.
9. Ministry of Telecommunications, New Delhi.
10. Ministry of Human Resources Development, Department of Education, Government of India.
11. National Health Profile, Central Bureau of Health Intelligence, Government of India.
12. National Human Development Report, 2001. Planning Commission, Government of India. March 2002.
13. National Sample Survey. 38th, 50th, 55th, 61st and 66th Rounds.
14. Reserve Bank of India. Quarterly Handout on Banking Statistics.
15. Socio-Economic Review, Gujarat State.
16. Statistical abstract of Gujarat. Directorate of Economics and Statistics, Government of Gujarat, Gandhinagar.

2.1.1b Data Source for District-wise Analysis of Gujarat

This part of the study deals with the data sources of district-wise data related to Infrastructure, Economic Growth and Human Development for the time points–1991, 2000-01 and 2009-10. Secondary data has been collected from - Statistical Abstract of Gujarat, Directorate of Economics and Statistics, Government of Gujarat, Gandhinagar and Socio-Economic Review, Gujarat State (for different Years).

2.1.2a Description of Variables related to Infrastructure, Economic Growth and Human Development in Gujarat

To analyse the role of Infrastructure Development to influence Economic Growth, seven sectors of **Infrastructure** with eleven components have been considered- **Transport** (consists Road Length and Rail Route Length), **Communication** (consists Telephone Connections and Post Offices), **Banking, Irrigation, Electricity,**

Education (consists Numbers of Educational Institutions and Numbers of Teachers per 100 Pupils) and **Health** (consists Numbers of Medical Institutions and Beds).

Here 'Total Road Length' is the aggregate of National Highways, State highways, Other PWD roads, Zila Parishad Roads, Village Panchayat roads, CD/Panchayat Samiti roads and Urban roads and 'Total Rail Route Length' is the aggregate of broad gauge, metre gauge and narrow gauge. The variable 'Number of Telephone Connection' includes Fixed Line, CDMA and Cellular Phones connections. As per availability of data 'Total Numbers of Banks' includes only the numbers of scheduled commercial banks. Again, the variable 'Number of Educational Institutions' include primary, secondary, high and higher secondary schools. The variable 'Number of Teachers per 100 Enrolled Pupils' is also based on the total numbers of teachers and total enrolled pupils in primary, secondary, high and higher secondary schools. Further, the variable 'Number of Medical Institutions' includes the number of Primary Health Centres (PHCs), Community Health Centres (CHCs), Sub-centres and Hospitals in rural and urban areas. The variable 'Number of Beds in Medical Institutions' includes the number of beds in Government Hospitals in rural and urban areas.

Here, '**Economic Growth'** has been represented by the variable **'Per Capita Net State Domestic Product at factor cost and constant prices'.**

To examine Gujarat's performance in '**Human Development'** tabular and graphical analysis has been done with respect to different indicators related to Human Development as well as India's state-wise Human Development Index (HDI) for different years.

To analyse **'Standard of living'** in Gujarat, the data regarding 'Per Capita NSDP' and 'Monthly Per Capita Consumption Expenditure' have been analysed. The data regarding 'Poverty', 'Unemployment' and 'Working Children' have been also analysed here. To discuss **'Educational Attainment'** in Gujarat, data regarding 'Literacy rate', 'Gross Enrollment Ratio', 'Pupil-Teacher Ratio at Primary and Upper Primary Levels' have been examined. Some other data relevant to Human Development like 'Housing', 'Electricity', 'Sanitation' and 'Drinking Water Facility' have also been examined. To analyse the **'Health Facility'** in Gujarat, data regarding **'**Infant Mortality Rate', 'Life Expectancy at Birth', 'Under Five Mortality Rate', 'Anaemia among Children (0-5 Years)' and Women, 'Maternal Mortality Rate' and 'Body-Mass Index for women' have been analysed. The data regarding 'Vaccination of Children', Total Fertility Rate (TFR), 'Percentage of Malnourished and Severely Malnourished Children', 'Population', 'Sex Ratio' have also been studied.

2.1.2b Description of Variables (District-Wise Analysis of Gujarat)

For district-wise analysis of Infrastructure, Economic Growth and Human Development, secondary data for three time points-1991, 2000-01 and 2009-10 have been collected. To analyse district-wise infrastructure development in Gujarat fourteen components of **Infrastructure** have been considered.

Transport (Road length with respect to area as well as population), **Irrigation**, **Villages with Clean Drinking Water facility**, **Villages with Electricity Connections**, **Banking** (Scheduled Commercial Banks with respect to area as well as population), **Education** (Number of Primary Schools, Number of High and Higher Secondary Schools, Pupil-Teacher Ratio in Primary Schools, Pupil-Teacher Ratio in High and Higher Secondary Schools), **Health** (Number of Allopathic Medical Institutions, Population Served per Medical Institution and Number of Beds) for three time points- 1991, 2000-01 and 2009-10.

Here, district-wise **'Total Road Length'** is basically the aggregate of total surfaced and unsurfaced roads where surfaced roads include National highway, State highway, District roads and Village approach roads.

'Number of Allopathic Medical Institutions' includes Hospitals, Primary Health Centres (PHCs), Dispensaries and Others. **'Number of Beds in Medical Institutions'** includes only the beds in Hospitals and Primary Health Centre (PHCs).

Though, **Economic Growth** is generally expressed by Per Capita Income or Per Capita Consumption Expenditure but district-wise data of Per Capita Income or Expenditure is not available in Gujarat. So, nine indicators related to economic growth have been considered as proxy of **Economic Growth** in this study.

As per **'Gujarat Human Development Report, 2004,'** when the data of Per Capita Income or Expenditure is unavailable then as proxy the indicators like–**'Per capita output in agriculture and industries together', Per capita bank deposits' or 'Percentage of households having specified assets'** can be used.

On the basis of these three sectors–Agriculture, Industry and Banking (suggested by **Gujarat Human Development Report, 2004),** nine indicators have been taken into account as per availability of data:

Agriculture- It includes Irrigation Intensity, Cropping Intensity, Per Capita Net Area Sown and Average Yield of Food Grains.

Industry- It includes Number of Registered Small Scale Industries with respect to Area as well as Population.

Banking- It includes Per Capita Bank Deposits, Per Capita Bank Credit and Credit-Deposit Ratio.

To prepare the district-wise **Human Development Index** four indicators- Per Capita Bank Deposit, Educational Attainment (Literacy Rate and Adjusted Intensity of Formal Education (AIFE)) and Infant Mortality Rate are considered.

As district-wise data of Per Capita Income or Expenditure of Gujarat state is not available, 'Per Capita Bank Deposit' has been used as a proxy variable of **'Standard of Living'** (ref: Gujarat Human Development Report, 2004).

Literacy Rate for 7+ age group of population and calculated **'Adjusted Intensity of Formal Education (AIFE)'** has been used to calculate '**Educational Attainment Index'**. 35 per cent weight is given to literacy rate and 65 per cent weight is given to Adjusted Intensity of Formal Education (AIFE) to calculate the 'Educational Attainment Index'. Due to unavailability of district-wise data of 'Life Expectancy at Birth', the variable **'Infant Mortality Rate'** has been considered as the health indicator in this study.

2.2 Relative Indexation Technique for Graphical Analysis of Infrastructure Development and Economic Growth in Gujarat

To analyse the trend of infrastructure development for the period 1980-81 to 2009-10 in Gujarat as compared to India's average graphically, the relative infrastructure index (with respect to each components of infrastructure under consideration) has been constructed which is basically the relative position of Gujarat in the scale of infrastructure development in India. It has been calculated by relating Gujarat's proportion in total infrastructure stock (or service) of India to its proportion of total population (or area) of India.

$$\textbf{Relative Index of Infrastructure Development} = \frac{Y_i / \Sigma Y_i}{P / \Sigma P} \times 100 \quad \text{.........(2.1)}$$

Where, Y_i = i^{th} infrastructure stock (or service) of Gujarat

ΣY_i = the corresponding stock (or service) of India

P = population (or area) of Gujarat

ΣP = the corresponding population (or area) of India

2.3 Principal Component Analysis

The 'Principal Component Analysis (PCA)' provides a convenient way of aggregating the indicators with the weights assigned to the indicators being determined in a relatively objective manner on the basis of correlation matrix. This procedure comprises mainly of redefining a set of original variables into a set of newly constructed variables (called principal components) are then used to calculate component scores.

Principal component Analysis follows from the fact that every set of correlated variables can be replaced by a set of uncorrelated variables. These new variables are obtained as linear combinations of original variables. They are referred to as principal components of the given set of variables.

To determine the weights of different components (for the analysis of Gujarat state and its district-wise analysis) considered in this study, the principal component analysis has been used. Statistical Package for the Social Sciences (**SPSS 18) software** has been used for this analysis.

$$\mathbf{P_i = \Sigma a_{ij} Z_j} \qquad ...(2.2)$$

Here, P_i = Principal Component; a_{ij} = Factor Loading of ith variable; Z_j = Standardised variable.

In this study, in the calculation of the scores, instead of using standardised variables (as usual practice) as it distorts the dispersion of the original indicator, each indicator has been divided by its mean in order to remove the scale bias in the data (ref: K Seeta Prabhu and P.C. Sarkar, EPW, Sept 5, 1992, pp 1927-1937).

Derivation and Interpretation of the Principal Components

The aim of the method of principal components is the construction of set of variables Z_j's of new variables (P_i) called principal components which are linear combinations of the Z's:

$$P_1 = a_{11} Z_1 + a_{12} Z_2 + ... + a_{1k} Z_k$$

$$P_2 = a_{21} Z_1 + a_{22} Z_2 + ... + a_{2k} Z_k$$

.

.

.

$$P_k = a_{k1} Z_1 + a_{k2} Z_2 + ... + a_{kk} Z_k$$

Therefore, $P_i = \Sigma a_{ij} Z_j$ where, i,j=1,2...k and a_{ij} =loadings

The problem is to obtain the estimates of a's (loadings), with which it is possible to transform the Z's into orthogonal artificial variables, the principal components. It is needed to estimate the coefficients at first and then to conduct some tests of significance to decide whether the estimates a_{ij} statistically significant or not. Finally it is required some rule of decision, some criterion, on the basis of which to decide how many of the principal components (how many of all possible P's) to retain into the analysis.

To estimate the loadings (a's), simple correlation coefficients between the k explanatory variables need to be estimated. These correlation coefficients may be arranged in a table which is known as 'correlation table'. The main diagonals include units since the elements of the diagonal are the self-correlation, i.e., the correlations of each Z_j with itself. The correlation matrix is symmetrical, i.e., the elements of each row are identical to the elements of the corresponding columns,

$$\text{Since,} \quad r_{xi\,xj} = r_{xj\,xi} \qquad \ldots(2.3)$$

The next step is to sum each column (or row) of the correlation table, obtaining k sums of simple correlation coefficients

$$\sum_{j}^{k} r_{xi\,xj} = \sum^{k} r_{xi\,xj} \qquad \ldots(2.4)$$

Then total sum of the column (or rows) is computed.

$$\sum_{i}^{k}\sum_{j}^{k} r_{xi\,xj} \qquad \ldots(2.5)$$

Finally, to obtain the loadings of first principal component P_1, each column or row sum need to be divided by the square root of grand total.

$$a_{1j} = (\sum_{j}^{K} r_{xi\,xj}) \sqrt{\sum\sum r_{xi\,xj}} \qquad ..(2.6)$$

Here, $r_{xi\,xj}$ = simple correlation coefficients between the k explanatory variables (where, i,j=1,2...k).

(ref: Theory of Econometrics, second edition, A. Koutsoyiannis, pp. 426-427)

The loadings are used as component scores i.e., weights of different components. The percentage of total variance of a principal component can be obtained by dividing the latent root (λ) with number of components (k).

The latent root (λ) (or Eigen value or Characteristic root) is the sum of the squares of loadings of each principal component.

The principal components are uncorrelated (orthogonal). The first principal component absorbs and accounts for the maximum possible proportion of total variation in the set of all Z's. Similarly, the second principal component absorbs the maximum remaining variation in Z's and so on.

To obtain the second principal component it is essential to form residual correlation table, from the original one, by removing the part of total variation which has been absorbed by first principal component. From the residual correlation table the loadings and the variance of second principal component can be obtained in the same way as first principal component.

Again, the drawback of principal component analysis is that, though the first component explains the maximum variance in the series, the proportion of variance hardly exceeds 50 per cent and in most of the studies only the first principal component scores are used. **To overcome this deficiency with first principal component, other principal component scores (second, third etc.) have been used here, which together explain above 70 per cent of variance. The aggregation of the scores of the components, whenever necessary, was done on the basis of weights assigned to the components, the weights being the proportion of variance, explained by the component. The aggregate weighted index of infrastructure is derived by summing up the component scores.**

The aggregation of the scores of the components, whenever necessary, is done on the basis of weights assign to the components, the weights being the proportion of variance explained by the component (K Seeta Prabhu and Sarkar, EPW, Sept 5, 1992, pp. 1927-1937).

The weights of principal components are calculated by the given formula:

$$\mathbf{W_{pj} = (100/TV_i)^*V_{pj}} \quad \ldots(2.7)$$

Here, W_{pj} = Weight of the jth principal component ;

TV_i = Total variance of ith indicator (where i= infrastructure or economic growth);

V_{pj} = Variance of jth principal component;

Where, p_j = j^{th} principal component and j=1, 2....n.

(Here, total variance of ith indicator means aggregate variance of all the principal components (p_j) taken into account).

2.4 Methodology of Time Series Data Analysis-Infrastructure and Economic Growth in Gujarat

To analyse the causal relationship between infrastructure and economic growth for the time period 1980-81 to 2009-10, the time series data analysis technique has been adopted. The log values of the variables-weighted aggregate infrastructure index and per capita net state domestic product (at factor cost and constant prices) are considered in this study. Eviews 5 software has been used for this analysis.

To analyse the time series data, at first it is important to know that the time series are stationary or not. Because if a time series is non-stationary, its behaviour can be studied only for the time under consideration. Each set of time series data will therefore be for a particular episode. As a consequence, it is not possible to generalise it to other time periods.

2.4.1 Stationarity Test

A stochastic time series is said to be stationary, if its mean and variance are constant over time and the value of the covariance between two time periods depends on the distance or gap or lag between the two periods and not actual time at which the covariance is computed.

Dickey-Fuller test is a most common test for stationarity. Dicky and Fuller have computed the values of tau statistic on the basis of which stationarity of time series variable can be tested. In conducting Dickey-Fuller (DF) test it is assumed that the error term μ_t is uncorrelated. But in case it is correlated, Dickey-Fuller developed a test, known as Augmented Dickey-Fuller (ADF) test. This test is conducted by adding lagged values of the dependent variable (say, Y_t). **Augmented Dickey-Fuller test** has been used to test the stationarity of the time series variables of this study.

2.4.2 Cointegration

If the variables have same stochastic trends individually, but their linear combination cancels out the stochastic trends and become stationary, then the series of these variables are cointegrated. The choice of cointegration methodology over the classical Ordinary Least Square (OLS) procedure is governed by the fact that, in the time series framework, the application of OLS may yield inconsistent results. Generally there is a possibility of estimating spurious regression in which R-square is high enough and Durbin Watson (DW) is very low. Hence to obtain consistent long run estimates cointegration methodology is required to adopt.

There are several methods for testing cointegration. In a bivariate analysis **Engel-Granger** procedure is normally followed for the assertion of the cointegration between the two variables. In this procedure at first OLS regression need to be estimated between two variables and then it is required to estimate residuals. Then DF or ADF test is required to use to know the presence of unit root in the estimated residual series. If the residual series is stationary, i.e. it is I(0), then it is said that the variables are cointegrated. The model of cointegration in general form for the bivariate data given below:

1. OLS regression for the variables with same stochastic trend:

$$y_t = \alpha + \beta X_t + \varepsilon_t \quad ...(2.8)$$

2. Estimation of residual series:

$$\hat{\varepsilon}_t = Y_t - \hat{Y}_t \quad ...(2.9)$$

where, Y_t = weighted aggregate infrastructure index (in logarithmic form) and

X_t = per capita NSDP at factor cost and constant prices (in logarithmic form).

$\hat{\varepsilon}_t$ = Residual Series; $(Y_t - \hat{Y}_t)$ = Difference between the actual and estimated Y values.

Now the presence of unit root in residual series is tested and if the residual series is I(0) i.e. stationary, then the variables are cointegrated i.e., there is a long run relationship between these two variables under consideration.

2.4.3 Vector Error Correction Model

If the variables are cointegrated, then it is useful to consider specific parameterisations that support the analysis of the cointegration structure. The resulting models are known as Vector Error Correction Models (VECMs). To find out whether the model converges to its long run equilibrium path, the short run dynamic in the error correction model associated with the long run estimates is estimated. If two variables are cointegrated, there is long run equilibrium relationship between the two. Of course, in the short run there may be disequilibrium. Therefore, one can treat the 'Error Correction Term (ECT)' as the equilibrium error and this error term can be used to tie the short run behaviour of the variables under consideration to their long run behaviour. The 'Error Correction Mechanism (ECM)' first used by Sargan and later popularised by Engel and Granger corrects for disequilibrium. An important theorem Granger representation theorem states that, if two variables Y and X are cointegrated, then the relationship between the two can be expressed as ECM.

The Vector Error Correction Model (VECM) for bivariate data in general form is given below:

$$\Delta X_t = Y_2 + \sum_{l=1}^{n} \theta_{2,1} \Delta X_{t-1} + \sum_{l=1}^{n} \Psi_{2,1} \Delta Y_{t-1} + \Phi_2 \, ECT^1_{t-1} + \varepsilon_{2t} \quad ....(2.10)$$

$$\Delta Y_t = Y_1 + \sum_{l=1}^{n} \Psi_{1,l} \Delta Y_{t-l} + \sum_{l=1}^{n} \theta_{1,l} \Delta X_{t-l} + \Phi_1 ECT^2_{t-1} + \varepsilon_{1t} \quad ...(2.11)$$

Where, Δ =first difference operator; Y_t = weighted aggregate infrastructure index (in logarithmic form) and X_t = per capita NSDP at factor cost and constant prices (in logarithmic form); t = time period (t=1,2....T); l = Lag length (l=1,2...n);

ε = white noise error; Φ = coefficient of error correction term (ECT).

The lag lengths are determined by AIC or SIC technique (using Stata 12 software) so that white noise error terms are serially uncorrelated. The coefficient of error correction terms are expected to capture the adjustments of the variables under consideration towards long run equilibrium and the speed of adjustment.

2.4.4 Vector Error Correction Granger causality test or Wald test

Granger has introduced causality concept that has become quite popular in econometric literature. He defines a time series variable (say X) to be causal for the time series variable (Y) if the former helps to improve the forecasts of the latter. The existence of a relationship between the two variables does not prove the causality or direction of influence. If in a bivariate model, the cointegrating rank (r) is equal to 1, there must be Granger–causality in at least one direction i.e. either Y to X or X to Y or both.

In the presence of cointegration, granger causality test can be investigated in a vector error correction model (ref: 'Advanced Time Series Econometrics' (2004) by Helmut Lutkepohl, p.146) i.e. **between the variables Y_t and X_t**. Peter Rossini and Valerie Kupke of University of South Australia in their paper 'Granger Causality Test for the Relationship between House and Land Prices' presented in Eighteenth Annual Pacific-Rim Real Estate Society Conference (15-18 January, 2012) have used VEC Granger Causality–Wald Test to determine short run causal relationship between house and land prices and concluded that as per their sample data analysis house prices Granger cause land prices but not land prices Granger cause house prices.

Here, the short run causal relationship between infrastructure (here, weighted aggregate infrastructure index) **and economic growth has been tested using the Vector error correction (VEC) Granger causality or block exogeneity Wald test by using Eview-5 software.**

2.5 Methodology for District-wise Data Analysis of Gujarat

For district-wise analysis of data at three time points (1991, 2000-01 and 2009-10), on the basis of weights derived from Principal Component

Analysis, the weighted aggregate infrastructure index and weighted aggregate index of economic growth have been calculated. The district-wise Human Development Indices for three time points have also been calculated in this study. On the basis of the values of these indicators the districts have been classified into three categories–high, medium and low.

The classification of the districts into high, medium or low category with respect to each of the indicators of Infrastructure, Economic Growth as well as Human Development and also with respect to aggregate weighted indices of infrastructure and economic growth and with respect to calculated human development index have been done with the help of below given formulae:

$\bar{X}$ **+0.5S and** $\bar{X}$ **-0.5S** where, $\bar{X}$ = mean and S=standard deviation (ref: Hrima H. Thaker and R. L. Shiyani, 2009. Socio-Economic Development in Gujarat: Rosy Picture with Concerns. Journal of Rural Development, NIRD, Hyderabad. October–December 2009, Vol. 28, No. (4). pp. 515-528).

The high developed districts are those whose index values are greater than or equal to $\bar{X}+0.5S$ and the districts with index values less than or equal to $\bar{X}-0.5S$ are categorised as low developed districts. The districts, whose index values fall in between are categorised as medium developed districts.

To examine the association between the Weighted Aggregate Infrastructure Index and Weighted Aggregate Index of Economic Growth on one hand and Human Development Index and Weighted Aggregate Index of Economic Growth (considered in this study) on the other for the districts of Gujarat, double log cross section regression model has been applied. Simple Ordinary Least Square (OLS) regression analysis (with double log) has been used here. SPSS 18 software has been used for this analysis. The cross-section regressions are separately estimated for the two time points 2000-01 and 2009-10. Both way regression analyses have been done.

(a) When district-wise Weighted Aggregate Infrastructure Index is dependent variable and Weighted Aggregate Index of Economic Growth is independent variable.

$$\log I_t = \log c_1 + d_1 \log E_t + u_t \qquad ...(2.12)$$

(b) When district-wise Weighted Aggregate Index of Economic Growth is dependent variable and Weighted Aggregate Infrastructure Index is independent variable.

$$\log E_t = \log c_2 + d_2 \log I_t + u_t \qquad ...(2.13)$$

Where $\mathbf{I_t}$ = Weighted Aggregate Infrastructure Index; $\mathbf{E_t}$ = Weighted Aggregate Index of Economic Growth, c_1 and c_2 are constants; d_1 and d_2 are coefficients of log Weighted Aggregate Index of Economic Growth and log Weighted Aggregate Infrastructure Index respectively and t=Time.

(c) When district-wise Human Development Index is dependent variable and Weighted Aggregate Index of Economic Growth is independent variable.

$$\log HDI_t = \log m_1 + n_1 \log E_t + u_t \quad \text{...(2.14)}$$

(d) When district-wise Weighted Aggregate Index of Economic Growth is dependent variable and Human Development Index is independent variable.

$$\log E_t = \log m_2 + n_2 \log HDI_t + u_t \quad \text{...(2.15)}$$

Where, $\mathbf{HDI_t}$ = Human Development Index; $\mathbf{E_t}$ = Weighted Aggregate Index of Economic Growth, m_1 and m_2 are constants; n_1 and n_2 are coefficients of log Weighted Aggregate Index of Economic Growth and log Human Development Index respectively and t=Time.

2.6 Hypotheses

The following Hypotheses are adopted to use the given methodology in this study:

2.7 Methodology Used to Prepare District-wise Human Development Index of Gujarat

The district-wise Human Development Index of Gujarat has been calculated with four indicators–Per Capita Bank Deposit (as proxy of per capita income ref: Gujarat Human Development report, 2004), Literacy

Table 2.1: Hypotheses

Sr. No.	*Null Hypotheses H_0*	*Alternative Hypotheses H_1*
1.	No relationship between Infrastructure Development and Economic Growth in Gujarat.	Significant relationship between Infrastructure Development and Economic Growth in Gujarat.
2.	No relationship between district-wise Weighted Aggregate Infrastructure Index and Weighted Aggregate Index of Economic Growth in Gujarat.	Significant relationship between district-wise Weighted Aggregate Infrastructure Index and Weighted Aggregate Index of Economic Growth in Gujarat.
3.	No relationship between district-wise Human Development Index and Weighted Aggregate Index of Economic Growth in Gujarat.	Significant relationship between district-wise Human Development Index and Weighted Aggregate Index of Economic Growth in Gujarat.

Source: Framed elaborations.

Rate for the population of 7+ age group with 35 per cent of weight, Adjusted Intensity of Formal Education (AIFE) with 65 per cent weight and Infant Mortality Rate. The secondary data of all these indicators of human development (taken under consideration) are available except AIFE. So AIFE has been calculated by the following method.

2.7.1 Adjusted Intensity of Formal Education (AIFE)

As per National Human Development Report (NHDR) 2001 methodology the Intensity of Formal Education (IFE) is estimated as a ratio between 'Weighted Average Enrolment (WAE)' of students from class I to class XII (where weights being assigned 1 for Class I, 2 for Class II and so on) to the 'Total Enrolment (TE)' in Class I to Class XII. IFE is multiplied with the proportion of Total Enrolment to Population in the age group 6-18 years. According to the formula suppose E_i be the number of children (rural and urban combined) enrolled in i^{th} standard in the given time, i=1 for Class I to 12 for Class XII). Then Weighted Average of the Enrolment (WAE) from Class I to Class XII is calculated as the weighted average of enrolment in a particular Class where weights are i = 1 for Class I to 12 for Class XII.

Now, suppose TE_i is the total enrolment of Children from Class I to Class XII in given time period. Then the Intensity of Formal Education (IFE) for children (rural and urban combined) becomes WAE expressed as a percentage of TE.

Therefore, **IFE = (WAE/TE)*100** ...(2.16)

Suppose P_i represents the Population of Children (rural and urban combined) in the age group 6 to 18 years in the given time. Then we can determine the Adjusted Intensity of Formal Education (AIFE) for children by the formula given below:

AIFE= IFE*(TE/ P_i) ...(2.17)

(**ref:** Mukherjee, Sacchidananda. Chakraborty, Debashis. 2010. Is there any relationship between Economic Growth and Human Development? Evidence from Indian States. MPRA Paper No. 22997. Source: http://mpra.ub.uni-muenchen.de/22997/).

In the present analysis, though Adjusted Intensity of Formal Education (AIFE) has been calculated according to the given methodology of NHDR, some modifications have been implemented because of unavailability of necessary data.

1. As per availability of district-wise data in Gujarat population of Children (district-wise) in the age group 5 to 19 years has been taken into account (district-wise data of population in the age group of 6-18 years is not available in Gujarat).

2. Again, in Gujarat, district-wise data of number of students enrolled in different classes are not available separately for each class from I to XII. Here the data is available for total numbers of students enrolled in primary and high and higher secondary classes. So the weights are being assigned in this study in the way given below:
   (i) In Gujarat class I to class VII are considered as primary classes. As district–wise Enrolment data for each class are not available in Gujarat, the average weight i.e. (1+2+3+4+5+6+7)/7 has been used as the weight of Enrolment in primary classes. The weight is being assigned as 4 for total numbers of students enrolled in primary classes.
   (ii) In Gujarat class VIII to class XII are considered as high and higher secondary classes. So the average weight (8+9+10+11+12)/5 has been used as average weight of total Enrolment in high and higher secondary classes. The weight is being assigned as 10 for total numbers of students enrolled in high and higher secondary classes.

2.7.2 Measurement of Human Development Index (HDI)

(i) For the positive indicators i.e. **per capita bank deposits (PBD) and educational attainment I_x = (Actual Value–Minimum Value)/ (Maximum Value–Minimum Value)**

(ii) As **infant mortality rate (IMR)** is negative indicators, I_x for this indicator is-**I_x = (Maximum Value - Actual Value)/ (Maximum Value–Minimum Value)**

Where, **I_x = Dimension Index of 'X'.**

HDI is obtained in terms of the arithmetic mean of its subindices as follows-

HDI = 1/3*(PBD Index + Educational Attainment Index + IMR Index) ...(2.18)

2.8 Limitations

1. This study is based on time series data of eleven infrastructural components and district-wise data of fourteen infrastructural components. More infrastructural components can be used to extend this study.
2. Due to limitation of data, different indicators related to human development have been studied for the time points as per their availability.
   (i) The data regarding percentage of children with anaemia, percentage of women with anaemia and percentage of women with B.M.I.<18.5 have been discussed only for two time points–1998-99 and 2005-06.

(ii) The data regarding state-wise (for 15 major states) Human Development Index has been discussed for the years 1991, 1999-00 and 2007-08. Again, the data regarding Health Index, Income Index and Education Index have been discussed for the years 1999-00 and 2007-08.

(iii) The data regarding percentage of malnourished and severely malnourished children has been discussed for the time points– 1994, 2005-06, 2007 and 2011.

(iv) The state-wise data (15 major states) regarding percentage of households has no latrine within premises use, percentage of households have improved source of drinking water, percentage of population with respect to India, population per square km. of area and sex ratio have been discussed as per Census 2011 data.

3. As district-wise data of per capita income is not available for the state Gujarat, weighted aggregate index of nine components related to economic growth (i.e. weighted aggregate index of economic growth) has been used as the proxy of Economic Growth in this study.
4. There were 19 districts in Gujarat in 1991 and later they bifurcated to 26 of which 25 (except Tapi) are considered to analyse the district-wise data for the time points 2000-01 and 2009-10. Again the data source of some variables in 1991 is different than the data source of the variables for the time points 2000-01 and 2009-10. So, district-wise performance with respect to different indicators related to infrastructure, economic growth or human development are compared and cross district regression analyses between weighted aggregate infrastructure index and weighted aggregate index of economic growth as well as human development index and weighted aggregate index of economic growth have been done in two time points- 2000-01 and 2009-10.
5. Further, due to unavailability of district-wise data of per capita income or per capita consumption expenditure in Gujarat, for the calculation of district-wise Human Development Index per capita bank deposit index has been used as proxy of standard of living.
6. Again, the data of district-wise Infant mortality Rate (IMR) in the state Gujarat is available only for the year 1991. In this study the data of district-wise IMR has been calculated for the years 2000-01 and 2009-10.

3

Quantitative Analysis of Infrastructure and Economic Growth in Gujarat

The present chapter is aimed to analyse the socio-economic infrastructural facilities and economic growth in Gujarat with the help of thirty years of time series data (1980-81 to 2009-10). To examine the trends of eleven components related to seven sectors of infrastructure (considered in this study), economic growth and their relative indices (with respect to India's average) for the given time period, the graphical analysis has been done. The causal relationship (short run as well as long run) between the weighted aggregate infrastructure index and economic growth has also been examined in this chapter.

3.1 Infrastructure Indicators

To examine the trend of infrastructure development as well as long run and short run causal relationship between infrastructure and economic growth in Gujarat, eleven infrastructure components have been considered in this study. The infrastructure indicators are given below:

I1. Road Length per 100 sq. km. of Area
I2. Rail Route Length per 100 sq. km. of Area
I3. Number of Post Offices per 100 sq. km. of Area
I4. Number of Telephone Connections per 100 People
I5. Per Capita Annual Consumption of Electricity
I6. Number of Scheduled Commercial Banks per 100 sq. km. of Area
I7. Gross Irrigated Area as Percentage of Gross Cropped Area
I8. Number of Schools per 100 sq. km. of Area
I9. Number of Teachers per 100 Enrolled Pupils

I10. Number of Medical Institutions per 100 sq. km. of Area
I11. Number of beds in Medical Institutions per 100 People

3.2 Trend of Infrastructure Development in Gujarat

To examine the trend of infrastructure development in Gujarat graphical analysis has been done in this study. For graphical analysis, the annual indicators of each of eleven infrastructure components have been estimated both for Gujarat and India for thirty years, from 1980-81 to 2009-10, the ratio of which yields the relative infrastructure development index of the particular component for Gujarat with respect to India's average.

Between the seven sectors of infrastructure (transport, communication, electricity, scheduled commercial banks, irrigation, education and health) there are four sectors–transport, communication, education and health, each of which has two components. Simple average of the relative indices of these components is used to get the Composite Relative Index of each of these four sectors. The aggregate average of relative indices of four components of education and health yield the relative aggregate average social infrastructure index and the aggregate average of relative indices of remaining seven components give relative aggregate average economic infrastructure index.

In Figures 3.1(a) to 3.7(c), the lower panel shows the relative indicator and the upper panel, the respective infrastructure index of Gujarat and India. The relative index greater than one hundred indicates a higher level of infrastructure stock (with respect to area or population) of Gujarat than India's average and the relative index lower than one hundred indicates a lower level of infrastructure stock (with respect to area or population) of Gujarat than India's average.

3.2.1 Transportation

In this study two indicators of transportation—road length and rail route length have been considered. The graphical representations of 'road length per 100 sq. km. of area' of Gujarat, India and Gujarat's relative index (with respect to India's average) with respect to this indicator are given below:

From the graphical analysis [Figure 3.1(a) (part 1)] it is clearly seen that, Gujarat's road length per 100 sq. km. of area was comparatively lower than India's average for all the years (1980-81 to 2009-10) except in 1999-00. Though Gujarat's road length per 100 sq. km. of area varied between 28.54 km. and 39.87 km. in the time period 1980-81 to 1990-91 and between 40.48 km. and 44.71 km. in the time period 1991-92 to 1998-99, yet it gets a sudden hike in 1999-00 which not only increased significantly the road length of Gujarat but also makes it slightly higher than India's average. The road length per 100 sq. km. of area in Gujarat

Figure 3.1(a): Road Length (in km)

Part-1:

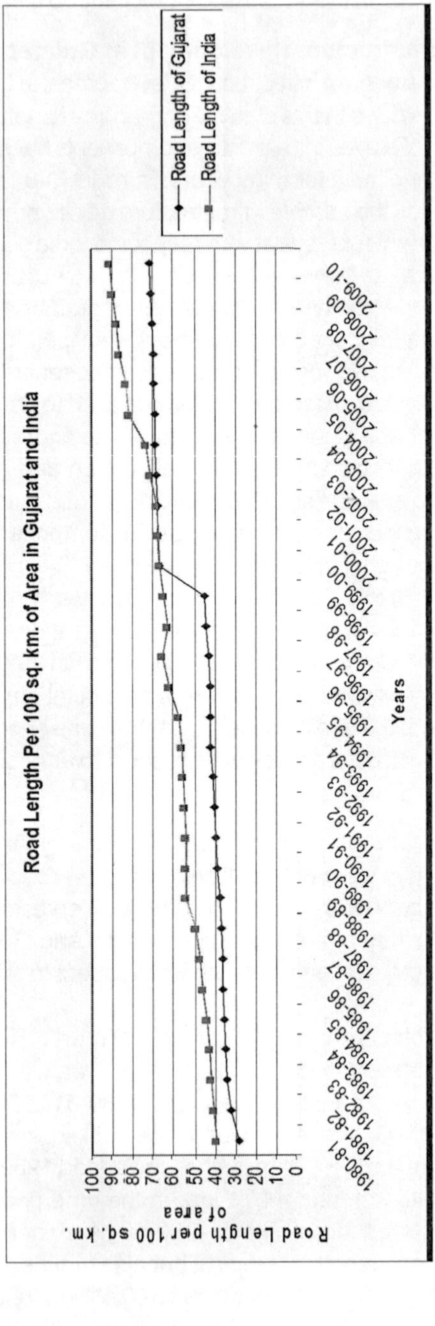

Figure 3.1(a): Road Length (in km)
Part-2:

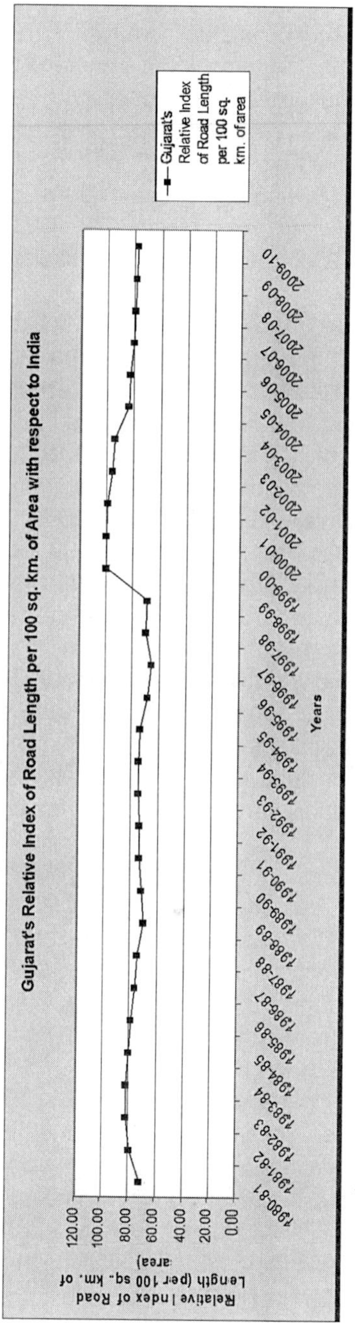

was 67.11 km. against India's average 66.99 km. in 1999-00. Gujarat's road length per 100 sq. km. of area increased from 67.42 km. in 2000-01 to 71.30 km. in 2009-10 against India's average 67.50 km. and 91.54 km. respectively. Though, Gujarat's road length per 100 sq. km. of area was lower than India's average in the given time period, yet the compound annual growth rate (CAGR) of road length in Gujarat (3.36 per cent between 1980-81 and 2009-10) was higher than India's 2.84 per cent because Gujarat increased its road length rapidly (specifically, between the years 1998-99 and 1999-2000) as compared to India's average in the given time period.

Further, it is found from Figure 3.1(a) (part 2) that Gujarat's relative index of road length per 100 sq. km. of area (with respect to India's average) increased steadily from 71.26 to 82.10 between the years 1980-81 and 1983-84, but from 1984-85 it started to decline and became 69.52 in 1988-89. Again, from 1989-90 it started to increase and raised continuously up to the period of 1993-94 (became 74.59). Between the years 1994-95 (relative index 73.58) and 1996-97 (relative index 66.01), the trend was decreasing in nature. In 1999-00, Gujarat's relative index of road length increased significantly and became 100.18, i.e. higher than India's average. From 2000-01 it again started to decline and was less than 100 for the rest of the years.

It is clear from the analysis that, except in 1999-00, Gujarat's relative index of road length per 100 sq. km. of area was less than 100 for all the other years considered in this study.

So, it can be concluded that Gujarat's road length per 100 sq. km. of area was below India's average in the given time period (except in 1999-00).

Another component of transportation infrastructure considered in this study is the rail route length. The graphical representations of 'rail route length per 100 sq. km. of area' in Gujarat, India and Gujarat's relative index (with respect to India's average) are given below.

It is found from Figure 3.1 (b) (part 1) that Gujarat's rail route length per 100 sq. km. of area increased from 2.85 km (India's average1.86 km) in 1980-81 to 2.87 km (India's average1.881 km.) in 1985-86 and remained stagnant up to the year 1987-88. In 1988-89, Gujarat's rail route length per 100 sq. km. of area declined to 2.675 km. (India's average 1.885 km.) due to decline in its metre gauge and narrow gauge and remained stagnant up to 1989-90 (India's average 1.8925 km). In 1990-91, it increased to 2.727 km. (India's average 1.897 km.) due to increase in its metre gauge and then started to decline and became 2.686 km. (India's average 1.908 km.) in 1996-97 due to further decline in its metre

Figure 3.1(b): Rail Route Length (in km)
Part 1:

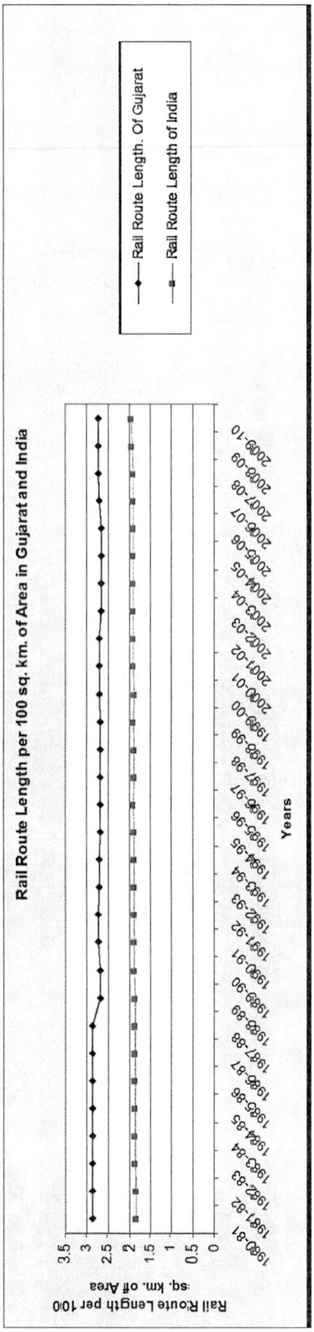

Figure 3.1(b): Rail Route Length (in km)
Part 2:

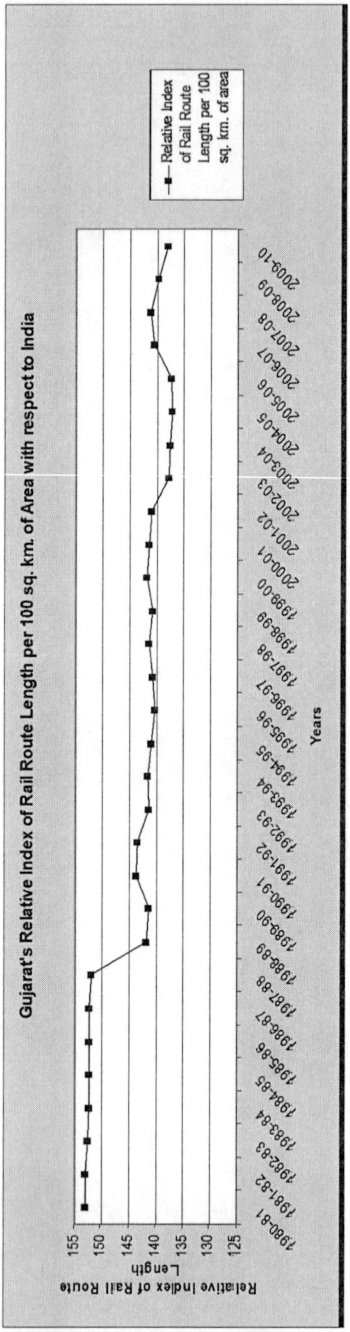

Figure 3.1(c): Relative Transportation Index

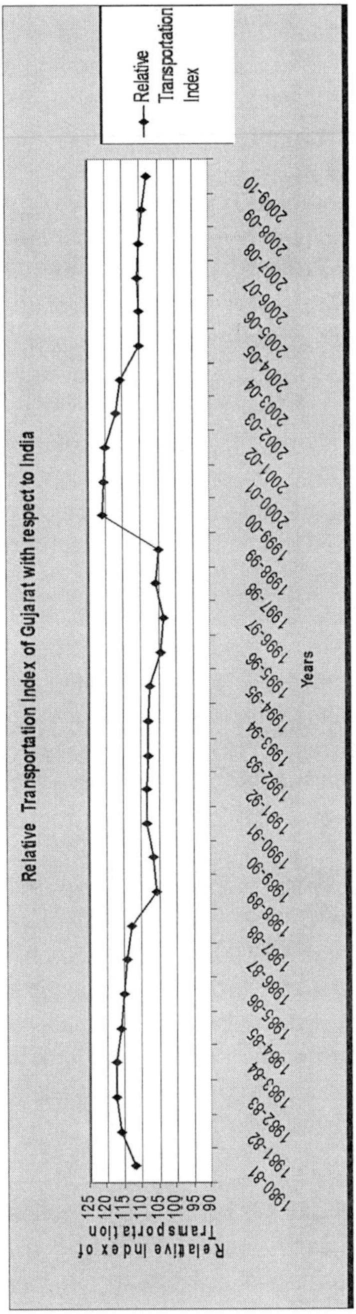

Source: Based on the data given in Appendix 1.

gauge. From 1997-98, it again started to increase due to increase in broad gauge and became 2.7099 km. (India's average 1.9174 km.) in 2000-01. From 2001-02 it started to decline and became 2.7089 km. (India's average 1.9208 km.) due to decrease in its metre gauge. It was 2.6466 km. (India's average 1.9266 km.) in 2005-06. From 2006-07 it again started to increase due to increase in its broad gauge and became 2.718 km. (India's average 1.97 km.) in 2009-10.

Though, rail route length in Gujarat decreased from 2.85 km. per 100 sq. km. of area in 1980-81 to 2.718 km. per 100 sq. km. of area in 2009-10 (due to decrease in its metre gauge or narrow gauge given in Appendix 3), it was comparatively higher than India's average (1.86 km. and 1.97 km. in 1980-81 and 2009-10 respectively) and accounting for about 8.4 per cent of total rail route length of India.

It is found from Figure 3.1 (b) (part 2) that, Gujarat's relative index of rail route length per 100 sq. km. of area was much above hundred (153.02 in 1980-81 and 137.97 in 2009-10). So, it can be concluded that Gujarat's rail route length per 100 sq. km. of area was higher than India's average in the given time period.

Gujarat's aggregate average of relative indices of road length and rail route length gives the relative index of transportation infrastructure (with respect to India's average), which is given in Figure 3.1(c).

It is evident from the Figure 3.1(c) that, the relative transportation index of Gujarat (with respect to India's average) increased from 112.14 in 1980-81 to 117.29 in 1983-84. Then, it started to decline and became 105.70 in 1988-89. It started to increase again from 1989-90 and became 108.50 in 1991-92.

Though, the relative transportation index varied between 103.40 and 108.06 in the time period 1992-93 to 1998-99, yet it increased steadily in 1999-2000 and became 121.06 due to sudden hike in road length in Gujarat. Then it again started to decline and became 107.93 in 2009-10.

So it can be concluded that, the relative transportation index of Gujarat was above hundred for the whole period considered in this study (1980-81 to 2009-10) i.e. Gujarat's transportation infrastructure stock (with respect to area) was higher than all India's average for the given time period.

3.2.2 Communication

In modern era of globalisation communication infrastructure has tremendous importance to narrow down the global distance. Here, two types of important communication infrastructure have been considered- post offices and telecommunication.

Figure 3.2(a): Post Offices
Part 1:

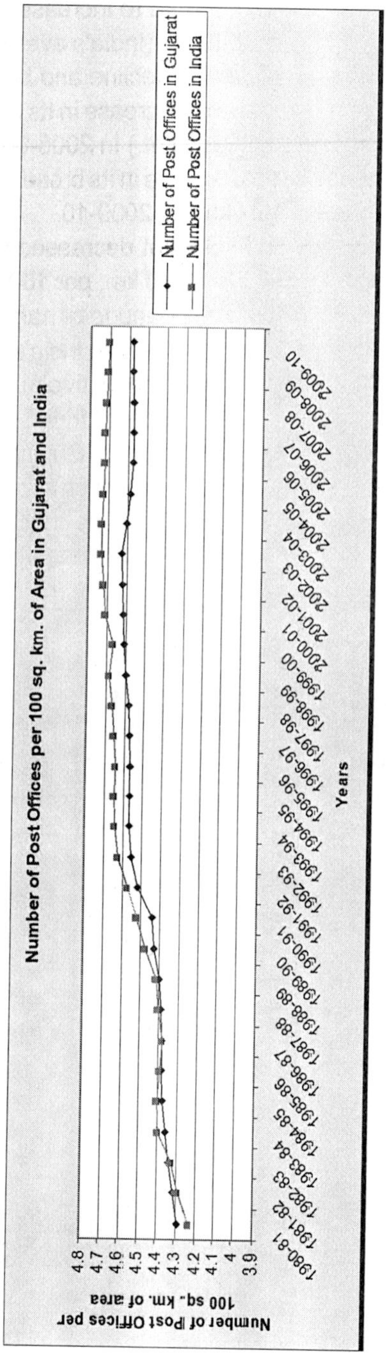

Figure 3.2(a): Post Offices
Part 2:

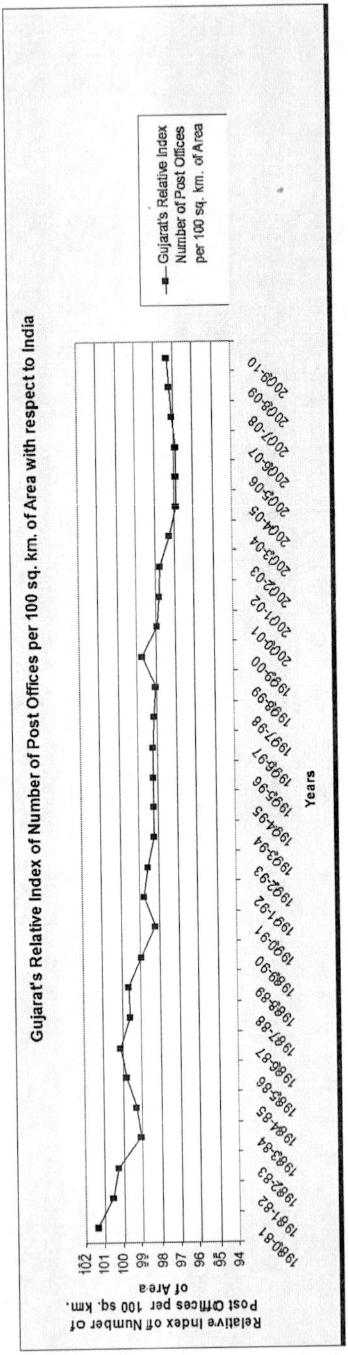

Effectiveness of postal network is an important indicator to discuss the communication infrastructure of a state. The graphical representations of 'number of post offices per 100 sq. km. of area' in Gujarat, India and Gujarat's relative index (with respect to India's average) are given below.

It is found from the Figure 3.2(a) (part 1) that, the number of post offices per 100 sq. km. of area in Gujarat was 4.29 in 1980-81 against India's average 4.24. It increased gradually and became 4.62 in 2002-03 in Gujarat (India's average 4.72). After that it started to decline and became 4.579 (India's average 4.706) in 2009-10. The compound annual growth rate (CAGR) of number of post offices per 100 sq. km. of area in the time period 1980-81 to 2009-10 was 0.30 per cent in Gujarat against India's 0.40 per cent.

It is found from the Figure 3.2(a) (part 2) that, the relative index of number of post offices per 100 sq. km. of area the state Gujarat (with respect to India's average) was above 100 only up to the year 1982-83 (relative index 100.29) and then it started to decline and fell below 100. Except for the year 1986-87 (relative index 100.14), Gujarat's relative index with respect to this indicator was below 100 in the time period 1983-84 (99.09) to 2009-10 (97.40). Therefore, Gujarat's 'number of post offices per 100 sq. km. of area' was lower than India's average in the time period 1983-84 to 2009-10 (except in the year 1986-87).

The graphical representations of 'number of telephone connections per 100 people' in Gujarat, India and Gujarat's relative index (with respect to India's average) are given below.

It is found from the Figure 3.2(b) (part 1) that, Gujarat's telephone connections per 100 people increased from 0.58 in 1980-81 to 52.12 in 2009-10 against India's average 0.31 and 45.69 respectively. Though, the number of telephone connections per 100 people in Gujarat increased slowly between the years 1980-81 (0.58) and 2002-03 (7.77), yet it increased rapidly from 2003-04 (10.14) and became 52.12 in 2009-10 (against India's 7.08 in 2003-04 and 45.69 in 2009-10). The compound annual growth rate (CAGR) of telephone connections per 100 people in Gujarat was 15.72 per cent against India's 18.41 per cent in the time period 1980-81 to 2009-10.

It is found from the Figure 3.2(b) (part 2) that, though the trend of relative index of number of telephone connections per 100 people in Gujarat (with respect to India's average) was decreasing, yet it was always above one hundred in the given time period (185.41 in 1980-81 and 114.07 in 2009-10). So, we can conclude that Gujarat's number telephone connections per 100 people was higher than India's average in the given time period.

Figure 3.2(b): Telephone Connections
Part 1:

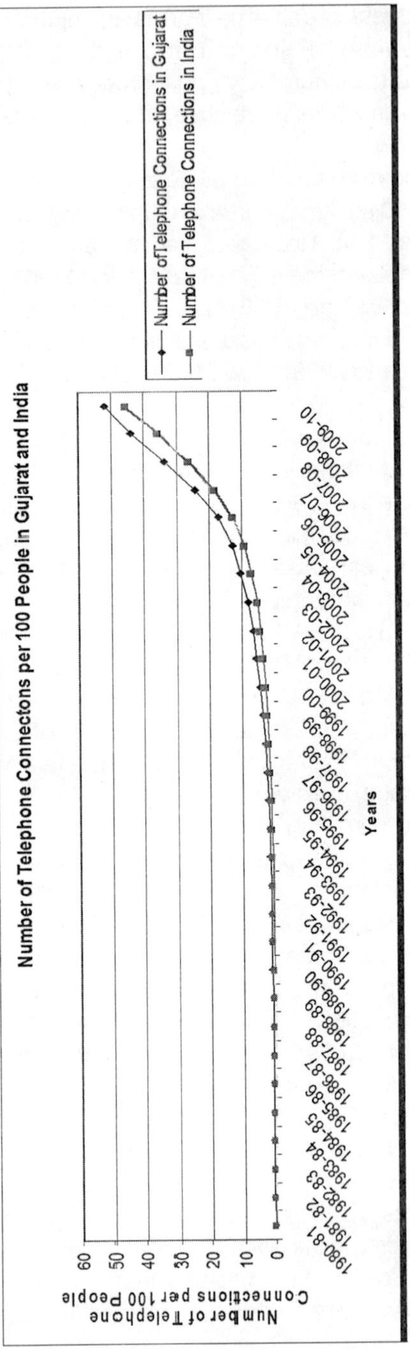

Figure 3.2(b): Telephone Connections Part 2:

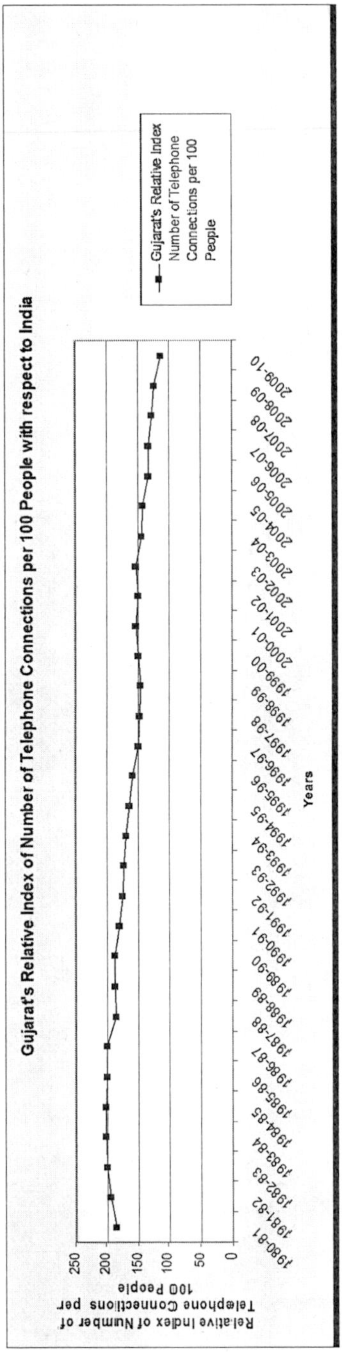

Figure 3.2(c): Relative Communication Index

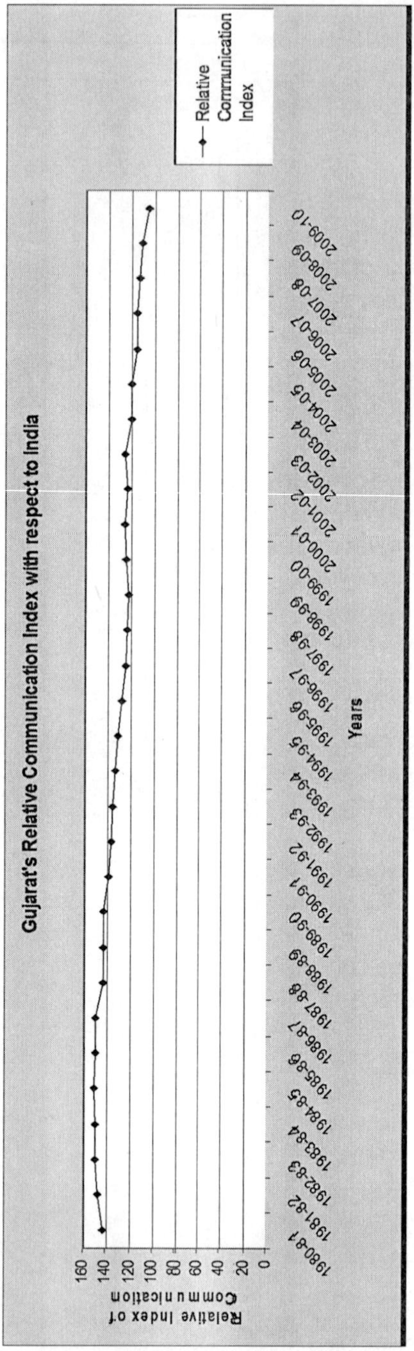

Source: Based on the data given in Appendix 1.

The Relative Communication index is the aggregate average of relative indices of telephone connections per 100 people and number of post offices per 100 sq. km. of area of Gujarat.

From Figure 3.2(c) it is clear that, the relative communication index of Gujarat was above100 but with decreasing trend (decreased from 143.39 in 1980-81 to 105.70 in 2009-10) in the given time period (1980-81 to 2009-10). The decreasing relative index of both the indicators- 'number of telephone connections per 100 people' and 'number of post offices per 100 sq. km. of area' of the state Gujarat is the reason behind this falling relative index. As the relative communication index of Gujarat was above 100 in the given time period, it can be concluded that, Gujarat's communication infrastructure stock was higher than India's average in the given time period.

3.2.3 Electricity

Gujarat has one of the most developed power sector with 24 hours power supply to 98 per cent of villages. Gujarat has taken numerous measures on Power Sector Reforms and has moved towards corporatisation/unbundling of Generation, Transmission and Distribution activities of the Gujarat Electricity Board. The state is endowed with high solar power radiation levels and the State Government proposes to encourage solar power generation projects as a means for socio-economic development.

The graphical representations of 'per capita electricity consumption' in Gujarat, India and Gujarat's relative index (with respect to India's average) are given below.

It is found from the Figure 3.3 (part 1) that, Gujarat's per capita annual consumption of electricity increased from 245.2 KWH in 1980-81 to 1491 KWH in 2009-10 against India's average 144.82 KWH and 523 KWH respectively. In 1985-86 both Gujarat and India experienced sudden hike and per capita consumption of electricity increased from 281.80 KWH (India's average 167.30 KWH) in 1984-85 to 580.32 KWH (India's average 340.96 KWH) in 1985-86. Though, in 1986-87 it decreased significantly to 320.21 KWH (India's average191 KWH) in Gujarat, yet from 1987-88 it again stated to increase and became 963 KWH (India's average 366.12 KWH) in 2001-02. In Gujarat, it decreased to 944 KWH in 2002-03 and 932 KWH in 2003-04. In 2004-05, Gujarat experienced again a sudden rise in per capita electricity consumption and it increased from 932 KWH (India's average 390.03 KWH) in 2003-04 to 1321 KWH (India's average 411.04 KWH) in 2004-05. So, there is increasing trend of per capita electricity consumption in the state Gujarat in the given time period (except for the year 1986-87 and for the time period 2002-03 to

Figure 3.3: Electricity
Part 1:

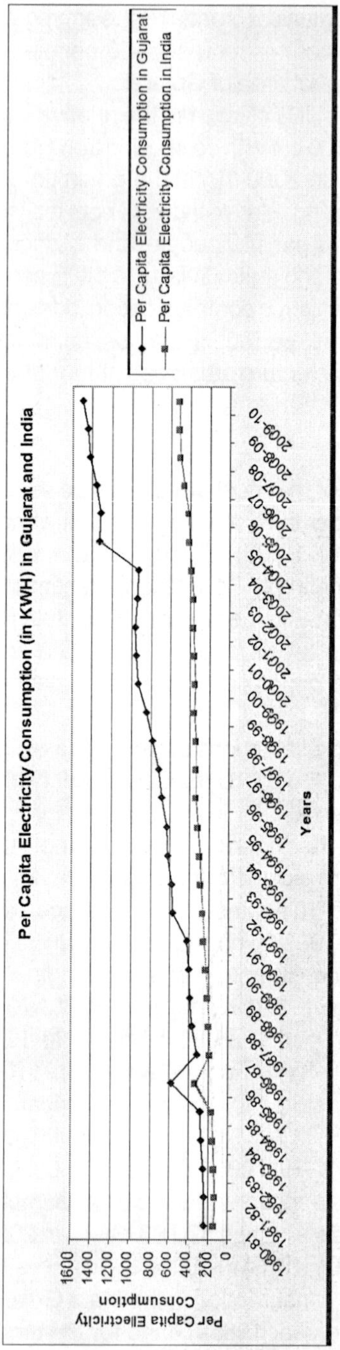

Figure 3.3: Electricity
Part 2:

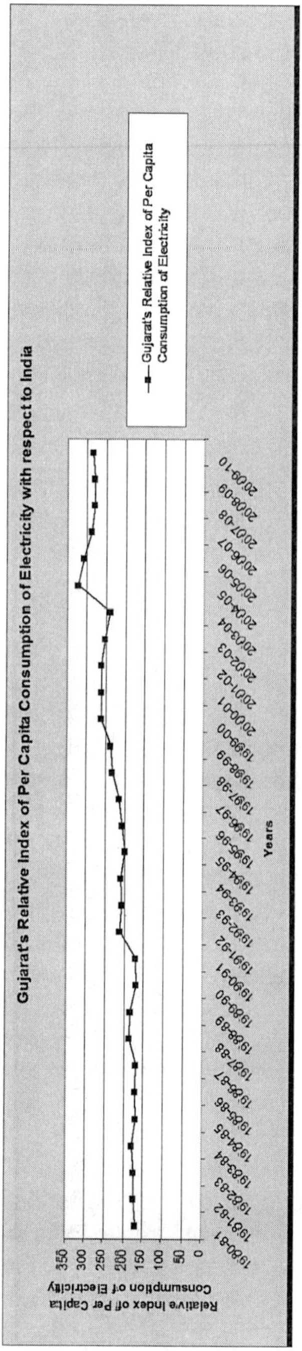

2003-04). The Compound Annual Growth Rate (CAGR) of this indicator in the time period 1980-81 to 2009-10 was 6.82 per cent in Gujarat and 4.39 per cent in India.

It is found from the Figure 3.3 (part 2) that, the relative index with respect to this indicator of the state Gujarat (with respect to India's average) was significantly higher than 100 in the given time period. The relative index varied between 169 and 185 in the time period 1980-81 to 1990-91. It was 321.38 in 2004-05 and 285.09 in 2009-10 which indicates that in 2004-05 Gujarat's per capita electricity consumption was more than triple and in 2009-10 it was more than double as compared to India's average. So it can be concluded that Gujarat's per capita electricity consumption was significantly higher than India's average for the given time period.

3.2.4 Banking

In this study banking facility is represented by 'number of scheduled commercial banks per 100 sq. km. of area'. The graphical representations of 'number of scheduled commercial banks per 100 sq. km. of area' in Gujarat, India and Gujarat's relative index (with respect to India's average) are given below.

It is evident from the Figure 3.4 (part 1) that, the number of scheduled commercial bank offices per 100 sq. km. of area in Gujarat increased from 1.259 to 2.332 in the time period 1980-81 to 2009-10 against India's average 1.074 in 1980-81 and 2.628 in 2009-10.

Though, it is evident from the graphical representation that there was increasing trend with respect to this indicator for the given time period both for Gujarat and India, yet Gujarat's number of scheduled commercial bank offices per 100 sq. km. of area was higher than India's average only for the time period 1980-81 to 1983-84. From 1984-85 Gujarat's number of scheduled commercial bank offices per 100 sq. km. of area (1.566) became lower than India's average (1.604) and it was below India's average for rest of the time period (from 1985-86 to 2009-10) also.

The compound annual growth rate (CAGR) of Gujarat was 1.41 per cent against India's 2.12 per cent with respect to this indicator in the given time period.

It is found from the Figure 3.4 (part 2) that, the relative index of number of scheduled commercial bank offices per 100 sq. km. of area in the state Gujarat was above 100 for the time period 1980-81 to 1983-84 i.e. it was higher in Gujarat as compared to India's average in the time period 1980-81 to 1983-84. It was less than 100 for the rest of the time period (1984-85 to 2009-10) i.e. it was lower in Gujarat as compared to India's average in the given time period (1984-85 to 2009-10).

Figure 3.4: Scheduled Commercial Bank Offices
Part 1:

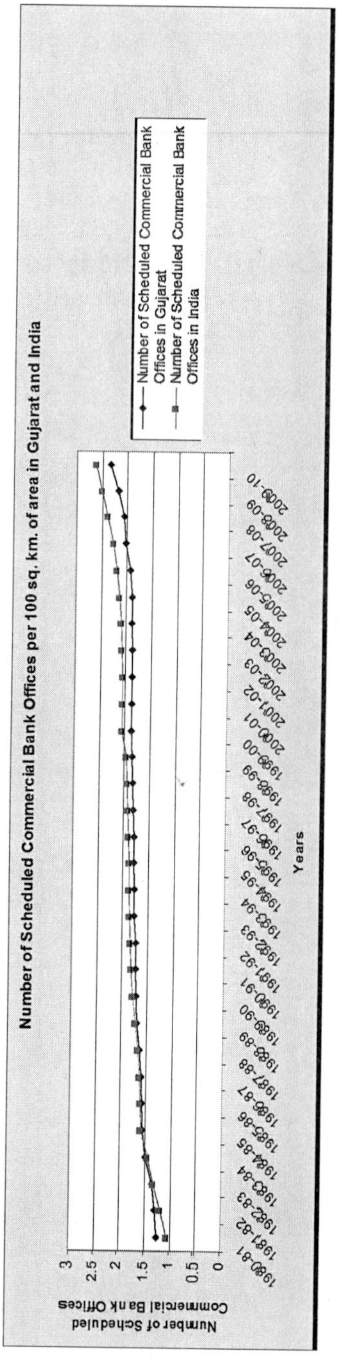

Figure 3.4: Scheduled Commercial Bank Offices
Part 2:

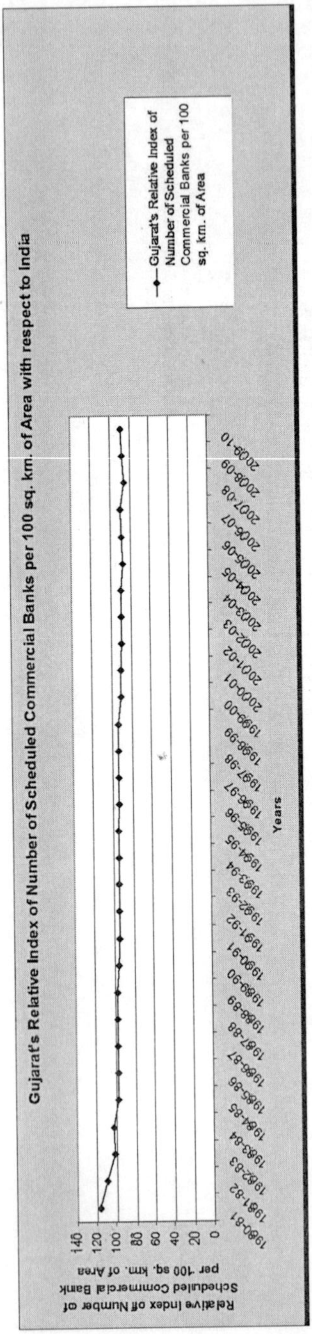

Figure 3.5: Irrigation
Part 1:

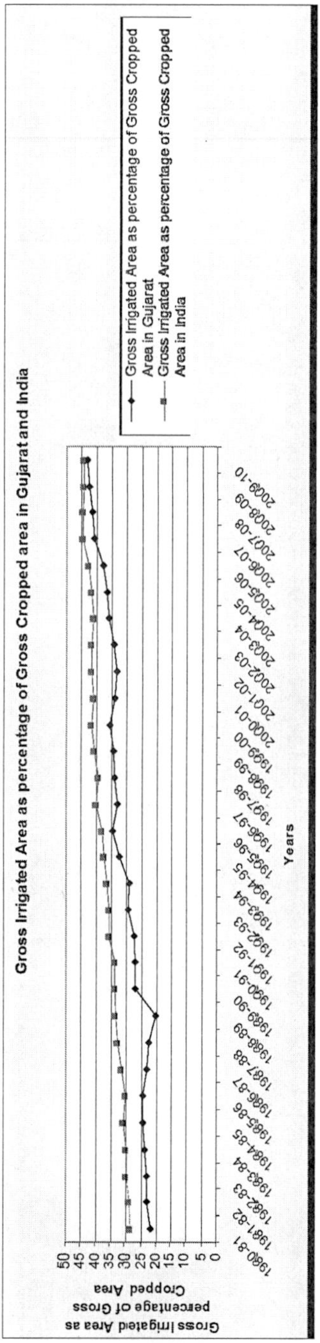

Figure 3.5: Irrigation
Part 2:

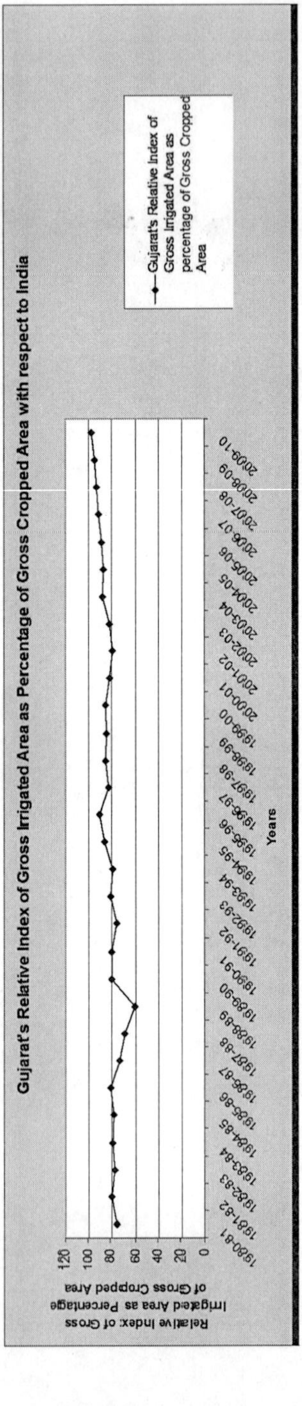

3.2.5 Irrigation

In this study, the variable 'gross irrigated area as percentage of gross cropped area' has been considered as proxy of irrigation facility. The graphical representations of gross irrigated area as percentage of gross cropped area in Gujarat, India and Gujarat's relative index (with respect to India's average) are given below.

It is evident from the Figure (3.5, part 1) that, though Gujarat experienced an increasing trend with respect to 'gross irrigated area as percentage of gross cropped area' for the time period 1980-81 to 2009-10, yet it was lower than India's average for the given time period.

Gujarat's gross irrigated area as percentage of gross cropped area increased from 21.83 per cent (India's average 28.83 per cent) in 1980-81 to 24.64 per cent (India's average 30.42 per cent) in 1985-86, then it started to decline in Gujarat and became 20.23 per cent (India's average 33.53 per cent) in the year 1988-89. From the year 1989-90, it again started to increase and became 34.71 per cent (India's average 38.25 per cent) in 1995-96 from 27.21 per cent (India's average 33.93 per cent) in 1989-90. It varied between 33.11 per cent (India's average 39.7 per cent) and 36.47 per cent (India's average 41.89 per cent) in the time period 1996-97 to 2004-05 and from 2005-06 it again started to increase and became 43.22 per cent (India's average 44.4 per cent) in 2009-10.

The compound annual growth rate (CAGR) of this indicator was 2.43 per cent in Gujarat against India's 1.61 per cent in the given time period.

It is evident from the Figure (3.5, part 2) that, though the relative index of this indicator increased from 75.72 in 1980-81 to 97.34 in 2009-10, yet it remained always below 100 i.e. the 'gross irrigated area as percentage of gross cropped area' in Gujarat was lower than India's average in the given time period.

3.2.6 Education

Educational infrastructure is one of the key ingredients of social infrastructure. Two indicators of this sector have been considered in this study- 'Number of schools per 100 sq. km of area' and 'Number of teachers per 100 enrolled pupils' (where primary, middle, high and higher secondary schools, teachers and pupils have been considered). The graphical representations of the number of schools per 100 sq. km of area in Gujarat, India and Gujarat's relative index (with respect to India's average) are given below.

It is evident from the Figure [3.6(a), part 1] that, Gujarat experienced an increasing trend with respect to 'number of schools per 100 sq. km. of area' in the given time period. It increased from 14.054 in 1980-81 to 24.514 in 2009-10 against India's average 19.882 and 37.296 respectively.

Figure 3.6(a): Schools
Part 1:

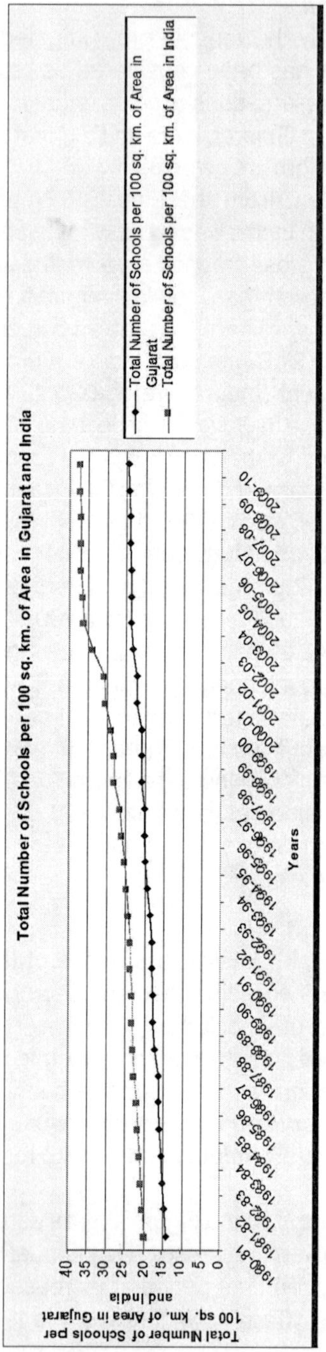

Figure 3.6(a): Schools
Part 2:

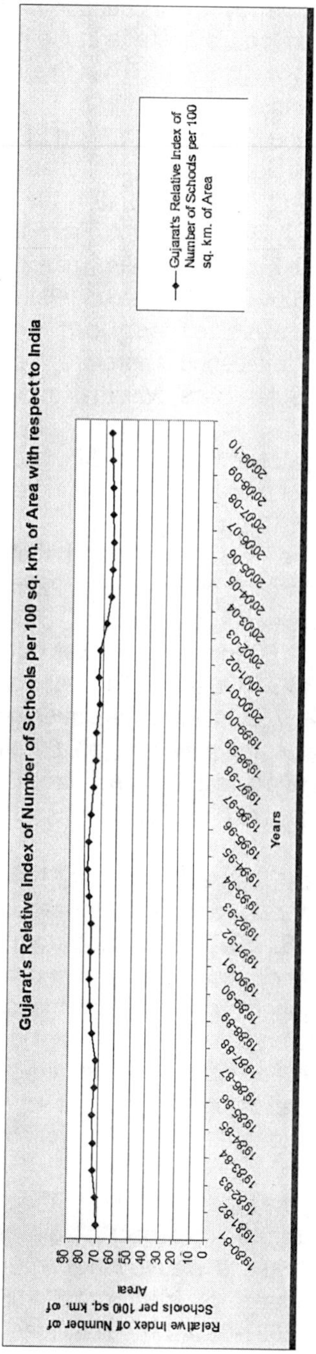

Therefore, Gujarat's number of schools per 100 sq. km. of area was significantly lower than India's average in the given time period. The Compound Annual Growth Rate (CAGR) of this indicator in Gujarat was 2.02 per cent against India's 2.42 per cent.

It is evident from the Figure [3.6(a), part 2] that, Gujarat's relative index of number of schools per 100 sq. km. of area (with respect to India) increased from 70.69 in 1980-81 to 73.49 in 1984-85 and then it started to decline and became 71.85 in 1986-87. From 1987-88, it again started to increase and became 78.28 in 1993-94. Then it again started to decline and became 65.73 in 2009-10. The trend of relative index of Gujarat with respect to this indicator was significantly lower than 100, varied between 65 and 78 in the given time period. Therefore, the number of schools per 100 sq. km. of area in Gujarat was lower than India's average in the given time period.

The second indicator of Educational infrastructure (considered in this study) is 'Number of teachers per 100 enrolled pupils' which is given in graphical form [Figure 3.6(b)].

It is evident from the Figure 3.6(b) (part 1) that, in Gujarat the number of teachers per 100 enrolled pupils was 2.722 in 1980-81 and 3.198 in 2009-10 against India's average 2.964 and 2.870 respectively. Gujarat's number of teachers per 100 enrolled pupils was higher than India's average for the time period 1983-84 (Gujarat's 2.768 against India's average 2.723) to 1986-87 (Gujarat's 2.719 against India's average 2.714), from 1988-89 (Gujarat's 2.754 against India's average 2.666) to 1996-97 (Gujarat's 2.628 against India's average 2.537) and from 2002-03 (Gujarat's 2.710 against India's average 2.701) to 2009-10 (Gujarat's 3.198 against India's average 2.870).

The relative index [Figure 3.6(b), part 2] of the state Gujarat with respect to this Indicator was above 100 for all the years except for nine years (1980-81 to 1982-83, 1987-88 and from 1997-98 to 2001-02). Therefore, it can be concluded that Gujarat's number of teachers per 100 enrolled pupils was higher than India's average for twenty one years and lower than India's average for rest of the years in the given time period.

The relative index of education is the aggregate average of the relative indices of these two indicators–'Number of schools per 100 sq. km of area' and 'Number of teachers per 100 enrolled pupils' which is given below in graphical form.

It is evident from the Figure 3.6(c) that, though the trend of relative education index in Gujarat (with respect to India) was increasing in nature for the time period 1980-81 (relative index 81.26) to 1993-94 (relative index 94.31), yet it started to decline from 1994-95 (relative index 92.37) and became 81.68 in 2001-02. It varied between 82 and 89 in the rest of

Figure 3.6(b): Number of Teachers per 100 Enrolled Pupils Part 1:

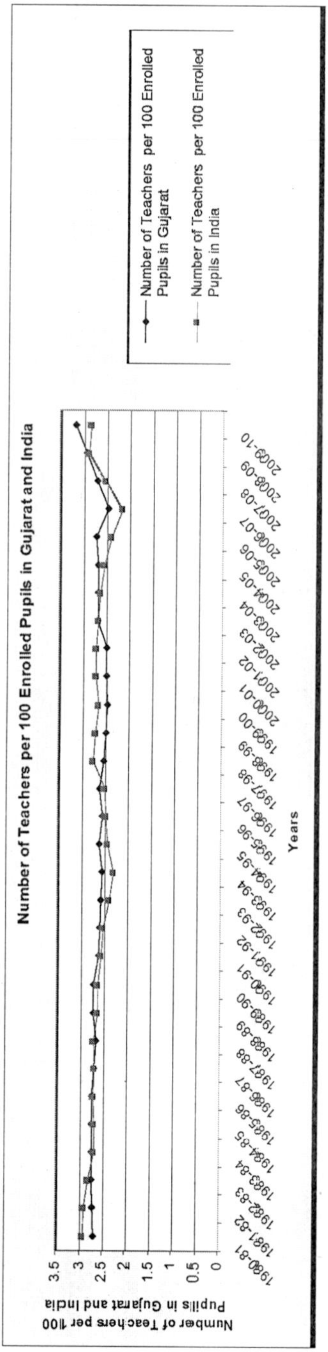

Figure 3.6(b): Number of Teachers per 100 Enrolled Pupils Part 2:

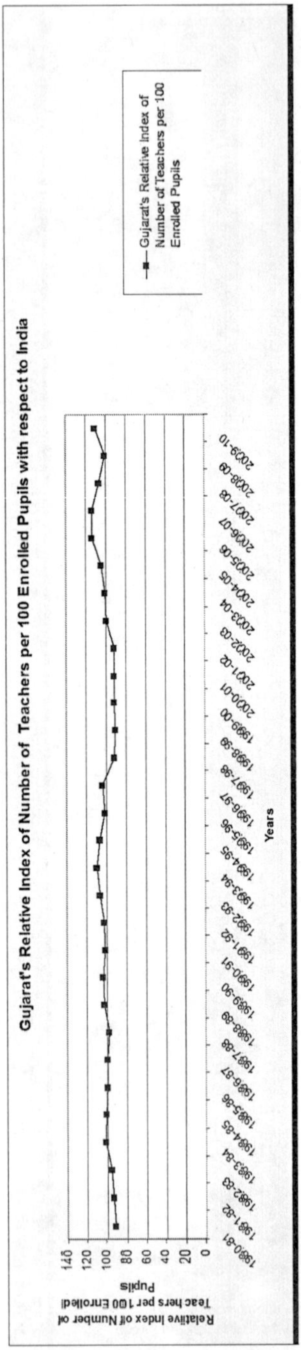

Figure 3.6(c): Relative Education Index

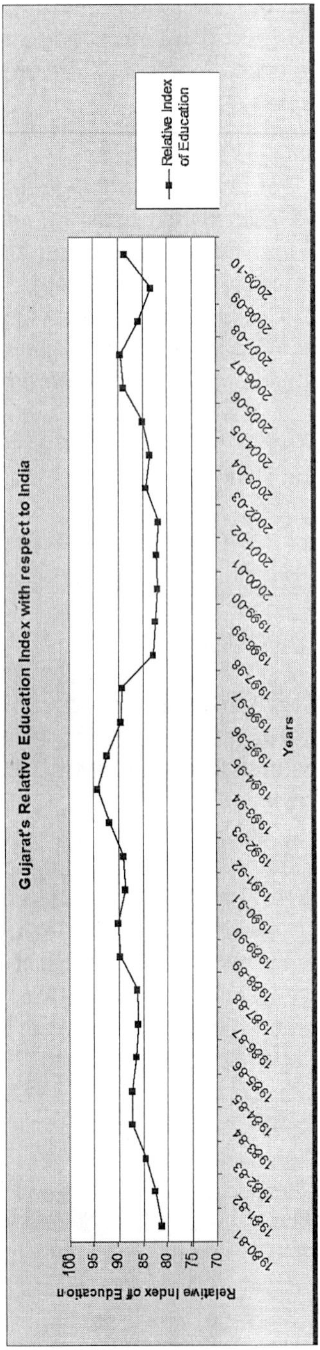

Source: Based on the data given in Appendix 1.

the time period. It was 88.58 in 2009-10. As the composite relative index of education of Gujarat was below 100 for whole period considered in this study, it can be concluded the educational infrastructure stock of the state Gujarat was lower than India's average in the given time period.

3.2.7 Health

Health infrastructure is another important ingredient of social infrastructure. In this study two indicator of health infrastructure have been considered– 'number of medical institutions per 100 sq. km. of area', [where medical institutions included Primary Health Centres (PHCs), Community Health Centres (CHCs), Sub-centres and Hospitals in rural and urban areas] and 'number of beds in medical institutions per 100 people' (where, medical institutions include government hospitals in rural and urban area) in the state. The graphical representations of the 'number of medical institutions per 100 sq. km. of area' in Gujarat, India and Gujarat's relative index (with respect to India's average) are given below.

It is evident from the Figure 3.7(a) part (1) that, in Gujarat number of medical institutions per 100 sq. km. of area increased from 1.582 in 1980-81 to 5.635 in 2002-03 against India's average 1.935 and 5.457 respectively. Then, it started to decline and became 4.651 in Gujarat in 2003-04 against India's average 5.307. From 2004-05, though the number of medical institutions per 100 sq. km. of area in India again started to rise and became 5.67 in 2009-10, yet Gujarat experienced declining trend with respect to this indicator between the years 2004-05 (4.654) and 2009-10 (4.588). Decrease in number of PHCs, CHCs and urban government hospitals in Gujarat are some major reasons behind it. In India, number of medical institutions per 100 sq. km. of area decreased between the years 2001-02 (5.457) and 2003-04 (5.307) because of heavy decreases in total hospitals in Madhya Pradesh, decrease in CHCs and also non-reporting by some states. Gujarat's number of medical institutions per 100 sq. km. of area was lower than India's average for all the years considered in this study, except for the time period 1983-84 (Gujarat's 2.75 against India's average 2.70) to 1987-88 (Gujarat's 4.27 against India's average 4.13) and 1991-92 (Gujarat's 5.17 against India's average 5.08) to 2002-03(Gujarat's 5.64 against India's average 5.46). The Compound Annual Growth Rate (CAGR) of medical institutions in the state Gujarat, in the given time period (1980-81 to 2009-10) was 2.74 per cent against India's 2.94 per cent.

It is evident from the Figure 3.7(a) part (2) that, the relative index of numbers of medical institutions per 100 sq. km. of area of the state Gujarat (with respect to India's average) was lower than 100 for all the

Figure 3.7(a): Medical Institutions Part 1:

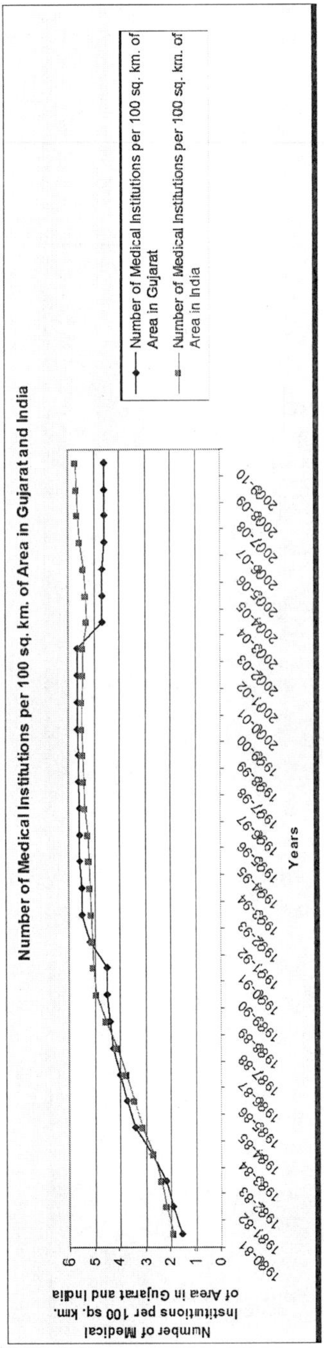

Figure 3.7(a): Medical institutions
Part 2:

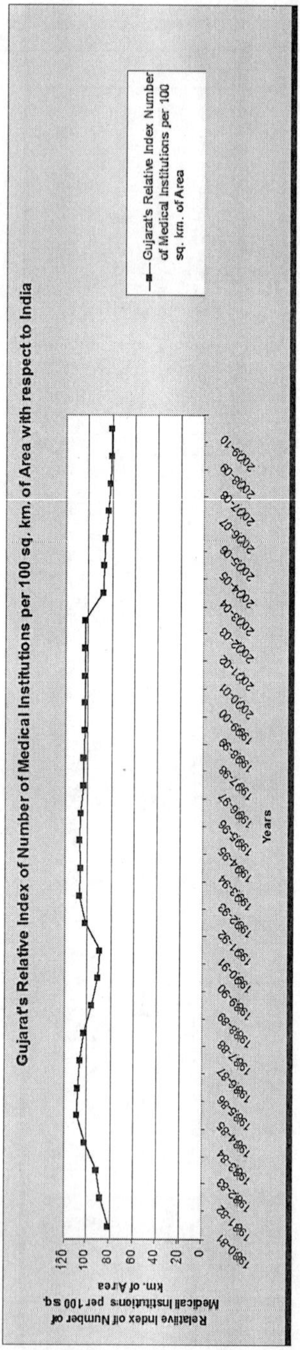

years in the time period 1980-81 to 2009-10 except from 1983-84 (relative index 102) to 1987-88 (relative index 103.17) and from 1991-92 (relative index 101.65) to 2002-03 (relative index 103.26). Therefore, except fifteen years (from 1983-84 to 1987-88 and from 1991-92 to 2002-03) for rest of the years in the given time period (1980-81 to 2009-10), Gujarat's number of medical institutions per 100 sq. km. of area was lower than India's average.

The graphical representations of the number of beds in medical institutions per 100 people in Gujarat, India and Gujarat's relative index (with respect to India's average) are given below.

It is evident from the Figure 3.7(b) (part 1) that, Gujarat's number of beds in medical institutions per 100 people was 0.0941 (against India's average 0.0683) in 1980-81 which increased to 0.141 in 1994-95 (against India's average 0.0679) and then started to decrease and became 0.0487 in 2009-10 (against India's average 0.0515). In 2003-04, both Gujarat and India experienced a sudden decline in number of beds in medical institution due to decrease in number of urban hospitals. Beds in medical institutions in Gujarat also abolished due to dots treatment in National T.B. control programme. In India, it decreased due to non-reporting by some states also.

It is evident from the Figure 3.7(b) (part 2) that, the relative index of this indicator for Gujarat was above 100 for the time period 1980-81 to 2008-09. In 2009-10 it became 94.55 i.e. lower than India's average. Therefore, Gujarat's number of beds in medical institutions per 100 people was higher than India's average for all the years except in 2009-10.

Gujarat's relative health index is aggregate average of the relative indices of these two indicators-number of medical institutions per 100 sq. km. of area and number of beds in medical institutions per 100 people which is represented below graphically.

It is evident from Figure 3.7(c) that, Gujarat's relative health index was greater than 100 for the time period 1980-81 (relative health index 109.75) to 2006-07(relative health index 101.47) i.e. Gujarat's health infrastructure stock was higher than India's average for the time period 1980-81 to 2006-07. It was less than 100 (i.e. lower than India's average) for the time period 2007-08 (relative health index 94.56) to 2009-10 (relative index 87.44).

3.3 Relative Aggregate Average Infrastructure Indices

Relative aggregate average infrastructure index is nothing but the simple average of all infrastructure components which have been considered in this study. Here, three types of relative aggregate average indices have been represented graphically-Relative Aggregate Average

Figure 3.7(b): Numbers of Beds in Medical Institutions per 100 People

Part 1:

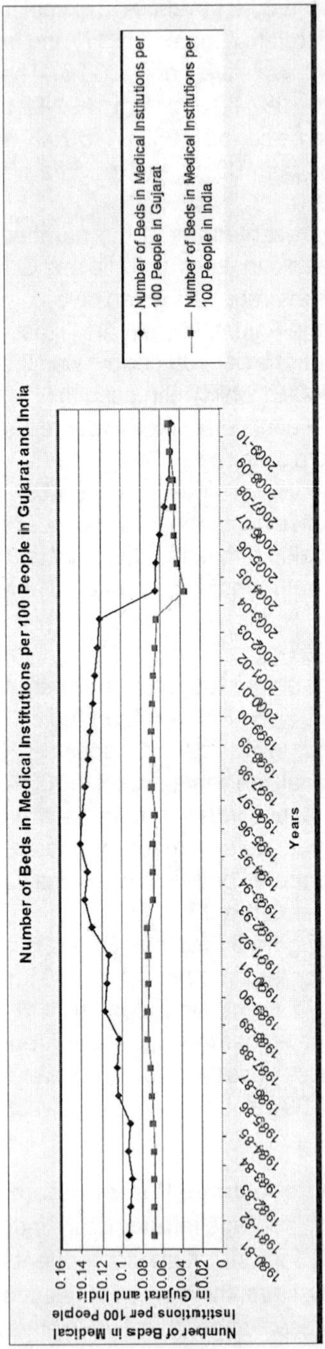

Figure 3.7(b): Numbers of Beds in Medical Institutions per 100 People Part 2:

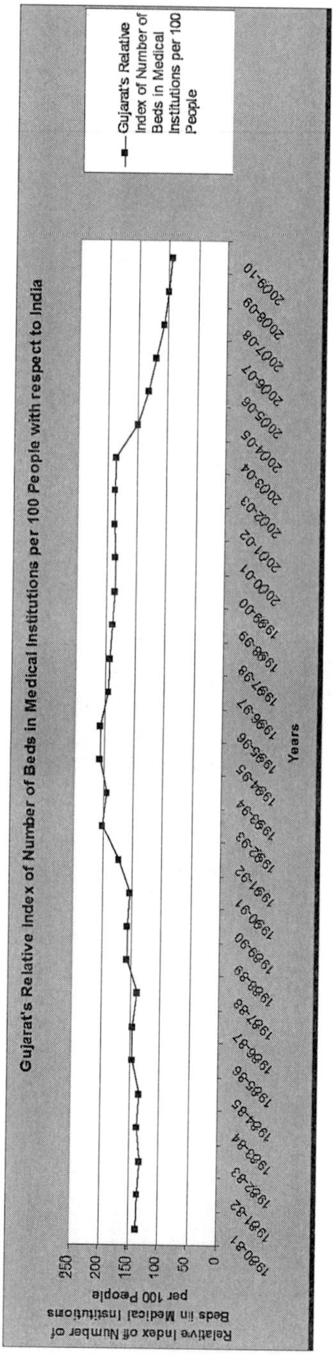

Figure 3.7(c): Relative Health Index

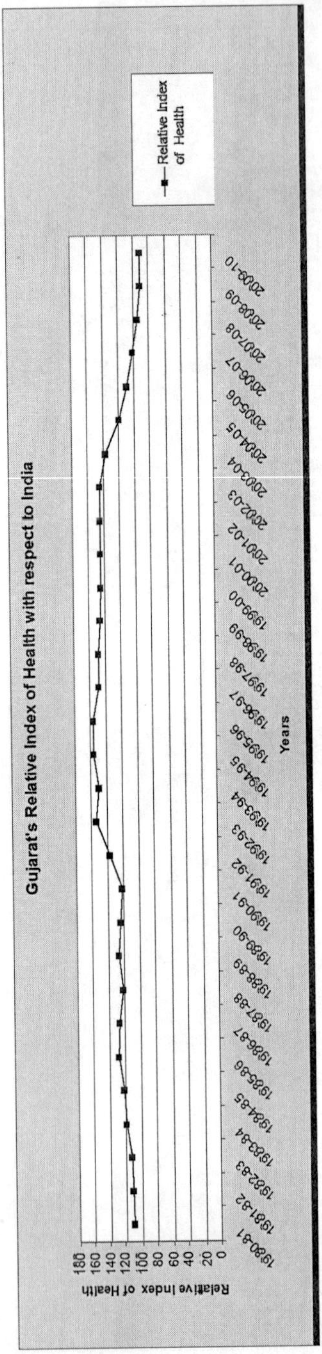

Source: Based on the data given in Appendix 1.

Economic Infrastructure Index (simple average of relative indices of all the economic infrastructure indicators related to transportation, communication, electricity, banking and irrigation), Relative Aggregate Average Social Infrastructure Index (simple average of all the relative indices of social infrastructure components related to education and health) and Relative Aggregate Average Infrastructure Index (simple average of relative indices of all the eleven components of infrastructure considered in this study).

It is evident from Figure 3.8(a) that Gujarat's relative aggregate average economic infrastructure was above 100 for the given time period. It was 124.76 in 1980-81 and decreased to 119.80 in 1988-89. It again started to increase from the year 1989-90 (120.58) and became 136.65 in 2004-05. From 2005-06 (relative index 133.43), it again stated to decline and became 128.34 in 2009-10. Therefore, Gujarat's economic infrastructure stock was higher than India's average for the given time period.

In the case of Gujarat's relative aggregate average social infrastructure index [given in Figure 4.8(b)], though it remained above 100 in the time period 1983-84 (relative index 103.54) to 2004-05 (relative index 101.87), yet it was below 100 for the rest of the time period under consideration, i.e. from 1980-81 to 1982-83 (varied between 95.5 and 98.4) and from 2005-06 to 2009-10 (varied between 87 and 98). Therefore, Gujarat's social infrastructure stock was higher than India's average for the time period 1983-84 to 2004-05 and lower than India's average for the time period 1980-81 to 1982-83 and 2005-06 to 2009-10.

So, it can be concluded that, as compared to India's average, Gujarat's economic infrastructure stock was higher than its social infrastructure stock in the given time period because Gujarat's relative aggregate average economic infrastructure index varied between 119.8 and 136.65 and its relative aggregate average social infrastructure index varied between 87.08 and 124.78 in the time period 1980-81 to 2009-10.

Gujarat's relative aggregate average infrastructure index [Figure 3.8 (c)] was above 100 for all the years in the given time period. It varied between 113.55 and 125.64 in the time period 1980-81 to 2009-10. Therefore, Gujarat's infrastructure stock in average was higher than India's average in the given time period.

3.4 Economic Growth

In this study per capita net State Domestic Product (NSDP) at factor cost and constant prices (base: 1999-2000) has been used as proxy of economic growth in Gujarat. The graphical representations of per capita

Figure 3.8(a): Relative Aggregate Average Economic Infrastructure Index

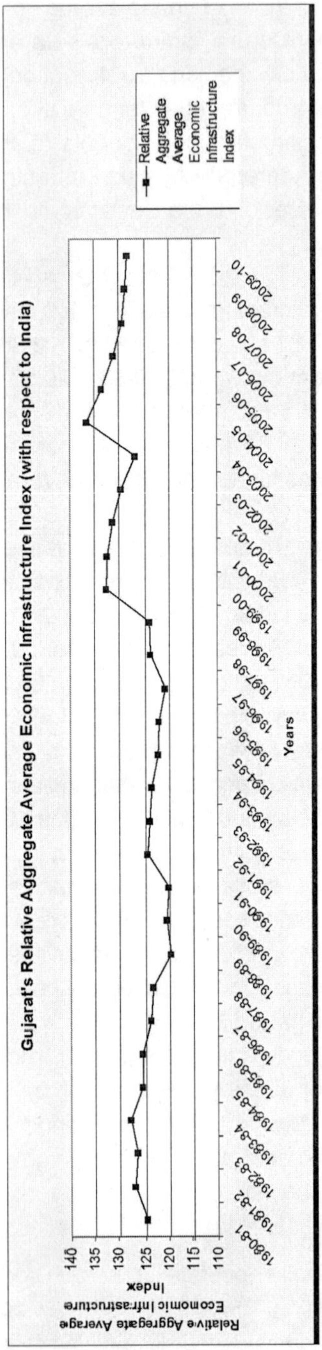

Figure 3.8(b): Relative Aggregate Average Social Infrastructure Index

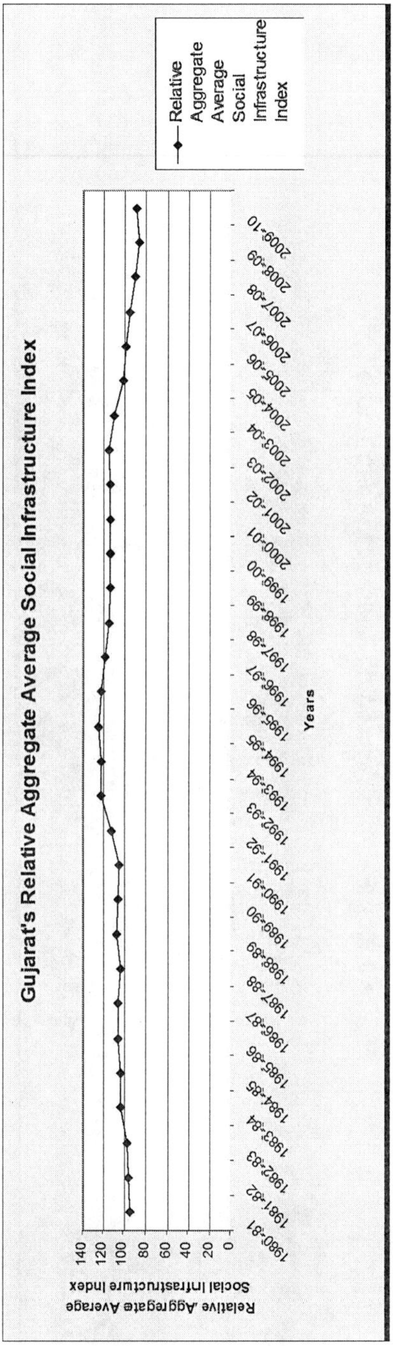

Figure 3.8(c): Relative Aggregate Average Infrastructure Index

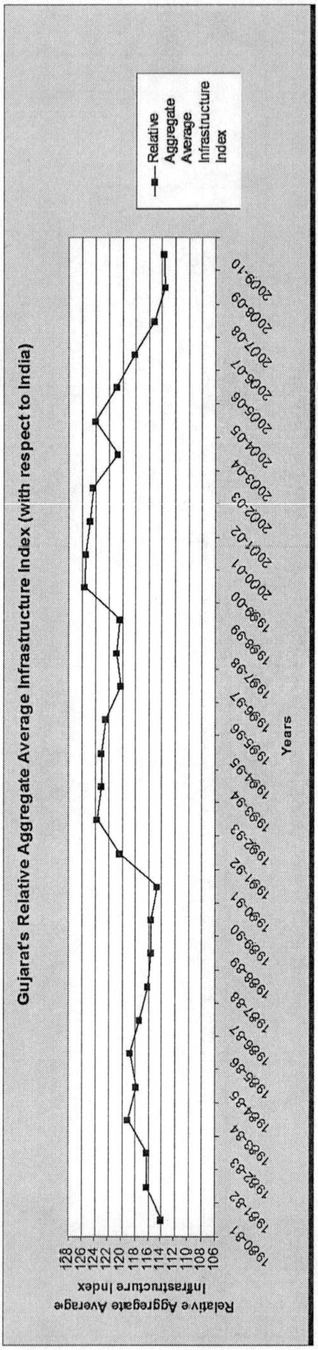

Source: Based on the data given in Appendix 2.

Figure 3.9: Per Capita NSDP at Factor Cost and Constant Prices (base:1999-2000)

Part 1:

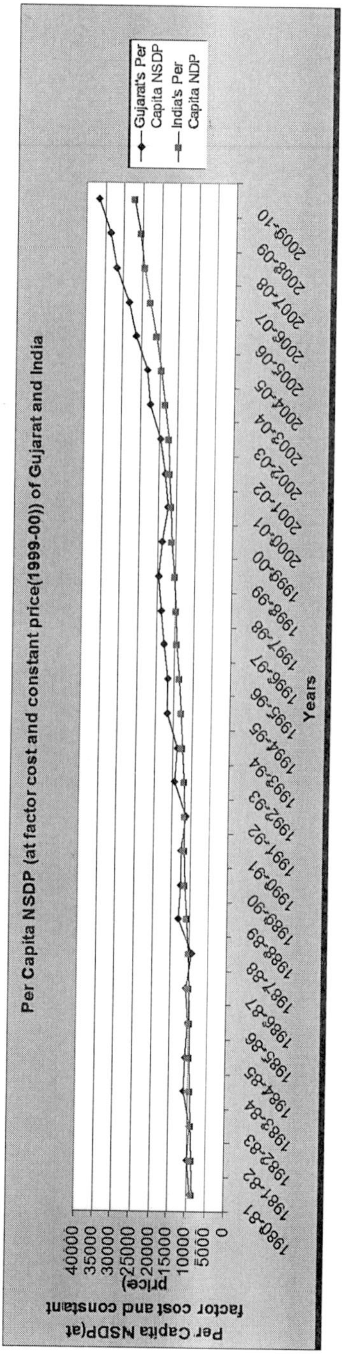

Figure 3.9: Per Capita NSDP at Factor Cost and Constant Prices (base:1999-2000) Part 2:

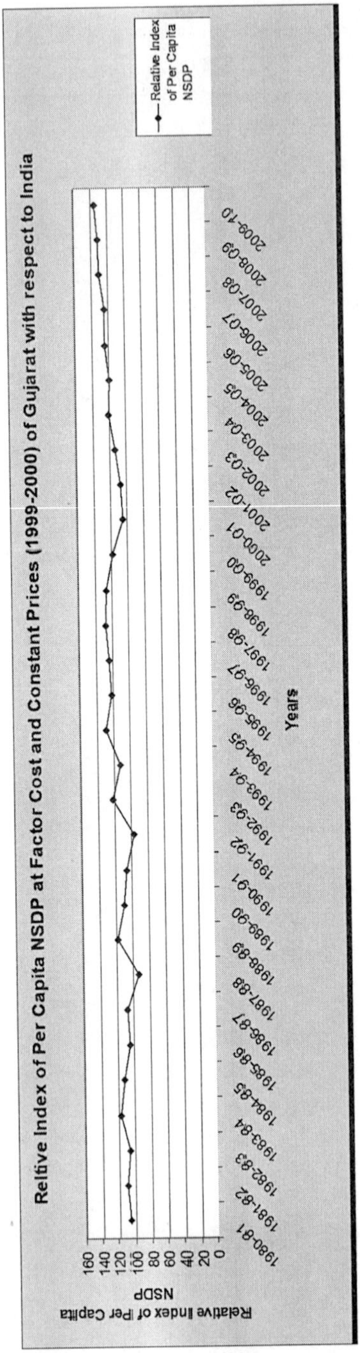

Source: Based on the data given in Appendix 3.

NSDP of Gujarat, India and Gujarat's relative index with respect to India's per capita Net Domestic Product (NDP) are given below.

It is evident from Figure 3.9 (part 1) that, Gujarat's per capita NSDP at factor cost and constant prices (base: 1999-00) was Rs 9157 (against India's Rs 8594) in 1980-81, increased to Rs 11059 (against India's Rs 9464) in 1983-84. From 1984-85 it started to decline (Rs 10823 in Gujarat against India's Rs 9609) and became Rs 9374 in Gujarat (against India's Rs 10083) in 1987-88. In 1988-89, it increased significantly to Rs12919 in Gujarat (against India's Rs 10916) and then it again declined to Rs 11239 (against India's Rs 11600) in 1991-92. From 1992-93 it increased significantly in Gujarat (Gujarat's Rs14590 against India's Rs 11989) and became Rs 19484 (against India's Rs 15372) in 1998-99. In 1999-00 it again started to decline in Gujarat and became Rs18864 (against India's Rs 16035). It was Rs 17227 in Gujarat in 2000-01 (against India's Rs 16393). From 2001-02 both Gujarat and India experienced consistently increasing per capita NSDP (at factor cost and constant prices (base: 1999-00)). It increased from Rs 18200 in Gujarat (against India's Rs 16963) in 2001-02 to Rs 36665 (against India's Rs 27101) in 2009-10. Therefore, except in 1987-88 and 1991-92, for all the years (in the given time period), Gujarat's per capita NSDP [at factor cost and constant prices (base: 1999-00)] was higher than India's per capita NDP [at factor cost and constant prices (base: 1999-00)].

It is evident from Figure 3.9 (part 2) that, the relative index of per capita NSDP [at factor cost and constant prices (base: 1999-00)] was above 100 for all the years in the given time period (1980-81 to 2009-10) except in the year 1987-88 (relative index 92.97) and 1991-92 (relative index 96.89). So, it may be concluded that Gujarat's per capita NSDP [at factor cost and constant prices (base: 1999-00)] was higher than India's per capita NDP [at factor cost and constant prices (base: 1999-00)] in the given time period (1980-81 to 2009-10) except for the years 1987-88 and 1991-92.

3.5 Gujarat's Infrastructure Index Score and Rank among Major States in India

To determine the rank of the state Gujarat in infrastructure development among 15 major states of India, the state-wise data with respect to Weighted Aggregate Economic Infrastructure Index (WAEII), Weighted Aggregate Social Infrastructure Index (WASII) and Weighted Aggregate Infrastructure Index (WAII) in 2009-10 is given below in Table 4.1. Here, Weighted Aggregate Economic Infrastructure Index is the weighted aggregation of seven components of economic infrastructure (Road Length per 100 sq. km. of area, Rail Route Length per 100 sq. km. of area, Number of Post Offices per 100 sq. km. of area, Number of

Table 3.1: Infrastructure Index and Rank of Fifteen Major States in India in 2009-10

States	*WAEII*	*Rank*	*WASII*	*Rank*	*WAII*	*Rank*
Andhra Pradesh	55.678	8	1.050	6	56.728	8
Assam	25.931	14	0.732	13	26.663	14
Bihar	68.670	3	0.689	14	69.359	3
Gujarat	**80.054**	**2**	**1.144**	**4**	**81.198**	**2**
Haryana	104.439	1	0.888	11	105.327	1
Karnataka	28.737	12	1.346	2	30.083	12
Kerala	16.590	15	1.411	1	18.001	15
Madhya Pradesh	64.232	5	0.806	12	65.038	6
Maharashtra	35.265	10	0.964	9	36.229	10
Orissa	25.960	13	0.919	10	26.879	13
Punjab	67.573	4	1.006	8	68.579	4
Rajasthan	64.066	6	1.123	5	65.189	5
Tamil Nadu	54.445	9	1.248	3	55.693	9
Uttar Pradesh	57.305	7	0.528	15	57.833	7
West Bengal	34.162	11	1.0237	7	35.1857	11

Source: Self Calculated.

(*Note*: Here, WAEII = Weighted Aggregate Economic Infrastructure Index, WASII = Weighted Aggregate Social Infrastructure Index and WAII = Weighted Aggregate Infrastructure Index)

Telephone Connections per 100 People, Per Capita Electricity Consumption, Gross Irrigated Area as percentage of Gross Cropped Area and Number of Scheduled Commercial Banks per 100 sq. km. of area), Weighted Aggregate Social Infrastructure Index is the weighted aggregation of four components of social infrastructure components Number of Schools per 100 sq. km. of Area (include primary, secondary, high and higher secondary schools.), Number of Teachers per 100 Enrolled Pupils (based on the total numbers of teachers and total enrolled pupils in primary, secondary, high and higher secondary school), Number of Medical Institutions (PHCs, CHCs, sub-centres and hospitals in rural and urban areas) per 100 sq. km. of area and Numbers of Beds in Medical Institutions (government hospitals of rural and urban areas) per 100 People and Weighted Aggregate Infrastructure Index (weighted aggregation of all the eleven components of infrastructure considered here), where weights are assigned with the help of Principal Component Analysis.

It is evident from the Table 3.1 that, Gujarat obtained second rank with respect to Weighted Aggregate Economic Infrastructure Index as well as Weighted Aggregate Infrastructure Index (only after Haryana). Gujarat's improved transportation, communication, electricity infrastructure are the reason behind the comparatively better economic infrastructure in the state. Again, the state obtained fourth rank with respect to Weighted Aggregate Social Infrastructure Index (after Kerala, Karnataka and Tamil Nadu). The comparatively low education infrastructure and health infrastructure (with respect to number of medical institutions per 100 sq. km. of area) is the reason behind it.

3.6 Empirical Results

To examine the causal relationship between infrastructure and economic growth in Gujarat with the help of time series data (1980-81 to 2009-10), the weighted aggregate infrastructure index of Gujarat has been calculated. The weights have been assigned to each of the eleven selected infrastructure components according to their importance by using Principal Component Analysis. SPSS-18 software has been used for this analysis. According to K Seeta Prabhu and PC Sarkar (*EPW*, Sept 5, 1992, pp. 1927-1937), in the calculation of the principal component scores, instead of using standardised variables (as usual practice) as it distorts the dispersion of the original indicator, each indicator should be divided by its mean in order to remove the scale bias in the data and in this study the same has been done. Again both first and second principal component scores have been used here, which together explain above 80 per cent of variance. The inter-correlation matrix, principal component scores, communalities, eigen values, percentage of variances etc. with respect to thirty years time series data (1980-81 to 2009-10) of eleven components infrastructure (considered in this study) of the state Gujarat are given below.

3.6.1 Principal Component Analysis

From the given inter-correlation matrix of infrastructure [Table 3.2(a)], it is observed that most of the variables are significantly positively correlated. The positive correlation explains that all the variables move in the same direction.

The variable I1 is significantly, positively correlated with I3, I4, I5, I6, I7, I8 and I10. The variable I3 is significantly, positively correlated with I1, I4, I5, I6, I7, I8 and I10. Similarly, the variable I4 is significantly, positively correlated with I1, I3, I5, I6, I7, I8 and I9. Again, the variable I5 is significantly, positively correlated with I1, I3, I4, I6, I7, I8 and I10. The variable I7 is significantly, positively correlated with I1, I3, I4, I5, I6, I8 and I10. The variable I8 has significant positive correlated with the variables I1, I3, I4, I5, I6, I7 and I10. Further, the variable I10 is significantly positively correlated with I1, I3, I5, I6, I7, I8 and I11.

There are few variables which are negatively correlated. The variable I2 is significantly negatively correlated with the variables I1, I3, I4, I5, I6, I7, I8 and I10. It may be the decreasing trend of 'Rail-Route Length per 100 sq. km. of area (I2)' in Gujarat, is the reason behind this negative relationship. Similarly, the variable I11 is negatively and significantly correlated with I1, I4, I5, I6, I7, I8 and I9. The decreasing 'Number of Beds in Medical Institutions per 100 People (I11)' due to increasing population may be one of the important reasons behind this negative relationship.

The principal component matrix derived from this inter-correlation matrix is given in Table 3.2(b).

It is evident from the Table 3.2(b) that, for the thirty years of time series data (1980-81 to 2009-10) of this study, principal component matrix retained two principal components which together explain 89.07 per cent of the total variance. The first principal component (P1) explains 64.268 per cent of total variance and the second principal component (P2) explains 24.802 per cent of total variance. As both the first and second principal component scores have been used here, with respect to given proportion of variances of these two principal components 72 per cent of weight has been given to first principal component and 28 per cent weight has been given to second principal component (formula given in Chapter 2). It is evident from the last column of the table that all the Communalities (h^2) are very high ranging, varied from +0.699 to +0.979. Therefore, each variable taken for analysis are significantly correlated with other variables.

Table 3.2(a): Inter-correlation Matrix of Infrastructure

	I1	*I2*	*I3*	*I4*	*I5*	*I6*	*I7*	*I8*	*I9*	*I10*	*I11*
I1	1.000										
I2	-.594***	1.000									
I3	.779***	-.833***	1.000								
I4	.707***	-.251*	.404***	1.000							
I5	.924***	-.604***	.783***	.818***	1.000						
I6	.826***	-.680***	.832***	.776***	.900***	1.000					
I7	.874***	-.647***	.844***	.768***	.950***	.902***	1.000				
I8	.965***	-.759***	.892***	.697***	.950***	.924**	.939***	1.000			
I9	.057	.231	-.290*	.587***	.132	.156	.055	.010	1.000		
I10	.471***	-.765***	.873**	.102	.487***	.689***	.557***	.649***	-.426***	1.000	
I11	-.484***	-.106	.061	-.742***	-.518***	-.317**	-.397***	-.365**	-.604***	.417***	1.000

Source: Self Calculated.

Note: *** means significant at 1 per cent level, ** means significant at 5 per cent level and * means significant at 10 per cent level.

Table 3.2 (b): Principal Component Scores of Infrastructural Indicators in Gujarat

Infrastructure Indicators	*First Principal Component Scores (P1)*	*Second Principal Component Scores (P2)*	*Communa-lities (h^2)*
1. Road Length per 100 sq. km. of area (I1)	0.922	0.120	0.864
2. Rail Route Length per 100 sq. km. of area (I2)	-0.747	0.452	0.762
3. Number of Post Offices per 100 sq. km. of Area (I3)	0.893	-0.421	0.975
4. Number of Telephone Connections per 100 People (I4)	0.745	0.617	0.935
5. Per Capita Electricity Consumption (I5)	0.962	0.177	0.957
6. Number of Scheduled Commercial Banks per 100 sq. km. of Area (I6)	0.958	0.029	0.918
7. Gross Irrigated Area as Percentage of Gross Cropped Area (I7)	0.961	0.065	0.928
8. Number of Schools per 100 sq. km. of Area (I8)	0.989	-0.022	0.979
9. Number of teachers per 100 enrolled pupils (I9)	0.055	0.834	0.699
10. Number of Medical Institutions per 100 sq. km. of Area (I10)	0.658	-0.684	0.901
11. Number of Beds in Medical Institutions per 100 People (I11)	-0.357	-0.867	0.879
Eigen Values	7.070	2.728	
Percentage of Variance	64.268	24.802	
Cumulative Variance (per cent)	64.268	89.070	

Source: Self Calculated.

The Weighted Aggregate Infrastructure Index Scores and Per Capita Income [i.e. Per Capita NSDP at factor cost and constant prices (base year 1999-00)] of Gujarat for thirty years (1980-81 to 2009-10) is given below.

Table 3.2(c): Weighted Aggregate Infrastructure Index and Per Capita Income of Gujarat

Years	*Weighted Aggregate Infrastructure Index*	*Per Capita Net State Domestic Product at factor cost and constant prices (base year 1999-00)*
1980-81	2.1820	9157
1981-82	2.3517	9837
1982-83	2.4636	9478
1983-84	2.6023	11059
1984-85	2.7177	10823
1985-86	3.0073	10318
1986-87	2.7457	10743
1987-88	2.8634	9374
1988-89	2.8677	12919
1989-90	3.0832	12480
1990-91	3.1393	12466
1991-92	3.2689	11239
1992-93	3.3743	14590
1993-94	3.4773	13896
1994-95	3.5908	16667
1995-96	3.7484	16601
1996-97	3.8026	17932
1997-98	3.9787	18767
1998-99	4.1355	19484
1999-00	4.6563	18864
2000-01	4.7999	17227
2001-02	4.8922	18200
2002-03	5.1103	19509
2003-04	5.5829	22387
2004-05	6.2143	23346
2005-06	6.6631	26268
2006-07	7.4289	28335
2007-08	8.4212	31780
2008-09	9.4589	33547
2009-10	10.3337	36665

Source: **Self Calculated** (Weighted Aggregate Infrastructure Index Scores) and **Central Statistical Organisation** (Per Capita NSDP at factor cost and constant prices).

Table 3.3: Results of the Augmented Dicky Fuller Test of the Time Series Variables

Variables	*At Levels*			*At First Difference*		
	WODT	*WID*	*WDT*	*WODT*	*WID*	*WDT*
Log Weighted Aggregate Infrastructure Index (Y_t)	7.809509 (1.0000)	3.101007 (1.0000)	2.390377 (1.0000)	0.329366 (0.7727)	-0.550517 (0.8648)	-5.704770*** (0.0004)
Log Per Capita NSDP (X_t)	3.436897 (0.9996)	1.031966 (0.9958)	-2.70013 (0.2437)	-1.32626 (0.1661)	-8.12989*** (0.0000)	-8.41446*** (0.0000)

Source: Self Calculated.

Notes:

(i) WODT = Without drift and trend

(ii) WID = With Drift

(iii) WDT = With drift and trend

(iv) ***, ** and * implies significance at 1 per cent, 5 per cent and 10 per cent level respectively.

(v) Lag lengths are determined by using SIC criteria.

(vi) t-values are given (with probability given in bracket).

To examine the long run as well as short run causal relationship between Weighted Aggregate Infrastructure Index and Economic Growth (here, Per Capita Net State Domestic Product at factor cost and constant prices) the time series analysis has been done with respect to logarithmic values of these variables. Eviews-5 software has been used for this analysis.

3.6.2 Stationarity Test

The presence of unit root has been tested in the time series data by using Augmented Dickey-Fuller test. The results of stationarity test have been given below in Table 3.3. The **logarithmic form of the variables** (natural log has been taken here), are used in this analysis.

From the above table it is observed that both the variables- log weighted aggregate infrastructure index and log per capita NSDP are non-stationary i.e. they have unit roots. However, both the variables are found stationary at first difference- log weighted aggregate infrastructure index is stationary at first difference with drift and trend and log per capita NSDP is stationary at first difference both with drift and with trend and drift, as their t-values are significant at 1 per cent level. Therefore, both the variables are I(1) which implies that cointegration test for these variables is appropriate to determine the long run relationship between the variables.

3.6.3 Determination of Cointegration

The next step is to detect whether the two variables are cointegrated or not. So the OLS regression analysis has been done with **log weighted aggregate infrastructure index** as independent variable and **log per capita NSDP** as dependent variable.

From the above table it is observed that there is positive significant relationship between these two variables. The R-square is very high 0.9448 which implies that 94.48 per cent of changes in log per capita NSDP is explained by changes in log weighted aggregate infrastructure index. The coefficient of log weighted aggregate infrastructure index is positive and significant (at 1 per cent level).

To determine the cointegrating relationship between these two variables residual series of this OLS regression has been calculated and tested for the unit root by using Augmented Dickey-Fuller test. The stationarity test result of residual series has been given below.

Therefore, from the above table it is clear that the residual series is a stationary series i.e. it is stationary at level with 1 per cent level of significance. **This result implies that the two variables taken under consideration are cointegrated i.e. the linear combination of these**

Table 3.4 (a): Regression Result [Where, Log Weighted Aggregate Infrastructure Index (Y_t) is independent Variable and Log Per capita NSDP (X_t) is Dependent Variable]

R square	*F*	*Constant*	*Coefficient of Y_t*
0.944758	478.8590*** (0.000)	8.386035*** (0.000)	0.931458*** (0.000)

Source: Self Calculated.

Note:-

(i) ***, ** and * implies significance at 1 per cent, 5 per cent and 10 per cent level respectively.

(ii) Probabilities are given in the bracket.

Table 3.4(b): Results of the Augmented Dicky Fuller Test of the Residual Series

Variable	*At Level and without Drift and trend*
Residual series	-3.783773*** (0.0005)

Source: Self Calculated.

Note:

(i) The t-ratio of the variable is given here and the probability is given in the bracket.

(ii) ***, ** and * implies significance at 1 per cent, 5 per cent and 10 per cent level respectively.

two variables- log weighted aggregate infrastructure index and log per capita NSDP is I(0). So there is significant long run relationship between these two variables.

3.6.4 Vector Error Correction Model

Though, the two variables of the study have long run equilibrium relationship, yet in short run there may be deviations from this equilibrium and it is essential to verify whether such disequilibrium converges to the long run equilibrium or not. Vector Error Correction Model can be used to generate this short run dynamics. Error correction mechanism provides a means whereby a proportion of disequilibrium is corrected in the next period. Thus error correction mechanism is a means to reconcile the short run and the long run behaviour.

The estimation of Vector Error Correction requires selection of an appropriate lag length. The number of lags in the model has been determined according to AIC criterion (using Stata12 software). Two lag lengths have been considered in this model (suggested by AIC criterion).

Table 3.5: Vector Error Correction Estimates
Included Observations: 27 after adjustments Y_t = log weighted aggregate infrastructure index and X_t = log per capita NSDP at factor cost and constant prices. **Standard errors given in ( ) and t-statistics given in [ ].**

Included Observations: 27 after adjustments
Y_t = log weighted aggregate infrastructure index and X_t = log per capita NSDP at factor cost and constant prices.
Standard errors given in ( ) and t-statistics given in [ ].

Variables	ΔX_t	ΔY_t
Error Correction Terms	ECT^1_{t-1} = **-0.334780***** (0.11285) [-2.96668]	ECT^2_{t-1} = **-0.095776*** (0.05376) [-1.78150]
ΔX_{t-1}	**-0.174764** (0.1774) [-0.98516]	**0.260579***** (0.08451) [3.08328]
ΔX_{t-2}	**0.101305** (0.18255) [0.55494]	**0.186297**** (0.08697) [2.14210]
ΔY_{t-1}	**-0.3095** (0.48757) [-0.63478]	**-0.241422** (0.23229) [-1.03933]
ΔY_{t-2}	**-1.35319***** (0.41532) [-3.25821]	**0.157157** (0.19786) [0.79428]
Constant (C)	**0.137017***** (0.03594) [3.81272]	**0.03762**** (0.01712) [2.17642]
R-squared	0.53245	0.444861
Adj. R-squared	0.421129	0.312686
Sum sq. residuals	0.134759	0.030586
S.E. equation	0.080107	0.038164
F-statistics	4.783003	3.365679
Log-Likelihood	33.24009	53.25989
Akaike AIC	-2.017784	-3.500733
Schwartz SC	-1.729821	-3.212769

Source: Self Calculated.

Note: ***, ** and * implies significance at one per cent, five per cent and ten per cent level respectively.

The Vector Error Correction Model with the computed t-values and standard error of the regression coefficients is estimated by using Eviews-5 software and the results are given in Table 3.5.

It is evident from Table 3.5 that, Error correction terms are significant and negative for both of the models i.e. when log per capita NSDP is dependent variable and log weighted aggregate infrastructure index is independent variable and vice versa. This result provides the evidence of long run bi-directional causality between the variables in this study. Further, it is evident that there is a convergence to a long run equilibrium path for both of the models.

Among these two variables log per capita NSDP has significant positive impact on log weighted aggregate infrastructure index both for first and second lag periods. Though, the impact of log weighted aggregate infrastructure index on log per capita NSDP is insignificant at first lag, yet it has positive and significant impact on log per capita NSDP at second lag period. Therefore, there is short run bi-directional significant relationship between these two variables.

3.6.5 Vector Error Correction Granger Causality Test or Wald Test

In the presence of cointegration, granger causality can also be investigated in a vector error correction model (ref: 'Advanced Time Series Econometrics' (2004) by Helmut Lutkepohl, pp. 146) i.e. between the variables ΔY_t and ΔX_t. So in the present study, Granger Causality has been tested in the Vector Error Correction model to show the short run causality between the two variables (under consideration) given in Table 3.6.

From Table 3.6 it is clear that in short run weighted aggregate infrastructure index (in logarithmic form) granger causes per capita NSDP (in logarithmic form) on one hand and per capita NSDP (in logarithmic form) granger causes weighted aggregate infrastructure index (in logarithmic form) on the other and both the results are highly significant at 1 per cent level. Therefore, there is bi-directional short run causal relationship between these two variables.

So it can be concluded that, the state Gujarat's infrastructure

Table 3.6: VEC Granger Causality Test or Wald Test

Dependent Variable: ΔX_t

Excluded	*Chi-sq.*	*Degree of freedom*	*Probability*
ΔY_t	10.61771	2	.0049***

Dependent Variable: ΔY_t

Excluded	*Chi-sq.*	*Degree of freedom*	*Probability*
ΔX_t	10.18302	2	.0061***

Source: Self Calculated.

Note: ***Significant at 1% level. Here, X_t = log per capita NSDP at factor cost and constant prices and Y_t = log weighted aggregate infrastructure index.

stock with respect to transportation, communication and per capita electricity consumption was higher than India's average in the given time period. Gujarat's infrastructure stock with respect to irrigation and banking was comparatively lower than India's average. Gujarat's education infrastructure stock was lower than India's average in the given time period. In the case of health infrastructure though Gujarat was above India's average in terms of number of beds in medical institutions per 100 people in the given time period (except in the year 2009-10), yet with respect to number of medical institutions per 100 sq. km. of area Gujarat was below India's average for the time periods 1980-81 to 1982-83, 1988-89 to 1990-91 and 2003-04 to 2009-10.

It is also evident from the analysis that, though Gujarat was above India's average with respect to relative aggregate average economic infrastructure index and relative aggregate average infrastructure index for the whole period considered in this study, yet Gujarat's social infrastructure stock was higher than India's average for the time period 1983-84 to 2004-05 and lower than India's average for the time period 1980-81 to 1982-83 and 2005-06 to 2009-10.

Further, Gujarat's per capita net state domestic product at factor cost and constant prices was higher than India's per capita net domestic product at factor cost and constant prices in the given time period–1980-81 to 2009-10 (except for two years–1987-88 and 1991-92).

It is also found that, in 2009-10 among fifteen major states of India, though the state Gujarat obtained second rank with respect to weighted aggregate economic infrastructure index as well as weighted aggregate infrastructure index, yet it obtained fourth rank with respect to weighted aggregate social infrastructure index.

From empirical analysis it is found that both the variables–log weighted aggregate infrastructure index and log per capita NSDP (at factor cost and constant prices) are stationary at first difference and the linear combination of these two variables is I(0) i.e. they are cointegrated and there is significant long run relationship between these two variables.

Error correction terms are significant and negative for both of the models i.e. when log per capita NSDP is dependent variable and log weighted aggregate infrastructure index is independent variable and vice versa. This result provides the evidence of long run bi-directional causality between the variables in this study. Further, it is evident that there is a convergence to a long run equilibrium path for both of the models. From Vector Error Correction Granger Causality Test, it is proved that there is bi-directional short run causal relationship between these two variables. In brief, long run as well as short run bi-directional positive and significant causal relationship between the variables log weighted aggregate infrastructure index and log per capita NSDP in Gujarat has been found in this study.

4

Human Development in Gujarat

The term 'Human Development' has become to be accepted in the development economics literature as an expansion of human capabilities, widening of choices, an enhancement of freedom and fulfillment of human rights. Human requires a development path or development strategy that is conducive to the development of human capabilities and opportunities. Human development has four essential components: equality, sustainability, productivity and empowerment. It regards economic growth as essential but emphasises the need to pay attention to its quality and distribution, analyses at length its link with human lives and questions its long term sustainability.

The United Nations Development Programmes (UNDP) has called this a human-centred development paradigm. The various annual global Human Development Reports (HDRs) of the UNDP have discussed at length different aspects of this paradigm. The United Nations Development Programme (UNDP) has been preparing the global Human Development Report (HDR) since 1990. Each year, the HDR focuses on a distinct theme that has implications in explaining and measuring of multidimensional nature and process of human development. The HDR presents a concise indicator on the level of human development in each country.

In the context of India, human development implies promoting basic capabilities among those who lack them. It also means supporting those, who are marginalised and excluded from the mainstream of development. It is now widely accepted that human development and not economic growth, is the ultimate goal of any society and that economic growth per se does not ensure human development.

In this study an attempt has been made to map the state of human development in Gujarat. The quality of life and the level of human well-being, in terms of changes in a range of indicators, have been tracked across States at different points of time and Gujarat has been ranked and analysed with respect to these different indicators related to human development. The choice of indicators has been governed by the need to evaluate the development process in terms of its overall impact on the quality of life and the standard of living of people.

4.1 Standard of Living

Standard of living means economic attainments of individuals and their well-being and it is conventionally captured through indicators like per capita income or per capita GDP of an economy. UNDP uses per capita GDP (at ppp dollar) to capture an individual's command over resources, as well as the opportunities and attainments that it facilitates in other aspects of well-being.

There are several limitations in the use of per capita income in evaluating social well-being, and also some conceptual and methodological ambiguities to measure economic attainments and well-being of individuals through this indicator. Despite of these limitations, the inclusion of economic indicator, such as per capita income or GDP of an economy, in composite human development index is generally explained on the ground that they are indirect but good measures of other valued attainments. Per capita GDP is also useful in capturing the stock of available resources or means that, in a sense, facilitate other attainments for individuals and the society at large.

In 'National Human Development Report' of India per capita consumption expenditure instead of per capita income has been used. The choice of this indicator is governed as much by the consideration of having an indicator that is potentially available at state and sub-state levels of desegregations, as by the conceptual requirement of having an indicator and this is a direct and better measure of economic well-being.

In this study Gujarat's standard of living is examined with the help of per capita income and per capita consumption expenditure.

4.1.1 Per capita Net State Domestic Product (NSDP) at factor cost and constant price

The State Domestic Product (SDP) and its related aggregates reflected the economic growth process of the State. The estimates of State Domestic Product over a period of time reveal the extent and direction of changes in the levels of economic growth of the State. The per capita NSDP of Gujarat as well as India at factor cost and constant prices (base year 1999-00) has been given below for the five time points in the time period 1991-92 to 2009-10 in tabular as well as graphical form.

Table 4.1.1(a): Per capita NSDP at Factor Cost and Constant Prices (base: 1999-00) of Gujarat and India

Year	*Gujarat's per capita NSDP*	*India's per capita NDP*
1991-92	11239	11600
1995-96	16601	13582
2000-01	17227	16393
2005-06	26268	21055
2009-10	36665	27101

Source: Central Statistical Organisation (CSO), New Delhi.

Figure 4.1.1(a)

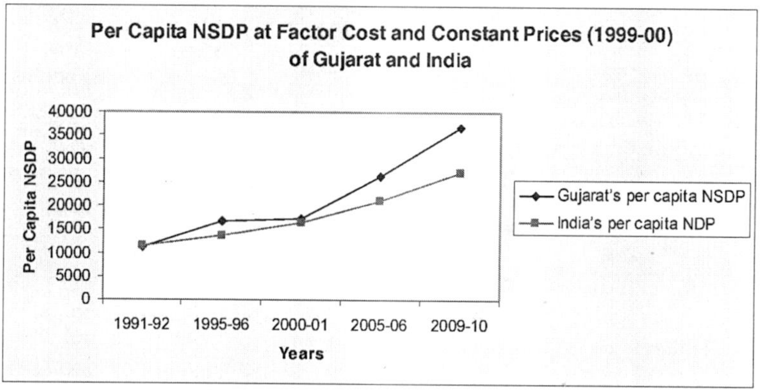

Source: Based on the data given in Table 4.1.1 (a).

It is evident from the Table and Figure 4.1.1(a) that Gujarat's per capita Net State Domestic Product (NSDP) at factor cost and constant price (base year 1999-00) was significantly high for all the years considered here (except in 1991-92), as compared to India. It is also clear that the difference in per capita NSDP between Gujarat and India increased significantly between the years 2005-06 and 2009-10. The clear picture of Gujarat's high per capita NSDP and its increasing trend (significantly higher than India) are found here.

It is evident from Table and Figure 4.1.1(b) that during the time period 1991-92 to 1995-96 Gujarat's compound annual growth rate (CAGR) was 9.527 per cent (against India's 3.977). It decreased to 1.106 per cent (against India's 3.769 per cent) in the time period 1995-96 to 2000-01. Then again increased to 8.981 per cent (against India's 5.127

Table 4.1.1 (b): Compound Annual Growth Rate (CAGR) of Per Capita Net State Domestic Product (NSDP) at factor cost and constant prices (base:1999-00) of Gujarat and India

Periods	*Compound Annual Growth Rate of Gujarat's per capita NSDP (per cent)*	*Compound Annual Growth Rate of India's per capita NDP (per cent)*
1991-92 to 1995-96	9.527	3.977
1995-96 to 2000-01	1.106	3.769
2000-01 to 2005-06	8.981	5.127
2005-06 to 2009-10	8.763	6.396

Figure 4.1.1(b)

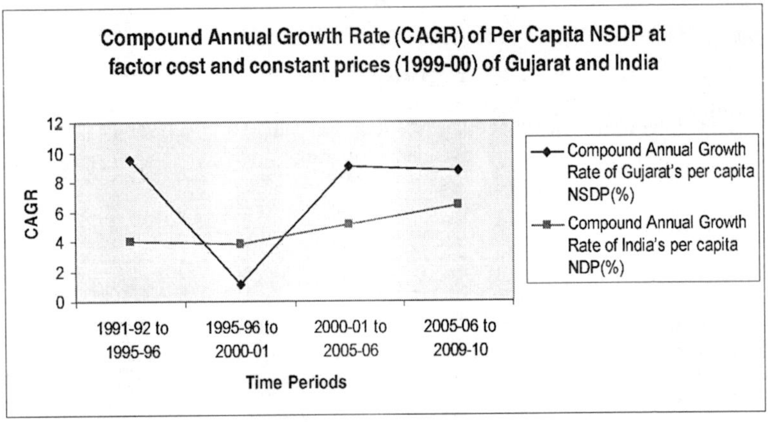

Source: Based on the data given in Table 4.1.1 (b).

per cent) in the time period 2000-01 to 2005-06 and became 8.763 per cent (against India's 6.396 per cent) in the time period 2005-06 to 2009-10.

The Compound Annual Growth Rate of Gujarat in per capita NSDP (at factor cost and constant prices) was better than India for all the time periods considered here, except in the time period 1995-96 to 2000-01.

To examine Gujarat's rank with respect to per capita net state domestic product (NSDP) among 15 major states of India, the state-wise data of per capita NSDP at factor cost and constant prices (base: 2004-05) and their ranks for the year 2009-10 are given in the Table 4.1.1(c).

It is evident from the Table 4.1.1(c) that Gujarat obtained 3rd rank (with per capita NSDP Rs 48511) among 15 major states, after Maharashtra (achieved first rank with Rs 57458 per capita NSDP) and Haryana (achieved second rank with Rs 54884 per capita NSDP) in

Table 4.1.1 (c): Per Capita Net State Domestic Product at Factor Cost and Constant Prices (base: 2004-05) of 15 Major States in India in 2009-10 (in rupees)

States	*Per Capita NSDP*	*Rank*
Andhra Pradesh	37061	8
Assam	20193	13
Bihar	12012	15
Gujarat	**48511**	**3**
Haryana	54884	2
Karnataka	38646	7
Kerala	45908	5
Madhya Pradesh	21095	12
Maharashtra	57458	1
Orissa	24275	10
Punjab	42727	6
Rajasthan	24166	11
Tamil Nadu	46692	4
Uttar Pradesh	16374	14
West Bengal	30372	9
India	**33843**	-

Source: State Statistical Bureau and Central Statistical Organisation, New Delhi.

2009-10. Bihar was at bottom (15th rank) with significantly lower per capita NSDP- Rs 12012 in 2009-10.

4.1.2 Monthly Per Capita Consumption Expenditure (MPCE)

Although UNDP considers Real GDP Per Capita in PPP USD for generating the HDI, the NHDR 2001 has preferred inflation and inequality adjusted average monthly per capita consumption expenditure (MPCE) of a state over that. Here, the MPCE of Gujarat and India are given in the Table and Figure (4.1.2(a)) for the years 1993-94, 1999-2000, 2004-05 and 2009-10 and compared with respect to India graphically.

From the Table and Figure 4.1.2(a) it is observed that, Gujarat's MPCE was with increasing trend (varied between Rs 356.87 in 1993-94 to Rs 1490 in 2009-10 against India's Rs 328.18 and Rs 1405 respectively) and better than India for all the years considered here.

To understand Gujarat's actual performance with respect to MPCE, we have to compare the state with India's major states with respect to this indicator. So, in this study the data of 15 major states of India has been taken into account for the year 2009-10. The states have been ranked in descending order.

Table 4.1.2(a): Monthly Per Capita Consumption Expenditure of Gujarat and India at current prices (in Rupees)

Year	Gujarat's MPCE	India's MPCE
1993-94	356.87	328.18
1999-00	678.27	590.98
2004-05	872.47	700.33
2009-10	1490	1405

Source: NSS 50th, 55th, 61st and 66th Rounds.

Note: MPCE of Gujarat and India in 2009-10 is the Average of Rural and Urban MPCE.

Figure 4.1.2(a):

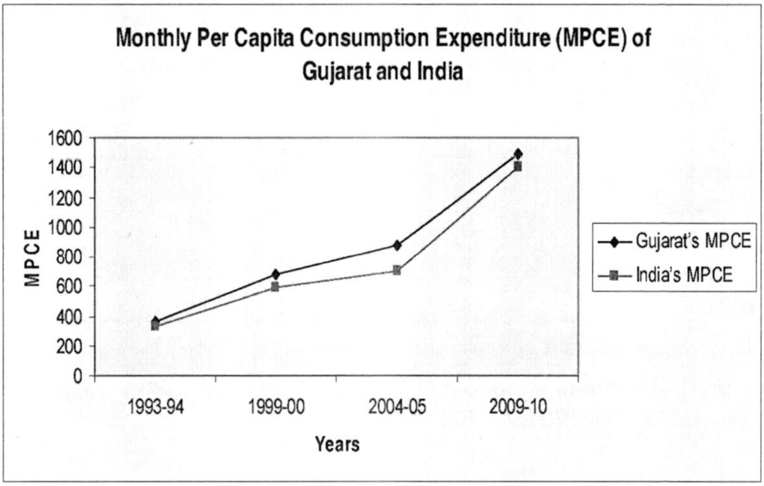

Source: Based on the data given in Table 4.1.2(a).

It is evident from the Table 4.1.2 (b) that, Gujarat obtained Fifth rank with respect to rural MPCE (Rs1065.40) below Kerala (Rs 1763.14), Punjab (Rs 1565.53), Haryana (Rs 1423.27) and Andhra Pradesh (Rs 1090.28) in 2009-10. Though there was little difference between Andhra Pradesh and Gujarat's MPCE, but it was significantly lower than Kerala, Punjab and Haryana.

Again, in the case of urban MPCE Gujarat's rank was Seventh (Rs 1914.17) in 2009-10 and it was behind the six major states – Kerala (Rs 2267.16), Maharashtra (Rs 2251.44), Punjab (Rs 2072.11), Karnataka (Rs 2060.32), Andhra Pradesh (Rs 2015.44) and Haryana (Rs 2008.16).

4.2 Poverty

The concept of poverty is multidimensional. To better understand the nature of poverty, several related poverty concepts are employed.

Table 4.1.2(b): Monthly Per Capita Consumption Expenditure ($MPCE_{MRP}$) of 15 Major States in India in 2009-10 (in Rupees) at current prices

States	*Rural MPCE*	*Rank*	*Urban MPCE*	*Rank*
Andhra Pradesh	1090.28	4	2015.44	5
Assam	866.57	10	1604.06	10
Bihar	689.37	15	1096.56	15
Gujarat	**1065.40**	**5**	**1914.17**	**7**
Haryana	1423.27	3	2008.16	6
Karnataka	887.86	9	2060.32	4
Kerala	1763.14	1	2267.16	1
Madhya Pradesh	802.79	13	1529.82	12
Maharashtra	1048.41	6	2251.44	2
Orissa	715.59	14	1468.84	14
Punjab	1565.53	2	2072.11	3
Rajasthan	1035.15	7	1576.60	11
Tamil Nadu	1017.07	8	1794.52	9
Uttar Pradesh	832.18	12	1512.16	13
West Bengal	857.77	11	1801.03	8
India	**953.05**	-	**1856.01**	-

Source: NSS 66th Round.

These include–

1. **Human poverty:** The lack of essential human capabilities, notably literacy and nutrition.
2. **Income poverty:** The lack of sufficient income to meet minimum consumption needs.
3. **Absolute poverty:** The degree of poverty below which the minimal requirements for survival are not being met.

This is a fixed measure in terms of a minimum calorific requirement plus essential non-food components. While absolute poverty is often used interchangeably with extreme poverty, the meaning of the later may vary, depending on local interpretations or calculations.

Planning Commission estimated the proportion and number of poor separately for rural and urban India at national and state levels, following the recommendations of the Task Force on Projections of Minimum Needs and Effective Consumption Demand (1979). The methodology behind these estimates often termed as the Official Methodology. According to this methodology poverty line is estimated as per capita expenditure level at which the calorie norms (2400 calories per capita per day for rural areas and 2100 calories per capita per day for urban areas) are met on the basis of the all India consumption basket for rural and urban areas. As per officially released estimates Gujarat's below poverty line (BPL) population was with decreasing trend and also significantly lower than India for both the years 1983-84 (Gujarat's BPL population was 24.3 per cent against India's 37.4 per cent) and 1987-88 (Gujarat's BPL population was 18.4 per cent against India's 29.9 per cent).

The Planning Commission (December 2005) appointed a committee known as Tendulkar Committee (chaired by Professor Suresh D. Tendulkar) to review the alternate concepts of estimation of poverty line and recommended changes in the existing official methodology. The percentage of below poverty line population (calculated by using Tendulkar

Table 4.2.1: Percentage of Population Below Poverty Line (in Total i.e. Rural-Urban Combined) in Gujarat and India for 1993-94, 2004-05 and 2009-10

Year	*Gujarat's percentage of Population*	*India's percentage of Population*
1993-94	37.8	45.3
2004-05	31.6	37.2
2009-10	23.0	29.8

Source: Data for use of Deputy Chairman, Planning Commission, GOI, 3rd May 2013.

Figure 4.2.1

Percentage of Population Below Poverty Line (in Total) in Gujarat and India

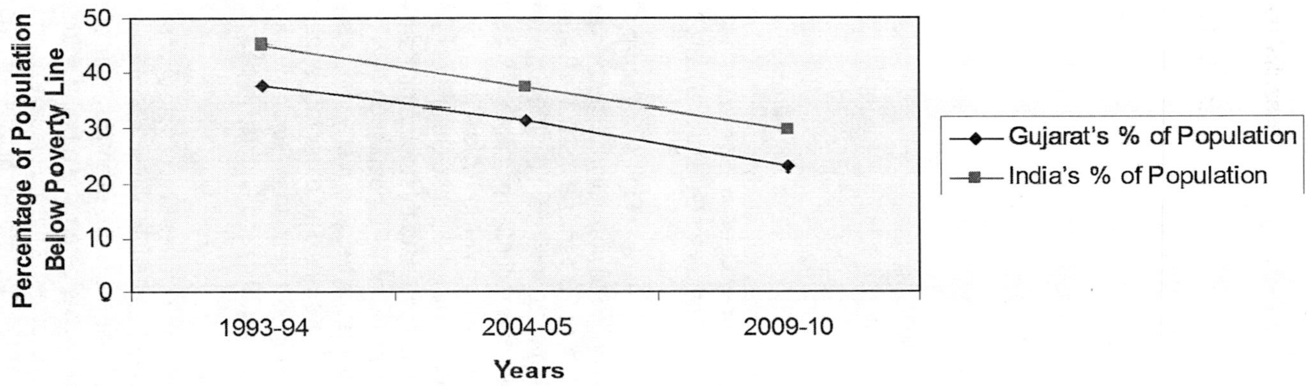

Source: Based on the data given in Table 4.2.1.

Note: Here, 'in Total' means Rural-Urban Combined.

Table 4.2.2: Percentage of Population Below Poverty Line (in Total i.e. Rural-Urban Combined) of 15 Major States in India in 2009-10

States	*Percentage of Population*	*Rank*
Andhra Pradesh	21.1	5
Assam	37.9	14
Bihar	53.5	15
Gujarat	**23.0**	**6**
Haryana	20.1	4
Karnataka	23.6	7
Kerala	12	1
Madhya Pradesh	36.7	11
Maharashtra	24.5	8
Orissa	37.0	12
Punjab	15.9	2
Rajasthan	24.8	9
Tamil Nadu	17.1	3
Uttar Pradesh	37.7	13
West Bengal	26.7	10
Indla	**29.8**	-

Source: Data for use of Deputy Chairman, Planning Commission, GOI, 3rd May 2013.

Methodology) is given below for Gujarat and India for the years 1993-94, 2004-05 and 2009-10.

It is evident from Table and Figure 4.2.1 that, Gujarat's percentage of below poverty line (BPL) population decreased significantly from 37.8 per cent in 1993-94 to 23 per cent in 2009-10 against India's 45.3 per cent (in 1993-94) and 29.8 per cent (in 2009-10) respectively.

The state-wise data regarding percentage of below poverty line (BPL) population for 2009-10 is given in Table 4.2.2.

It is evident from Table 4.2.2 that, Gujarat obtained sixth rank among 15 major states with respect to this indicator. Kerala obtained first rank with lowest percentage of BPL population (12) in 2009-10. Gujarat's percentage of population below poverty line was 23.0 in 2009-10, i.e. almost two times of Kerala. The other four states with comparatively lower BPL population (per cent) than Gujarat were- Punjab (15.9), Tamil Nadu (17.1), Haryana (20.1) and Andhra Pradesh (21.1).

4.3 Unemployment

Economic attainment refers to access to or command over resources by households and individuals, which enhances their capabilities. At most elementary level, the status of employment of household members and ownership of assets determine a household's income, which to a very large extent determines the individual's command over resources.

In this section the unemployment rate per thousand labour force is discussed for Gujarat and India on one hand and also with respect to 15

Table 4.3.1: Unemployment Rate Per Thousand of Labour Force according to Usual Principal and Subsidiary Status by Gender in Rural and Urban Areas in Gujarat and India in 1993-94, 2004-05 and 2009-10

	Gujarat (Rural)			*India (Rural)*		
Year	*Male*	*Female*	*Persons*	*Male*	*Female*	*Persons*
1993-94	12	3	8	15	8	12
2004-05	8	2	5	16	18	17
2009-10	8	7	8	16	16	16
	Gujarat (Urban)			*India (Urban)*		
Year	*Male*	*Female*	*Persons*	*Male*	*Female*	*Persons*
1993-94	30	46	32	41	63	45
2004-05	23	29	24	37	69	44
2009-10	15	31	18	28	57	34

Source: **NSSO 50th, 61st and 66th Round.** (**Note**:- For population with age 15 years and above).

Figure 4.3.1(a)

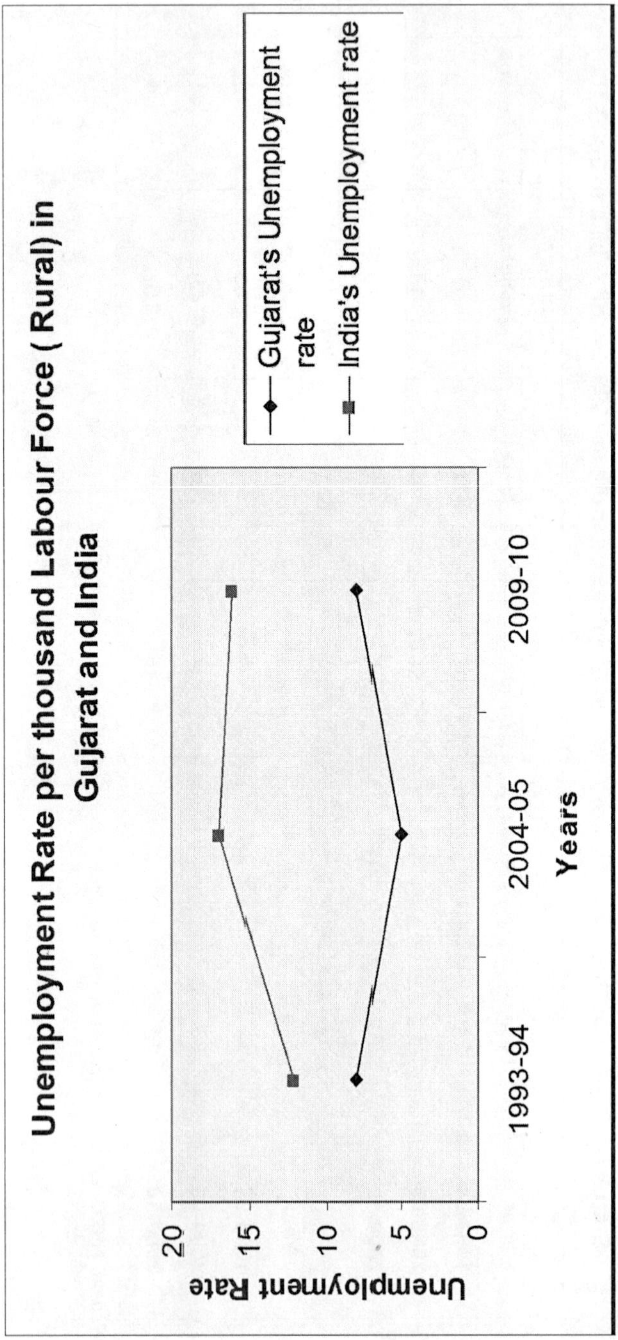

Source: Based on the data given in Table 4.3.1.

Figure 4.3.1(b)

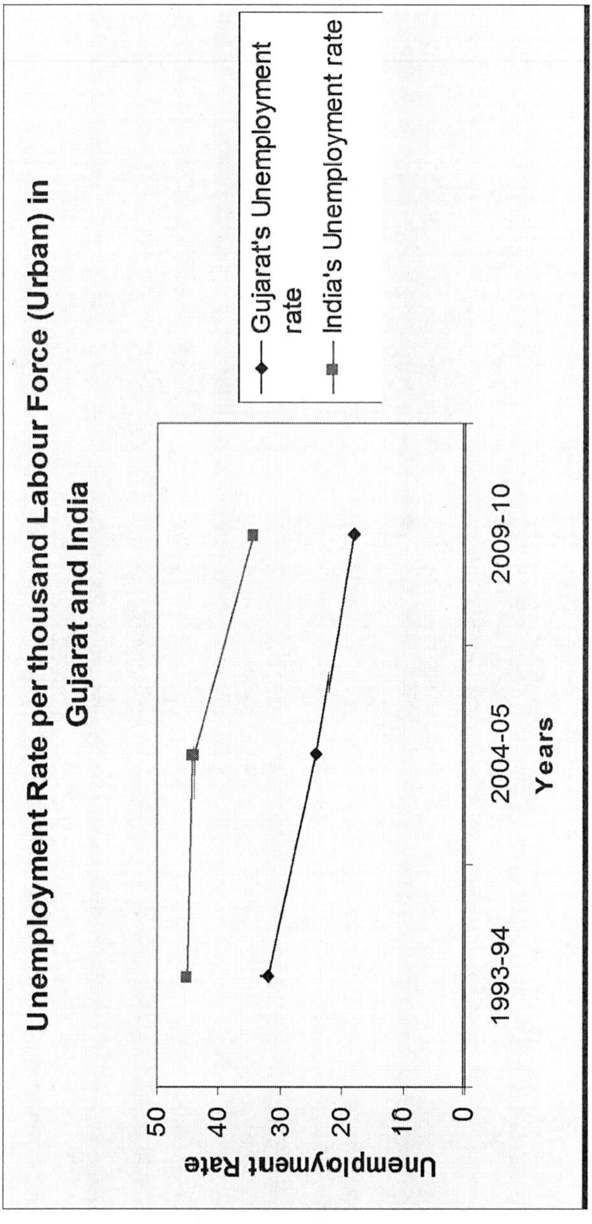

Source: Based on the data given in Table 4.3.1.

Table 4.3.2: Unemployment Rate Per Thousand of Labour Force according to Usual Principal and Subsidiary Status by Gender in Rural and Urban Areas in 15 Major Indian States in 2009-10

	Rural			Urban		
States	*Males*	*Females*	*Persons*	*Males*	*Females*	*Persons*
Andhra Pradesh	13 (7)	9 (7)	12 (7)	25 (6)	51 (8)	31 (6)
Assam	34 (15)	56 (14)	39 (14)	40 (12 / 13)	125 (13)	52(13)
Bihar	21 (10 / 11)	13 (9)	20 (10)	63 (15)	160 (14)	73(14 /15)
Gujarat	**8 (4 / 5)**	**7 (6)**	**8 (5)**	**15 (1)**	**31 (1)**	**18 (1)**
Haryana	21 (10 / 11)	11 (8)	18 (9)	22 (3)	38 (4)	25 (3)
Karnataka	5 (1)	4 (2/ 3 /4)	5 (2)	24 (4 / 5)	40 (5)	27 (4)
Kerala	32 (14)	161 (15)	75 (15)	29 (9 / 10)	168 (15)	73(14 / 15)
Madhya Pradesh	8 (4 / 5)	4 (2/ 3 /4)	7 (4)	27 (7)	36 (3)	29 (5 /6)
Maharashtra	7 (3)	4 (2/ 3 /4)	6 (3)	28 (8)	50 (7)	32 (8 / 9)
Orissa	31 (13)	27 (12)	30 (13)	40 (12 / 13)	54 (9 /10)	42(11)
Punjab	28 (12)	22 (11)	26 (12)	44 (14)	66 (12)	48(12)
Rajasthan	6 (2)	1 (1)	4 (1)	17 (2)	44 (6)	22 (2)
Tamil Nadu	15 (8)	15 (10)	15 (8)	24 (4 / 5)	54 (9 /10)	32 (8 / 9)
Uttar Pradesh	12 (6)	5 (5)	10 (6)	29 (9 /10)	34 (2)	29(5 /6)
West Bengal	17 (9)	28 (13)	19 (11)	35 (11)	65 (11)	40(10)
India	**16**	**16**	**16**	**28**	**57**	**34**

Source: NSS 66th Round.

Note: Ranks of the states are given in the bracket.

major Indian states (for rural and urban areas) both for males and females separately (to determine Gujarat's rank among them) on the other.

It is evident from Table 4.3.1 and Figures [4.3.1(a) and 4.3.1(b)] that Gujarat's unemployment rate was significantly lower than India (both for rural and urban areas) for all the years considered here. Gujarat's unemployment rate (per thousand labour force) for persons in rural areas was eight in 1993-94, became five in 2004-05 and it again increased to eight in 2009-10 against India's 12 (in 1993-94), 17 (in 2004-05) and 16 (in 2009-10) respectively.

Further, for urban areas the unemployment rate of persons of Gujarat was 32 in 1993-94, 24 in 2004-05 and 18 in 2009-10 against India's 45 (in 1993-94), 44 (in 2004-05) and 34 (in 2009-10) respectively.

The state-wise data regarding unemployment rate per thousand labour forces both for rural and urban areas in 2009-10 is given in Table 4.3.2.

As this is a negative indicator the ranking of the states has been done in ascending order i.e. the state with lowest unemployment rate is ranked first and so on.

It is evident from the Table 4.3.2 that Gujarat obtained fifth rank with respect to unemployment rate of persons for rural areas (behind Rajasthan, Karnataka, Maharashtra and Madhya Pradesh). It obtained fourth rank for rural males (behind Karnataka, Rajasthan, and Maharashtra) and sixth rank for rural females (behind Rajasthan, Karnataka, Maharashtra, Madhya Pradesh and Uttar Pradesh) in 2009-10. It is observed that, in urban unemployment rate Gujarat obtained first rank with lowest unemployment rate for urban males, urban females and also with respect to unemployment rate of persons in 2009-10. Though, the unemployment rate of female (31) was more than two times as compared to male unemployment rate (15), yet the urban unemployment rate of persons was 18 in 2009-10. As compared to all-India the unemployment rate of the state in 2009-10, was significantly lower both for rural and urban areas with respect to males, females and persons in Gujarat.

4.4 Working Children

A child is classified as labourer if the child is in the age group 5-14 years and is 'economically active' i.e. works on regular basis for which he or she receives remuneration. In India, despite acceptance of international standards and commitments on restricting the use of child labour, the existence of a national child labour policy, wide-spread national and state level laws and regulations, millions of children are engaged in work, often under hardship or hazardous conditions. It deprives them of their childhood and their dignity and is detrimental to their health,

Table 4.4.1: Gujarat and India's Percentage of Working Children (age 5 to 14 Years)

Year	*Gujarat's Working Children (per cent)*	*India's Working Children (per cent)*
1991	5.3	5.4
1993-94	3.4	6.2
2004-05	2.5	3.3
2007-08	2.6	2.4
2009-10	3.26	1.92

Source: Computed from Census 1991, 2001 data and NSS 50th, 61st and 66th unit level data.

Figure 4.4.1

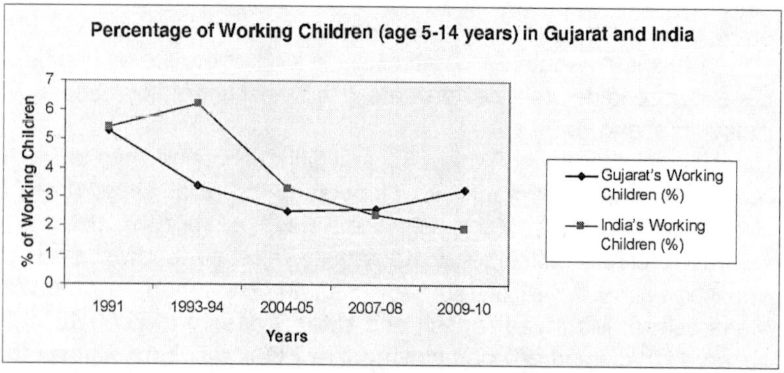

Source: Based on the data given in Table 4.4.1.

education, and more importantly, in developing capabilities and availing opportunities as normal individuals in the society.

It is evident from the Table and Figure 4.4.1 that in Gujarat, percentage of working children was 5.3 in 1991, 3.4 in 1993-94, 2.5 in 2004-05, 2.6 in 2007-08 and 3.26 in 2009-10 against India's 5.4, 6.2, 3.3, 2.4 and 1.92 respectively. Though Gujarat's percentage of working children was lower than India's average upto the year 2005-06, yet from 2007-08 it became higher than India's average.

The state-wise percentage of working children (for 5-14 years old children) is given in Table 4.4.2. As this is a negative indicator ranking has been done in ascending order.

It is evident from the Table 4.4.2 that, Gujarat obtained 14th rank (among 15 major states of India) with almost 6.4 times higher percentage of working children (which was also higher than India) as compared to Kerala (which obtained first rank with the lowest percentage of working children 0.05 in 2009-10) and it was also higher than all the major states

Table 4.4.2: Percentage of Working Children (age 5 to 14 years) in 15 Major States of India in 2009-10

States	*State-Wise Percentage of Working Children*	*Rank*
Andhra Pradesh	1.51	8
Assam	2.69	12
Bihar	0.95	3
Gujarat	**3.26**	**14**
Haryana	1.40	7
Karnataka	2.06	10
Kerala	0.05	1
Madhya Pradesh	1.13	5
Maharashtra	1.27	6
Orissa	1.60	9
Punjab	0.99	4
Rajasthan	2.47	11
Tamil Nadu	0.15	2
Uttar Pradesh	3.49	15
West Bengal	3.17	13
India	**1.92**	-

Source: Computed from Data on Child Labour based on Employment Unemployment Survey During NSS 66th Round (2009-10).

considered in this study except Uttar Pradesh (3.49 per cent) in 2009-10.

4.5 Education

In this study three types of educational indicators- Literacy Rate, Gross Enrolment Ratio and Pupil-Teacher Ratio have been used to know the performance of Gujarat in Education (with respect to these indicators).

4.5.1 Literacy Rate

In this study literacy rate in Gujarat and India has been given in tabular and graphical form for males, females and in total for the years 1991, 2001 and 2011.

It is evident from the Table 4.5.1(a) and Figures 4.5.1(a)(i), 4.5.1(a)(ii) and 4.5.1(a)(iii) that, Gujarat's male literacy rate increased from 73.13 per cent (against India's 64.13 per cent) in 1991 to 87.23 per cent (against India's 82.14 per cent) in 2011. Gujarat's female literacy rate was 48.64 per cent (against India's 39.29 per cent) in 1991 and it increased to 70.73 per cent (against India's 65.46 per cent) in 2011. Gujarat's overall literacy rate was 61.29 per cent (against India's 52.21 per cent) in 1991 and 79.31 per cent (against India's 74.04 per cent) in 2011.

Table 4.5.1(a): Literacy Rate

Year	*Gujarat's Male Literacy Rate*	*India's Male Literacy Rate*	*Gujarat's Female Literacy Rate*	*India's Female Literacy Rate*	*Gujarat's Literacy Rate (in total)*	*India's Literacy Rate (in total)*
1991	73.13	64.13	48.64	39.29	61.29	52.21
2001	80.50	75.85	58.60	54.16	69.97	65.38
2011	87.23	82.14	70.73	65.46	79.31	74.04

Source: Census of India (1991, 2001 and 2011).

Figure 4.5.1 (a)(i)

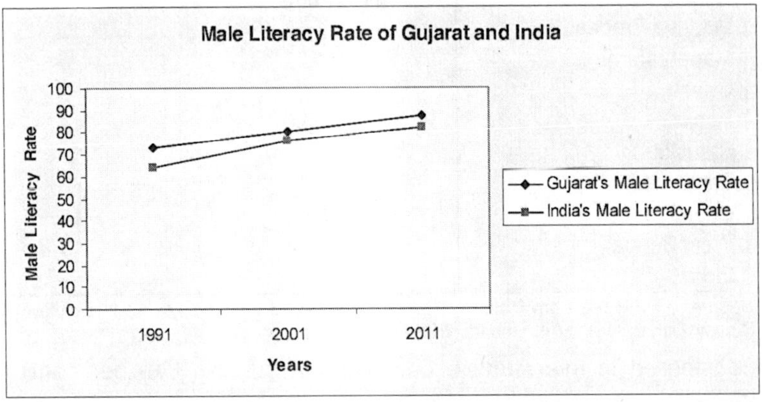

Source: Based on the data given in Table 4.5.1(a).

Figure 4.5.1(a)(ii)

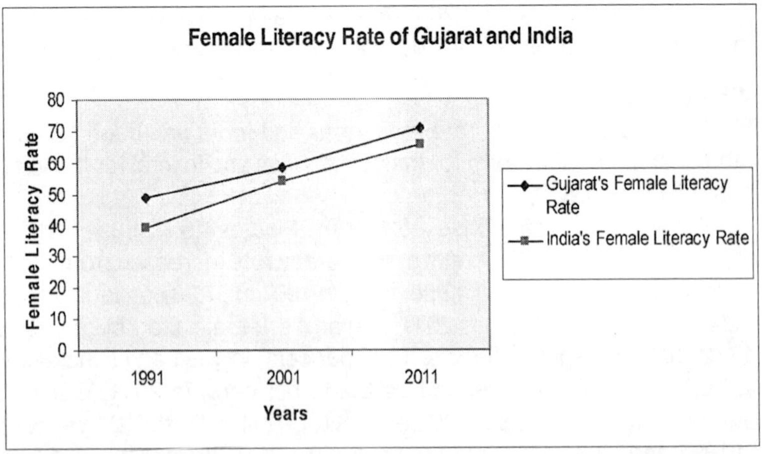

Source: Based on the data given in Table 4.5.1(a).

Figure 4.5.1 (a)(iii)

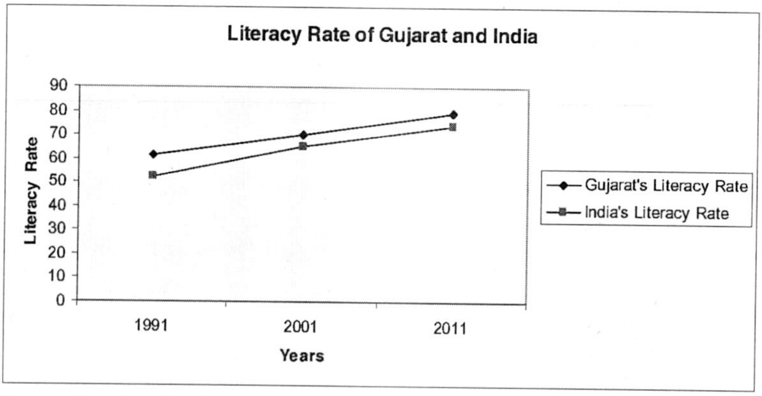

Source: Based on the data given in Table 4.5.1(a).

The literacy rate (gender-wise as well as in total) has been given in Table 4.5.1(b) for 15 major states of India as per 2011 census.

It is evident from Table 4.5.1 (b) that, Gujarat obtained fourth rank in overall literacy rate (79.31 per cent), third rank in male literacy rate (87.23 per cent) and sixth rank in female literacy rate (70.73 per cent). As per 2011 census data Gujarat's overall literacy rate was lower than three states- Kerala, Maharashtra and Tamil Nadu. In male literacy rate Gujarat was just behind two states- Kerala and Maharashtra. Though in female literacy rate Gujarat improved significantly, yet the state was

Table 4.5.1(b): Gender-wise Literacy Rate of 15 Major States in India as per Census 2011

States	*Persons*	*Males*	*Females*
Andhra Pradesh	67.66 (13)	75.56(14)	59.74(12)
Assam	73.18(10)	78.81(13)	67.27(8)
Bihar	63.82(15)	73.39(15)	53.33(14)
Gujarat	**79.31(4)**	**87.23(3)**	**70.73(6)**
Haryana	76.64(7)	85.38(5)	66.67(9)
Karnataka	75.60(8)	82.85(6)	68.13(7)
Kerala	93.91(1)	96.02(1)	91.98(1)
Madhya Pradesh	70.63(11)	80.53(10)	60.02(11)
Maharashtra	82.91(2)	89.92(2)	75.48(2)
Orissa	73.45(9)	82.40(8)	64.36(10)
Punjab	76.68(6)	81.48(9)	71.34(4)
Rajasthan	67.06(14)	80.51(11)	52.66(15)
Tamil Nadu	80.33(3)	86.61(4)	73.86(3)
Uttar Pradesh	69.72(12)	79.24(12)	59.26(13)
West Bengal	77.08(5)	82.67(7)	71.16(5)
India	**74.04**	**82.14**	**65.46**

Source: **Census of India** (**Note:** Ranks of the states are given in brackets).

still behind five states–Kerala, Maharashtra, Tamil Nadu, Punjab and West Bengal.

The state Kerala, with male literacy rate 96.02 per cent, female literacy rate 91.98 per cent and overall literacy rate 93.91 per cent obtained first rank among 15 major states of India as per 2011 census data.

4.5.2 Gross Enrolment Ratio (GER)

The two most important indicators regarding Enrolment of pupils are **Gross Enrollment Ratio** (GER) and **Net Enrolment Ratio** (NER). GER is defined as the ratio of students enrolled in a particular level of education (regardless of age) to the population of official school age for that level of education. Since both the over-aged and under-aged population for a specific level of education are included in the calculation of GER, its value can exceed 100. NER is on the other hand is the ratio of students belonging to the official age of Enrolment (as required for a particular level of education) who are enrolled to the population of official school age for that level of education. The essential difference between GER and NER is that net Enrolment excludes enrolled children who fall outside the age range (as specified for a certain level of education), while they are included in the calculation of GER.

In this study Gross Enrolment Ratio (GER) of Gujarat and India on one hand and for 15 major states of India on the other, have been discussed. The tabular and graphical representations are given below.

It is evident from the Table [4.5.2(a)] and Figures [4.5.2(a)(i)] and [4.5.2(a)(ii)] that Gujarat's Gross Enrolment Ratio (GER) both in primary and upper primary classes was higher than India for all the years considered in this study except in 1990-91. Gujarat's Gross Enrollment Ratio (GER) in primary classes (I-V) increased from 110.9 (against

Table 4.5.2(a): Gross Enrolment Ratio (GER) at Primary and Upper Primary Levels in Gujarat and India

Years	*Gujarat's GER at Primary Classes*	*India's GER at Primary Classes*	*Gujarat's GER at Upper Primary Classes*	*India's GER at Upper Primary Classes*
1990-91	110.9	114	68.26	76.6
1995-96	131.4	104.3	71.6	67.6
2000-01	126.16	95.66	66.51	58.64
2004-05	118.65	107.80	73.77	69.93
2009-10	120.42	115.47	86.51	81.52

Source: Economic Survey of India (for different years).

Figure 4.5.2 (a)(i)

Gross Enrollment Ratio (GER) in Primary Classes (I-V) in Gujarat and India

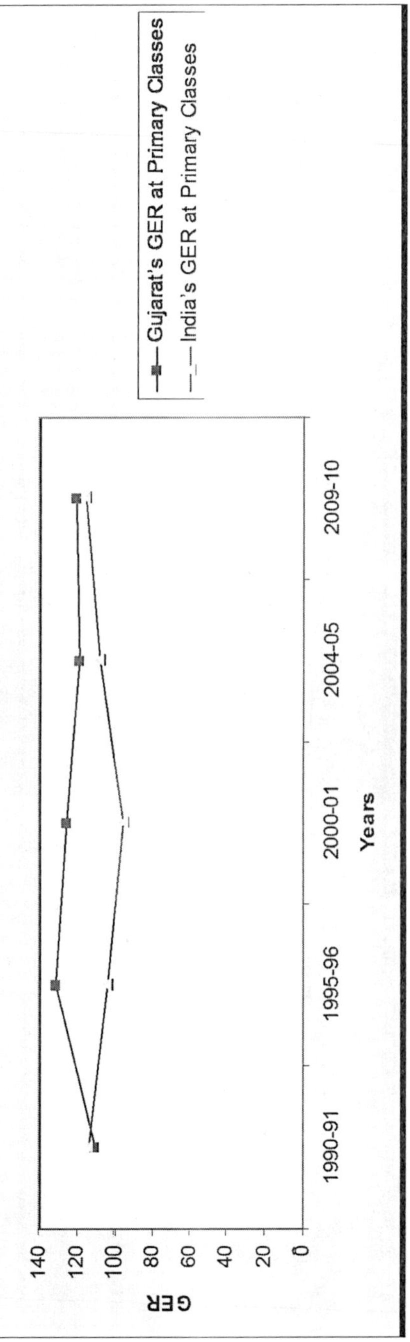

Source: Based on the data given in Table 4.5.2(a).

Figure 4.5.2 (a)(ii)

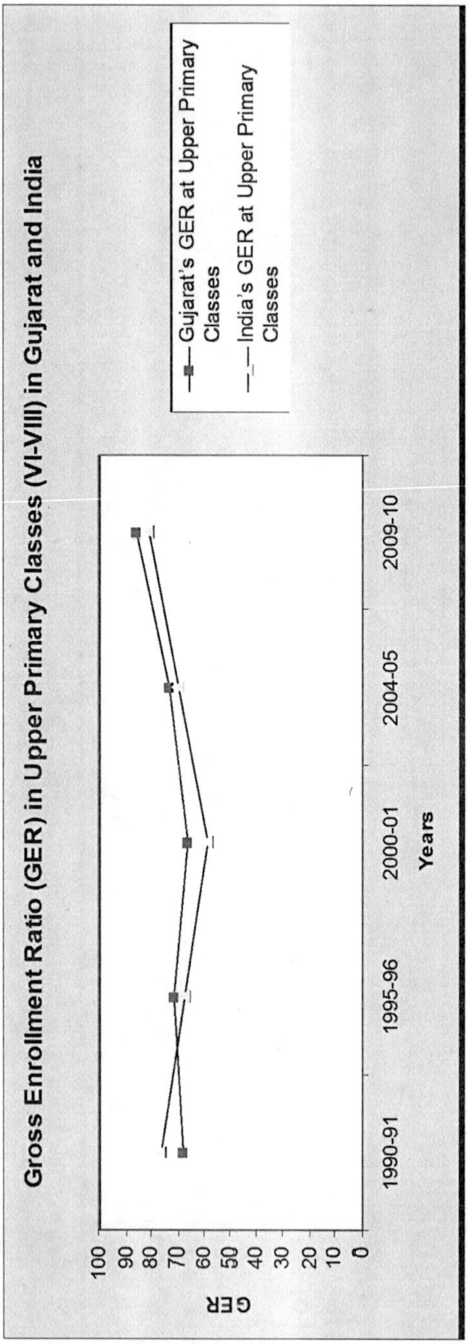

Source: Based on the data given in Table 4.5.2(a).

India's 114) in 1990-91 to 131.4 (against India's 104.3) in 1995-96, then decreased to 126.16 (against India's 95.66) in 2000-01 and became 118.65 (against India's 107.8) in 2004-05. In 2009-10, it increased to 120.42 against India's 115.47. Again, Gujarat's GER in Upper Primary Classes increased from 68.26 (against India's 76.6) in 1990-91 to 71.6 (against India's 67.6) in 1995-96, decreased to 66.51 (against India's 58.64) in 2000-01 and became 73.77 (against India's 69.93) in 2004-05. In 2009-10, gross Enrolment ratio in upper primary classes increased significantly both in Gujarat (86.51) and India (81.52).

The GER in primary and upper primary classes of 15 major states in India in 2009-10 is given in Table 5.5.2(b).

It is evident from the Table 4.5.2(b) that, whether Gujarat obtained third rank among 15 major states with respect to GER of primary classes (120.42), the state obtained seventh rank with respect to the GER in upper primary classes (86.51). The states with comparatively higher

Table 4.5.2 (b): Gross Enrolment Ratio, by Level of Education in 15 Major Indian States in 2009-10

States	*Primary (I-V) (6-11 years)*	*Rank*	*Upper Primary (VI-VIII) (11-14 years)*	*Rank*
Andhra Pradesh	98.16	12	77.65	12
Assam	92.89	14	68.80	14
Bihar	117.83	5	55.46	15
Gujarat	**120.42**	**3**	**86.51**	**7**
Haryana	90.10	15	78.86	11
Karnataka	104.71	10	89.34	5
Kerala	93.65	13	104.77	2
Madhya Pradesh	149.67	1	101.87	3
Maharashtra	103.66	11	89.32	6
Orissa	118.84	4	83.74	9
Punjab	108.09	9	91.84	4
Rajasthan	117.19	6	84.38	8
Tamil Nadu	114.79	7	113.22	1
Uttar Pradesh	110.42	8	70.25	13
West Bengal	125.59	2	83.59	10
India	**115.47**	-	**81.52**	-

Source: Economic Survey of India, 2011-12.
(Available in Data for use of Deputy Chairman, Planning Commission, GOI, 10th April 2012, pp. 162).

GER in primary classes than Gujarat were- Madhya Pradesh (149.67) and West Bengal (125.59). Again, the states with comparatively higher GER in upper primary classes than Gujarat in 2009-10 were–Tamil Nadu (113.22), Kerala (104.77), Madhya Pradesh (101.87), Punjab (91.84), Karnataka (89.34) and Maharashtra (89.32).

It is clear from the above analysis that Gujarat's GER in primary classes (120.42) was significantly higher than its GER in upper primary classes (86.51) in 2009-10. It may be the high drop out rate, which is a major reason behind this contradictory picture of GER in primary and upper primary classes in Gujarat. To understand the actual reason it is required to examine the drop out rate of the state in primary and upper primary classes.

The data of drop out rate in primary and upper primary classes for 15 major states of India in 2009-10 is given in the below Table.

It is evident from the Table 4.5.2(c) that with drop out rate 25.66 in primary classes Gujarat obtained 10th rank (in ascending order) among 15 major states in India. Gujarat's drop out rate in primary classes was significantly higher than 9 states– Punjab (-18.07), Kerala (-12.52),

Table 4.5.2(c): Drop Out Rate, by Level of Education in 15 Major Indian States in 2009-10

States	*Primary*	*Rank*	*Upper Primary*	*Rank*
Andhra Pradesh	15.80	6	41.29	9
Assam	35.89	12	61.21	14
Bihar	42.45	13	66.02	15
Gujarat	**25.66**	**10**	**39.70**	**8**
Haryana	-1.64	3	14.37	4
Karnataka	11.12	5	25.86	6
Kerala	-12.52	2	-14.14	2
Madhya Pradesh	21.16	8	21.44	5
Maharashtra	21.31	9	25.88	7
Orissa	26.45	11	54.30	13
Punjab	-18.07	1	-19.12	1
Rajasthan	50.51	15	50.32	11
Tamil Nadu	0.35	4	8.67	3
Uttar Pradesh	42.06	14	52.78	12
West Bengal	20.52	7	50.46	10
India	**28.86**	**-**	**42.39**	**-**

Source: Elementary Education in India, DISE 2009-10: Flash Statistics.
(Available in Data for use of Deputy Chairman,Planning Commission, GOI, 3rd May 2013, pp. 194)

Haryana (-1.64), Tamil Nadu (0.35), Karnataka (11.12), Andhra Pradesh (15.80), West Bengal (20.52), Madhya Pradesh (21.16) and Maharashtra (21.31). The states Punjab, Kerala and Haryana's drop out rates were negative i.e. there were no drop outs in these states in primary classes in 2009-10, rather there were some additional Enrolment in primary classes in these states. Drop out rate of Gujarat was lower than India's average (28.86) in 2009-10.

Further, in upper primary classes the drop out rate of Gujarat was 39.70 in 2009-10 and it obtained eighth rank among 15 major states in India. Drop out rate of the state in upper primary classes was significantly higher than 7 states– Punjab (-19.12), Kerala (-14.14), Tamil Nadu (8.67), Haryana (14.37), Madhya Pradesh (21.44), Karnataka (25.86) and Maharashtra (25.88). In upper primary classes also the drop out rates were negative for the states Punjab and Kerala i.e. there were no drop outs in these states, rather there are some additional Enrollment in upper primary classes in these states. Gujarat's drop out rate in upper primary classes was lower than India's average (42.39) in 2009-10.

It may be concluded that, instead of Gujarat's high GER in primary classes, the GER was significantly low in upper primary classes due to its high drop out rate.

4.5.3 Pupil-Teacher Ratio at Primary and Upper Primary Levels

In this section Pupil-Teacher Ratio of Gujarat and India has been studied on one hand and to determine the rank of Gujarat among 15 major states, the state-wise data of this indicator has been discussed on the other.

It is evident from the Table 4.5.3 (a) and Figure 4.5.3(a)(i) that, the pupil-teacher ratio of Gujarat at primary level of education was 44 in 1991-92, 47 in 1997-98 against India's 45 and 42 respectively. But it decreased significantly in Gujarat and became 30 in 2007-08 against India's 47. In 2009-10 it was 32 in Gujarat against India's 33.

Again, from the Table 4.5.3 (a) and Figure 4.5.3(a)(ii) it is observed that, in upper primary education Gujarat's pupil-teacher ratio was 42 in 1991-92, 41 in 1997-98 and reduced to 37 in 2007-08 against India's 43, 37 and 35 respectively. In 2009-10, it was 33 in Gujarat against India's average 31.

The pupil-teacher ratio of 15 major states in primary and upper primary classes has been given in Table 4.5.3 (b) for the year 2009-10.

It is evident from the Table 4.5.3(b) that, Gujarat obtained ninth rank with respect to pupil teacher ratio both in primary classes (32) and upper primary classes (33) in 2009-10.

The eight major states with comparatively lower pupil teacher ratio than Gujarat in primary classes were Kerala (24), Assam (25), Andhra

Table 4.5.3 (a): Pupil-Teacher Ratio at Primary and Upper Primary Levels in Gujarat and India

Time Periods	*1991-92*		*1997-98*		*2007-08*		*2009-10*	
State /Country	*Primary*	*Upper Primary*	*Primary*	*Upper Primary*	*Primary*	*Upper Primary*	*Primary*	*Upper Primary*
Gujarat	44	42	47	41	30	37	32	33
India	45	43	42	37	47	35	33	31

Source: Selected Educational Statistics (for different years). Department of Education. Ministry of Human Resource Development. Statistics of School Education, Ministry of Human Resource Development, 2007-08. Elementary Education in India Progress towards UEE, Flash Statistics, DISE 2009-10, pp. 14 (Published by: 'National University of Educational Planning and Administration' in 2011).

Figure 4.5.3 (a)(i)

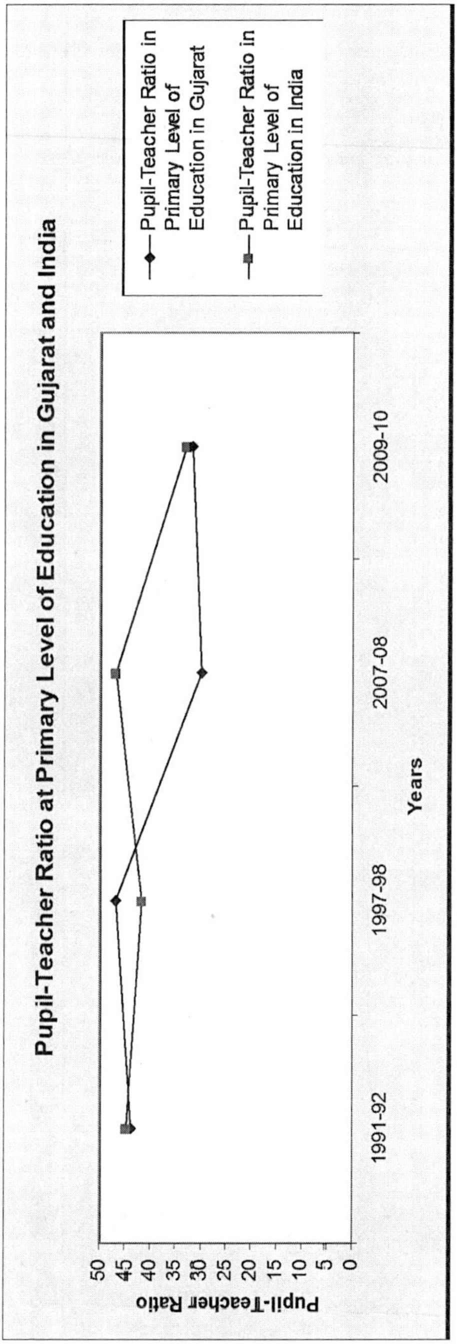

Source: Based on the data given in Table 5.5.3(a).

Figure 4.5.3 (a)(ii)

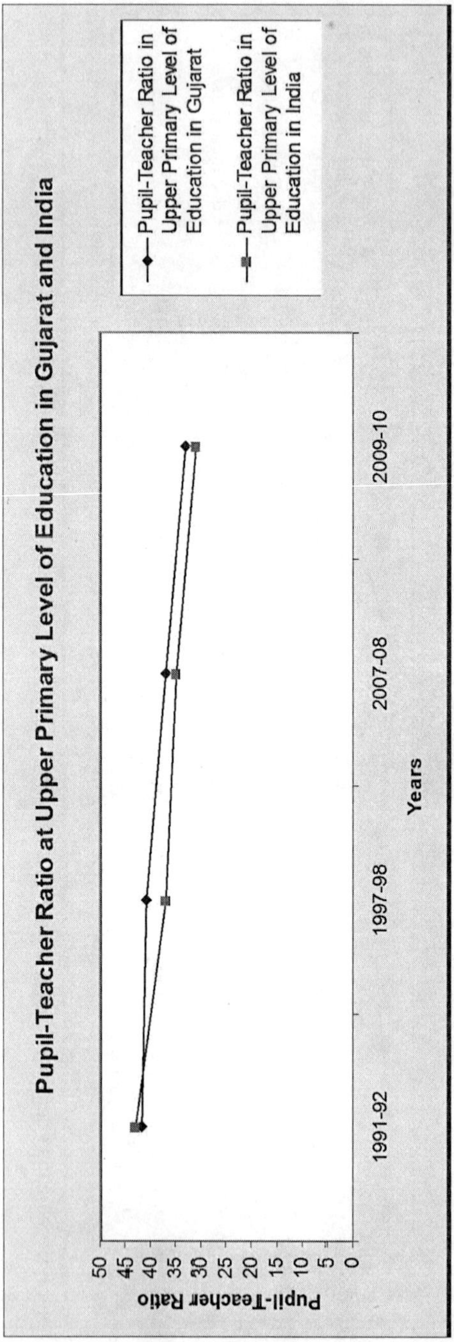

Source: Based on the data given in Table 4.5.3(a).

Table 4.5.3(b): Pupil-Teacher Ratio at Primary and Upper Primary Level of Education in 15 Major States of India in 2009-10

States	Primary	Rank	Upper Primary	Rank
Andhra Pradesh	25	2/3	18	1
Assam	25	2/3	20	2
Bihar	57	15	61	15
Gujarat	**32**	**9/10**	**33**	**9/10**
Haryana	37	13	26	3/4/5
Karnataka	28	5	30	7/8
Kerala	24	1	26	3/4/5
Madhya Pradesh	35	12	33	9/10
Maharashtra	30	7	30	7/8
Orissa	32	9/10	37	12
Punjab	31	8	28	6
Rajasthan	27	4	26	3/4/5
Tamil Nadu	29	6	34	11
Uttar Pradesh	47	14	44	13
West Bengal	34	11	51	14
India	**33**	-	**31**	-

Source: Elementary Education in India Progress towards UEE, Flash Statistics, DISE 2009-10, pp. 14 (Published by: 'National University of Educational Planning and Administration' in 2011).

Pradesh (25), Rajasthan (27), Karnataka (28), Tamil Nadu (29), Maharashtra (30) and Punjab (31).

Similarly, the eight major states with comparatively lower pupil teacher ratio than Gujarat in upper primary classes were Andhra Pradesh (18), Assam (20), Haryana (26), Kerala (26), Rajasthan (26), Punjab (28), Maharashtra (30) and Karnataka (30).

4.6 Housing

In this study the data of the percentage of households live in pucca houses in Gujarat and India as well as with respect to 15 major states of India have been discussed.

The data on quality of houses are based on the material used for construction of walls and roof separately. If both the walls and roof are made of *pucca* material (burnt brick, G.I sheets or other metal sheets, stone or cement concrete), a house is classified as *pucca*.

It is observed from the Table and Figure 4.6.1 that, Gujarat's percentage of households with pucca house was significantly higher

Table 4.6.1: Distribution of Households (per cent) by Pucca House

State/ Country	*Year 1991*	*Year 2002*	*Year 2009*
Gujarat	56.93	56.4	75.7
India	41.61	47.4	66.1

Source: Housing and Amanities, Paper 2 of 1993; p. 37, Census of India, 1991. NSSO 58th and 65th Round.

Figure 4.6.1

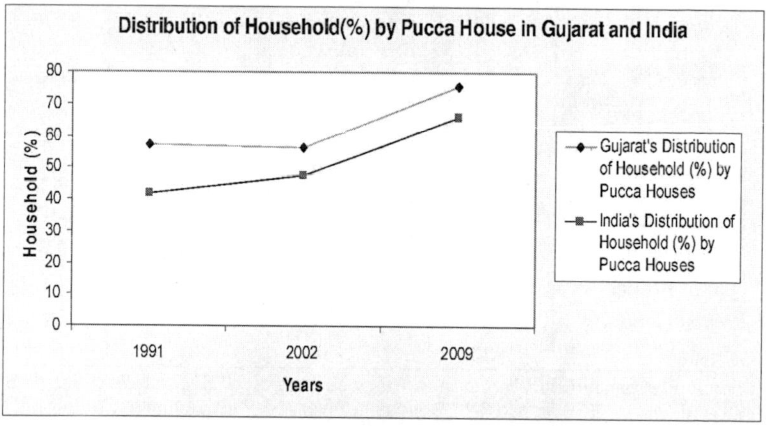

Source: Based on the data given in Table 4.6.1.

than India for all the years considered in this study. Gujarat's percentage of households with pucca house was 56.93 per cent (against India's 41.61 per cent) in 1991. Though, in 2002 it decreased slightly to 56.4 per cent (against India's 47.4 per cent), yet in 2009 it registered a significant improvement and became 75.7 per cent against India's 66.1 per cent.

It is evident from the Table 4.6.2 that Gujarat obtained sixth rank with 75.7 per cent of households obtained pucca house among 15 major states of India in 2009. The five states with comparatively higher percentage of households with pucca house than Gujarat were- Haryana (94.8), Punjab (93.4), Kerala (80.3), Maharashtra (78.9) and Andhra Pradesh (77.1) in 2009. Though, there is impressive improvement in percentage of households with pucca house in Gujarat during the given time period (1991-2009), yet the state is far behind than Haryana and Punjab.

Table 4.6.2: Distribution of Households (per cent) by Pucca House of 15 Major States in India in 2009

States	*Household (per cent) with Pucca House (2009)*	*Rank*
Andhra Pradesh	77.1	5
Assam	27	15
Bihar	48.3	13
Gujarat	**75.7**	**6**
Haryana	94.8	1
Karnataka	63.5	10
Kerala	80.3	3
Madhya Pradesh	56.9	11
Maharashtra	78.9	4
Orissa	40.3	14
Punjab	93.4	2
Rajasthan	73.8	7
Tamil Nadu	73.5	8
Uttar Pradesh	67.8	9
West Bengal	50.3	12
India	**66.1**	-

Source: NSS 65th Round.

4.7 Electricity

In this section the data regarding percentage of households with electricity connection has been discussed for Gujarat and India as well as for 15 major states of India to determine the rank of Gujarat among them.

It is observed from the Table and Figure (4.7.1) that, though both for Gujarat and India, the percentage of households with electricity connection increased significantly in the given time period (1991 to 2009), yet it was significantly higher in Gujarat than India. In the case of Gujarat it increased from 65.93 per cent in 1991 to 87.5 per cent in 2002 and became 93.4 per cent in 2009 against India's 42.37 per cent, 63.9 per cent and 75 per cent respectively.

Table 4.7.1: Distribution of Households (per cent) with Electricity Connection in Gujarat and India

Year State/Country	*1991*	*2002*	*2009*
Gujarat	65.93	87.5	93.4
India	42.37	63.9	75

Source: Housing and Amenities, Paper 2 of 1993: Table 3.3, p. 46, Census of India 1991. (Ref: National Human Development Report, p. 178) and NSS 58th and 65th Round.

Figure 4.7.1

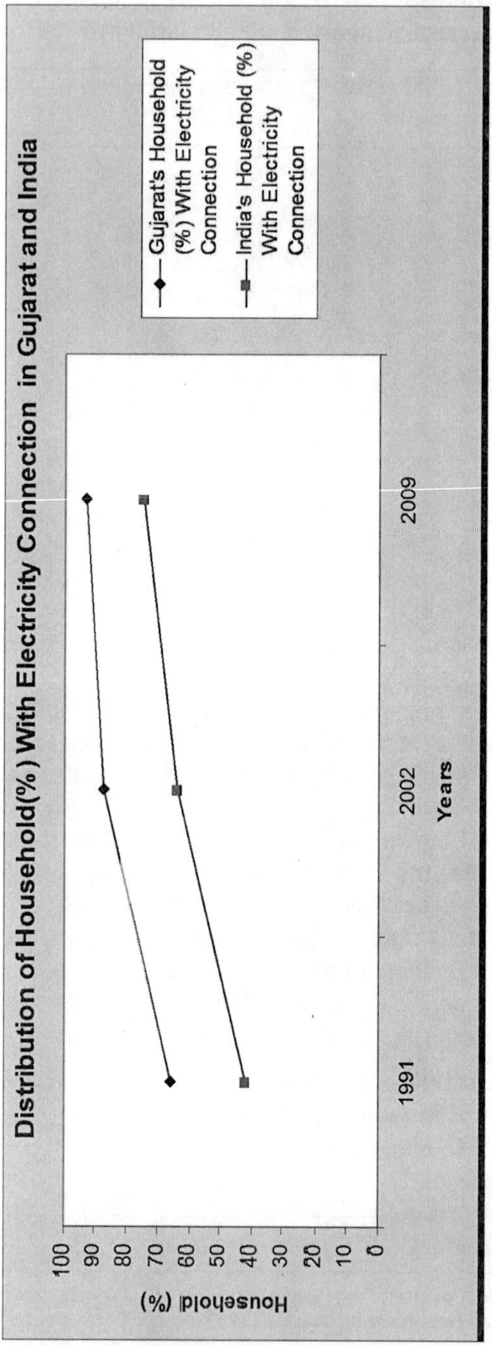

Source: Based on the data given in Table 4.7.1.

Table 4.7.2: Distribution of Households (per cent) With Electricity Connection in 15 Major States in India in 2009

States	*Percentage of Households With Electricity Connection in 2009*	*Rank*
Andhra Pradesh	94.5	5
Assam	46.6	14
Bihar	30.5	15
Gujarat	**93.4**	**7**
Haryana	95	3/4
Karnataka	95.5	2
Kerala	94.1	6
Madhya Pradesh	85.1	9
Maharashtra	89.3	8
Orissa	52.1	12
Punjab	97.6	1
Rajasthan	72.6	10
Tamil Nadu	95	3/4
Uttar Pradesh	49	13
West Bengal	60.8	11
India	**75**	-

Source: NSS 65th Round.

It is found from the Table 4.7.2 that, though Gujarat was with significantly higher percentage of household with electricity connection (93.4 per cent) than India (75 per cent) in 2009, yet the state obtained seventh rank among 15 major states.

The six states, with comparatively higher percentage of households with electricity connection than Gujarat were– Punjab (97.6 per cent), Karnataka (95.5 per cent), Haryana (95 per cent), Tamil Nadu (95 per cent), Andhra Pradesh (94.5 per cent) and Kerala (94.1 per cent) in 2009.

4.8 Toilet Facility

A majority of India's population does not have access to toilet facilities in their dwellings and lacks sanitation facilities for the disposal of waste water. In this section the data regarding 'percentage of households has no toilets within premises use' has been discussed for Gujarat and India as well as for 15 major states of India.

It is evident from the Table and Figure (4.8.1) that, Gujarat's percentage of households with no latrine within premises use was significantly lower than India for all the years considered here. Gujarat experienced decreasing trend with respect to this indicator-decreased

Table 4.8.1: Percentage of Households has No Latrine within premises use (use either public latrine or in Open) in Gujarat and India

Years	*Gujarat's Percentage of Households with No Latrine*	*India's Percentage of Households with No Latrine*
1991	69.3	76.3
2002	50.6	59.8
2009	43.6	49.2

Source: Housing and Amenities, Paper 2 of 1993; Table 3.5, page 48, Census of India, 1991, 2011 and NSS 58th, 65th Rounds.

Figure 4.8.1

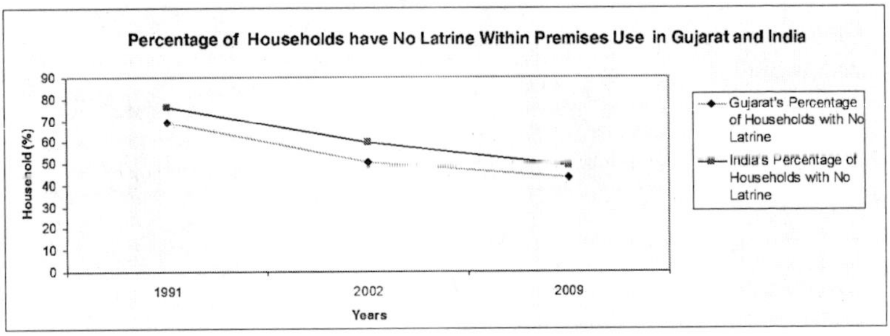

Source: Based on the data given in table 4.8.1

significantly from 69.3 per cent (against India's average 76.3 per cent) in 1991 to 43.6 per cent (against India's average 49.2 per cent) in 2009.

It is observed from the Table 4.8.2 that Gujarat obtained 6th rank with 42.65 per cent of households with no latrine within premises use among 15 major states of India.

Table 4.8.2: State-wise Percentage of Households have No Latrine within premises use (use either public latrine or in Open) in 2011

States	*Percentage of Households have no Latrine*	*Rank*
Andhra Pradesh	50.42	9
Assam	35.11	4
Bihar	76.94	14
Gujarat	**42.65**	**6**
Haryana	31.37	3
Karnataka	48.79	8

(Contd.)

(Contd. Table 4.8.2)

States	*Percentage of Households have no Latrine*	*Rank*
Kerala	4.80	1
Madhya Pradesh	71.18	13
Maharashtra	46.90	7
Orissa	77.96	15
Punjab	20.71	2
Rajasthan	65.03	12
Tamil Nadu	51.71	10
Uttar Pradesh	64.35	11
West Bengal	41.15	5
India	**53.08**	-

Source: Census 2011 (downloaded from indiastat.com on 28.10.2013).

It was significantly higher than five states–Kerala (4.8 per cent), Punjab (20.71 per cent), Haryana (31.37 per cent), Assam (35.11 per cent) and West Bengal (41.15 per cent). Gujarat's percentage of households with no latrine within premises use was almost nine times higher than the state Kerala.

Though Gujarat's position vis-à-vis fifteen major states of the country is encouraging, yet nearly two-fifth of its population is not having the latrine facilities within the premises use.

4.9 Drinking Water Facility

In this section percentage of households have access to safe drinking water has been discussed for Gujarat and India as well as for 15 major states (to determine Gujarat's rank among them).

It is observed from the Table and Figure (4.9.1) that, Gujarat's percentage of households with access to safe drinking water was greater than India for all the years considered in this study. Gujarat was with increasing trend in the time period (1991 to 2011) with respect this indicator- increased from 69.8 per cent (against India's 62.3 per cent) in

Table 4.9.1: Percentage of households have access to Safe Drinking Water Facility in Gujarat and India

Year	*Gujarat's Households (percentage)*	*India's Households (percentage)*
1991	69.8	62.30
2001	84.1	77.9
2011	90.3	85.5

Source: Data for use of Deputy Chairman,Planning Commission, GOI, 3rd May 2013, p. 188.

Figure 4.9.1

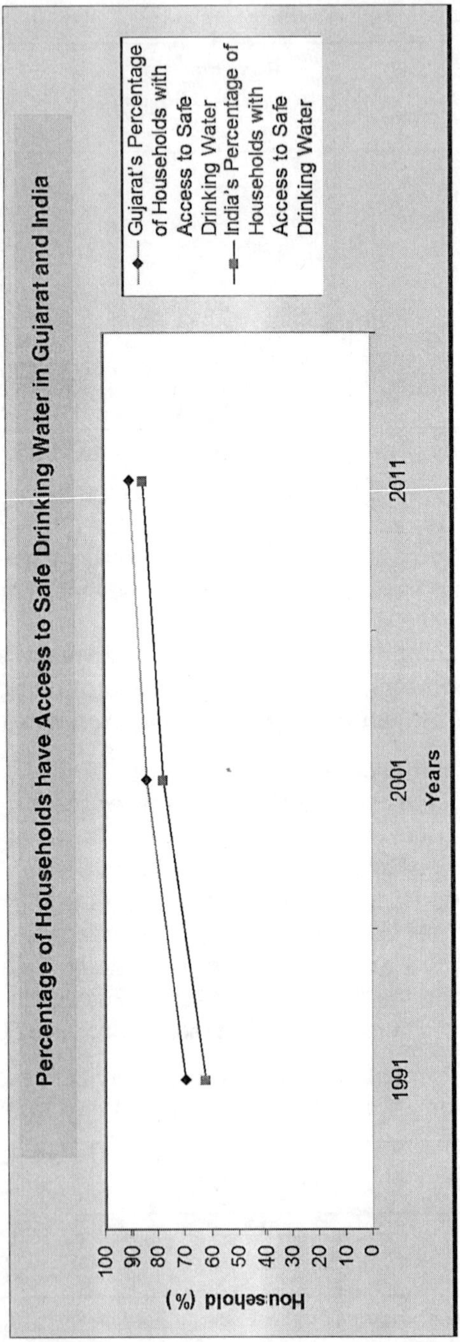

Source: Based on the data given in Table 4.9.1.

Table 4.9.2: State-wise Percentage of Households have Improved Source of Drinking Water Facility in 2011

States	Percentage of Households have Improved source of Drinking Water Facility	Rank
Andhra Pradesh	90.5	7
Assam	69.9	14
Bihar	94	3
Gujarat	**90.3**	**8**
Haryana	93.8	4
Karnataka	87.5	9
Kerala	33.5	15
Madhya Pradesh	78	12
Maharashtra	83.4	10
Orissa	75.3	13
Punjab	97.6	1
Rajasthan	78.1	11
Tamil Nadu	92.5	5
Uttar Pradesh	95.1	2
West Bengal	92.2	6
India	**85.5**	-

Source: Data for use of Deputy Chairman,Planning Commission, GOI, 3rd May 2013, p. 188.

1991 to 84.1 per cent (against India's average 77.9 per cent) in 2001 and became 90.3 per cent (against India's average 85.5 per cent) in 2011.

It is observed from the Table 4.9.2 that, in 2011 Gujarat obtained 8th rank among 15 major states with respect to percentage of households have access to safe drinking water (90.3 per cent) and it was lower than seven states– Punjab (97.6 per cent), Uttar Pradesh (95.1 per cent), Bihar (94 per cent), Haryana (93.8 per cent), Tamil Nadu (92.5 per cent), West Bengal (92.2 per cent) and Andhra Pradesh (90.5 per cent).

4.10 Health

To discuss the health status of Gujarat, the state has been compared with India as well as with 15 major states of India with respect to indicators like- Infant Mortality Rate, Life Expectancy at Birth, Under Five Mortality Rate, Percentage of Children (0 to 5 years) with Anaemia, Maternal Mortality Rate, Percentage of Women with Anaemia, Percentage of Women with BMI<18.5, Malnutrition among Children and Percentage of Children not Immunised.

4.10.1 Infant Mortality Rate (IMR)

Infant mortality rate (IMR) refers to the number of deaths per thousand live births in the first year of a child's life. It reflects the probability of a child dying before attaining the age one year. In this section, the IMR of Gujarat and India as well as for 15 major states of India (to determine the rank of Gujarat among them) has been discussed.

It is evident from the Table and Figure 4.10.1(a) that, in 1991, Gujarat's IMR was 78 against India's 77 i.e. it was slightly higher than India. Later it decreased rapidly and became 61 in Gujarat against India's 72 in 1996. In 2001 Gujarat's IMR increased to 64 against India's 66. But in 2006 it decreased to 53 (against India's 57) and became 44 in 2010 against India's 47.

From the Table 4.10.1(b) it is evident that, Gujarat obtained seventh rank among 15 major states in 2009 as well as in 2010 with respect to IMR and the states with comparatively lower IMR than Gujarat were– Kerala, Tamil Nadu, Maharashtra, Punjab, West Bengal and Karnataka in these years. Gujarat's IMR was almost 3.4 times higher than the

Table 4.10.1(a): Infant Mortality Rate (IMR) of Gujarat and India

Year	*Gujarat's IMR*	*India's IMR*
1991	78	77
1996	61	72
2001	64	66
2006	53	57
2010	44	47

Source: Vital Statistics, NFHS; Economic Survey 2012-13, Sample Registration System 46, 47 dated December 2011; October, 2012, Office of Registrar General, Ministry of Home Affairs. (Ref: Data for use of Deputy Chairman,Planning Commission, GOI, 3rd May 2013, p. 173).

Figure 4.10.1(a)

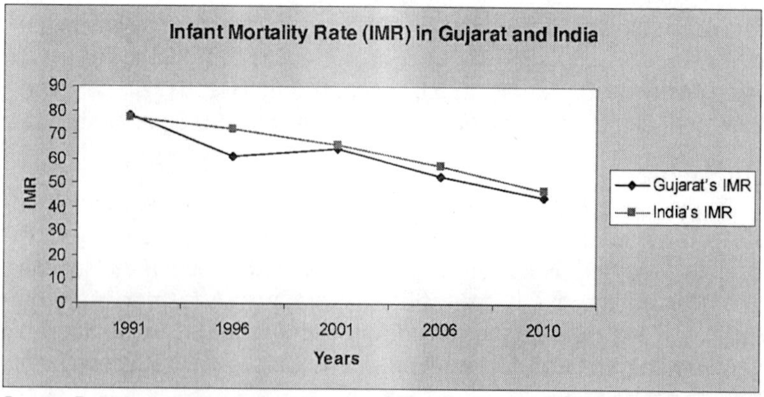

Source: Based on the data given in Table 5.10.1(a).

Table 4.10.1(b): State-wise IMR in 2009 and 2010

States	*IMR 2009*	*Rank*	*IMR 2010*	*Rank*
Andhra Pradesh	49	8	46	8
Assam	61	12	58	12
Bihar	52	10	48	9 /10
Gujarat	**48**	**7**	**44**	**7**
Haryana	51	9	48	9 /10
Karnataka	41	6	38	6
Kerala	12	1	13	1
Madhya Pradesh	67	15	62	15
Maharashtra	31	3	28	3
Orissa	65	14	61	13 /14
Punjab	38	5	34	5
Rajasthan	59	11	55	11
Tamil Nadu	28	2	24	2
Uttar Pradesh	63	13	61	13 /14
West Bengal	33	4	31	4
India	**50**	-	47	-

Source: **SRS Bulletin, Vol. 46, No. 1 (Dec 2011); Vol. 47 (Oct, 2012)** (Ref: Data for use of Deputy Chairman,Planning Commission, GOI, 3rd May 2013, p. 173).

state Kerala [the state with lowest IMR (13)] in 2010. Though, there was impressive decline in IMR in Gujarat in the given time period, yet there is urgent need to improve the health facilities to obtain IMR comparable with Kerala.

4.10.2 Life Expectancy at Birth (LEB)

Life expectancy at birth is the average number of years that a newborn could expect to live, if he or she was to pass through life exposed to the age and sex-specific death rates prevailing at that time of his or her birth, for a specific year, in a given country, territory, or geographical area.

The tabular and graphical representations of life expectancy at birth for Gujarat and India are given below:

Table 4.10.2(a): Life Expectancy at Birth (LEB) in Gujarat and India

Time Period	*Gujarat's LEB*	*India's LEB*
1986-91	59.9	58.6
1997-01	63.3	62.2
2001-05	63.9	63.1
2006-10	69.1	66.95

Source: Compendium of India's Fertility and Mortality Indicators, based on Sample Registration System, Register General India.

Figure 4.10.2(a)

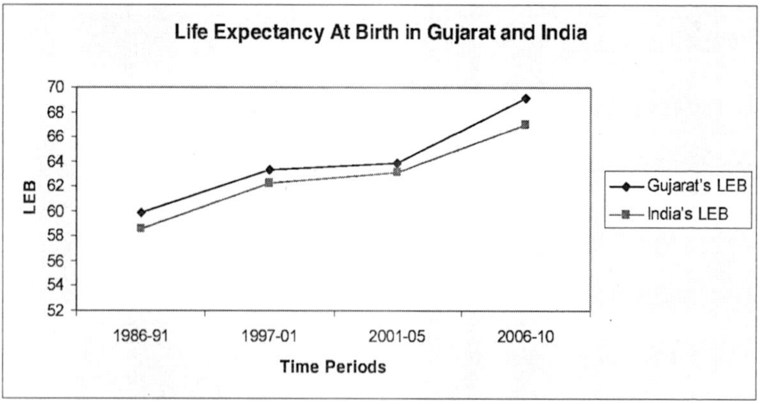

Source: Based on the data given in table 4.10.2 (a)

It is evident from the Table and Figure (4.10.2(a)) that Gujarat's LEB was with increasing trend in the given time period- increased from 59.9 (against India's 58.6) in 1986-1991 to 63.3 (against India's 62.2) in

Table 4.10.2(b): State-wise Life Expectancy at Birth (LEB) in the Time Period 2006–10

States	*LEB*	*Rank*
Andhra Pradesh	67.4	10
Assam	63.2	14
Bihar	66.9	11
Gujarat	**69.1**	**5 / 6**
Haryana	68.85	7
Karnataka	68.8	8
Kerala	74.4	1
Madhya Pradesh	62.9	15
Maharashtra	69.6	3
Orissa	64.05	13
Punjab	70.15	2
Rajasthan	67.65	9
Tamil Nadu	69.1	5 / 6
Uttar Pradesh	64.2	12
West Bengal	69.55	4
India	**66.95**	-

Source: Compendium of India's Fertility and Mortality Indicators, based on Sample Registration System, Register General India.

1997-2001, became 63.9 (against India's 63.1) in 2001-2005 and further increased to 69.1 (against India's 66.95) in 2006-2010. Though Gujarat's LEB was higher than India's avearge for all the time periods considered here, but the differences were not very significant.

It is evident from the Table 4.10.2(b) that, both the states Gujarat and Tamil Nadu obtained fifth rank with respect to LEB among 15 major states in the given time period (2006-10).

Whereas, the state Kerala obtained first rank with highest LEB (74.4), the other three states-Punjab (70.15), Maharashtra (69.6) and West Bengal (69.55) obtained second, third and fourth ranks respectively with comparatively higher LEB than Gujarat (69.1).

4.10.3 Under-Five Mortality Rate (U5MR)

U5MR refers to the probability of children born in a specific period dying before reaching the age of five years and is expressed as numbers of deaths per 1000 live births. The U5MR of Gujarat and India has been given in tabular and graphical form.

It is observed from the Table and Figure [4.10.3(a)] that, in Gujarat U5MR was with decreasing trend- it reduced from 101 in 1991, 85.1 in 1999 and 60.9 in 2006 to 60 in 2008 against India's 94, 94.9, 74.3 and 69 respectively. It increased slightly in 2009 and became 61 in Gujarat against India's 64. Except in 1991, for all the years considered here, Gujarat's U5MR was lower than India's average.

Table 4.10.3(a): Under-Five Mortality Rate of Gujarat and India

Year	*Gujarat*	*India*
1991	101	94
1999	85.1	94.9
2006	60.9	74.3
2008	60	69
2009	61	64

Source: For 1981, Child Mortality Estimates of India, Occasional Paper No.5 of 1988, Statement 2, page 5, Census of India and for 1991, Occasional Paper No.1 of 1997, Table 3, pages 112-113, Census of Indian (Ref: National Human Development Report, India, p. 2001); NFHS 2, 3 and Sample Registration System-Registar General, India.

Figure 4.10.3 (a)

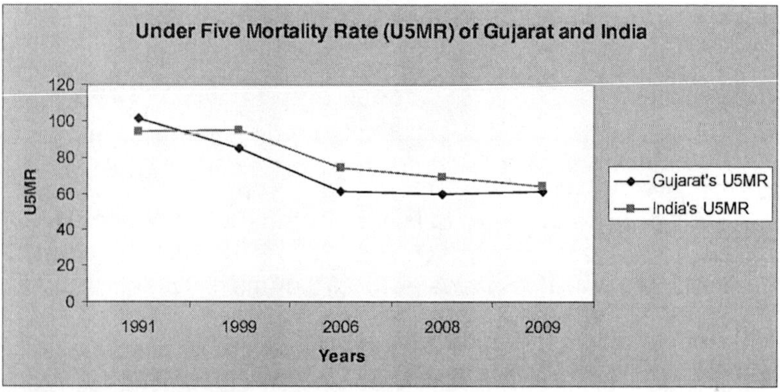

Source: Based on the data given in Table 4.10.3(a).

Table 4.10.3(b): State-wise Under-Five Mortality Rate (U5MR) in 2009

States	*U5MR*	*Rank*
Andhra Pradesh	52	7
Assam	87	14
Bihar	70	10
Gujarat	**61**	**9**
Haryana	60	8
Karnataka	50	6
Kerala	14	1
Madhya Pradesh	89	15
Maharashtra	36	3
Orissa	84	12
Punjab	46	5
Rajasthan	74	11

(Contd.)

[Contd. Table 4.10.3(b)]

States	U5MR	Rank
Tamil Nadu	33	2
Uttar Pradesh	85	13
West Bengal	40	4
India	**64**	-

Source: Sample Registration System-Registar General, India. (Ref: Family Welfare Statistics in India, 2011, Ministry of Health and Family Welfare, Government of India, Table A 40).

It is observed from the Table 4.10.3(b) that, Gujarat obtained 9th rank with respect to U5MR in 2009. Instead of impressive decline in U5MR in Gujarat in the given time period, it was significantly higher (by 4.3 times) than Kerala [the state with lowest U5MR(14)]. So there is urgent need to improve the health facilities in Gujarat to obtain U5MR comparable with Kerala.

The other seven states with comparatively lower U5MR than Gujarat were- Tamil Nadu (33), Maharashtra (36), West Bengal (40), Punjab (46), Karnataka (50), Andhra Pradesh (52) and Haryana (60).

4.10.4 Anaemia among Children (0-5 years)

Anaemia among children (haemoglobin level < 11.0 g/dL) was associated with iron deficiency (low ferritin level), maternal anaemia, and food insecurity. The data on percentage of children with anaemia in Gujarat and India as well as for 15 major Indian states (to determine the rank of Gujarat state between them) have been studied.

Table 4.10.4 (a): Percentage of Children with Anaemia in Gujarat and India

Years	Children (percentage) with Anemia in Gujarat	Children (percentage) with Anemia in India
1998-99	74.5	74.3
2005-06	69.7	69.5

Source: National Family Health Survey 2 (ref: National Human Development Report, 2001, p. 245).

It is evident form the Table and Figure [4.10.4(a)] that, whether Gujarat's percentage of anaemic children was 74.5 per cent (against India's 74.3 per cent) in 1998-99, it decreased to 69.7 per cent (against India's 69.5 per cent) in 2005-06. Both in 1998-99 and 2005-06 Gujarat's percentage of anaemic children was higher than India's average.

It is observed from Table 4.10.4(b) that, Gujarat obtained 8th rank among 15 major states with 69.7 per cent anaemic children in 2005-06.

Figure 4.10.4(a)

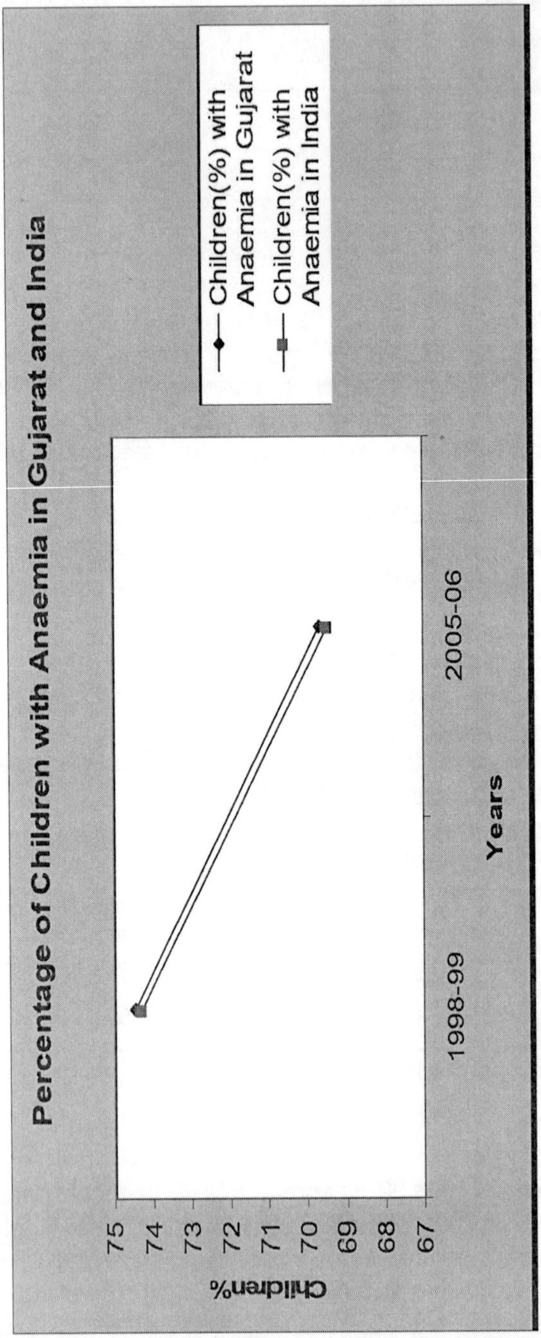

Source: Based on the data given in Table 4.10.4 (a).

Table 4.10.4(b): State-wise Percentage of Children with Anaemia (0-5 years) in 2005-06

States	*Children with Anemia (percentage)*	*Rank*
Andhra Pradesh	70.8	11
Assam	69.6	7
Bihar	78	15
Gujarat	**69.7**	**8 / 9**
Haryana	72.3	12
Karnataka	70.4	10
Kerala	44.5	1
Madhya Pradesh	74.1	14
Maharashtra	63.4	3
Orissa	65	5
Punjab	66.4	6
Rajasthan	69.7	8 / 9
Tamil Nadu	64.2	4
Uttar Pradesh	73.9	13
West Bengal	61	2
India	**69.5**	-

Source: National Family Health Survey 3. (ref: India Human Development Report, 2011, p. 276.)

The lowest percentage of anaemic children found in Kerala (44.5 per cent), significantly lower than Gujarat.

The other six states with comparatively lower percentage of anaemic children than Gujarat were-West Bengal (61 per cent), Maharashtra (63.4 per cent), Tamil Nadu (64.2 per cent), Orissa (65 per cent), Punjab (66.4 per cent) and Assam (69.6 per cent).

4.10.5 Percentage of Women with Anaemia

Anaemia is the late manifestation of deficiency of nutrients needed for haemoglobin synthesis. In women, anaemia may become the

Table 4.10.5(a): Percentage of Women with Anaemia in Gujarat and India

Years	*Women (percentage) with Anaemia in Gujarat*	*Women (percentage) with Anaemia in India*
1998-99	46.3	51.8
2005-06	55.3	55.3

Source: National Family Health Survey 2 and 3.
(ref: India Human Development Report, 2011, p. 272).

Figure 4.10.5(a)

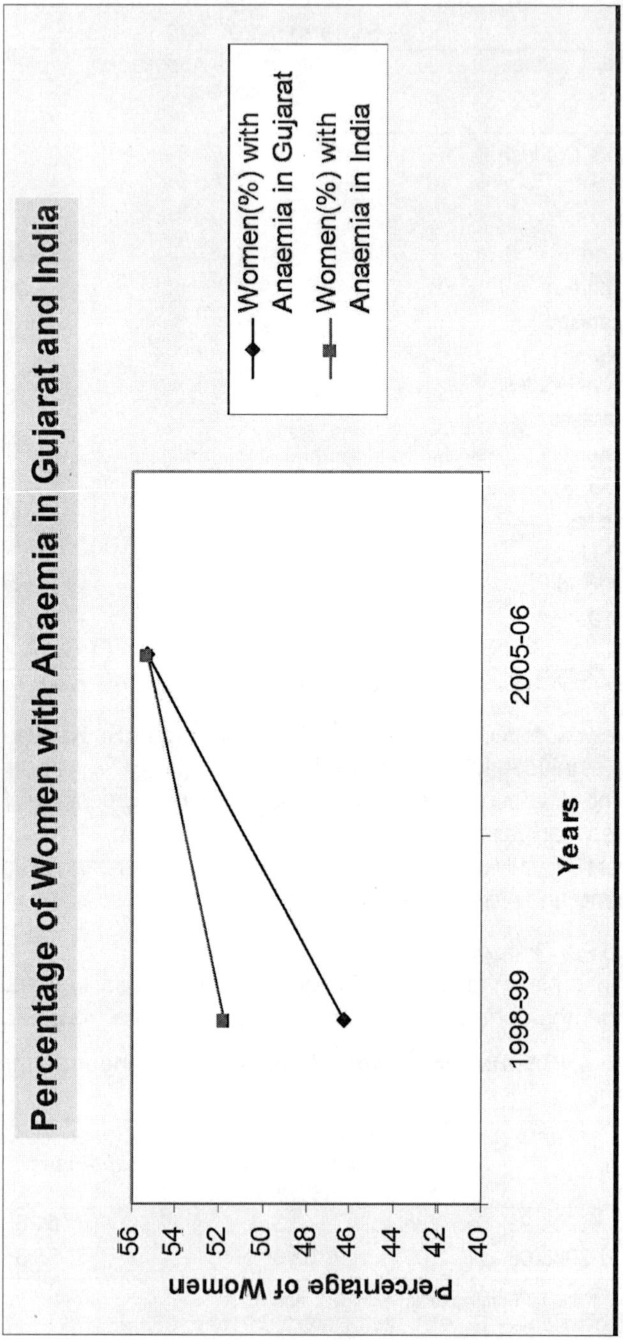

Source: Based on the data given in Table 4.10.5 (a).

Table 4.10.5(b):State-wise Percentage of Women with Anaemia in 1998-99 and 2005-06

States	*Women (percentage) with Anaemia in 1998-99*	*Women(percentage) with Anaemia in 2005-06*
Andhra Pradesh	49.8(9)	62.9(13)
Assam	69.7(15)	69.5(15)
Bihar	63.4(14)	67.4(14)
Gujarat	**46.3(4)**	**55.3(8)**
Haryana	47(5)	56.1(10)
Karnataka	42.4(3)	51.5(5)
Kerala	22.7(1)	32.8(1)
Madhya Pradesh	54.3(10)	56(9)
Maharashtra	48.5(6 or7)	48.4(3)
Orissa	63(13)	61.2(11)
Punjab	41.4(2)	38(2)
Rajasthan	48.5(6 or 7)	53.1(6)
Tamil Nadu	56.5(11)	53.2(7)
Uttar Pradesh	48.7(8)	49.9(4)
West Bengal	62.7(12)	63.2(12)
India	**51.8**	**55.3**

Source: National Family Health Survey 3 (ref: India Human Development Report, 2011, p. 272).

Note: Ranks of the states are given in bracket.

underlying cause of maternal mortality and prenatal mortality. Anaemia also results in an increased risk of premature delivery and low birth weights.

The percentage of women with anaemia in Gujarat and India for the years 1998-99 and 2005-06 are given in tabular and graphical form.

It is observed from the Table and Figure [4.10.5 (a)] that, the percentage of women with anaemia in Gujarat was 46.3 in 1998-99 and 55.3 in 2005-06 against India's 51.8 and 55.3 respectively. Though, Gujarat's percentage of women with anaemia was lower than India in 1998-99, it increased to 55.3 in 2005-06 and became equal to India.

The state-wise (for 15 major states) percentage of anaemic women has given in tabular form to determine the rank of Gujarat among them.

It is evident from the Table 4.10.5(b) that, though Gujarat obtained fourth rank with respect to this indicator in 1997-98 with 46.3 per cent of anaemic women, its rank deteriorated to eighth in 2005-06 with 55.3 per cent of anaemic women.

In 2005-06 the seven states with comparatively lower percentage of anaemic women than Gujarat were Kerala (32.8 per cent), Punjab (38 per cent), Maharashtra (48.4 per cent), Uttar Pradesh (49.9 per cent), Karnataka (51.5 per cent), Rajasthan (53.1 per cent) and Tamil Nadu (53.2 per cent).

4.10.6 Maternal Mortality Rate (MMR)

The maternal mortality rate (MMR) is defined as the number of maternal deaths in a given year, in a particular area (which can be a whole country, or a region, or a community), divided by the number of live births in the same year and area. The result is multiplied by 100,000 live births. The maternal mortality rates are discussed here for Gujarat and India.

It is evident from the Table and Figure 4.10.6(a) that, Gujarat experienced decreasing trend with respect to MMR in the given time period- decreased from 389 in 1992-93 to148 in 2007-09 against India's 458 and 212 respectively. Gujarat's maternal mortality rate was significantly lower than India for all the time periods considered here.

The MMR for 15 major states of India for the time period 2007-09 is given in Table 4.10.6(b).

It is evident from the Table 4.10.6(b) that, with 148 MMR in the time period 2007-09 Gujarat obtained sixth rank among 15 major states. The state Kerala, with lowest MMR (81) obtained first rank in the given time

Table 4.10.6(a): Maternal Mortality Rate in Gujarat and India

Years/ Time Periods	*Maternal Mortality Rate in Gujarat*	*Maternal Mortality Rate in India*
1992-93	389	458
1999-01	202	327
2001-03	172	301
2004-06	160	254
2007-09	148	212

Source: Registrar General of India, Ministry of Home Affairs (SRS Estimates).
(Ref: Status of Health and Nutrition in Gujarat: Some Issues by Indira Hirway and Darshini Mahadevia, p. 5, Table 1 and Family Welfare Statistics in India, 2011, Ministry of Health and Family Welfare, Government of India, Table A 39).

Figure 4.10.6(a)

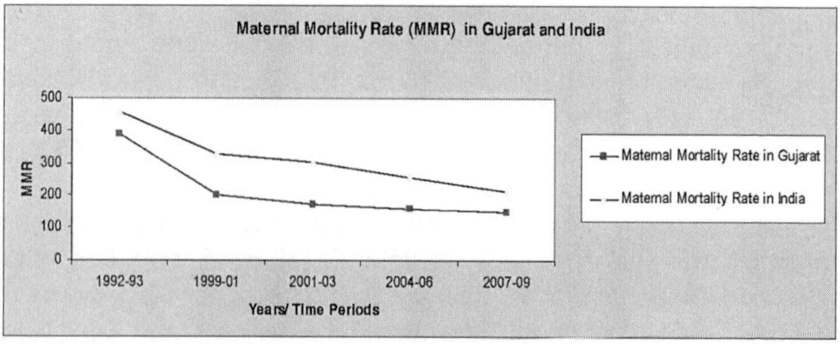

Source: Based on the data given in Table 4.10.6(a)

Table 4.10.6(b): Maternal Mortality Rate in 15 Major States (2007–09)

States	*Maternal Mortality Rate*	*Rank*
Andhra Pradesh	134	4
Assam	390	15
Bihar	261	11
Gujarat	**148**	**6**
Haryana	153	7
Karnataka	178	9
Kerala	81	1
Madhya Pradesh	269	12
Maharashtra	104	3
Orissa	258	10
Punjab	172	8
Rajasthan	318	13
Tamil Nadu	97	2
Uttar Pradesh	359	14
West Bengal	145	5
India	**212**	-

Source: Registrar General of India, Ministry of Home Affairs (SRS Estimates). (Ref: Family Welfare Statistics in India, 2011, Ministry of Health and Family Welfare, Government of India, Table A 39).

period and Gujarat's MMR was almost 1.83 times higher than the state Kerala.

The other four major states with comparatively lower MMR as compared to Gujarat in the given time period were Tamil Nadu (97), Maharashtra (104), Andhra Pradesh (134) and West Bengal (145).

4.10.7 Body Mass Index (BMI) of Women

The body mass index (BMI), or Quetelet index, is a heuristic proxy for human body fat based on an individual's weight and height. It is defined as the individual's body mass divided by the square of his or her height (kilogram/meter^2). A person with BMI of 18.5 to 24.9 may indicate that the person is with optimal weight; the BMI lower than 18.5 suggest that the person is underweight.

Table 4.10.7(a): Percentage of Women with BMI<18.5 in Gujarat and India

Years	*Women (percentage) with BMI<18.5 in Gujarat*	*Women (percentage) with BMI<18.5 in India*
1998-99	37	35.8
2005-06	36.3	33

Source: National Family Health Survey 2 and 3. (ref: India Human Development Report, 2011, p. 269).

Figure 4.10.7(a)

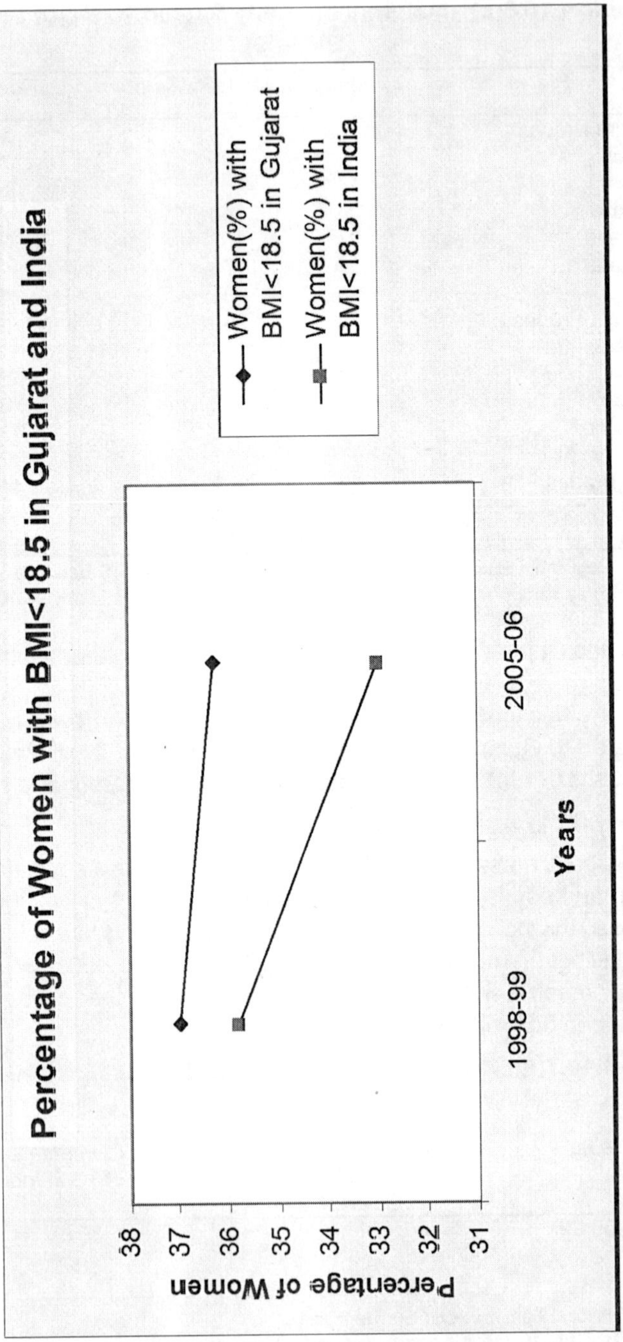

Source: Based on the data given in table 4.10.7 (a).

In this study the percentage of women with less than 18.5 BMI has been studied for Gujarat and India for 1998-99 and 2005-06 as well as for 15 major Indian states.

The tabular as well as graphical representation of data regarding women with less than 18.5 B.M.I for Gujarat and India is given below.

It is evident from the above Table and Figure 4.10.7(a) that Gujarat's percentage of women with BMI<18.5 was higher than India for both the years considered here– 37 per cent (against India's 35.8 per cent) in 1998-99 and 36.3 per cent (against India's 33 per cent) in 2005-06.

Table 4.10.7(b):State-wise Percentage of Women with BMI<18.5 in 2005-06

States	*Women (percentage) with BMI<18.5 in 2005-06*	*Rank*
Andhra Pradesh	33.5	5
Assam	36.5	10
Bihar	45.1	15
Gujarat	**36.3**	**9**
Haryana	31.3	4
Karnataka	35.5	6
Kerala	18	1
Madhya Pradesh	41.7	13
Maharashtra	36.2	8
Orissa	41.4	14
Punjab	18.9	2
Rajasthan	36.7	11
Tamil Nadu	28.4	3
Uttar Pradesh	36	7
West Bengal	39.1	12
India	**33**	-

Source: National Family Health Survey 2 and 3.
(ref: India Human Development Report, 2011, p. 269).

It is evident from the Table 4.10.7(b) that, Gujarat obtained 9th rank in 2005-06 with 36.3 per cent of women with BMI <18.5. The states with comparatively lower percentage of women with BMI <18.5 than Gujarat in 2005-06 were– Kerala (18 per cent), Punjab (18.9 per cent), Tamil Nadu (28.4 per cent), Haryana (31.3 per cent), Andhra Pradesh (33.5 per cent), Karnataka (35.5 per cent), Uttar Pradesh (36 per cent) and Maharashtra (36.2 per cent). It is clear from the above Table that Gujarat's percentage of women with BMI<18.5 per cent was significantly higher (almost two times) than Kerala and Punjab.

4.10.8 Malnutrition Among Children

As per 'Harvard Standard, a child weighing 80 per cent and above of the median weight for his age group treated as normal in standard deviation

Table 4.10.8(a): Percentage of Malnourished and Severely Malnourished Children (0-5 Years) in Gujarat and India

Year	*Gujarat*		*India*	
	Malnourished	*Severely Malnourished*	*Malnourished*	*Severely Malnourished*
1994*	**50.8**	**11.9**	**45.1**	**11.1**
2005-06**	**44.6**	**16.3**	**42.5**	**15.8**
2007***	**70.69**	**0.85**	**50.10**	**0.55**
2011***	**38.77**	**4.56**	**41.16**	**3.33**

Source: * Government of Gujarat (1994) (ref: Status of Health and Nutrition in Gujarat: Some Issues by Indira Hirway and Darshini Mahadevia, p. 13, Table 7) ; ** Data as per NFHS-3 and *** Data as per Ministry.
(ref: CAG, Report No. 22,Chapter VI, Supplementary Nutrition, p. 76).

Note: Percentage of malnourished children covers all malnourished children including severely malnourished in 2005-06, 2007 and 2011. Following WHO growth standard National Family Health Survey 3 (NFHS 3) conducted by Ministry of Health and Family Welfare provides the data of malnourished children of 0-5 years of age group for the year 2005-06, 2007 and 2011.

Figure 4.10.8(a)(i)

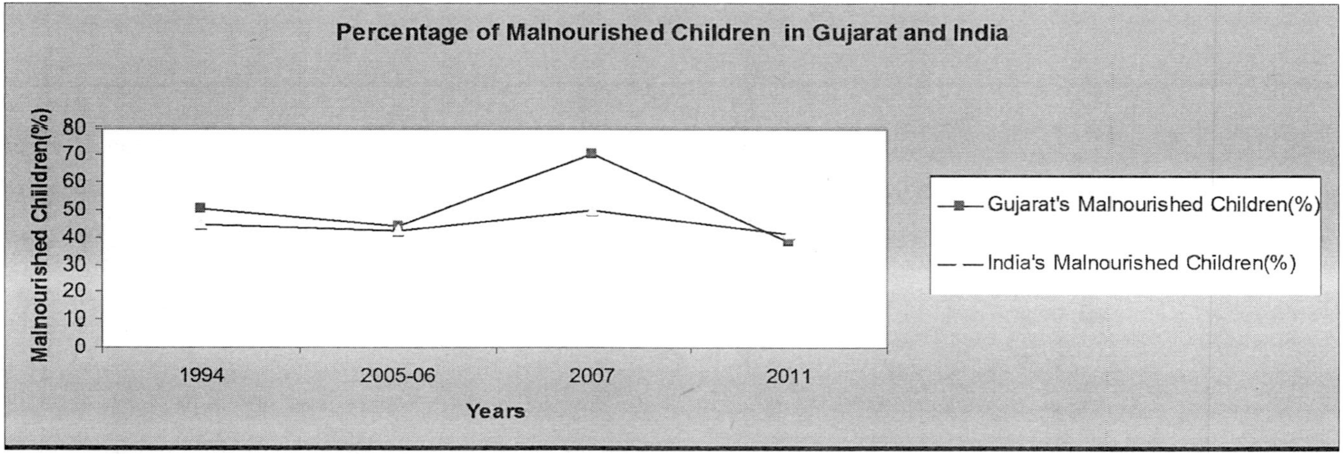

Source: Based on the data given in Table 4.10.8 (a).

Figure 4.10.8(a)(ii)

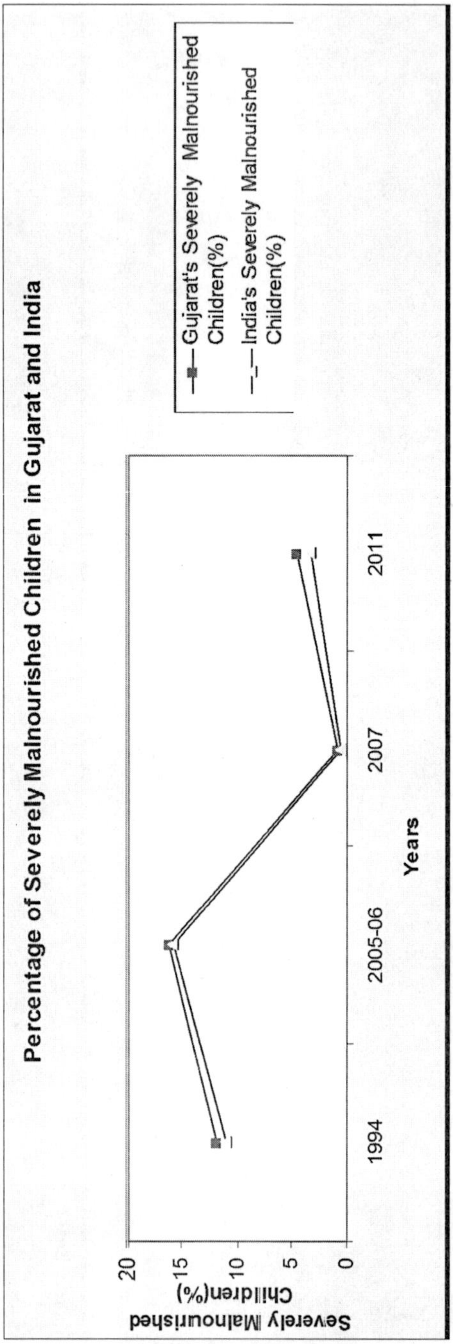

Source: Based on the data given in Table 4.10.8 (a).

Table 4.10.8(b): Percentage of Malnourished and Severely Malnourished Children (0-5 Years) in 15 Major States of India in 2011(as on 31st March)

States	*Malnourished*	*Rank*	*Severely Malnourished*	*Rank*
Andhra Pradesh	48.72	13	0.08	4 or 5
Assam	31.32	3	0.46	8
Bihar	82.12	15	25.94	15
Gujarat	**38.77**	**8**	**4.56**	**14**
Haryana	42.95	11	0.05	2 or 3
Karnataka	39.50	9	2.84	12
Kerala	36.92	6 or 7	0.08	4 or 5
Madhya Pradesh	28.49	2	1.88	10
Maharashtra	23.32	1	2.61	11
Orissa	50.43	14	0.72	9
Punjab	33.63	4	0.05	2 or 3
Rajasthan	43.13	12	0.33	7
Tamil Nadu	35.22	5	0.02	1
Uttar Pradesh	40.93	10	0.21	6
West Bengal	36.92	6 or 7	4.08	**13**
India	**41.16**	-	**3.33**	-

Source: CAG of India, Report No. 22,Chapter VI, Supplementary Nutrition, p. 76.

Note: Percentage of malnourished children covers all malnourished children including severely malnourished.

units (Z-scores) from the median of the reference population. Children whose weight-for-age is below minus two standard deviation (-2SD) from the median of the reference population are classified as underweight. Children whose weight-for-age is below minus three standard deviation (-3SD) from the median of the reference population are considered to be severely underweight' (ref: CAG, Report No. 22, Chapter VI, Supplementary Nutrition, p. 75).

The percentage of malnourished and severely malnourished children is given below in tabular and graphical form for Gujarat and India.

It is observed from the given Table and Figures that, though Gujarat's percentage of malnourished children (0-5 years) decreased from 50.8 per cent (against India's 45.1 per cent) in 1994 to 44.6 per cent (against India's 42.5 per cent) in 2005-06, yet in 2007 the state experienced a major hike and it increased to 70.69 per cent (against India's 50.1 per cent). Later it decreased significantly and became 38.77 per cent (against India's 41.16 per cent) in 2011. It is also found that, Gujarat's percentage of malnourished children was higher than India for all the years considered here except in 2011.

Gujarat obtained 11.9 per cent of severely malnourished children (against India's 11.1 per cent) in 1994, which increased to 16.3 per cent (against India's 15.8 per cent) in 2005-06. In 2007, though it decreased significantly to 0.85 per cent (against India's 0.55 per cent) yet it increased again in 2011 and became 4.56 per cent (against India's 3.33 per cent).

It is observed from the Table 4.10.8(b) that, with 38.77 per cent of malnourished children (0-5 years), Gujarat obtained eighth rank among 15 major states in 2011.

The states with comparatively lower percentage of malnourished children than Gujarat in 2011 were- Maharashtra (23.32 per cent), Madhya Pradesh (28.49 per cent), Assam (31.32 per cent), Punjab (33.63 per cent), Tamil Nadu (35.22 per cent), Kerala (36.92 per cent) and West Bengal (36.92 per cent).

Again, with 4.56 per cent of severely malnourished children Gujarat obtained 14th rank among 15 major states i.e. the state was only better than the state Bihar (25.94 per cent) in 2011. The states with comparatively lower percentage of severely malnourished children than Gujarat were– Tamil Nadu (0.02 per cent), Haryana (0.05 per cent), Punjab (0.05 per cent), Andhra Pradesh (0.08 per cent), Kerala (0.08 per cent), Uttar Pradesh (0.21 per cent), Rajasthan (0.33 per cent), Assam (0.46 per cent), Orissa (0.72 per cent), Madhya Pradesh (1.88 per cent), Maharashtra (2.61 per cent), Karnataka (2.84 per cent) and West Bengal (4.08 per cent).

4.10.9 Vaccination of Children

Though, vaccination among children is rising over time, yet it is also true that, a large proportion of the children are still not fully immunised in India. In this study 'percentage of children with complete immunisation' has been examined for Gujarat and India as well as for 15 major states of India, to determine the rank of Gujarat among them. The tabular and graphical representations of it for Gujarat and India are given below.

Table 4.10.9(a): Percentage of Children (12 to 23 months of age) Fully Immunised

Years	*Children(percentage) with complete Vaccination in Gujarat*	*Children(percentage) with complete Vaccination in India*
1992	49.8	35.4
1998-99	58.1	54.2
2002-04	54.0	45.9
2007-08	54.9	54.1
2009	56.6	61

Source: National Family Health Survey I & II. District Level Household Survey (DLHS) Estimates I, II, III and Coverage Estimates Survey (CES) 2009 by United Nations Children's Fund (UNICEF) 2009: national Fact Sheet. (Ref: Data for use of Deputy Chairman, Planning Commission, GOI, 3rd May 2013, p. 178 and p. 180).

Figure 4.10.9(a)

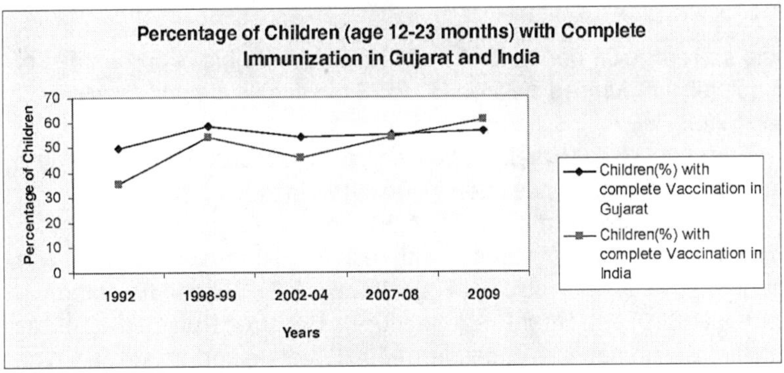

Source: Based on the data given in Table 4.10.9 (a).

It is evident from the Table and Figure 4.10.9(a) that, the percentage of completely immunised children increased from 49.8 per cent in 1992 to 58.1 per cent in 1998-99 in Gujarat (against India's average 35.4 per cent and 54.2 per cent in 1992-93 and 1998-99 respectively). It decreased to 54 per cent (against India's average 45.9 per cent) in 2002-04 and then again increased from 54.9 per cent (against India's average 54.1 per cent) in 2007-08 and became 56.6 per cent in 2009 in Gujarat (against

Table 4.10.9(b): State-wise Percentage of children (12 to 23 months) Fully Immunised in 2009

States	*Children (percentage) with Complete Immunisation*	*Rank*
Andhra Pradesh	68	7
Assam	59.1	10
Bihar	49	13
Gujarat	**56.6**	**11**
Haryana	71.7	6
Karnataka	78	4
Kerala	81.5	2
Madhya Pradesh	42.9	14
Maharashtra	78.6	3
Orissa	59.5	9
Punjab	83.6	1
Rajasthan	53.8	12
Tamil Nadu	77.3	5
Uttar Pradesh	40.9	15
West Bengal	64.9	8
India	**61**	-

Source: Coverage Estimates Survey (CES) 2009 by United Nations Children's Fund (UNICEF) 2009: national Fact Sheet.

(Ref: Data for use of Deputy Chairman,Planning Commission, GOI, 3rd May 2013, p. 180).

India's average 61 per cent). As per 2009 data Gujarat's percentage of completely immunised children (12 to 23 months) was significantly lower than India.

The state-wise (15 major states) percentage of children with complete immunisation in 2009 has been given below in tabular form.

It is observed from the Table 4.10.9(b) that Gujarat obtained 11th position among 15 major states with respect to this indicator i.e. it was better than only four states– Rajasthan (53.8), Bihar (49), Madhya Pradesh (42.9) and Uttar Pradesh (40.9). The state Punjab (83.6) was with highest percentage of children with complete immunisation which was also significantly higher than Gujarat (56.6) in 2009. The other nine states with comparatively higher percentage of children with complete immunisation than Gujarat in 2009 were– Kerala (81.5), Maharashtra (78.6), Karnataka (78), Tamil Nadu (77.3), Haryana (71.7), Andhra Pradesh (68), West Bengal (64.9), Orissa (59.5), Assam (59.1).

4.11 Total Fertility Rate (TFR)

The total fertility rate (TFR) is defined as the number of live births a woman would expect to deliver if she was to live through her reproductive

Table 4.11.1: Total Fertility Rate in Gujarat and India

Time Period	*Gujarat*	*India*
1990-92	3.2	3.7
1995-97	3.1	3.4
1998-00	3	3.2
2008-10	2.5	2.6

Source: Data for use of Deputy Chairman,Planning Commission, GOI, 3rd May 2013, p. 160.

years (age 15-49 years) and to bear children at each age in accordance with the prevailing age specific fertility rate.

The relationship between the total fertility rate (TFR) and socio-economic development, which is measured by the human development index (HDI), is the subject of debate in social sciences. Many studies conducted to examine the relationship between them. According to the empirical findings of Mikko Myrskylä, Hans-Peter Kohler, Francesco C. Billari's (2000, pp. 1-2) study 'Advances in Development Reverse Fertility Declines', in countries with a medium or low human development index, higher levels of HDI tend to be associated with lower fertility rates and the countries with very high human development index (above 0.9) higher levels of HDI tend to be associated with higher level of fertility rates (Ref: Downloaded from www.ccpr.ucla.edu/.../Kohler-advances per cent20in per cent 20development.pdf on 26.12.2013)ý.

In India Human Development Report 2011, the importance has been given on declining fertility rate and achievement of replacement level. Replacement level fertility is the total fertility levels of about 2.1 children per woman. This value represents the average number of children a woman would need to have to reproduce by bearing a daughter who survives to childbearing age. If replacement level fertility is sustained over a sufficiently long period, each generation will exactly replace itself in the absence of migration.

It is observed from the Table and Figure 4.11.1 that, the TFR of Gujarat decreased from 3.2 in 1990-92 to 2.5 in 2008-10 against India's 3.7 (in 1990-92) and 2.6 (2008-10) respectively. Though, Gujarat's TFR is lower than India, yet it is to reach the replacement level of TFR (2.1).

TFR for 15 major Indian states for the time period 2008-10 is given in Table 4.11.2.

It is evident from the Table 4.11.2 that, Gujarat obtained 10th rank (among 15 major states) with TFR 2.5 in the time period 2008-10. The nine states with comparatively lower TFR than Gujarat in the given time period were Kerala (1.7), Tamil Nadu (1.7), Punjab (1.8), Andhra Pradesh (1.8), Maharashtra (1.9), West Bengal (1.9), Karnataka (2.0), Orissa

Figure 4.11.1

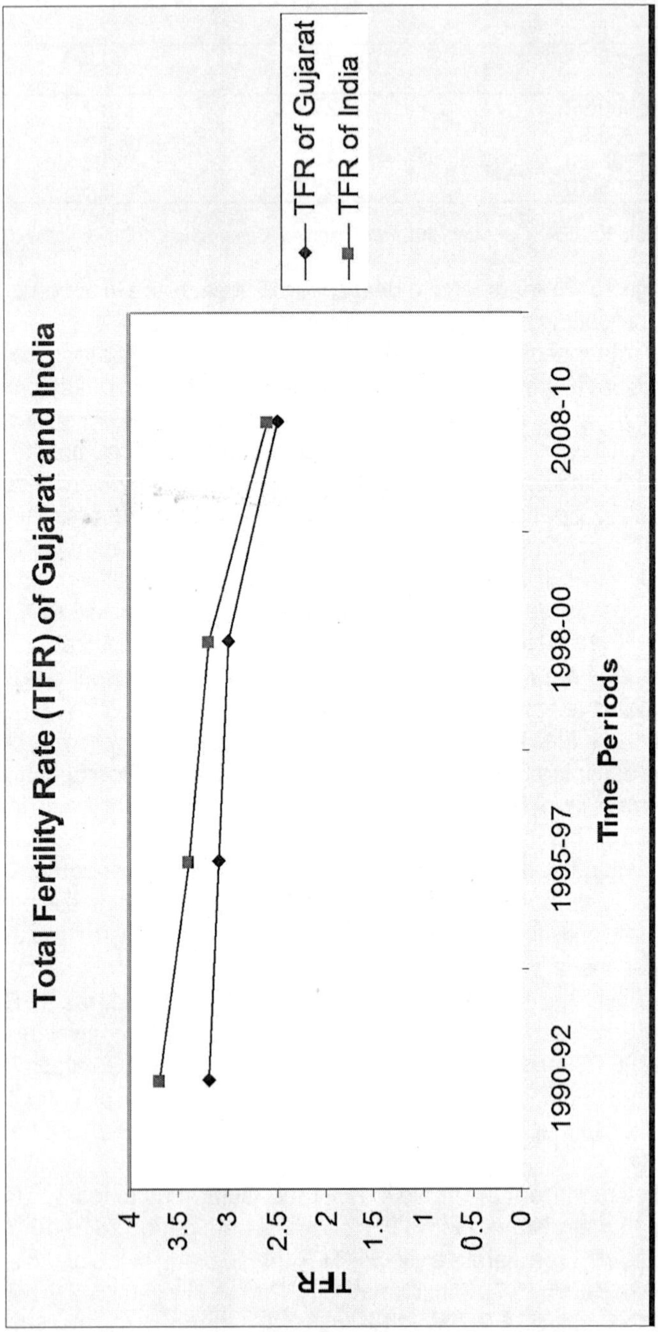

Source: Based on the data given in Table 4.11.1.

Table 4.11.2: State-wise Total Fertility Rate (TFR) in 2008-10

States	*Total Fertility Rate*	*Rank*
Andhra Pradesh	1.8	3 or 4
Assam	2.6	11
Bihar	3.6	14 or15
Gujarat	**2.5**	**10**
Haryana	2.4	9
Karnataka	2.0	7
Kerala	1.7	1 or 2
Madhya Pradesh	3.2	12 or 13
Maharashtra	1.9	5 or 6
Orissa	2.3	8
Punjab	1.8	3 or 4
Rajasthan	3.2	12 or 13
Tamil Nadu	1.7	1 or 2
Uttar Pradesh	3.6	14 or 15
West Bengal	1.9	5 or 6
India	**2.6**	-

Source: Data for use of Deputy Chairman, Planning Commission, GOI, 3rd May 2013, p. 160.

(2.3) and Haryana (2.4). Among these nine major states, seven states have already been attained replacement level 2.1.

4.12 Population

In this study the absolute numbers of population of Gujarat and India, and Gujarat's percentage of population with respect to India for the years 1991, 2001 and 2011 are given in the below Table.

It is observed from the Table 4.12.1 that, Gujarat's absolute population increased from 41.31 million to 60.38 million against India's 846.30 million to 1210.19 million in the period 1991 to 2011. India's percentage of population residing in Gujarat varied between 4.88 per cent to 4.99 per cent in the time period 1991 to 2011 i.e. the percentage of India's total population residing in Gujarat was almost remained stagnant from the past two decades.

The growth rates of population (in 10 years) in India and Gujarat are given below in Table 4.12.2.

From the above Table it is evident that the growth rate of population in Gujarat was 22.49 per cent (against India's 21.35 per cent) in the time period 1991 to 2001. Gujarat's population growth rate decreased from 22.49 per cent (against India's average 21.35 per cent) to 19.33 per cent (against India's 17.84 per cent) in the time period 2001-2011. So, Gujarat's population growth rate (per cent) was higher than India.

Table 4.12.1: Total Population of Gujarat and India

Years	*Total Population of Gujarat (in million)*	*Total Population of India (in million)*	*Gujarat's percentage of Population with respect to India*
1991	41.31	846.30	4.88
2001	50.60	1027.02	4.93
2011	60.38	1210.19	4.99

Source: Census of India (of different years).

Table 4.12.2: Growth Rates of Population (in ten years) in Gujarat and India

Time Periods	*Growth rate Population in Gujarat (percentage)*	*Growth rate Population in India (percentage)*
1991-2001	22.49	21.35
2001-2011	19.33	17.84

Source: Self calculated.

State-wise (15 major states) data regarding population as per census 2001 and 2011 are given in Table 4.12.3.

It is evident from Table 4.12.3 that, the population per square kilometer of area of Gujarat was 258 in 2001 and increased to 308 in 2011 which was not only lower than India (312 in 2001 and 368 in 2011), but also lower than most of the major states (considered in this study) due to its comparatively larger area.

The rank of Gujarat was 12th in 2001 and 11th in 2011 (among 15 major states) with respect to this indicator. Though in 2001, there were three states– Rajasthan, Madhya Pradesh and Orissa with comparatively lower population density than Gujarat, in 2011 with these three states the state Andhra Pradesh's population density also became lower than Gujarat.

The percentage of India's total population residing in Gujarat was 4.93 per cent in 2001 and increased to 4.99 per cent in 2011. Gujarat obtained 10th rank with respect to this indicator for both the years considered in this study.

4.13 Sex Ratio

The sex ratio is defined as 'numbers of females per 1000 males'. India is a developing country with comparatively lower female population than males. The sex ratio of Gujarat and India are given below in tabular and graphical form.

It is evident from the Table and Figure 4.13.1 that, though India's sex ratio has an increasing trend between 1991 to 2011, the state experienced comparatively lower sex ratio which was not only lower than India (except in 1991) but also with a decreasing trend. In 1991, 2001 and 2011 the sex ratios of Gujarat were 934, 921 and 918 respectively.

From the Table 4.13.2 it is found that, Gujarat obtaind 11th rank among 15 major states in 2011 with significantly lower sex ratio. Kerala was the only state with very high sex ratio 1034 in 2011 i.e. female population is more than male population. Gujarat's sex ratio was lower

Table 4.12.3 State-wise Population of India

States	*Percentage of Population with respect to India 2001*	*Rank of the States with respect to Percentage of Population with respect to India 2001*	*Percentage of Population with respect to India 2011*	*Rank of the States with respect to Percentage of Population with respect to India 2011*	*Population Per sq. km. of area 2001*	*Rank of the States with respect to Population Per sq. km. of area 2001*	*Population Per sq. km. of area 2011*	*Rank of the States with respect to Population Per sq. km. of area 2011*
Andhra Pradesh	7.37	5	7.00	5	275	10	307	12
Assam	2.59	13	2.58	13	340	8	397	8
Bihar	8.07	3	8.58	3	880	2	1102	1
Gujarat	**4.93**	**10**	**4.99**	**10**	**258**	**12**	**308**	**11**
Haryana	2.05	15	2.09	15	477	7	573	5
Karnataka	5.13	9	5.05	9	275	11	319	10
Kerala	3.10	12	2.76	12	819	3	859	3
Madhya Pradesh	5.88	7	6.00	6	196	14	236	14
Maharashtra	9.42	2	9.23	2	314	9	365	9
Orissa	3.57	11	3.47	11	236	13	269	13
Punjab	2.37	14	2.29	14	482	5	550	7
Rajasthan	5.50	8	5.67	8	165	15	201	15
Tamil Nadu	6.05	6	5.96	7	478	6	555	6
Uttar Pradesh	16.17	1	16.49	1	689	4	828	4
West Bengal	7.81	4	7.55	4	904	1	1029	2
India	**100**	-	**100**		**312**	-	**368**	-

Source: Census of India, 2011.

Table 4.13.1: Sex-Ratio in Gujarat and India

Years	*Gujarat's Sex ratio*	*India's Sex Ratio*
1991	934	926
2001	921	933
2011	918	940

Source: Census of India (1991, 2001, 2011).

Figure 4.13.1

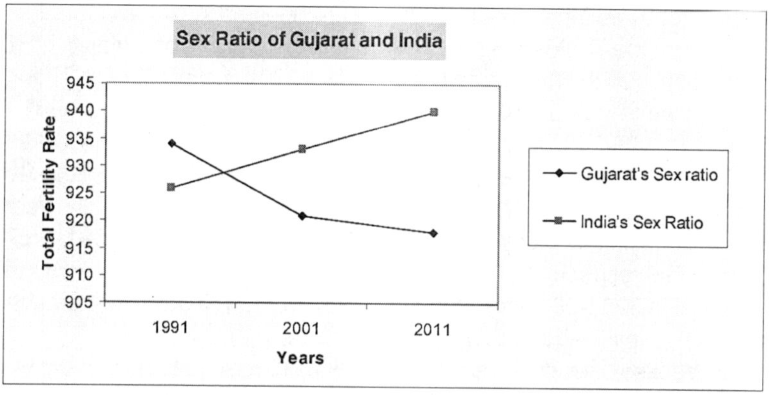

Source: Based on the data given in Table 4.13.1.

Table 4.13.2: State-wise Sex Ratio in 2011

States	*Sex ratio*	*Rank*
Andhra Pradesh	992	3
Assam	954	6
Bihar	916	12
Gujarat	**918**	**11**
Haryana	877	15
Karnataka	968	5
Kerala	1084	1
Madhya Pradesh	930	8
Maharashtra	925	10
Orissa	978	4
Punjab	893	14
Rajasthan	926	9
Tamil Nadu	995	2
Uttar Pradesh	908	13
West Bengal	947	7
India	**940**	-

Source: Census of India, 2011.

than 10 major states– Kerala, Tamil Nadu, Andhra Pradesh, Orissa, Karnataka, Assam, West Bengal, Madhya Pradesh, Rajasthan and Maharashtra.

4.14 Human Development Index (HDI) and its Components for 15 Major States of India

In this section the human development indices and the components of HDI i.e. health Index, income index and education index of 15 major Indian states and India has been discussed.

4.14.1 Human Development Index (HDI)

In this section the state-wise Human Development Indices are given below for three time points– 1991, 1999-2000 and 2007-08.

From the Table 4.14.1 it is evident that, the rank of Gujarat in HDI was sixth in all the three time points 1991, 1999-00 and 2007-08. Though the absolute value of Gujarat's HDI increased from 0.431 in 1991 to 0.466 in 1999-2000 and became 0.527 in 2007-08 against India's 0.381, 0.387 and 0.467 respectively, yet the state was still behind the five major states of India. The state Kerala obtained first rank in all the years considered in this study with human development indices 0.591, 0.677 and 0.790 respectively. The states with comparatively higher HDI than Gujarat in 2007-08 were– Kerala (0.790), Punjab (0.605), Maharashtra (0.572), Tamil Nadu (0.570) and Haryana (0.552).

We also discuss the score and rank of 15 major states of India with respect to its three indicators (health index, income index and education index), to obtain the rank of Gujarat among them with respect to each of these three components of HDI.

4.14.2 Health Index

As per national human development report of the year 2001, two components were used to construct the state-wise health index– Life expectancy at age 1 (with 0.65 weight) and the reciprocal of Infant mortality rate (with 0.35 weight). As per NHDR 2001, the maximum and minimum values of 'life expectancy at age one' were 80 years and 50 years respectively. Similarly, the minimum value of 'Infant mortality rates' was 20 per thousand life births.

However, in NHDR 2011, the 'Life expectancy at birth' was considered as single component of health index and the normalisation of the indicator was done by subtracting the minimum value (50 years) from the actual value (state-wise) of that indicator and then divide it by the difference between maximum (80 years) and minimum (50 years) value of this indicator.

It is evident from the Table 4.14.2 that, Gujarat's health indices were 0.562 and 0.633 against India's 0.497 and 0.563 for the years 1999-2000 and 2008 respectively. The rank of the state among 15 major states of India was eighth in 1999-00 and improved to sixth position in 2008 by overtaking Haryana and Karanataka (which were with sixth and

Table 4.14.1 State-wise Human Development Index (HDI) in 1991, 1999-2000 and 2007-08

States	*HDI 1991*	*Rank*	*HDI 1999-00*	*Rank*	*HDI 2007-08*	*Rank*
Andhra Pradesh	0.377	9	0.368	10	0.473	9
Assam	0.348	10	0.336	11	0.444	10
Bihar	0.308	15	0.292	14	0.367	14
Gujarat	**0.431**	**6**	**0.466**	**6**	**0.527**	**6**
Haryana	0.443	5	0.501	3 / 4	0.552	5
Karnataka	0.412	7	0.432	7	0.519	7
Kerala	0.591	1	0.677	1	0.790	1
Madhya Pradesh	0.328	13	0.285	13	0.375	13
Maharashtra	0.452	4	0.501	3 / 4	0.572	3
Orissa	0.345	12	0.275	15	0.362	15
Punjab	0.475	2	0.543	2	0.605	2
Rajasthan	0.347	11	0.387	9	0.434	11
Tamil Nadu	0.466	3	0.480	5	0.570	4
Uttar Pradesh	0.314	14	0.316	12	0.380	12
West Bengal	0.404	8	0.422	8	0.492	8
India	**0.381**	-	**0.387**	-	**0.467**	-

Source: India Human Development Report, 2011.

Table 4.14.2: State-wise Health Index in 1999-2000 and 2008

States	*Health Index 1999-00*	*Rank*	*Health Index 2008*	*Rank*
Andhra Pradesh	0.521	9	0.580	10
Assam	0.339	15	0.407	15
Bihar	0.506	11	0.563	11
Gujarat	**0.562**	**8**	**0.633**	**6**
Haryana	0.576	6	0.627	7 / 8
Karnataka	0.567	7	0.627	7 / 8
Kerala	0.782	1	0.817	1
Madhya Pradesh	0.363	14	0.430	14
Maharashtra	0.601	3	0.650	3 / 4
Orissa	0.376	13	0.450	13
Punjab	0.632	2	0.667	2
Rajasthan	0.520	10	0.587	9
Tamil Nadu	0.586	5	0.637	5
Uttar Pradesh	0.398	12	0.473	12
West Bengal	0.600	4	0.650	3 / 4
India	**0.497**	-	**0.563**	-

Source: India Human Development Report, 2011.

seventh rank respectively in 1999-2000). Gujarat's health index in 2008 was comparatively lower than Kerala (0.817), Punjab (0.667), West Bengal (0.650), Maharashtra (0.650) and Tamil Nadu (0.637).

4.14.3 Income Index

In National Human Development Report 2001, monthly per capita consumption expenditure was used (with maximum and minimum values Rs 325 and Rs 65 respectively) to determine standard of living. Again, as per India Human Development Report 2011, the per capita real consumption expenditure was used (with maximum and minimum values Rs 1091 and Rs 255 respectively) to determine standard of living. As this is positive indicator the normalisation has been done by subtracting minimum value from the actual value and then divide it by difference between maximum and minimum value of it.

It is observed from the Table 4.14.3 that, Gujarat obtained fourth rank in income index for both the years 1999-2000 and 2007-08 with the income index score 0.323 and 0.371 against India's 0.223 and 0.271 respectively. Gujarat's income index was comparatively lower than Kerala (0.458 and 0.629 in 1999-2000 and 2007-08 respectively), Punjab (with income index 0.455 in 1999-2000 and 0.495 in 2007-08) and Haryana (with income index 0.417 in 1999-2000 and 0.408 in 2007-08).

4.14.4 Education Index

According to NHDR 2001, the educational attainment index is a weighted composite index of two components- literacy rate for the age group of seven years and above (with 0.35 weight) and adjusted intensity of formal education (with 0.65 weight). The scaling norm in NHDR 2001 for education was such that- the maximum and minimum values of literacy rate were 100 and 0 and for adjusted intensity of formal education they were seven and 0 respectively. According to NHDR 2011, the educational attainment index is a weighted composite index of two components- literacy rate for the age group of seven years and above (having weight of 1/3) and adjusted mean years of schooling (having weight of 2/3). Here, the mean years of schooling is the average number of years of school education of population aged seven years and above, adjusted for out of school children in the school going age 6-17 years by multiplying mean years of schooling with one minus percentage of the out of school children.

It is evident from the Table 4.14.4 that, Gujarat's rank in its educational attainment index deteriorated from sixth to eighth between the time points 1999-00 (with educational attainment index 0.512) and 2007-08 (with educational attainment index 0.577). Though the educational indices were significantly higher than India (0.442 in 1999-2000 and 0.568 in

Table 4.14.3 State-wise Income Index in 1999-2000 and 2007-08

States	*Income Index 1999-00*	*Rank*	*Income Index 2007-08*	*Rank*
Andhra Pradesh	0.197	10	0.287	9
Assam	0.152	12	0.288	8
Bihar	0.100	14	0.127	15
Gujarat	**0.323**	**4**	**0.371**	**4**
Haryana	0.417	3	0.408	3
Karnataka	0.260	8	0.326	7
Kerala	0.458	1	0.629	1
Madhya Pradesh	0.127	13	0.173	13
Maharashtra	0.297	5	0.351	6
Orissa	0.076	15	0.139	14
Punjab	0.455	2	0.495	2
Rajasthan	0.293	6	0.253	10
Tamil Nadu	0.285	7	0.355	5
Uttar Pradesh	0.179	11	0.175	12
West Bengal	0.210	9	0.252	11
India	**0.223**	-	**0.271**	-

Source: India Human Development Report, 2011.

Table 4.14.4: State-wise Education Index in 1999-2000 and 2007-08

States	*Education Index 1999-00*	*Rank*	*Education Index 2007-08*	*Rank*
Andhra Pradesh	0.385	10	0.553	10
Assam	0.516	5	0.636	5
Bihar	0.271	15	0.409	15
Gujarat	**0.512**	**6 / 7**	**0.577**	**8**
Haryana	0.512	6 / 7	0.622	6
Karnataka	0.468	8	0.605	7
Kerala	0.789	1	0.924	1
Madhya Pradesh	0.365	13	0.522	11
Maharashtra	0.606	2	0.715	3
Orissa	0.372	11	0.499	12
Punjab	0.542	4	0.654	4
Rajasthan	0.348	14	0.462	14
Tamil Nadu	0.570	3	0.719	2
Uttar Pradesh	0.371	12	0.492	13
West Bengal	0.455	9	0.575	9
India	**0.442**	-	**0.568**	-

Source: India Human Development Report, 2011.

Table 4.15: Matrix of Different Indicators of Human Development

Indicators	*Year*	*State with Maximum Score*	*State with Minimum Score*	*Gujarat (Score and Rank)*
Per Capita NSDP (at factor cost and constant price) in rupees	2009-10	Maharashtra 57458	Bihar 12012	48511 (3rd)
MPCE (Rural) in rupees	2009-10	Kerala 1763.14	Bihar 689.37	1065.4 (5th)
MPCE (Urban) in rupees	2009-10	Kerala 2267.16	Bihar 1096.56	1914.7 (7th)
Poverty (per cent)	2009-10	Bihar 53.5	Kerala 12	23 (6th)
Unemployment Rate (Rural) (per 1000 Labour Force)	2009-10	Kerala 75	Rajasthan 4	8 (5th)
Unemployment Rate (Urban) (per 1000 Labour Force)	2009-10	Bihar and Kerala 73	Gujarat 18	18 (1st)
Per cent of Working Children	2009-10	Uttar Pradesh 3.49	Kerala 0.05	3.26 (14th)
Literacy Rate	2011	Kerala 93.91	Bihar 63.82	79.31 (4th)

(Contd.)

(Contd. Table 4.15)

Indicators	*Year*	*State with Maximum Score*	*State with Minimum Score*	*Gujarat (Score and Rank)*
Gross Enrolment Ratio (Primary)	2009-10	Madhya Pradesh 149.67	Haryana 90.1	120.42 (3rd)
Gross Enrolment Ratio (Upper Primary)	2009-10	Tamil Nadu 113.22	Bihar 55.46	86.51 (7th)
Drop Out Rate (Primary)	2009-10	Rajasthan 50.51	Punjab -18.07	25.66 (10th)
Drop Out Rate (Upper Primary)	2009-10	Bihar 66.02	Punjab -19.12	39.7 (8th)
Pupil-Teacher Ratio (Primary Classes)	2009-10	Bihar 57	Kerala 24	32 (9th/10th)
Pupil-Teacher Ratio (Upper Primary Classes)	2009-10	Bihar 61	Andhra Pradesh 18	33 (9th/10th)
Distribution of Households (per cent) by Pucca House	2009	Haryana 94.8	Assam 27	75.6 (6th)
Households (per cent) with Electricity for Domestic Use	2009	Punjab 97.6	Bihar 30.5	93.4 (7th)
Households (per cent) with No Latrine	2011	Odisha 77.96	Kerala 4.80	42.65 (6th)
Households (per cent) with improved source of Drinking Water	2011	Punjab 97.6	Kerala 33.5	90.3 (8th)

Note: In third and fourth column scores are given below the name of the states and in fifth column the rank of the state Gujarat is given in bracket.

Table 4.15: Matrix of Different Indicators of Human Development (Contd.)

Indicators	*Year*	*State with Maximum Score*	*State with Minimum Score*	*Gujarat (Score and Rank)*
Infant Mortality Rate	2010	Madhya Pradesh 62	Kerala 13	44 (7th)
Life Expectancy at Birth	2006-10	Kerala 74.4	Madhya Pradesh 62.9	69.1 (6th)
Under Five Mortality Rate	2009	Madhya Pradesh 89	Kerala 14	61 (9th)
Children (per cent) with Anaemia	2005-06	Bihar 78	Kerala 44.5	69.7 (8th)
Maternal Mortality Rate	2007-09	Assam 390	Kerala 81	148 (6th)
Women (per cent) with Anaemia	2005-06	Assam 69.5	Kerala 32.8	55.3 (8th)
Per cent of Women have B.M.I <18.5	2005-06	Bihar 45.1	Kerala 18	36.3 (9th)
Per cent of Malnourished Children (0-5 years)	2011	Bihar 82.12	Maharashtra 23.32	38.77 (8th)

(Contd.)

(Contd. Table 4.15)

Indicators	*Year*	*State with Maximum Score*	*State with Minimum Score*	*Gujarat (Score and Rank)*
Per cent of Severely Malnourished Children (0-5 years)	2011	Bihar 25.94	Tamil Nadu 0.02	4.56 (14th)
Children (per cent) fully Immunized	2009	Punjab 83.6	Uttar Pradesh 40.9	56.6 (11th)
Total Fertility Rate	2008-10	Bihar & Uttar Pradesh 3.6	Kerala & Tamil Nadu 1.7	2.5 (10th)
Population (per cent) with respect to India	2011	Uttar Pradesh 16.49	Haryana 2.09	4.99 (10th)
Population per square Km. of area	2011	Bihar 1102	Rajasthan 201	308 (11th)
Sex Ratio	2011	Kerala 1084	Haryana 877	918 (11th)
Human Development Index	2007-08	Kerala 0.790	Odisha 0.362	0.527 (6th)
Health Index	2008	Kerala 0.817	Assam 0.407	0.633 (6th)
Income Index	2007-08	Kerala 0.629	Bihar 0.127	0.371 (4th)
Education Index	2007-08	Kerala 0.924	Bihar 0.409	0.577 (8th)

Note: In third and fourth column scores are given below the name of the states and in fifth column the rank of the state Gujarat is given in bracket.

2007-08) in both the years considered in this study, yet it was significantly lower than Kerala (0.924), Tamil Nadu (0.719), Maharashtra (0.715), Punjab (0.654), Assam (0.636), Haryana (0.622) and Karnataka (0.605) in 2007-08.

Further, there was small increment (0.065) in Gujarat's educational attainment index between the given time points against India's 0.126 and Kerala's 0.135, which were almost two times than Gujarat.

As shown in the above Tables it can be concluded that, the ranking of Gujarat remains same on the basis of income index (fourth) for both of the two time points– 1999-00 and 2007-08. The state obtained eighth rank with respect to educational attainment index and sixth rank with respect to health index in 2007-08 which are comparatively lower than the rank of Gujarat with respect to income index. It may be the comparatively low health index and educational attainment index are the major reasons behind Gujarat's sixth rank with respect to HDI score among 15 major states both in 1999-00 and 2007-08.

4.16 Distribution of Fifteen Major States of India into Virtuous Cycle, Lopsided Economic Growth, Lopsided Human Development and Vicious Cycle with respect to their Categories in HDI and Economic Growth

The influential work by Ranis, Gustav; Stewart, Francis and Ramirez, Alejandro (RSR) provides evidence for the connections between Economic Growth (EG) and Human Development (HD) (ref: Ranis, Gustav; Stewart, Francis and Ramirez, Alejandro. 2000. Economic Growth and Human Development. World Development. Vol. 28, No. 2. pp. 197-219). As per classification of country performance given by RSR, fifteen major states of India are distributed into four categories– Virtuous Cycle, Lopsided Economic Growth, Lopsided Human Development and Vicious Cycle with respect to their categories in Economic growth i.e. per capita NSDP at factor cost and constant prices and Human Development Index scores (to determine Gujarat's position).

1. **Virtuous Cycle:** States with high HDI as well as high Per Capita NSDP at factor cost and constant prices. In this cycle good HD enhances economic growth, which in turn promotes further HD and so on.
2. **Lopsied Economic Growth:** States with high Per Capita NSDP at factor cost and constant prices but medium or low HDI. This will occur if good EG does not bring about good HD because of weak linkages such as low social expenditure ratio.
3. **Lopsied Human Development:** States with high HDI but medium or low Per Capita NSDP at factor cost and constant prices. It may happen when good HD performance does not generate good EG,

due to a dearth of complementary resources arising from low investment.

4. Vicious Cycle: States with medium or low HDI as well as Per Capita NSDP at factor cost and constant prices. In this cycle poor performance of HD tends to poor economic growth which in turn depressed further HD achievements and so on.

Here the states are categorised into high, medium and low categories by applying the below given formulae :

$\bar{X}$ + 0.5S and X - 0.5S; where X= Mean and S=Standard Deviation.

The score and category of the states with respect to their per capita NSDP and HDI are given for the three time points– 1991, 1999-00 and 2007-08.

As per the given data of per capita NSDP at factor cost and constant prices (base: 1993-94) in 1991.

$\bar{X}$ + 0.5S = 8380 and $\bar{X}$ - 0.5S = 6006

The states with per capita NSDP greater than or equal to Rs 8380 are categorised as high per capita income states. The states with per capita NSDP lower than or equal to Rs 6006 are categorised as low per capita income states. The states with per capita NSDP lower than Rs 8380 but higher than Rs 6006 are categorised as medium per capita income states.

As per given data of per capita NSDP in 1991, the high per capita income states were Punjab, Haryana, Maharashtra, and Gujarat. Medium per capita income states were Andhra Pradesh, Karnataka, Kerala, Madhya Pradesh, Rajasthan and Tamil Nadu. The states with low per capita NSDP were Assam, Bihar, Orissa, Uttar Pradesh and West Bengal.

Similarly, with respect to the given data of state-wise Human Development Index (HDI) in 1991 :

$\bar{X}$ + 0.5S = 0.441 and $\bar{X}$ - 0.5S = 0.364

In the same way (as given above) the states with HDI greater than or equal to 0.441 are categorised under high HDI states. The states with HDI lower than or equal to 0.364 are categorised as low HDI states. The states with HDI lower than 0.441 but higher than 0.364 are categorised as medium HDI states.

As per given data of HDI in 1991, the states under high category with respect to HDI were Haryana, Kerala, Maharashtra, Punjab and Tamil Nadu. The states under Medium category with respect to HDI were Gujarat, Andhra Pradesh, Karnataka and West Bengal. The states

Table 4.16.1(a): Per Capita NSDP at factor cost and constant prices (base: 1993-94) and Human Development Index of 15 major States of India in 1990-9

States	*Per Capita NSDP in 1991*	*Category of the States*	*HDI in 1991*	*Category of the States*
Andhra Pradesh	6845	Medium	0.377	Medium
Assam	5574	Low	0.348	Low
Bihar	3568	Low	0.308	Low
Gujarat	**8788**	**High**	**0.431**	**Medium**
Haryana	11114	High	0.443	High
Karnataka	6631	Medium	0.412	Medium
Kerala	6890	Medium	0.591	High
Madhya Pradesh	6366	Medium	0.328	Low
Maharashtra	10159	High	0.452	High
Orissa	4388	Low	0.345	Low
Punjab	11776	High	0.475	High
Rajasthan	6760	Medium	0.347	Low
Tamil Nadu	7901	Medium	0.466	High
Uttar Pradesh	5147	Low	0.314	Low
West Bengal	5991	Low	0.404	Medium

Source: CSO, New Delhi and National Human Development Report 1991;
(Categorisation of the states:- Self Computed)

under low category with respect to HDI were Assam, Bihar, Madhya Pradesh, Orissa, Rajasthan and Uttar Pradesh.

As per the given data of per capita NSDP at factor cost and constant prices (base: 2004-05) in 1999-00

$\overline{X}$ **+ 0.5S = 24186.3 and** $\overline{X}$ **- 0.5S = 16966.9.**

Therefore, the states with per capita NSDP greater than or equal to 24186.3 are categorised under high per capita income states. The states with per capita NSDP lower than or equal to 16966.9 are categorised as low per capita income states. The states with per capita NSDP lower than 24186.3 but higher than 16966.9 are categorised as medium per capita income states.

As per given data of per capita NSDP, in 1999-00 the states with high per capita income were Haryana, Gujarat, Kerala, Maharashtra, Punjab and Tamil Nadu. Medium per capita income states were Andhra Pradesh, Karnataka and West Bengal. The states with low per capita income were Assam, Bihar, Madhya Pradesh, Orissa, Rajasthan and Uttar Pradesh.

Similarly, with respect to the given data of state-wise Human Development Index (HDI) in 1999-00

$\overline{X}$ **+ 0.5S = 0.475 and** $\overline{X}$ **- 0.5S = 0.362**

In the same way (as given above) the states with HDI greater than or equal to 0.475 are categorised as the states with high HDI. The states with HDI lower than or equal to 0.362 are categorised as low HDI states. The states with HDI lower than 0.475 but higher than 0.362 are categorised as medium HDI states.

As per given data of HDI in 1999-00 the high HDI states were Haryana, Kerala, Maharashtra, Punjab and Tamil Nadu. Medium HDI states were Gujarat, Andhra Pradesh, Rajasthan, Karnataka and West Bengal. The states with low HDI were Assam, Bihar, Madhya Pradesh, Orissa and Uttar Pradesh.

Further, as per the given data of per capita NSDP at factor cost and constant prices (base: 2004-05) in 2007-08

$\overline{X}$ **+ 0.5S = 37151 and** $\overline{X}$ **- 0.5S = 24308.4**

Therefore, the states with per capita NSDP greater than or equal to Rs 37151 were categorised as high per capita income states. The states with per capita NSDP lower than or equal to Rs 24308.4 were categorised as low per capita income states. The states with per capita NSDP lower than Rs 37151 but higher than Rs 24308.4 were categorised as medium per capita income states.

Table 4.16.1(b): Per Capita NSDP at factor cost and constant prices (base: 2004-05) and Human Development Index of 15 major States of India in 1999-00

States	*Per Capita NSDP in 1999-00*	*Category of the States*	*HDI in 1999-00*	*Category of the states*
Andhra Pradesh	19568	Medium	0.368	Medium
Assam	14780	Low	0.336	Low
Bihar	6762	Low	0.292	Low
Gujarat	**25874**	**High**	**0.466**	**Medium**
Haryana	28732	High	0.501	High
Karnataka	23714	Medium	0.432	Medium
Kerala	24689	High	0.677	High
Madhya Pradesh	15894	Low	0.285	Low
Maharashtra	31066	High	0.501	High
Orissa	14084	Low	0.275	Low
Punjab	30405	High	0.543	High
Rajasthan	16960	Low	0.387	Medium
Tamil Nadu	25426	High	0.480	High
Uttar Pradesh	12115	Low	0.316	Low
West Bengal	18580	Medium	0.422	Medium

Source: CSO, New Delhi and National Human Development Report 2001;
(Categorisation of the states:- Self Computed)

Table 4.16.1(c) : Per Capita NSDP at factor cost and constant prices (base: 2004-05) and Human Development Index of 15 major States of India in 2007-08

States	*Per Capita NSDP in 2007-08*	*Category of the States*	*HDI in 2007-08*	*Category of the States*
Andhra Pradesh	33239	Medium	0.473	Medium
Assam	18089	Low	0.444	Medium
Bihar	9685	Low	0.367	Low
Gujarat	**42498**	**High**	**0.527**	**Medium**
Haryana	47054	High	0.552	Medium
Karnataka	35574	Medium	0.519	Medium
Kerala	40288	High	0.790	High
Madhya Pradesh	17572	Low	0.375	Low
Maharashtra	50532	High	0.572	High
Orissa	21640	Low	0.362	Low
Punjab	39567	High	0.605	High
Rajasthan	21922	Low	0.434	Low
Tamil Nadu	41314	High	0.570	High
Uttar Pradesh	14875	Low	0.380	Low
West Bengal	27094	Medium	0.492	Medium

Source: State Statistical Bureaus and Central Statistical Organisation, New Delhi and India Human Development Report 2011;
(Categorisation of the states:- Self Computed)

Table 4.16.2: Distribution of States according to Four Categories of Development with Reference to Per capita NSDP at factor cost and constant prices and HDI

1991	*1999-00*	*2007-08*
Virtuous Cycle (States with High HDI and High Per Capita NSDP)		
Haryana, Maharashtra, Punjab	Haryana, Kerala, Maharashtra, Punjab and Tamil Nadu	Kerala, Maharashtra, Punjab and Tamil Nadu
Lopsided Economic Growth (States with Medium or Low HDI and High Per Capita NSDP)		
Gujarat	Gujarat	Gujarat and Haryana
Lopsided Human Development (States with Medium or Low Per Capita NSDP and High HDI)		
Kerala, Tamil Nadu	Nil	Nil
Vicious Cycle (States with Medium or Low HDI and Medium or Low Per Capita NSDP)		
Andhra Pradesh, Assam, Bihar, Karnataka, Madhya Pradesh, Orissa, Rajasthan, Uttar Pradesh and West Bengal.	Andhra Pradesh, Assam, Bihar, Karnataka, Madhya Pradesh, Orissa, Rajasthan, Uttar Pradesh and West Bengal.	Andhra Pradesh, Assam, Bihar, Karnataka, Madhya Pradesh, Orissa, Rajasthan, Uttar Pradesh and West Bengal.

Source: Self calculated.

As per given data of per capita NSDP in 2007-08, the high per capita income states were Haryana, Gujarat, Kerala, Maharashtra, Punjab and Tamil Nadu. Medium per capita income states were Andhra Pradesh, Karnataka and West Bengal. The states with low per capita income were Assam, Bihar, Madhya Pradesh, Orissa, Rajasthan and Uttar Pradesh.

Similarly, with respect to the given data of state-wise Human Development Index :

(HDI) in 2007-08 (ref: India Human Development Report, 2011)

$\bar{X}$ **+ 0.5S = 0.5548 and** $\bar{X}$ **- 0.5S = 0.440**

In the same way (as given above) the states with HDI greater than or equal to 0.5548 are categorised as the states with high HDI. The states with HDI lower than or equal to 0.440 are categorised as low HDI states. The states with HDI lower than 0.5548 but higher than 0.440 are categorised as medium HDI states.

As per given data of HDI in 2007-08 the high HDI states were Kerala, Maharashtra, Punjab and Tamil Nadu. Medium HDI states were Gujarat, Haryana, Andhra Pradesh, Assam, Karnataka and West Bengal. The states with low HDI were Bihar, Madhya Pradesh, Orissa, Rajasthan and Uttar Pradesh.

From the above Table (4.16.2), it is evident that Gujarat was under Lopsided Economic Growth for all the three time points 1991, 1999-00 and 2007-08 with high Economic Growth but medium Human Development Index. It means Gujarat's Economic Growth is not transforming into Human Development and it may be due to comparatively low expenditure on health and education in Gujarat.

5

District-wise Quantitative Analysis of Infrastructure, Economic Growth and Human Development in Gujarat

The present chapter is aimed to analyse the socio-economic Infrastructural Facilities, Economic Growth and Human Development at district level in Gujarat at three time points- 1991, 2000-01 and 2009-10. In 1991 there were 19 districts in Gujarat and later the districts were bifurcated and the numbers increased to 26 of which 25 districts (except Tapi) are considered in this study for the time points 2000-01 and 2009-10. The data source for some variables in 1991 is also different from the data source in 2000-01 and 2009-10. So the performance of the districts in 1991 is not comparable with the performance of the districts in 2000-01 and 2009-10. Though, the districts are categorised and ranked with respect to selected indicators of infrastructure, economic growth and human development for all the time points considered in this study, yet the performance of the districts are compared for the time points 2000-01 and 2009-10 and the relationship between district-wise Weighted Aggregate Infrastructure Index and Weighted Aggregate Index of Economic Growth as well as Human Development Index and Weighted Aggregate Index of Economic Growth are analysed with the help of cross district regression analysis for the time points 2000-01 and 2009-10.

5.1 District-wise Infrastructure Development in Gujarat

In this section the district-wise analysis of Infrastructure Development in Gujarat has been done with the help of fourteen infrastructure components as well as Weighted Aggregate Infrastructure Index. The districts are categorised into High, Medium and Low Developed districts with respect to different infrastructure components as well as Weighted Aggregate Infrastructure Index. The indicators of infrastructure which are considered in this study are given in Section 5.1.1.

5.1.1 Infrastructure Indicators

ID1 Road length per 100 sq. km. of area
ID2 Road length per lakh population
ID3 Gross irrigated area as percentage of gross cropped area
ID4 Percentage of villages has access to clean drinking water to total inhabited villages
ID5 Percentage of electrified villages to total inhabited villages
ID6 Number of scheduled commercial banks per 100 sq. km. of area
ID7 Number of scheduled commercial banks per lakh population
ID8 Number of primary schools per 100 sq. km. of area
ID9 Number of secondary and higher secondary schools per 100 sq. km. of area
ID10 Pupil teacher ratio in primary schools
ID11 Pupil teacher ratio in secondary and higher secondary schools
ID12 Number of allopathic medical institutions per 100 sq. km. of area
ID13 Population served per medical institution
ID14 Number of beds available in allopathic medical institutions per one lakh people.

Among these indicators ID1 to ID7 represent the Economic Infrastructure and ID8 to ID14 represent the Social Infrastructure.

5.1.2 District-wise Infrastructure Devlopment Index: Principal Component Analysis

To analyse the performance of the districts in Infrastructure Development for the time points 1991, 2000-01 and 2009-10, it is required to calculate Weighted Aggregate Infrastructure Index (WAII). The district-wise data (based on which the WAII of the three time points have been calculated) are given in Appendix 16 (for 1991), Appendix 18 (for 2000-01) and Appendix 20 (for 2009-10).

Here, Principal Component Analysis (PCA) has been applied which gives mathematical weightage in a purely objective manner and provides solution to the problem of multicollinerity. The districts are ranked on the basis of the components which explained at least 70 per cent of the total variance.

The inter-correlation matrices of selected 14 variables of Infrastructure are given separately for the years 1991, 2000-01 and 2009-10 in Table 5.1 (a), 5.1 (b) and 5.1 (c) respectively. The inter correlation matrices

Table 5.1 (a): Inter-correlation Matrix of Infrastructure (1991)

	ID1	*ID2*	*ID3*	*ID4*	*ID5*	*ID6*	*ID7*	*ID8*	*ID9*	*ID10*	*ID11*	*ID12*	*ID13*	*ID14*
ID1	1.000													
ID2	-.044	1.000												
ID3	.293	-.545***	1.000											
ID4	.253	-.609***	.274	1.000										
ID5	.221	.078	.311*	.065	1.000									
ID6	.624***	-.512***	.615***	.494**	.230	1.000								
ID7	-.173	.465***	-.103	-.177	.184	.091	1.000							
ID8	.824***	-.301	.426**	.174	.046	.667***	-.341*	1.000						
ID9	.627***	-.512***	.688***	.356*	.134	.761***	-.270	.855***	1.000					
ID10	-.407**	-.573***	.145	.216	-.086	.162	-.090	-.244	-.104	1.000				
ID11	-.388**	-.058	-.226	.304	-.068	-.097	.418**	-.626**	-.569**	.318*	1.000			
ID12	.585***	-.541***	.570***	.421**	.133	.667***	-.265	.599***	.578***	.082	-.003	1.000		
ID13	.181	.240	-.124	-.192	.013	.180	.068	.280	.181	-.006	-.410**	-.398*	1.000	
ID14	-.111	-.500**	.171	.388**	.086	.449***	.118	-.042	.031	.599***	.402**	.487**	-.345*	1.000

Source: Self calculated.

Note: *** means significant at one per cent level, ** means significant at five per cent level, * means significant at one per cent level

bring out the fact that most the variables are positively correlated. The positive correlation explains that the variables move in same direction.

On the basis of **inter-correlation matrix (1991),** it can be inferred that, the variable ID1 is significantly positively correlated with ID6, ID8, ID9, ID12 and negatively correlated with ID10, ID11. The variable ID2 is significantly positively correlated with ID7 and negatively correlated with ID3, ID4, ID6, ID9, ID10, ID12 and ID14. The variable ID3 is significantly and positively correlated with the variables ID5, ID6, ID8, ID9 and ID12. Further, the variable ID4 is significanty, positively correlated with ID6, ID9, ID12 and ID14. The variable ID6 has significantly positive correlation with ID8, ID9, ID12 and ID14. The variable ID7 is positively and significantly correlated with ID11 and negatively correlated with ID8. The variable ID8 is positively and significantly correlated with the variables ID9, ID12 and negatively correlated with the variable ID11. The variable ID9 is significantly positively correlated with the variable ID12 and negatively correlated with the variable ID11. Again the variable ID10 is positively and significantly correlated with the variables ID11 and ID14. Both the variables ID11 and ID12 are significantly negatively correlated with ID13 and positively correlated with ID14. The variables ID13 and ID14 are significantly negatively correlated with each other. Most of the variables are significantly positively correlated i.e. they move in same direction.

On the basis of **inter-correlation matrix (2000-01),** it is observed that, the variable ID1 has significant positive correlation with the variables ID3, ID4, ID5, ID6, ID8, ID9 and ID12. The variable ID2 is significantly positively correlated with ID14. The variable ID3 is significantly and positively correlated with ID1, ID4, ID5, ID6, ID7, ID8, ID9, ID11 and ID12. The variable ID4 has significant positive correlation with ID1, ID3, ID5, ID6, ID8, ID9 and ID12. Further, the variable ID6 has significant positive correlation with ID1, ID3, ID4, ID7, ID8, ID9 and ID12. The variable ID7 and ID8 are positively and significantly correlated with each other and also with the variables ID3, ID6 and ID12. The variables ID8 and ID9 are significantly, positively correlated with each other. Similarly, the variables ID10 and ID11 have significant positive correlation with each other.

Therefore, most of the variables are significantly positively correlated i.e. they move in same direction.

Though, there exists positive correlation between most of the variables, there are also few variables between which significant negative relationship prevails.

The variable ID2 has negative correlation with most of the variables– ID1, ID3, ID6, ID8, ID9, ID12 and ID13. Again, the variable ID14 is negatively correlated with ID1, ID3, ID8 and ID12. The decreasing 'Road

Table 5.1 (b): Inter-correlation Matrix of Infrastructure (2000-01)

	ID1	*ID2*	*ID3*	*ID4*	*ID5*	*ID6*	*ID7*	*ID8*	*ID9*	*ID10*	*ID11*	*ID12*	*ID13*	*ID14*
ID1	1.000													
ID2	-.330*	1.000												
ID3	.578***	-.481**	1.000											
ID4	.500***	-.187	.382**	1.000										
ID5	.276*	-.024	.295*	.848***	1.000									
ID6	.586***	-.634**	.670***	.331*	.150	1.000								
ID7	-.027	.233	.414**	-.086	-.174	.631***	1.000							
ID8	.727***	-.505**	.359**	.415**	.166	.575***	.024	1.000						
ID9	.742***	-.633**	.659***	.452**	.327*	.746***	.215	.731***	1.000					
ID10	.041	-.234	.100	.047	.166	.138	.003	.156	.261	1.000				
ID11	-.025	-.206	.335**	.033	.076	.118	.091	-.024	.082	.312*	1.000			
ID12	.830***	-.543**	.763***	.426**	.206	.809***	.346**	.621***	.854***	.094	.209	1.000		
ID13	-.308*	-.511**	.113	-.084	-.047	.257	.129	-.197	.039	.071	-.075	-.058	1.000	
ID14	-.306*	.419***	-.361**	-.066	-.063	-.165	.045	-.389**	-.253	.043	.049	-.286*	.068	1.000

Source: Self calculated.

Note: *** means significant at one per cent level, ** means significant at five per cent level, * means significant at one per cent level.

Table 5.1(c): Inter-correlation Matrix of Infrastructure (2009-10)

	ID1	*ID2*	*ID3*	*ID4*	*ID5*	*ID6*	*ID7*	*ID8*	*ID9*	*ID10*	*ID11*	*ID12*	*ID13*	*ID14*
ID1	1.000													
ID2	-.290*	1.000												
ID3	.542***	-.632***	1.000											
ID4	.470***	-.410**	.162	1.000										
ID5	.165	-.070	.137	.165	1.000									
ID6	.522***	-.633***	.640***	.231	.170	1.000								
ID7	.097	-.247	.373**	.274*	-.072	.534***	1.000							
ID8	.754***	-.558***	.519***	.395**	.207	.651***	-.042	1.000						
ID9	.649***	-.621***	.596***	.317*	.249	.817***	.137	.806***	1.000					
ID10	-.163	.188	-.092	.038	.109	-.288**	-.331*	-.188	-.323**	1.000				
ID11	-.174	..060	-.055	.099	-.140	-.311**	-.312*	-.171	-.383**	.461**	1.000			
ID12	.880***	-.564***	.650***	.361**	.229	.709***	.132	.902***	.837***	-.155	-.203	1.000		
ID13	-.311*	-.534***	.177	.035	-.054	.538***	.387**	.005	.327**	-.287*	-.236	-.073	1.000	
ID14	-.124	.203	-.345**	.125	-.524**	-.066	.272*	-.253	-.222	-.182	-.218	-.279*	.135	1.000

Source: Self calculated.

Note: *** means significant at one per cent level, ** means significant at five per cent level, * means significant at one per cent level.

length per lakh population (ID2)' and 'Number of beds available in allopathic medical institutions per one lakh people (ID14)' due to increasing population may be one of the important reasons behind this negative relationship.

It is observed from the **inter-correlation matrix (2009-10)** that, a high degree of positive correlation prevails between most of the variables. The variable ID1 has significant positive correlation with the variables ID3, ID4, ID6, ID8, ID9 and ID12. Again, the variable ID7 has significant positive correlation with ID3, ID4, ID6, ID13 and ID14. The variable ID11 is positively and significantly correlated with ID10. The variable ID13 has significant and positive correlation with ID6, ID7 and ID9. Therefore, most of the variables are significantly positively correlated i.e. they move in same direction.

There are few variables which are negatively correlated with other variables. The variable ID2 is negatively correlated with most of the variables- ID1, ID3, ID4, ID6, ID8, ID9, ID12 and ID13. The variable ID7 is significantly and negatively correlated with ID10 and ID11. The variable ID10 and ID11 are negatively and significantly correlated with ID6, ID7 and ID9. There is significant and negative correlation between the variables ID10 and ID13. The variables ID3, ID5 and ID12 have significant negative correlation with ID14.

5.1.3 Principal Component Scores of Infrastructure Variables

On the basis of these inter-correlation matrices the final factor loadings of the variables (included in this study) have been derived. The component loadings which represent the correlation between the original variables and the derived component variables are mainly used to calculate the scores. The aggregation of the scores are done on the basis of weights (depended on proportion of variance) assigned to the components.

The Principal Component Matrix of Infrastructure variables for the year 1991 is given in the Table 5.2(a). With respect to the Principal Component Scores of fourteen variables (under consideration) the respective Eigen values, Percentage of Variances, Cumulative Percentage of Variances and Communalities are also given in the table.

On the basis of Principal Component Matrix for the year **1991,** four principal components are retained for variables of **Infrastructure** which taken together explain 78.198 per cent of total variance. The Variance of First Principal Component is 35.802 per cent. Similarly, the variances of second, third and fourth principal components are 22.147 per cent, 11.315 per cent and 8.934 per cent respectively. Here, all the Principal Components are considered to calculate the Weighted Aggregate

Table 5.2 (a): Principal Component Matrix of Infrastructure (1991)

Variable	*P1*	*P2*	*P3*	*P4*	h^2
ID1	0.699	-0.468	0.240	-0.220	0.814
ID2	-0.663	-0.547	0.408	-0.104	0.916
ID3	0.727	0.097	0.102	0.071	0.554
ID4	0.529	0.467	0.010	-0.099	0.507
ID5	0.202	-0.059	0.613	0.044	0.422
ID6	0.864	0.098	0.327	0.266	0.934
ID7	-0.333	0.098	0.807	0.232	0.825
ID8	0.826	-0.470	-0.073	-0.002	0.909
ID9	0.901	-0.275	-0.054	0.106	0.901
ID10	0.080	0.714	-0.269	0.541	0.882
ID11	-0.338	0.753	0.317	-0.145	0.802
ID12	0.815	0.246	0.087	-0.368	0.868
ID13	0.003	-0.549	-0.002	0.759	0.877
ID14	0.312	0.773	0.165	0.117	0.736
Eigen Value	5.012	3.101	1.584	1.251	
Percentage of variance	35.802	22.147	11.315	8.934	
Cumulative Variance (in per cent)	35.802	57.949	69.264	78.198	

Source: Self calculated.

Note: Here P1 = First Prinicipal Component, P2= Second Principal Component, P3= Third Principal Component, P4=Fourth Principal Component and h^2 = Communalities.

Infrastructure Index. According to the given formula (ref: Chapter 3) 45.78 per cent, 28.32 per cent, 14.47 per cent and 11.43 per cent of weights are assigned to the Composite Infrastructure Scores with respect to P1, P2, P3 and P4 respectively. According to First Principal Component (P1) the variable 'Number of secondary and higher secondary schools per 100 sq. km. of area (ID9)' has the highest loading (0.901) and 'Number of scheduled commercial banks per 100 sq. km. of area (ID6)' has the second highest loading (0.864) in 1991. Communalities (h^2) are also moderate to high ranging (varied between 0.422 and 0.934).

The Principal Component Matrix of Infrastructure variables for the year 2000-01 is given below. The calculated Principal Component Scores, Eigen values, Percentage of Variances, Cumulative Percentage of Variances and Communalities with respect to the fourteen variables of Infrastructure (under consideration) are given in the Table 5.2(b).

On the basis of principal component matrix for the year **2000-01,** five principal components are retained for variables of **Infrastructure** which taken together explain 82.262 per cent of total variance. The First Principal Component (P1) explains 39.608 per cent of variance. The variances of Second, Third, Fourth and Fifth Principal Components explain 14.487 per cent, 10.835 per cent, 8.779 per cent and 8.553 per cent respectively. All the Principal Components are considered to calculate the Weighted Aggregate Infrastructure Index of 2000-01. According to the given formula (ref: Chapter 3) 48 per cent, 18 per cent, 13 per cent, 11 per cent and 10 per cent of weights are assigned to the composite infrastructure scores with respect to P1, P2, P3, P4 and P5 respectively. According to first principal component the variable 'Number of allopathic medical institutions per 100 sq. km. of area (ID12)' has the highest loading (0.923) and 'Number of secondary and higher secondary schools per 100 sq. km. of area (ID9)' has the second highest loading (0.914). The communalities (h^2) are high ranging varied between +0.621 and +0.937 which implies each of variables considered here, is significantly correlated with other variables.

The Principal Component Matrix of Infrastructure variables for the year 2009-10 is given in the below table. With respect to the Principal Component Scores of fourteen variables (under consideration) the respective Eigen values, Percentage of Variances, Cumulative Percentage of Variances and Communalities are also given in the Table 5.2(c).

On the basis of Principal Component Matrix for the year **2009-10,** five Principal components are retained for variables of **Infrastructure** which taken together explain 84.109 per cent of total variance. First Principal Component (P1) explains 39.5 per cent of variance. The variances of second, third, fourth and fifth Principal Components are 17.327 per cent, 10.389 per cent, 9.302 per cent and 7.591 per cent

Table 5.2 (b): Principal Component Matrix of Infrastructure (2000-01)

Variable	*P1*	*P2*	*P3*	*P4*	*P5*	h^2
ID1	0.812	0.332	-0.292	0.129	0.007	0.872
ID2	-0.686	0.445	0.068	0.386	0.264	0.892
ID3	0.800	-0.147	0.109	0.163	0.094	0.709
ID4	0.564	0.612	0.336	-0.197	0.233	0.898
ID5	0.366	0.637	0.555	-0.183	0.183	0.916
ID6	0.854	-0.340	0.039	0.040	0.255	0.913
ID7	0.326	-0.607	0.041	0.370	0.467	0.831
ID8	0.754	0.203	-0.326	-0.094	-0.205	0.767
ID9	0.914	0.026	-0.013	-0.053	-0.039	0.841
ID10	0.214	-0.067	0.498	0.101	-0.596	0.663
ID11	0.198	-0.139	0.463	0.545	-0.427	0.753
ID12	0.923	-0.034	-0.109	0.184	0.083	0.905
ID13	0.043	-0.605	0.392	-0.636	0.105	0.937
ID14	-0.381	0.039	0.506	0.262	0.387	0.621
Eigen Value	5.545	2.028	1.517	1.229	1.197	
Percentage of variance	39.608	14.487	10.835	8.779	8.553	
Cumulative Variance (in per cent)	39.608	54.095	64.930	73.709	82.262	

Source: Self calculated.

Note: Here P1 = First Prinicipal Component, P2= Second Principal Component, P3= Third Principal Component, P4=Fourth Principal Component, P5=Fifth Principal Component and h^2 = Communalities.

Table 5.2 (c): Principal Component Matrix of Infrastructure (2009-10)

Variable	*P1*	*P2*	*P3*	*P4*	*P5*	h^2
ID1	0.760	0.342	0.444	-0.098	0.200	0.942
ID2	-0.739	0.143	0.325	-0.411	0.055	0.844
ID3	0.754	0.019	-0.279	0.023	0.405	0.811
ID4	0.407	0.322	0.276	0.589	-0.391	0.846
ID5	0.268	0.371	-0.378	-0.454	-0.459	0.770
ID6	0.873	-0.306	-0.124	0.036	0.049	0.875
ID7	0.292	-0.703	-0.102	-0.177	0.424	0.801
ID8	0.859	0.274	0.175	0.110	-0.034	0.845
ID9	0.921	-0.023	0.020	-0.058	-0.160	0.878
ID10	-0.312	0.546	-0.302	0.236	0.188	0.578
ID11	-0.313	0.481	-0.298	0.512	0.358	0.809
ID12	0.915	0.262	0.170	-0.079	0.145	0.963
ID13	0.274	-0.697	-0.442	0.312	-0.313	0.952
ID14	-0.240	-0.547	0.627	0.336	0.000	0.863
Eigen Value	5.530	2.426	1.454	1.302	1.063	
percentage of variance	39.5	17.327	10.389	9.302	7.591	
Cumulative Variance (in per cent)	39.5	56.827	67.216	76.517	84.109	

Source: Self calculated.

Note: Here P1 = First Prinicipal Component, P2= Second Principal Component, P3= Third Principal Component, P4=Fourth Principal Component, P5=Fifth Principal Component and h^2 = Communalities.

respectively. All the Principal Components are considered to calculate the Weighted Aggregate Infrastructure Index. According to the given formula (given in Chapter-3) 47 per cent, 20.6 per cent, 12.4 per cent, 11 per cent and 9 per cent of weights have been assigned to the Composite Infrastructure Scores with respect to P1, P2, P3, P4 and P5 respectively. With respect to First Principal Component the variable 'Number of secondary and higher secondary schools per 100 sq. km. of area (ID9)' has the highest loading (0.921) and the variable 'Number of allopathic medical institutions per 100 sq. km. of area (ID12)' has the second highest loading (0.915) in 2000-01.

The increasing percentage of variance of Infrastructure Facilities in the district-wise analysis of Gujarat between 2000-01 and 2009-10 (as per Principal Component Analysis the total variance of Infrastructure was 82.262 per cent in 2000-01 which increased to 84.109 per cent in 2009-10) is the sign of increasing disparities between the districts of Gujarat with respect to infrastructure development.

All the communalities (h^2) are high ranging (varied between +0.578 and +0.963) implies each of the variables taken for analysis is significantly correlated with other variables.

5.1.4 Classification of Districts with respect to Different Components or Sectors of Infrastructure

In this section the categorisation of districts [High, Medium and Low (as per the formula given in Chapter-3) based on mean and standard deviation of each component] has been done on the basis of each sector of Infrastructure (with the help of Weighted Composite Infrastructure Indices of different Infrastructure indicators of the particular sector under consideration). Different sectors of Infrastructure on the basis of which the districts are categorised are given in Table 5.3(a).

On the basis of each sector of infrastructure given in the above table the classification of districts in three categories in the years 1991, 2000-01 and 2009-10 are given in the Tables 5.3(b), 5.3(c) and 5.3(d). The calculated values of different weighted composite indices (based on which the districts are categorised) are given in Appendix 25 (for 1991), Appendix 27 (for 2000-01) and Appendix 29 (for 2009-10).

According to Table 5.3 (b), the districts were concentrated under medium category with respect to 'Transportation Infrastructure index' in 1991. There were seven districts—Ahmedabad, Kheda, Surat, Vadodara, Mahesana, Valsad and Panch Mahals under high category, the districts–Kachchh and The Dangs under low category and rest of the districts under medium category with respect to this indicator.

Table 5.3 (a): Different Sectors of Infrastructure (on the basis of which the districts are ranked and categorised)

Infrastructure Sectors	*Indicators*
1. Transportation	Weighted composite index of i. Road length per 100 sq. km. of area. ii. Road length per one lakh population
2. Irrigation	Gross Irrigated Area as percentage of Gross Cropped Area.
3. Drinking Water	Percentage of villages have clean drinking water to total inhabited villages.
4. Electricity	Percentage of electrified villages to total inhabited villages.
5. Banking Facilities	Weighted composite index of i. Number of scheduled commercial banks per 100 sq. km. of area. ii. Number of scheduled commercial banks per Lakh population
6. Educational facilities	Weighted composite index of i. Number of primary and middle schools per 100 sq. km. of area ii. Number of secondary and higher secondary schools per 100 sq. km. of Area. iii. Pupil-Teacher Ratio in primary and middle schools iv. Pupil-Teacher Ratio in secondary and higher secondary schools.
7. Health Facilities	Weighted composite index of i. Number of allopathic medical institutions per 100 sq. km. of area ii. Population served per medical institution. iii. Number of beds available in allopathic medical institutions per lakh population.

Table 5.3 (b): Distribution of Districts by Infrastructure Development (1991)

Indicators	*High Category Districts*	*Medium Category Districts*	*Low Category Districts*
Transportation	Ahmedabad, Kheda, Surat, Vadodara, Mahesana, Valsad, Panch Mahals.	Gandhinagar, Sabar Kantha, Rajkot, Bhavnagar, Junagadh, Bharuch, Amreli, Jamnagar, Surendranagar, Banas Kantha.	Kachchh and The Dangs
Irrigation	Ahmedabad, Gandhinagar, Kheda, Surat, Mahesana, Banas Kantha.	Vadodara, Sabar Kantha, Rajkot, Valsad, Bhavnagar.	Junagadh, Bharuch, Amreli, Jamnagar, Surendranagar, Panch Mahals, Kachchh, The Dangs.
Drinking Water	Ahmedabad, Gandhinagar, Kheda, Vadodara, Mahesana, Rajkot, Valsad, Bhavnagar, Junagadh, Bharuch, Amreli, Surendranagar.	Panch Mahals, Surat, Jamnagar.	Sabar Kantha, Banas Kantha, Kachchh, The Dangs.
Electricity	Ahmedabad, Gandhinagar, Kheda, Mahesana, Rajkot, Valsad, Bhavnagar, Amreli, Jamnagar, Surendranagar, The Dangs.	Surat, Sabar Kantha.	Junagadh, Bharuch, Banas Kantha, Vadodara, Panch Mahals, Kachchh.

(Contd.)

[Contd. Table 5.3 (b)]

Indicators	*High Category Districts*	*Medium Category Districts*	*Low Category Districts*
Banking Facilities	Ahmedabad, Kheda, Surat, Vadodara, Valsad.	Gandhinagar, Mahesana, Rajkot, Bhavnagar, Junagadh, Amreli, Panch Mahals.	Sabar Kantha, Bharuch, Jamnagar, Surendranagar, Banas Kantha, Kachchh, The Dangs.
Educational Facilities	Ahmedabad, Kheda, Vadodara, Sabar Kantha, Valsad, Panch Mahals.	Gandhinagar, Surat, Mahesana, Rajkot, Junagadh.	Bhavnagar, Amreli, Jamnagar, Bharuch, The Dangs, Surendranagar, Banas Kantha, Kachchh.
Health Facilities	Ahmedabad, Kheda, Surat, Vadodara, Valsad.	Mahesana, Sabar Kantha, Rajkot, Bhavnagar, Junagadh, Bharuch, Amreli, Jamnagar, Surendranagar.	Gandhinagar, Banas Kantha, Kachchh, Panch Mahals, The Dangs.

Source: Self Calculated.

Again, with respect to 'Gross Irrigated Area as Percentage of Gross Cropped Area' most of the districts were under low category. There were only six districts– Ahmedabad, Gandhinagar, Kheda, Surat, Mahesana and Banas Kantha under high category with respect to this indicator.

Most of the districts were concentrated under high category with respect to the indicator 'Percentage of villages have clean drinking water to total inhabited villages' in 1991. There were only three districts– Surat, Jamnagar and Panch Mahals which were under medium category and four districts- Sabar Kantha, Banas Kantha, Kachchh and The Dangs which were under low category with respect to this indicator.

Further, with respect to 'Percentage of electrified villages to total inhabited villages' most of the districts were found under high category except eight districts of which two districts- Surat and Sabar Kantha were under medium category and other six districts-Vadodara, Junagadh, Bharuch, Banas Kantha, Panch Mahals and Kachchh were under low category.

With respect to 'Banking Facilities' most of the districts were found under medium and low categories. There were only five districts– Ahmedabad, Kheda, Surat, Vadodara, and Valsad which were under high category with respect to this indicator.

With respect to 'Educational Facilities', six districts (Ahmedabad, Kheda, Vadodara, Sabar Kantha, Valsad, Panch Mahals) were under high category, eight districts (Bhavnagar, Amreli, Jamnagar, Bharuch, The Dangs, Surendranagar, Banas Kantha, Kachchh) were under low category and the remaining five districts (Gandhinagar, Surat, Mahesana, Rajkot, Junagadh) were under medium category.

Most of the districts were concentrated under medium category with respect to 'Health Facilities' in 1991. There were only five districts– Ahmedabad, Kheda, Surat, Vadodara and Valsad under high category with respect to health facilities. The districts Gandhinagar, Banas Kantha, Panch Mahals, Kachchh and The Dangs were under low category in 1991 with respect to this indicator.

From the Tables 5.3 (c) and 5.3 (d) it is observed that, most of the districts were concentrated under medium category with respect to 'Transportation Infrastructure Index' for both the years 2000-01 and 2009-10. There were three districts which improved their categories between these two time points- Ahmedabad and Dahod, shifted from medium to high category, the district Patan shifted from low to medium category. The district Narmada is the only exception which deteriorated with respect to its category and shifted from medium to low category with respect to this indicator.

Table 5.3 (c): Distribution of Districts by Infrastructure Development (2000-01)

Indicators	*High Category Districts*	*Medium Category Districts*	*Low Category Districts*
Transportation	Gandhinagar, Kheda, Surat, Vadodara, Valsad, Anand and Navsari.	Ahmedabad, Mahesana, Sabar Kantha, Rajkot, Bhavnagar, Junagadh, Bharuch, Banas Kantha, Panch Mahals, Porbandar, Narmada and Dahod.	Amreli, Jamnagar, Surendranagar, Kachchh, The Dangs and Patan.
Irrigation	Gandhinagar, Kheda, Surat, Mahesana, Banas Kantha, Anand and Navsari.	Ahmedabad, Vadodara, Sabar Kantha, Rajkot, Valsad, Bharuch, Kachchh and Patan.	Bhavnagar, Junagadh, Amreli, Jamnagar, Surendranagar, The Dangs, Panch Mahals, Porbandar, Narmada and Dahod.
Drinking Water	Gandhinagar, Kheda, Surat, Rajkot, Valsad, Anand and Navsari.	Ahmedabad, Vadodara, Mahesana, Sabar Kantha, Bhavnagar, Bharuch, Amreli, Banas Kantha, Panch Mahals, Dahod, Patan.	Junagadh, Jamnagar, Surendranagar, Kachchh, Porbandar, The Dangs and Narmada

(Contd.)

[Contd. Table 5.3(c)]

Indicators	*High Category Districts*	*Medium Category Districts*	*Low Category Districts*
Electricity	Ahmedabad, Gandhinagar, Kheda, Mahesana, Sabar Kantha, Rajkot, Amreli, Panch Mahals, Surendranagar, The Dangs, Patan, Anand and Navsari.	Surat, Vadodara, Bhavnagar, Junagadh, Bharuch, Banas Kantha, Kachchh and Dahod.	Valsad, Jamnagar, Porbandar and Narmada
Banking Facilities	Ahmedabad, Gandhinagar, Surat, Vadodara, Anand and Navsari.	Kheda, Mahesana, Sabar Kantha, Rajkot, Valsad, Bharuch, Panch Mahals, Porbandar and Dahod.	Bhavnagar, Junagadh, Amreli, Jamnagar, Surendranagar, The Dangs, Banas Kantha, Kachchh, Patan and Narmada.
Educational Facilities	Ahmedabad, Gandhinagar, Kheda, Surat, Vadodara, Mahesana, Sabar Kantha, Valsad, Panch Mahals, Anand, Dahod and Navsari.	Junagadh and Rajkot.	Bhavnagar, Bharuch, Amreli, Jamnagar, Surendranagar, The Dangs, Banas Kantha, Kachchh, Patan, Porbandar and Narmada.
Health Facilities	Ahmedabad, Gandhinagar, Kheda, Vadodara, Mahesana, Valsad, Panch Mahals, Anand and Navsari.	Surat, Sabar Kantha, Junagadh, Bharuch and Narmada.	Rajkot, Bhavnagar, Amreli, Jamnagar, Surendranagar, The Dangs, Banas Kantha, Kachchh, Patan, Porbandar and Dahod.

Source: Self Calculated.

Again, in the case of 'Gross Irrigated area as per cent of gross cropped area' most of the districts were concentrated under medium and low category in 2000-01 as well as in 2009-10. The districts Bhavnagar, Junagadh and Narmada improved their categories and shifted from low to medium category between the given time points. But there were two medium category districts – Kachchh and Patan, which deteriorated with respect to their categories and shifted from medium to low category between the time points 2000-01 and 2009-10.

With respect to the indicator 'Percentage of villages have clean drinking water to total inhabited villages' though most of the districts were concentrated under medium category in 2000-01, yet in 2009-10, most of the districts were found under high category. The districts Ahmedabad, Vadodara, Mahesana, Sabar Kantha, Bhavnagar, Bharuch, Amreli, Panch Mahals, Dahod and Patan shifted from medium category to high category and the districts Junagadh, Jamnagar, Surendranagar, Porbandar, Narmada and The Dangs shifted from low to high category between the time points 2000-01 and 2009-10. In 2009-10, there were two districts Banas Kantha and Kachchh under medium category and low category respectively, which need further improvement in drinking water facility.

Further, it is evident from the given Tables that most of the districts were concentrated under high category with respect to the indicator 'Percentage of electrified villages to total inhabited villages' for both the time points 2000-01 and 2009-10. The districts Surat, Vadodara, Bhavnagar, Junagadh, Bharuch and Dahod which were under medium category in 2000-01 shifted to high category in 2009-10. The districts Jamnagar and Narmada shifted from low to medium category and the district Banas Kantha shifted from medium to low category between the given time points. In 2009-10, there were only three districts Jamnagar, Kachchh and Narmada which were under medium category and other three districts Valsad, Banas Kantha and Porbandar which were under low category with respect to this indicator.

Most of the districts were concentrated under medium and low categories with respect to 'Banking facilities' for both the time points 2000-01 and 2009-10. There were only six districts– Ahmedabad, Gandhinagar, Surat, Vadodara, Anand and Navsari under high category with respect to this indicator both in 2000-01 and 2009-10. The district Junagadh was the only district which improved its category and shifted from low category in 2000-01 to medium category in 2009-10.

Most of the districts were found either under high category or under low category with respect to 'Educational facilities' in 2000-01. The districts Ahmedabad, Gandhinagar, Kheda, Surat, Vadodara, Mahesana,

Table 5.3 (d): Distribution of Districts by Infrastructure Development (2009-10)

Indicators	*High Category Districts*	*Medium Category Districts*	*Low Category Districts*
Transportation	Ahmedabad, Gandhinagar, Kheda, Surat, Vadodara, Valsad, Anand, Dahod and Navsari.	Mahesana, Sabar Kantha, Rajkot, Bhavnagar, Junagadh, Bharuch, Banas Kantha, Panch Mahals, Patan and Porbandar.	Amreli, Jamnagar, Surendranagar, Kachchh, The Dangs and Narmada.
Irrigation	Gandhinagar, Kheda, Surat, Mahesana, Banas Kantha, Anand and Navsari.	Ahmedabad, Vadodara, Sabar Kantha, Rajkot, Valsad, Bhavnagar, Junagadh, Bharuch and Narmada.	Amreli, Jamnagar, Surendranagar, Kachchh, Patan, The Dangs, Panch Mahals, Porbandar and Dahod.
Drinking Water	Ahmedabad, Gandhinagar, Kheda, Surat, Mahesana, Sabar Kantha, Rajkot, Vadodara, Valsad, Bhavnagar, Junagadh, Bharuch, Amreli, Panch Mahals, Jamnagar, Surendranagar, The Dangs, Patan, Porbandar, Anand, Narmada, Dahod, Navsari.	Banas Kantha	Kachchh
Electricity	Ahmedabad, Gandhinagar, Kheda, Surat, Mahesana, Sabar Kantha, Rajkot, Vadodara, Bhavnagar, Junagadh, Bharuch, Amreli, Panch Mahals, Surendranagar, The Dangs, Patan, Anand, Dahod and Navsari.	Jamnagar, Kachchh and Narmada.	Valsad, Banas Kantha and Porbandar.

(Contd.)

[Contd. Table 5.3(d)]

Indicators	*High Category Districts*	*Medium Category Districts*	*Low Category Districts*
Banking Facilities	Ahmedabad, Gandhinagar, Surat, Vadodara, Anand and Navsari.	Kheda, Mahesana, Sabar Kantha, Rajkot, Valsad, Junagadh, Bharuch, Panch Mahals, Porbandar and Dahod.	Bhavnagar, Amreli, Jamnagar, Surendranagar, The Dangs, Banas Kantha, Kachchh, Patan and Narmada.
Educational Facilities	Ahmedabad, Gandhinagar, Kheda, Surat, Vadodara, Panch Mahals, Anand and Dahod.	Mahesana, Sabar Kantha, Valsad, Navsari, Junagadh and Rajkot.	Bhavnagar, Bharuch, Amreli, Jamnagar, Surendranagar, The Dangs, Banas Kantha, Kachchh, Patan, Porbandar and Narmada.
Health Facilities	Gandhinagar, Kheda, Surat, Mahesana, Valsad, Panch Mahals, Anand, Navsari and Dahod.	Ahmedabad, Vadodara, Sabar Kantha, Junagadh, and Narmada.	Bhavnagar, Bharuch, Amreli, Jamnagar, Surendranagar, The Dangs, Banas Kantha, Kachchh, Patan, Rajkot and Porbandar.

Source: Self Calculated.

Sabar Kantha, Valsad, Panch Mahals, Anand, Navsari and Dahod were under high category with respect to this indicator in 2000-01. The districts Bhavnagar, Bharuch, Amreli, Jamnagar, Surendranagar, The Dangs, Banas Kantha, Kachchh, Patan, Porbandar and Narmada were under low category and the districts Junagadh and Rajkot were under medium category with respect to this indicator in 2000-01. In 2009-10, though the districts Ahmedabad, Gandhinagar, Kheda, Surat, Vadodara, Panch Mahals, Anand and Dahod were under high category, yet there were four districts (Mahesana, Sabar Kantha, Valsad and Navsari) which shifted from high category to medium category with respect to this indicator.

Most of the districts were found under low category with respect to 'Health facilities' for both the time points 2000-01 and 2009-10. There were nine districts– Gandhinagar, Kheda, Surat, Mahesana, Valsad, Panch Mahals, Anand, Navsari and Dahod under high category with respect to this indicator in 2009-10. There were three districts Ahmedabad, Vadodara and Bharuch which deteriorated with respect to their categories. The districts Ahmedabad and Vadodara shifted from high to medium category and the district Bharuch shifted from medium to low category between the time points 2000-01 and 2009-10. The districts Dahod (under low category in 2000-01) and Surat (under medium category in 2000-01) improved their health facilities and shifted to high category in 2009-10.

From this discussion the district-wise facilities and lackunae with respect to different infrastructural sectors or components are clearly identified. So, with respect to this analysis it is easy to identify the requirement of improvement of the particular sector or component of infrastructure in the particular district and to widen the particular infrastructure facility which it lacks so that with the development of the districts, the district-wise disparities in infrastructure facilities can also be reduced.

5.1.5 Classification of Districts with respect to Weighted Aggregate Infrastructure Index

The districts are classified into high, medium and low developed districts with respect to infrastructure development in the way given below.

According to the mean (X) and standard deviation (S) of Weighted Aggregate Infrastructure Indices, the maximum and minimum values of it in **1991** are given below:

$$\bar{X} + 0.5S = 3.544 \text{ and } \bar{X} - 0.5S = 2.235$$

The districts with 'Weighted Aggregate Infrastructure Index' greater than or equal to 3.544 are considered as the districts with highly developed infrastructure. According to the above table the districts

Table 5.4 (a): District-wise Weighted Aggregate Infrastructure Index (WAII) Score Category and Rank in 1991

Districts	*WAII Score*	*Category*	*Rank*
Ahmedabad	5.162	High	1
Gandhinagar	2.969	Medium	8
Kheda	4.887	High	3
Surat	4.953	High	2
Vadodara	3.893	High	5
Mahesana	3.654	High	6
Sabar Kantha	3.047	Medium	7
Rajkot	2.598	Medium	11
Valsad	4.191	High	4
Bhavnagar	2.394	Medium	12
Junagadh	2.761	Medium	10
Bharuch	2.110	Low	15
Amreli	2.116	Low	13
Jamnagar	1.881	Low	17
Surendranagar	2.111	Low	14
Banas Kantha	2.066	Low	16
Panch Mahals	2.798	Medium	9
Kachchh	1.021	Low	18
The Dangs	0.289	Low	19

Source: Self calculated.

Ahmedabad, Kheda, Surat, Vadodara, Mahesana and Valsad were under high category with respect to **'Weighted Aggregate Infrastructure Index' score in 1991**.

The districts with 'Weighted Aggregate Infrastructure Index' varied between 3.544 and 2.235 i.e. lower than 3.544 but higher than 2.235 are categorised as medium with respect to this indicator. The districts **Gandhinagar, Sabar Kantha, Rajkot Bhavnagar, Panch Mahals and Junagadh were under medium category** with respect to this indicator. Similarly, the districts with Weighted Aggregate Infrastructure Index' less than or equal to 2.235 are categorised as low developed districts with respect to this indicator. The districts **Bharuch, Amreli, Jamnagar, Surendranagar, Banas Kantha, Kachchh and The Dangs** were under low category with respect to this indicator in 1991. According to the mean and standard deviation of 'Weighted Aggregate Infrastructure Index' in **2000-01** the calculated maxmimum and minimum values are given below:

$$\bar{X} + 0.5S = 3.9357 \text{ and } \bar{X} - 0.5S = 2.605$$

The districts with 'Weighted Aggregate Infrastructure Index' greater than or equal to 3.9357 are categorised as the districts with highly developed infrastructure.

The districts with 'Weighted Aggregate Infrastructure Index' lower than 3.9357 but higher than 2.605 are categorised as the districts with medium developed infrastructure.

Again, the districts with 'Weighted Aggregate Infrastructure Index' less than or equal to 2.605 are categorised as the districts with low developed infrastructure.

According to the analysis the districts **Ahmedabad, Gandhinagar, Kheda, Surat, Vadodara, Mahesana, Anand and Navsari** were under **high category** with respect to this indicator in 2000-01.

The districts **Sabar Kantha, Rajkot, Valsad, Bharuch, Panch Mahals and Dahod** were under **medium category** and the districts **Bhavnagar, Junagadh, Amreli, Jamnagar, Surendranagar, Banas Kantha, Kachchh, The Dangs, Patan, Porbandar and Narmada** were under **low category** with respect to this indicator in the given time point.

Similarly, as per the mean and standard deviation of 'Weighted Aggregate Infrastructure Index' in **2009-10:**

$$\bar{X} + 0.5S = 3.1095 \text{ and } \bar{X} - 0.5S = 1.7987$$

The districts with 'Weighted Aggregate Infrastructure Index' greater than or equal to 3.1095 have highly developed infrastructure.

Table 5.4 (b): District-wise Weighted Aggregate Infrastructure Index (WAII) Score, Category and Rank in 2000-01

Districts	*WAII Score*	*Category*	*Rank*
Ahmedabad	4.9318	High	4
Gandhinagar	5.8521	High	1
Kheda	4.5518	High	5
Surat	4.3488	High	7
Vadodara	4.2643	High	8
Mahesana	4.4300	High	6
Sabar Kantha	3.5507	Medium	10
Rajkot	2.6850	Medium	14
Valsad	3.8131	Medium	9
Bhavnagar	2.2558	Low	20
Junagadh	2.5538	Low	16
Bharuch	2.7398	Medium	13
Amreli	2.0957	Low	21
Jamnagar	1.7310	Low	23
Surendranagar	1.8205	Low	22
Banas Kantha	2.5653	Low	15
Panch Mahals	3.5416	Medium	11
Kachchh	1.3771	Low	25
The Dangs	1.5280	Low	24
Patan	2.4038	Low	17
Porbandar	2.3383	Low	19
Anand	5.5025	High	2
Narmada	2.3832	Low	18
Dahod	3.0127	Medium	12
Navsari	5.4829	High	3

Source: Self calculated.

The districts, with 'Weighted Aggregate Infrastructure Index' varies between 3.1095 and 1.7987, i.e. lower than 3.1095 but higher than 1.7987 are categorised as the districts with medium developed infrastructure.

Similarly, the districts with 'Weighted Aggregate Infrastructure Index' less than or equal to 1.7987 are categorised as the districts with low developed Infrastructure.

According to the analysis the districts **Ahmedabad, Gandhinagar, Kheda, Surat, Vadodara, Valsad, Anand and Navsari** were under **high category** with respect to this indicator in 2009-10.

The districts **Mahesana, Sabar Kantha, Rajkot, Junagadh, Banas Kantha, Panch Mahals and Dahod** were under **medium category** and the districts **Bhavnagar, Bharuch, Amreli, Jamnagar, Surendranagar, Kachchh, The Dangs, Patan, Porbandar and Narmada** were under **low category** with respect to this indicator in 2009-10.

Table 5.4 (c): District-wise Weighted Aggregate Infrastructure Index (WAII) Score, Category and Rank in 2009-10

Districts	*WAII Score*	*Category*	*Rank*
Ahmedabad	3.7749	High	5
Gandhinagar	4.8101	High	1
Kheda	3.5333	High	6
Surat	4.7758	High	2
Vadodara	3.2212	High	8
Mahesana	2.9955	Medium	10
Sabar Kantha	2.5930	Medium	12
Rajkot	2.0504	Medium	14
Valsad	3.3332	High	7
Bhavnagar	1.6855	Low	18
Junagadh	2.1288	Medium	13
Bharuch	1.7041	Low	17
Amreli	1.3048	Low	21
Jamnagar	0.9096	Low	23
Surendranagar	0.9831	Low	22
Banas Kantha	1.8240	Medium	15
Panch Mahals	2.9256	Medium	11
Kachchh	0.1070	Low	25
The Dangs	0.6752	Low	24
Patan	1.4329	Low	19
Porbandar	1.4094	Low	20
Anand	4.2743	High	3
Narmada	1.7108	Low	16
Dahod	3.0843	Medium	9
Navsari	4.1066	High	4

Source: Self calculated.

5.1.6 Comparison of District-wise Performances in Infrastructure Development between 2000-01 and 2009-10

To compare the district-wise performances in infrastructure development between 2000-01 and 2009-10, it is required to compare the ranks of the districts with respect to their 'Weighted Aggregate Infrastructure Index' scores in these two time points. The rank of the districts with respect to 'Weighted Aggregate Infrastructure Index' for the time points 2000-01 and 2009-10 are given in Table 5.5.

From Table 5.5 it is clear that, whereas some districts improved their rank with respect to WAII scores between the years 2000-01 and 2009-10, some of them sustained their rank and the ranks of some districts also deteriorated. The districts which sustained their ranks (between 2000-01 and 2009-10) were– Gandhinagar (1), Vadodara (8), Panch Mahals (11), Rajkot (14), Banas Kantha (15), Amreli (21), Surendranagar (22), Jamnagar (23), The Dangs (24) and Kachchh (25).

Table 5.5: Comparison of the District-wise Performances in Infrastructure Development ['Weighted Aggregate Infrastructure Index (WAII)'] between the time points 2000-01 and 2009-10 with respect to their ranks

Districts which sustained their ranks (with respect to WAII scores) between 2000-01 and 2009-10		
Name of the Districts	*Rank (with respect to WAII scores) in 2000-01*	*Rank (with respect to WAII scores) in 2009-10*
Gandhinagar	1	1
Vadodara	8	8
Panch Mahals	11	11
Rajkot	14	14
Banas Kantha	15	15
Amreli	21	21
Surendranagar	22	22
Jamnagar	23	23
The Dangs	24	24
Kachchh	25	25
Districts which improved their ranks (with respect to WAII scores) between 2000-01 and 2009-10		
Name of the Districts	*Rank (with respect to WAII scores) in 2000-01*	*Rank (with respect to WAII scores) in 2009-10*
Surat	7	2
Valsad	9	7
Dahod	12	9
Junagadh	16	13
Narmada	18	16
Bhavnagar	20	18
Districts with deteriorated ranks (with respect to WAII scores) between 2000-01 and 2009-10		
Name of the Districts	*Rank (with respect to WAII scores) in 2000-01*	*Rank (with respect to WAII scores) in 2009-10*
Anand	2	3
Navsari	3	4
Ahmedabad	4	5
Kheda	5	6
Mahesana	6	10
Sabar Kantha	10	12
Bharuch	13	17
Patan	17	19
Porbandar	19	20

Source: Self calculated.

Though, the rank of the district Banas Kantha remained same in the given time points, yet the category of the district improved from low (2000-01) to medium (2009-10).

The districts which improved their ranks between the time points 2000-01 and 2009-10 were– Surat, Valsad, Dahod, Junagadh, Narmada and Bhavnagar. The rank of these districts were 7, 9, 12, 16, 18 and 20 respectively in 2000-01 and improved to 2, 7, 9, 13, 16 and 18 respectively in 2009-10. There were some districts which improved their ranks as well as category between the given time points– Valsad shifted from medium to high and Junagadh shifted from low to medium.

The rank of the districts– Anand, Navsari, Ahmedabad, Kheda, Mahesana, Sabar Kantha, Bharuch, Patan and Porbandar were 2, 3, 4, 5, 6, 10, 13, 17 and 19 respectively in 2000-01 and deteriorated to 3, 4, 5, 6, 10, 12, 17, 19 and 20 respectively in 2009-10.

Though, the district Mahesana was under high category (with respect to WAII score) in 2000-01, it shifted to medium category in 2009-10. The district Bharuch also degraded with respect to its category and shifted from medium to low between the given time points.

5.2 District-wise Economic Growth in Gujarat

Generally economic growth is expressed by per capita income or per capita consumption expenditure. But for Gujarat, the district-wise data of per capita income or expenditure is not available. According to **'Gujarat Human Development Report, 2004,'** generally, in that case, **any one of these proxies can be used:**

(i) Per capita output in agriculture and industries together;
(ii) Per capita bank deposits;
(iii) Percentage of households having specified assets;

But it is also true that any single indicator among these given proxies can not express economic growth properly. **So, on the behalf on these given proxies nine selected indicators of economic growth have been used here and calculated weighted aggregate index of these indicators has been used as proxy of economic growth.**

The Indicators related to Economic Growth (considered in this study) are given below in Section 5.2.1.

5.2.1 Indicators related to Economic Growth

EG1 Per capita bank deposit
EG2 Per capita bank credit
EG3 Credit-deposit ratio
EG4 Cropping Intensity (in per cent)
EG5 Irrigation Intensity (in per cent)
EG6 Per capita net area sown (ha)

EG7 Average Yield of Food-Grains (kgs per hectare)

EG8 Number of registered small scale industries per 100 sq. km. of area

EG9 Number of registered small scale industries per lakh population

While selecting these indicators every care has been taken to select all these three sectors– banking, agriculture and industry which can be used as proxy of economic growth. The indicators EG1 to EG3 represent the performance of banking sector, EG4 to EG7 represent the performance of agriculture sector.

As small scale industrial sector, employs a large workforce, operates at a relatively low cost and has a significant share in exports, as per availability of data two indicators EG8 and EG9 (related to small scale industries) are taken into account as proxy of industrial sector.

5.2.2 District-wise Index of Economic Growth: Principal Component Analysis

In this section the indexation of selected indicators of economic growth has been done with the help of principal component analysis. The weights are assigned to each of the selected components and then Weighted Aggregate Index of Economic Growth (WAIEG) has been calculated.

The district-wise data of different indicators of economic growth (based on which WAIEG has been calculated for three time points) have been given in Appendix 17 (for 1991), Appendix 19 (for 2000-01) and Appendix 21 (for 2009-10).

The inter-correlation matrices of Economic Growth for the time points 1991, 2000-01 and 2009-10 are given in this section.

It is evident from the **inter-correlation matrix 1991** that, the variables EG1 and EG2 are significantly positively correlated with each other. Both the variables EG1 and EG2 have significant positive relationship with the variables EG5, EG7, EG8, EG9 and significant negative relationship with the variable EG6. Again, the variable EG3 is significantly, negatively correlated with EG5, EG6 and positively correlated EG8, EG9. The variable EG6 is significantly, negatively correlated EG1, EG3, EG7 and EG8. Further, the variables EG8 and EG9 are significantly, positively correlated with each other.

The inter-correlation matrix 1991 brings out the fact that, most the variables are positively correlated i.e., the variables move in same direction.

On the basis of **inter-correlation matrix of 2000-01**, it can be inferred that, the variable EG2 is significantly and positively correlated with EG1, EG3, EG8 and EG9. The variable EG3 is positively, significantly correlated with EG8 and EG9. The variables EG4 and EG5

Table 5.6 (a): Inter-correlation Matrix (Based on Indicators of Economic Growth) in 1991

	EG1	*EG2*	*EG3*	*EG4*	*EG5*	*EG6*	*EG7*	*EG8*	*EG9*
EG1	1.000								
EG2	.988***	1.000							
EG3	.264	.238	1.000						
EG4	.011	.130	-.172	1.000					
EG5	.326*	.327*	-.338*	.232	1.000				
EG6	-.362*	-.377*	-.467**	-.110	.117	1.000			
EG7	.319*	.344*	-.050	.089	-.061	-.314*	1.000		
EG8	.493**	.429**	.502**	-.216	-.157	-.537***	-.031	1.000	
EG9	.471**	.422**	.368*	-.206	-.210	-.237	-.102	.850***	1.000

Source: Self calculated.

Note: *** means significant at one per cent level, **means significant at five per cent level and * means significant at ten per cent level.

Table 5.6(b): Inter-correlation Matrix (Based on Indicators of Economic Growth) in 2000-01

	EG1	*EG2*	*EG3*	*EG4*	*EG5*	*EG6*	*EG7*	*EG8*	*EG9*
EG1	1.000								
EG2	0.614***	1.000							
EG3	0.021	0.747***	1.000						
EG4	-0.004	-0.125	-0.087	1.000					
EG5	0.042	-0.032	-0.211	0.452**	1.000				
EG6	-0.228	-0.345	-0.171	-0.276*	-0.303*	1.000			
EG7	0.253	-0.058	-0.275*	0.565***	0.338**	-0.358**	1.000		
EG8	0.224	0.635***	0.591***	0.041	-0.026	-0.489***	0.128	1.000	
EG9	0.118	0.436**	0.511***	-0.131	-0.237	-0.173	-.057	0.841***	1.000

Source: Self calculated.

Note: *** means significant at one per cent level, **means significant at five per cent level and * means significant at ten per cent level.

Table 5.6(c): Inter-correlation Matrix (Based on Indicators of Economic Growth) in 2009-10

	EG1	*EG2*	*EG3*	*EG4*	*EG5*	*EG6*	*EG7*	*EG8*	*EG9*
EG1	1.000								
EG2	0.782***	1.000							
EG3	0.150	0.668***	1.000						
EG4	-0.078	-0.111	-0.072	1.000					
EG5	-0.022	0.106	0.129	0.604***	1.000				
EG6	-0.375**	-0.375**	-0.131	-0.295*	0.033	1.000			
EG7	0.107	0.031	-0.002	0.231	0.247	-0.146	1.000		
EG8	0.373**	0.596***	0.566***	-0.084	-0.035	-0.540***	0.162	1.000	
EG9	0.283*	0.474***	0.475***	-0.275*	0.007	-0.204	0.235	0.718***	1.000

Source: Self calculated.

Note: *** means significant at one per cent level, **means significant at five per cent level and * means significant at ten per cent level.

are significantly, positively correlated with each other. The variable EG7 is positively and significantly correlated with EG4 and EG5. The variables EG8 and EG9 are positively and significantly correlated with each other. Some variables are also negatively correlated. The variable EG6 is significantly, negatively correlated with EG4, EG5, EG7 and EG8. The variable EG7 is significantly and negatively correlated with EG3 and EG6.

Therefore, most the variables are positively correlated i.e., the variables move in same direction.

From the **inter-correlation matrix of 2009-10,** it is observed that the variable EG1 is significantly, positively correlated with the variables EG2, EG8 and EG9. The variable EG2 is significantly, positively correlated with the variables EG3, EG8 and EG9. The variable EG3 is significantly, positively correlated with the variables EG8 and EG9. The variables EG4 and EG5 are positively and significantly correlated with each other. The variables EG8 and EG9 are also positively and significantly correlated with each other. There was also significant negative correlation between some of the variables in 2009-10. The variable EG6 is significantly and negatively correlated with the variables EG1, EG2, EG4 and EG8. The variables EG4 and EG9 are also significantly and negatively correlated with each other. Therefore, most the variables are positively correlated i.e., the variables move in same direction.

5.2.3 Principal Component Scores of Indicators of Economic Growth

The final factor loadings of all the selected variables are derived on the basis of the inter-correlation matrices given above. The districts are ranked on the basis of components which explained at least 70 per cent of total variance.

On the basis of principal component matrix for the year **1991,** three principal components have been retained for indicators of **Economic Growth.** The prinicipal component scores of indicators of economic growth in 1991 with Eigen Values, Variances, Cumulative Variances and communalities are given in Table 5.7(a).

It is evident from the above table that three principal components retained from indicators of **economic growth (1991),** explain 73.439 per cent of total variance. The first principal component (P1) explains 38.109 per cent of variance. The second principal component (P2) explains 21.639 per cent of variance and the third principal component (P3) explains 13.691 per cent of variance.

All of these three principal components (P1, P2, P3) are considered to calculate the Weighted Aggregate Index of Economic Growth. According to the given formula (given in Chapter-2) 51.89 per cent of weight is assigned to P1, 29.47 per cent of weight is assigned to P2

Table 5.7(a): Principal Component Matrix of Economic Growth (1991)

Variable	*P1*	*P2*	*P3*	h^2
EG1	0.830	0.460	0.172	0.929
EG2	0.799	0.525	0.109	0.927
EG3	0.586	-0.453	-0.214	0.594
EG4	-0.097	0.534	-0.257	0.361
EG5	-0.029	0.742	0.469	0.772
EG6	-0.648	0.015	0.525	0.696
EG7	0.249	0.415	-0.663	0.674
EG8	0.842	-0.347	0.158	0.855
EG9	0.746	-0.354	0.344	0.801
Eigen Value	**3.430**	**1.947**	**1.232**	
percentage of variance	**38.109**	**21.639**	**13.691**	
Cumulative Variance (in per cent)	**38.109**	**59.748**	**73.439**	

Source: Self calculated.

Note: Here, P1 = First Prinicipal Component, P2= Second Principal Component, P3= Third Principal Component and h^2 = Communalities.

and 18.64 per cent weight is assigned to P3 to get the weighted aggregate index of economic growth.

According to first principal component, the variable 'Number of registered small scale industries per 100 sq. km. of area (EG8)' has the highest loading (0.842) and the variable 'Per Capita Bank Deposit (EG1)' has the second highest loading (0.830) in 1991. It is also observed from the table that, communalities (h^2) are high ranging.

On the basis of principal component matrix for the year **2000-01,** three principal components have been retained for indicators of **Economic Growth.** The prinicipal component scores of economic growth indicators with Eigen Values, Variances, Cumulative Variances and Communalities are given below:

It is evident from the above table that three principal componets taken together explain 73.57 per cent of variance. The first principal component (P1) explains 35.629 per cent of variance, second (P2) and third (P3) principal components explain 25.466 per cent and 12.476 per cent of variance respectively.

All the principal components are considered to calculate the Weighted Aggregate Index of Economic Growth. According to the given formula (given in Chapter 3) 48 per cent, 35 per cent and 17 per cent of weights have been assigned to the composite scores of this indicator with respect to P1, P2 and P3 respectively. According to first principal component, the variable 'Number of registered small scale industries per 100 sq. km. of area (EG8)' has the highest loading (0.903) and the variable 'Per capita bank credits (EG2)' has the second highest loading (0.874) in 2000-01. All the communalities (h^2) are very high ranging, varied between +0.514 to +0.930, which indicates that each of the variables (considered for analysis) are significantly correlated with other variables.

Similarly, on the basis of principal component marix for the year **2009-10,** four principal components have been retained here. The principal component matrix based on indicators of Economic Growth for the year 2009-10 is given below.

It is evident from the above table that the four principal components retained in this analysis taken together explain 81.077 per cent of total variance. The first principal component (P1) explains 37.205 per cent of variance. The second (P2), third (P3) and fourth (P4) principal components explain 20.166 per cent, 12.516 per cent and 11.189 per cent of variance respectively.

All the principal components are considered to calculate the weighted aggregate index of Economic Growth. According to the given formula

Table 5.7(b): Principal Component Matrix of Economic Growth in 2000-01

Variable	*P1*	*P2*	*P3*	h^2
EG1	0.431	0.279	0.816	0.930
EG2	0.874	-0.006	0.360	0.894
EG3	0.772	-0.280	-0.200	0.715
EG4	-0.075	0.768	-0.305	0.688
EG5	-0.121	0.704	-0.058	0.514
EG6	-0.476	-0.584	0.083	0.575
EG7	0.002	0.815	0.017	0.665
EG8	0.903	0.114	-0.274	0.903
EG9	0.774	-0.178	-0.330	0.739
Eigen Value	3.207	2.292	1.123	
percentage of variance	35.629	25.466	12.476	
Cumulative Variance (in per cent)	35.629	61.095	73.570	

Source: Self calculated.

Note: Here P1 = First Prinicipal Component, P2= Second Principal Component, P3= Third Principal Component and h^2 = Communalities.

Table 5.7(c): Principal Component Matrix (Based on Economic indicators (2009-10))

Variable	*P1*	*P2*	*P3*	*P4*	h^2
EG1	0.664	-0.013	-0.506	0.182	0.731
EG2	0.883	-0.029	-0.093	0.364	0.922
EG3	0.688	-0.047	0.481	0.323	0.811
EG4	-0.102	0.904	0.121	0.129	0.859
EG5	0.048	0.797	0.354	0.302	0.854
EG6	-0.548	-0.297	0.570	0.196	0.751
EG7	0.204	0.496	0.142	-0.664	0.748
EG8	0.865	-0.031	0.074	-0.210	0.799
EG9	0.742	-0.158	0.374	-0.326	0.821
Eigen Value	3.348	1.815	1.126	1.007	
percentage of variance	37.205	20.166	12.516	11.189	
Cumulative Variance (in per cent)	37.205	57.371	69.888	81.077	

Source: Self calculated.

Note: Here P1 = First Prinicipal Component, P2= Second Principal Component, P3= Third Principal Component, P4=Fourth Principal Component and h^2 = Communalities.

(given in Chapter 3) 46 per cent, 25 per cent, 15 per cent and 14 per cent of weights have been assigned to the composite scores with respect to P1, P2, P3 and P4 respectively.

According to first principal component the variable 'Per capita bank credits (EG2)' has the highest loading (0.883) and the variable 'Number of registered small scale industries per 100 sq. km. of area (EG8)' has the second highest loading (0.865) in 2009-10.

All the communalities (h^2) are very high ranging, varied between +0.731 and +0.922, which indicates that each of the variables (considered for analysis) are significantly correlated with other variables.

It is an important fact that the total variance of principal components of the indicators related to economic growth in 2000-01 was 73.57 per cent, which increased to 81.077 per cent in 2009-10. It indicates that district–wise disparities with respect to these indicators of Economic Growth have increased between the given time points.

5.2.4 Classification of Districts with respect to Components of Economic Growth

In this section to analyse the district-wise economic growth in Gujarat, the districts are categorised with respect to three sectors of economic growth (Banking, Agriculture and Industry).

Different sectors of economic growth and their relevant indicators are given in the Table 5.8(a). On the basis of each sector the classification of districts in three categories- high, medium and low for the years 1991, 2000-01 and 2009-10 have been done.

The categorisation of districts with respect to different sectors of Economic Growth are given in the below tables for the years 1991, 2000-01 and 2009-10. The calculated of weighted composite indices of economic growth (based on which the districts are categorised for three time points) are given in Appendix 26 (for 1991), Appendix 28 (for 2000-01) and Appendix 30 (for 2009-10).

From Table-5.8(b) it is evident that in the year 1991, there were five districts– Ahmedabad, Gandhinagar, Vadodara, Valsad and Kachchh under high category, other five districts- Kheda, Surat, Rajkot, Junagarh, Jamnagar under medium category and rest of the nine districts– Mahesana, Sabar Kantha, Bhavnagar, Bharuch, Amreli, Surendranagar, Banas Kantha, Panch Mahals and The Dangs under low category with respect to 'Weighted Composite Banking Index'.

In the case of 'Weighted Composite Agricultural Index' most of the districts (eight districts- Ahmedabad, Gandhinagar, Kheda, Surat, Vadodara, Mahesana, Valsad, Panch Mahals) were concentrated under high category. There were five districts– Sabar Kantha, Bhavnagar, Junagadh, The Dangs and Kachchh under medium category and rest of

Table 5.8 (a): Different Sectors of Economic Growth (based on the indicators)

Sectors	*Indicators*
1. Banking (Scheduled Commercial Banks)	Weighted composite index of i. Per Capita Bank Deposits. ii. Per capita Bank Credits. iii. Credit-Deposit Ratio.
2. Agriculture	Weighted composite index of i. Cropping Intensity (per cent). ii. Irrigation Intensity (per cent). iii. Per Capita Net Area Sown. iv. Average Yield of Food-Grains.
3. Small Scale Industries	Weighted composite index of i. Number of Small Scale Industries per 100 sq. km. of Area ii. Number of Small Scale Industries per One Lakh Population.

the six districts Rajkot, Bharuch, Amreli, Jamnagar, Surendranagar, Banas Kantha under low category in 1991.

According to 'Weighted Composite Industrial Index' four districts– Ahmedabad, Surat, Rajkot and Valsad were under high category. There were eight districts– Gandhinagar, Kheda, Vadodara, Mahesana, Bhavnagar, Bharuch, Jamnagar, Surendranagar under medium category and rest of the seven districts– Sabar Kantha, Junagadh, Amreli, Banas Kantha, Panch Mahals, Kachchh, The Dangs were under low category.

From the Tables 5.8(c) and 5.8(d) it is observed that the districts were concentrated under low category in 2000-01 and under medium category in 2009-10 with respect to **'Weighted Composite Banking Index'**. As per the analysis there are some districts which improved their categories between these two time points with respect to 'Weighted Composite Banking Index'. The districts Gandhinagar and Rajkot shifted from medium to high category, the districts Mahesana, Sabar Kantha, Surendranagar, Banas Kantha, Panch Mahals, Patan shifted from low to medium category. The district Porbandar deteriorated with respect to its category between these two time points and shifted from high category to medium category.

As per **'Weighted Composite Agricultural Index'** the districts were concentrated under high and low categories in 2000-01. Though, in 2000-01 there were eleven districts under low category, in 2009-10 it reduced to six and the concentration of the districts were found under high and medium categories. The district Rajkot improved its category and shifted from low (2000-01) to high category (2009-10). The district

Table 5.8 (b) : Distribution of Districts by Different Sectors of Economic Growth (1991)

Indicators	*High Category Districts*	*Medium Category Districts*	*Low Category Districts*
Weighted Composite Banking Index	Ahmedabad, Gandhinagar, Vadodara, Valsad, Kachchh.	Kheda, Surat, Rajkot, Junagadh, Jamnagar.	Mahesana, Sabar Kantha, Bhavnagar, Bharuch, Amreli, Surendranagar, Banas Kantha, Panch Mahals, The Dangs.
Weighted Composite Agricultural Index	Ahmedabad, Gandhinagar, Kheda, Surat, Vadodara, Mahesana, Valsad, Panch Mahals.	Sabar Kantha, Bhavnagar, Junagadh, The Dangs, Kachchh.	Rajkot, Bharuch, Amreli, Jamnagar, Surendranagar, Banas Kantha.
Weighted Composite Industrial Index	Ahmedabad, Surat, Rajkot, Valsad.	Gandhinagar, Kheda, Vadodara, Mahesana, Bhavnagar, Bharuch, Jamnagar, Surendranagar.	Sabar Kantha, Junagadh, Amreli, Banas Kantha, Panch Mahals, Kachchh, The Dangs.

Source: Self calculated.

Table 5.8 (c): Distribution of Districts by Different Sectors of Economic Growth (2000-01)

Indicators	*High Category Districts*	*Medium Category Districts*	*Low Category Districts*
Weighted Composite Banking Index	Ahmedabad, Vadodara, Surat, Valsad, Porbandar, Kachchh.	Gandhinagar, Rajkot, Bhavnagar, Jamnagar, Bharuch, Anand and Navsari.	Kheda, Sabar Kantha, Mahesana, Junagadh, Amreli, Surendranagar, Banas Kantha, Panch Mahals, The Dangs, Patan, Narmada, Dahod.
Weighted Composite Agricultural Index	Ahmedabad, Gandhinagar, Kheda, Surat, Mahesana, Valsad, Junagadh, Anand and Navsari.	Vadodara, Sabar Kantha, Panch Mahals, Porbandar and Dahod.	Rajkot, Bhavnagar, Bharuch, Amreli, Jamnagar, Surendranagar, Banas Kantha, Kachchh, The Dangs, Patan and Narmada.
Weighted Composite Industrial Index	Ahmedabad, Kheda, Surat, Mahesana, Rajkot, Valsad,	Gandhinagar, Vadodara, Sabar Kantha, Bhavnagar, Junagadh, Bharuch, Amreli, Jamnagar, Surendranagar, Panch Mahals.	Banas Kantha, Kachchh, The Dangs, Patan, Porbandar, Anand, Dahod, Navsari and Narmada.

Source: Self calculated.

Table 5.8 (d): Distribution of Districts by Different Sectors of Economic Growth (2009-10)

Indicators	*High Category Districts*	*Medium Category Districts*	*Low Category Districts*
Weighted Composite Banking Index	Ahmedabad, Gandhinagar, Surat, Vadodara, Rajkot.	Mahesana, Sabar Kantha, Valsad, Bhavnagar, Bharuch, Amreli, Jamnagar, Surendranagar, Banas Kantha, Panch Mahals, Patan, Porbandar, Anand, Navsari.	Kheda, Junagadh, Panch Mahals, The Dangs, Narmada, Dahod.
Weighted Composite Agricultural Index	Ahmedabad, Gandhinagar, Kheda, Surat, Rajkot, Junagadh, Anand, Dahod, Navsari.	Vadodara, Mahesana, Sabar Kantha, Valsad, Bhavnagar, Jamnagar, Banas Kantha, Panch Mahals, Porbandar, Narmada.	Bharuch, Amreli, Kachchh, Surendranagar, The Dangs, Patan.
Weighted Composite Industrial Index	Ahmedabad, Kheda, Surat, Mahesana, Rajkot, Valsad, Bhavnagar, Junagadh, Bharuch.	Gandhinagar, Vadodara, Sabar Kantha, Jamnagar, Surendranagar, Panch Mahals, Navsari.	Amreli, Banas Kantha, Kachchh, The Dangs, Patan, Porbandar, Anand, Narmada, Dahod.

Source: Self calculated.

Dahod shifted from medium to high, the other four districts Bhavnagar, Jamnagar, Banas Kantha and Narmada shifted from low to medium category between these two time points with respect to this indicator. There were only two districts– Mahesana and Valsad, which deteriorated with respect to their categories and shifted from high to medium category.

Futher, in the case of **'Weighted Composite Industrial Index'** though most of the districts concentrated under medium and low categories in the given time points (2000-01 and 2009-10), the number of high category districts (with respect to this indicator) increased from six (2000-01) to nine in 2009-10. There were four districts which improved their categories – Bhavnagar, Junagadh and Bharuch (shifted from medium to high category) and Navsari (shifted from low to medium category) between these two time points. The district Amreli deteriorated with respect to its category and shifted from medium (2000-01) to low category (2009-10).

5.2.5 Classification of Districts with respect to Weighted Aggregate Index of Economic Growth (WAIEG)

In this section the classification of districts into high, medium and low category with respect to 'Weighted Aggregate Index of Economic Growth' in 1991, 2000-01 and 2009-10 has been discussed.

According to the mean and standard deviation of **'Weighted Aggregate Index of Economic Growth' in 1991** the maximum and minimum values are given below:

$$\bar{X} + 0.5S = 2.97 \text{ and } \bar{X} - 0.5S = 1.57$$

According to the maximum and minimum values, the districts with 'Weighted Aggregate Index of Economic Growth' greater than or equal to 2.97 are considered as high category districts. According to the analysis, the districts **Ahmedabad, Gandhinagar, Surat, Vadodara, Rajkot, Valsad and Kachchh were under high category** with respect to this indicator in 1991. The districts with 'Weighted Aggregate Index of Economic Growth' vary between 2.97 and 1.57 i.e. lower than 2.97 but higher than 1.57, are considered as medium category districts. The districts **Kheda, Mahesana, Bhavnagar, Junagadh and Jamnagar were under medium category** with respect to this indicator. Similarly, the districts with 'Weighted Aggregate Index of Economic Growth' less than or equal to 1.57 are known as low category districts. The districts **Sabar kantha, Bharuch Amreli, Surendranagar, Banas Kantha, Panch Mahals and The Dangs were under low category** with respect to this indicator in 1991.

Table 5.9 (a): Classification of Districts with respect to their Weighted Aggregate Index of Economic Growth (WAIEG) in 1991

Districts	*Weighted Aggregate Score*	*Category*	*Rank*
Ahmedabad	5.71	High	1
Gandhinagar	4.13	High	2
Kheda	2.72	Medium	8
Surat	3.88	High	3
Vadodara	3.35	High	5
Mahesana	1.59	Medium	12
Sabar Kantha	0.99	Low	16
Rajkot	3.05	High	6
Valsad	3.39	High	4
Bhavnagar	1.65	Medium	11
Junagadh	1.70	Medium	10
Bharuch	1.55	Low	13
Amreli	0.88	Low	17
Jamnagar	2.21	Medium	9
Surendranagar	1.06	Low	14
Banas Kantha	0.67	Low	18
Panch Mahals	1.02	Low	15
Kachchh	3.04	High	7
The Dangs	0.58	Low	19

Source: Self calculated.

Further, according to the mean and standard deviation of **'Weighted Aggregate Index of Economic Growth' (2000-01) the maximum and minimum values are-**

$\bar{X}$ + 0.5S = 2.8252 and $\bar{X}$ - 0.5S = 1.3149

The classification of Districts with respect to 'Weighted Aggregate Index of Economic Growth' score is given in the below table for the year 2000-01.

The districts with 'Weighted Aggregate Index of Economic Growth' greater than or equal to 2.8252 are considered as high category districts with respect to this indicator.

According to the analysis the districts **Ahmedabad, Vadodara, Surat, Valsad and Gandhinagar were under high category** with respect to this indicator.

The districts with 'Weighted Aggregate Index of Economic Growth' lower than 2.8252 but higher than 1.3149 are considered as medium category districts.

Table 5.9(b): Classification of Districts as per their Weighted Aggregate Index of Economic Growth (WAIEG) in 2000-01

Districts	*Aggregate Score*	*Category*	*Rank*
Ahmedabad	7.2479	High	1
Gandhinagar	2.8652	High	5
Kheda	2.2277	Medium	11
Surat	3.7821	High	3
Vadodara	4.3324	High	2
Mahesana	2.3042	Medium	10
Sabar Kantha	1.2719	Low	17
Rajkot	2.5324	Medium	6
Valsad	3.6618	High	4
Bhavnagar	1.8478	Medium	13
Junagadh	1.4416	Medium	16
Bharuch	2.4012	Medium	7
Amreli	0.7864	Low	21
Jamnagar	1.5654	Medium	15
Surendranagar	0.8777	Low	20
Banas Kantha	0.8897	Low	19
Panch Mahals	1.2588	Low	18
Kachchh	1.6474	Medium	14
The Dangs	0.3128	Low	25
Patan	0.6770	Low	22
Porbandar	2.3765	Medium	8
Anand	1.9843	Medium	12
Narmada	0.4916	Low	24
Dahod	0.6567	Low	23
Navsari	2.3108	Medium	9

Source: Self calculated.

The districts **Kheda, Mahesana, Rajkot, Bhavnagar, Junagadh, Bharuch, Jamnagar, Kachchh, Porbandar, Anand and Navsari were under medium category** with respect to this indicator in 2000-01.

Similarly, the districts with 'Weighted Aggregate Index of Economic Growth' less than or equal to 1.3149 are known as low category districts.

The districts **Sabar Kantha, Amreli, Surendranagar, Banas Kantha, Panch Mahals, The Dangs, Patan, Narmada and Dahod were under low category** with respect to this indicator in 2000-01.

Similarly, according to the mean and standard deviation of '**Weighted Aggregate Index of Economic Growth**' in **2009-10**:

$\bar{X}$ **+ 0.5S = 2.9043 and** $\bar{X}$ **- 0.5S = 1.5405**

The districts with 'Weighted Aggregate Index of Economic Growth' greater than or equal to 2.9043 are considered as high category districts.

According to the analysis the high category districts were **Ahmedabad, Gandhinagar, Surat, Vadodara, Rajkot and Valsad** in 2009-10.

The districts, with 'Weighted Aggregate Index of Economic Growth' lower than 2.9043 but higher than 1.5405 are medium category districts.

As per the analysis, the medium category districts were **Kheda, Mahesana, Sabar Kantha, Bhavnagar, Junagadh, Bharuch, Jamnagar, Anand and Navsari** with respect to this indicator in 2009-10.

Similarly, the districts under low category (with Weighted Aggregate Index of Economic Growth less than or equal to 1.5405) were **Amreli, Surendranagar, Banas Kantha, Panch Mahals, Kachchh, The Dangs, Patan, Porbandar, Narmada and Dahod in 2009-10**.

5.2.6 Comparison of Districts with respect to their Ranks in 'Weighted Aggregate Index of Economic Growth (WAIEG)' between the time points 2000-01 and 2009-10

It is required to compare the districts with respect their rank in 'Weighted Aggregate Index of Economic Growth' score between the time points 2000-01 and 2009-10 to know the improvement or degradation of the districts with respect to this indicator. The rank of the districts with respect to Weighted Aggregate Index of Economic Growth, for the time points 2000-01 and 2009-10 are given in Table 5.10.

It is evident from Table 5.10 that, the districts which sustained their rank between the time points 2000-01 and 2009-10 with respect to 'Weighted Aggregate Index of Economic Growth' are– Ahmedabad (1),

Table 5.9 (c): Classification of districts as per their Weighted Aggregate Index of Economic Growth (WAIEG) in 2009-10

Districts	*Aggregate Score*	*Category*	*Rank*
Ahmedabad	6.7855	High	1
Gandhinagar	2.9404	High	6
Kheda	2.1308	Medium	9
Surat	4.6916	High	2
Vadodara	4.1813	High	3
Mahesana	2.7041	Medium	7
Sabar Kantha	1.7660	Medium	14
Rajkot	3.3127	High	4
Valsad	3.2162	High	5
Bhavnagar	1.7968	Medium	11
Junagadh	1.6254	Medium	15
Bharuch	2.3099	Medium	8
Amreli	1.3817	Low	21
Jamnagar	1.7694	Medium	12
Surendranagar	1.3960	Low	20
Banas Kantha	1.5383	Low	16
Panch Mahals	1.4147	Low	18
Kachchh	1.5257	Low	17
The Dangs	0.7204	Low	25
Patan	1.1934	Low	22
Porbandar	1.4074	Low	19
Anand	1.7665	Medium	13
Narmada	1.1020	Low	23
Dahod	1.0331	Low	24
Navsari	1.8515	Medium	10

Source: Self calculated.

Panch Mahals (18), Surendranagar (20), Amreli (21), Patan (22) and The Dangs (25).

The districts Surat, Rajkot, Mahesana, Kheda, Bhavnagar, Jamnagar, Junagadh, Sabar Kantha, Banas Kantha and Narmada which obtained 3, 6, 10, 11, 13, 15, 16, 17, 19 and 24 ranks respectively in 2000-01

Table 5.10: Comparison of District-wise Performances in Economic Growth Between the time points 2000-01 and 2009-10 with respect to their Ranks in 'Weighted Aggregate Index of Economic Growth (WAIEG)'

Districts which sustained their ranks between 2000-01 and 2009-10		
Name of the Districts	*Rank (with respect to 'WAIEG' scores) in 2000-01*	*Rank (with respect to 'WAIEG' scores) in 2009-10*
Ahmedabad	1	1
Panch Mahals	18	18
Surendranagar	20	20
Amreli	21	21
Patan	22	22
The Dangs	25	25
Districts which improved their ranks between 2000-01 and 2009-10		
Name of the Districts	*Rank (with respect to 'WAIEG' scores) in 2000-01*	*Rank (with respect to 'WAIEG' scores) in 2009-10*
Surat	3	2
Rajkot	6	4
Mahesana	10	7
Kheda	11	9
Bhavnagar	13	11
Jamnagar	15	12
Junagadh	16	15
Sabar Kantha	17	14
Banas Kantha	19	16
Narmada	24	23
Districts with deteriorated ranks between 2000-01 and 2009-10		
Name of the Districts	*Rank (with respect to 'WAIEG' scores) in 2000-01*	*Rank (with respect to 'WAIEG' scores) in 2009-10*
Vadodara	2	3
Valsad	4	5
Gandhinagar	5	6
Bharuch	7	8
Porbandar	8	19
Navsari	9	10
Anand	12	13
Kachchh	14	17
Dahod	23	24

Source: Self calculated.

improved their rank to 2, 4, 7, 9, 11, 12, 15,14, 16 and 23 respectively in 2009-10.

Again, the district Rajkot which was under medium category in 2000-01, shifted to high category in 2009-10. The district Sabar Kantha which was under low category in 2000-01 shifted to medium category in 2009-10 with respect to this indicator.

Further, there were some other districts whose ranks are deteriorated between these two time points– the districts Vododara, Valsad, Gandhinagar, Bharuch, Porabandar, Navasari, Anand, Kachchh and Dahod which obtained 2, 4, 5, 7,8, 9, 12, 14 and 23 ranks respectively in 2000-01, degraded with respect to their ranks and became 3, 5, 6, 8, 19,10, 13, 17 and 24 respectively in 2009-10. The district Porbandar was one of the districts whose rank has diminished severely between these two time points. It obtained eighth rank in 2000-01 and deteriorated to 19th in 2009-10.

Again, there were two districts– Kachchh and Porbandar which deteriorated with respect to their categories and shifted from medium to low category between 2000-01 and 2009-10 with respect to this indicator.

5.3 District-wise Relationship between 'Weighted Aggregate Infrastructure Index' and 'Weighted Aggregate Index of Economic Growth' in Gujarat (with respect to score or category of the districts in these two indicators)

This section is devoted to analyse the inter-relationship between district-wise 'Weighted Aggregate Infrastructure Index' and 'Weighted Aggregate Index of Economic Growth'. The Weighted Aggregate Index of infrastructure and economic growth scores and categories of the districts are compared for the time points 2000-01 and 2009-10 so as to comprehend the relationship between them.

Table 5.11 presented the scores and category of the districts with respect to 'Weighted Aggregate Infrastructure Index' and 'Weighted Aggregate Index of Economic Growth' for the given time points.

It is evident from the Table 5.11 that, the districts **Ahmedabad, Gandhinagar, Surat and Vadodara** attained high category with respect to both of the indicators– 'Weighted Aggregate Infrastructure Index' as well as 'Weighted Aggregate Index of Economic Growth' for both the time points 2000-01 and 2009-10. Further, the 'Weighted Aggregate Infrastructure Index' score as well as 'Weighted Aggregate Index of Economic Growth' score declined marginally between the given time points (i.e. move in the same direction) in the districts Ahmedabad and Vadodara. So there is direct positive relationship between these two

Table 5.11: District-wise Values and Categories with Respect to Weighted Aggregate Infrastructure Index (WAII) and Weighted Aggregate Index of Economic Growth (WAIEG) in 2000-01 and 2009-10

Districts	*WAII 2000-01 (A)*	*Category (A)*	*WAIEG (2000-01) (B)*	*Category (B)*	*WAII 2009-10 (A1)*	*Category (A1)*	*WAIEG (2009-10) (B1)*	*Category (B1)*
Ahmedabad	4.9318	High	7.2479	High	3.7749	High	6.7855	High
Gandhinagar	5.8521	High	2.8652	High	4.8101	High	2.9404	High
Kheda	4.5518	High	2.2277	Medium	3.5333	High	2.1308	Medium
Surat	4.3488	High	3.7821	High	4.7758	High	4.6916	High
Vadodara	4.2643	High	4.3324	High	3.2212	High	4.1813	High
Mahesana	4.4300	High	2.3042	Medium	2.9955	Medium	2.7041	Medium
Sabar Kantha	3.5507	Medium	1.2719	Low	2.5930	Medium	1.7660	Medium
Rajkot	2.6850	Medium	2.5324	Medium	2.0504	Medium	3.3127	High
Valsad	3.8131	Medium	3.6618	High	3.3332	High	3.2162	High
Bhavnagar	2.2558	Low	1.8478	Medium	1.6855	Low	1.7968	Medium
Junagadh	2.5538	Low	1.4416	Medium	2.1288	Medium	1.6254	Medium
Bharuch	2.7398	Medium	2.4012	Medium	1.7041	Low	2.3099	Medium

(Contd.)

(Contd. Table 5.11)

Districts	*WAII 2000-01 (A)*	*Category (A)*	*WAIEG (2000-01) (B)*	*Category (B)*	*WAII 2009-10 (A1)*	*Category (A1)*	*WAIEG (2009-10) (B1)*	*Category (B1)*
Amreli	2.0957	Low	0.7864	Low	1.3048	Low	1.3817	Low
Jamnagar	1.7310	Low	1.5654	Medium	0.9096	Low	1.7694	Medium
Surendranagar	1.8205	Low	0.8777	Low	0.9831	Low	1.3960	Low
Banas Kantha	2.5653	Low	0.8897	Low	1.8240	Medium	1.5383	Low
Panch mahals	3.5416	Medium	1.2588	Low	2.9256	Medium	1.4147	Low
Kachchh	1.3771	Low	1.6474	Medium	0.1070	Low	1.5257	Low
The Dangs	1.5280	Low	0.3128	Low	0.6752	Low	0.7204	Low
Patan	2.4038	Low	0.6770	Low	1.4329	Low	1.1934	Low
Porbandar	2.3383	Low	2.3765	Medium	1.4094	Low	1.4074	Low
Anand	5.5025	High	1.9843	Medium	4.2743	High	1.7665	Medium
Narmada	2.3832	Low	0.4916	Low	1.7108	Low	1.1020	Low
Dahod	3.0127	Medium	0.6567	Low	3.0843	Medium	1.0331	Low
Navsari	5.4829	High	2.3108	Medium	4.1066	High	1.8515	Medium

Source: Self calculated.

indicators in the districts Ahmedabad and Vadodara. In Gandhinagar, though weighted aggregate score of Infrastructure Index declined from 5.85 in 2000-01 to 4.81 in 2009-10 and the 'Weighted Aggregate Index of Economic Growth' score increased from 2.865 in 2000-01 to 2.94 in 2009-10, yet the district was found under high category with respect to both of these two indicators in the given time points. So, it can be concluded that there is direct and positive relationship between these two indicators (under consideration) in this district also. In the district Surat 'Weighted Aggregate Infrastructure Index' score as well as 'Weighted Aggregate Index of Economic Growth' score increased between the given time points (2000-01 and 2009-10). So there is direct positive relationship between these two indicators in this district also.

The district **Mahesana** was under high category with respect to 'Weighted Aggregate Infrastructure Index' and was under medium category with respect to 'Weighted Aggregate Index of Economic Growth' in 2000-01. In 2009-10, though the district remained in the same category i.e. medium with respect to 'Weighted Aggregate Index of Economic Growth', it slipped to medium category from high with respect to 'Weighted Aggregate Index of Infrastructure'. So it may be concluded from this analysis that, as the district was under medium category in 2000-01 with respect to 'Weighted Aggregate Index of Economic Growth', the category and score of the district with respect to 'Weighted Aggregate Infrastructure Index' also declined in 2009-10.

Though the district **Sabar Kantha** was under medium category with respect to 'Weighted Aggregate Infrastructure Index', it was under low category with respect to 'Weighted Aggregate Index of Economic Growth' in 2000-01. In 2009-10, the district became categorically medium with respect to both in these two indicators. So, it can be concluded that with medium category infrastructure facilities, the category of the district in economic growth also improved from low to medium i.e. there is direct, positive relationship between these two indicators in this district.

With respect to 'Weighted Aggregate Infrastructure Index', though the district **Valsad** was under medium category, the category of the district was high with respect to 'Weighted Aggregate Index of Economic Growth' in 2000-01. In 2009-10, the district was under high category with respect to both of these two indicators. The weighted aggregate index scores of both the indicators declined (weighted aggregate index of infrastructure score declined from 3.81 to 3.33 and weighted aggregate index of economic growth score declined from 3.66 to 3.2162) between the given time points. So, there is direct, positive association between these two indicators in this district also.

The districts **Kachchh and Porbandar** were under low category with respect to 'Weighted Aggregate Infrastructure Index' and under medium category with respect to 'Weighted Aggregate Index of Economic Growth' in 2000-01. In 2009-10, the weighted aggregate score of both the indicators declined in these districts– 'Weighted Aggregate Infrastructure Index' score of Kachchh declined from 1.377 in 2000-01 to 0.10695 in 2009-10 and for Porbandar it declined from 2.338 in 2000-01 to 1.409 in 2009-10. Again, 'Weighted Aggregate Index of Economic Growth' score of Kachchh declined from 1.64 in 2000-01 to 1.526 in 2009-10 and for Porbandar it declined from 2.376 in 2000-01 to 1.407 in 2009-10. The districts became categorically low with respect to both of these two indicators in 2009-10. So, it can be concluded that, as these districts were under low category with respect to 'Weighted Aggregate Infrastructure Index' in 2000-01, consequently the category of these districts with respect to 'Weighted Aggregate Index of Economic Growth' also declined. So, there is direct positive relation between these two indicators in these districts also.

The districts **Anand and Navsari** were under high category with respect to 'Weighted Aggregate Infrastructure Index' and medium category with respect to 'Weighted Aggregate Index of Economic Growth' both in 2000-01 and 2009-10. The weighted aggregate index scores of infrastructure as well as economic growth for both the districts declined between the given time points. In Anand district the 'Weighted Aggregate Infrastructure Index' score declined from 5.5 to 4.27 and 'Weighted Aggregate Index of Economic Growth' score declined from 1.98 to 1.77 between 2000-01 and 2009-10. Similarly in Navsari 'Weighted Aggregate Infrastructure Index' score declined from 5.483 to 4.11 and 'Weighted Aggregate Index of Economic Growth' score declined from 2.31 to 1.85 between 2000-01 and 2009-10 i.e. both the districts Anand and Navsari moved in the same direction with respect to scores of weighted index of infrastructure and economic growth. So, there is direct, positive relationship between these two indicators for these districts also.

It is evident from the table that **Junagadh** district was under low category with respect to 'Weighted Aggregate Infrastructure Index' and medium category with respect to 'Weighted Aggregate Index of Economic Growth' in 2000-01. But in 2009-10 the district was under medium category with respect to both of these two indicators. So it can be concluded that the positive influence of medium category 'Weighted Aggregate Economic Growth Index' of the district was the reason behind the improvement of the district with respect to 'Weighted Aggregate Infrastructure Index' i.e. there is positive relationship between these two indicators in this district also.

It is evident from the table that the districts **Amreli, Surendranagar, The Dangs, Narmada and Patan** were under low category with respect to both of the indicators i.e. Weighted Aggregate Infrastructure as well as Economic Growth index in both the time points under consideration. So, there exists direct, positive relationship between these two indicators in these districts also.

The district **Jamnagar** was under low category with respect to 'Weighted Aggregate Infrastructure Index' and medium category with respect to 'Weighted Aggregate Index of Economic Growth' for both the time points. In Jamnagar, though the 'Weighted Aggregate Infrastructure Index' score decreased significantly from 1.731 to 0.9096, yet 'Weighted Aggregate Index of Economic Growth' increased from 1.5654 to 1.7694 between 2000-01 and 2009-10. So, in Jamnagar there is no such relationship between these two indicators.

The districts **Dahod and Panch Mahals** were under medium category with respect to 'Weighted Aggregate Infrastructure Index', but low category with respect to 'Weighted Aggregate Index of Economic Growth' in both the time points- 2000-01and 2009-10.

In the district Dahod, though the scores for both the indicators increased (Weighted Aggregate Infrastructure Index increased from 3.01 to 3.08 and Weighted Aggregate Index of Economic Growth increased from 0.657 to 1.033) between the time points 2000-01 and 2009-10, yet the picture was different in the district Panch Mahals.

In Panch Mahals, the 'Weighted Aggregate Infrastructure Index' score decreased from 3.54 to 2.925, but 'Weighted Aggregate Index of Economic Growth' increased from 1.259 to 1.415 between 2000-01 and 2009-10.

So, in Dahod district there is positive relationship between these two indicators, but in Panch Mahals there is no such relationship.

The district **Kheda** was under high category with respect to 'Weighted Aggregate Infrastructure Index', but under medium category with respect to 'Weighted Aggregate Index of Economic Growth', for both the time points 2000-01 and 2009-10. As the Weighted Aggregate scores of both the indicators declined ('Weighted Aggregate Infrastructure Index' score decreased from 4.55 to 3.53 and 'Weighted Aggregate Index of Economic Growth' score decreased from 2.23 to 2.13) between the time points 2000-01 and 2009-10, it indicates that decrease in the score of one indicator is the reason behind the decrease in the score of the other i.e. there is positive association between these two indicators in the district.

Though, the district **Banas Kantha** was under low category with respect to Weighted Aggregate Infrastructure as well as Economic Growth Index in 2000-01, but in 2009-10 the picture was different. In

2009-10, the category of the district with respect to 'Weighted Aggregate Infrastructure Index' improved from low to medium, but with respect to 'Weighted Aggregate Index of Economic Growth', the category of the district remained same. Again, the 'Weighted Aggregate Infrastructure Index' score decreased from 2.565 to 1.8239 and the 'Weighted Aggregate Index of Economic Growth' score increased from 0.889 to 1.538 between 2000-01 and 2009-10. So, there is no such relation prevailed in this district between these two indicators either category wise or direction of change in weighted aggregate score-wise.

Though the category of district **Bharuch** with respect to both the indicators (under consideration) was medium in 2000-01, but in 2009-10 the picture was different. In 2009-10, the category of the district with respect to 'Weighted Aggregate Infrastructure Index' deteriorated from medium to low, but the category of the district remained same, i.e. medium with respect to 'Weighted Aggregate Index of Economic Growth'. The weighted aggregate scores with respect to both the indicators decreased in this district (Weighted Aggregate score of Infrastructure index decreased from 2.7397 to 1.704 and the Weighted Aggregate Index of Economic Growth score decreased from 2.4011 to 2.3099 between 2000-01 and 2009-10). So, as per direction of change in aggregate scores, there is direct, positive relationship between these two indicators in this district.

It is evident from the table that, in the district **Bhavnagar**, though the category of the district with respect to 'Weighted Aggregate Infrastructure Index' was low but with respect to Weighted Aggregate Index of Economic Growth, the category was medium, both in 2000-01 and 2009-10. The 'Weighted Aggregate Infrastructure Index' score decreased from 2.25 to 1.685 and the 'Weighted Aggregate Index of Economic Growth' score also decreased from 1.847 to 1.796 between 2000-01 and 2009-10. So, there is inter-relationship between these two indicators in this district as per direction of change in Weighted Aggregate Index scores.

Though the district **Rajkot** was under medium category with respect to both of the two indicators in 2000-01, yet in 2009-10 the picture was different. In 2009-10, the category of the district with respect to 'Weighted Aggregate Infrastructure Index' remained same i.e. medium, but with respect to 'Weighted Aggregate Index of Economic Growth', the category of the district improved from medium to high. Further, the Weighted Aggregate Index score of Infrastructure decreased from 2.68 to 2.05 and the 'Weighted Aggregate Index of Economic Growth' score increased from 2.53 to 3.31 between the time points 2000-01 and 2009-10. So, there is no such relationship in this district between these two indicators either category-wise or direction of change in weighted aggregate index score-wise.

It can be concluded that there is direct, positive relationship between the 'Weighted Aggregate Infrastructure Index' and 'Weighted Aggregate Index of Economic Growth' in most of the districts of Gujarat. According to this analysis, except four districts– **Panch Mahals, Jamnagar, Banas Kantha and Rajkot** (which have no link between these two indicators, neither category-wise nor change in the direction of aggregate score-wise), in remaining twenty one districts there is positive relationship between these two indicators.

5.4 Cross Districts Regression Analysis between 'Weighted Aggregate Infrastructure Index' and 'Weighted Aggregate Index of Economic Growth' in 2000-01 and 2009-10

Cross districts regression analysis (double log) is required to examine the impact of 'Weighted Aggregate Infrastructure Index' on 'Weighted Aggregate Index of Economic Growth' on one hand and the impact of 'Weighted Aggregate Index of Economic Growth' on 'Weighted Aggregate Infrastructure Index' on the other for the years 2000-01 and 2009-10 separately for Gujarat. Simple Ordinary Least Square (OLS) regression analysis (with double log) has been used here.

The regression results on impact of 'log Weighted Aggregate Index of Economic Growth' on 'log Weighted Aggregate Infrastructure Index' is given in the Table 5.12.

In Table 5.12 the regression results are given where the variable **'log Weighted Aggregate Infrastructure Index'** has been considered as dependent variable and the variable **'log Weighted Aggregate Index of Economic Growth'** has been considered as independent variable. It is clearly observed from the above table that there is significant positive relationship between these two variables both in 2000-01 and 2009-10. In 2000-01 R-square value is 0.382 i.e.38.2 per cent changes in Weighted Aggregate Infrastructure Index is explained by changes in Weighted Aggregate Index of Economic Growth. F-value is also significant at one per cent level. In 2009-10, the value of R-square becomes 0.232 i.e. 23.2 per cent changes in Weighted Aggregate Infrastructure Index is explained by changes in Weighted Aggregate Index of Economic Growth. F-value is significant at five per cent level.

It is evident from the table that the coefficients of log Weighted Aggregate Index of Economic Growth (log E_t) is not only positive and highly significant for both the years 2000-01 and 2009-10, but it has also increased from 0.352 in 2000-01 to 0.760 in 2009-10 i.e. **Weighted Aggregate Index of Economic Growth** elasticity of **Weighted**

Table 5.12: The Impact of log Weighted Aggregate Index of Economic Growth (log E_t) on log Weighted Aggregate Infrastructure Index (log I_t) in 2000-01 and 2009-10

Year	*R square*	*F*	*log (constant)*	*coefficient of (log E_t)*
2000-01	0.382	14.211***	0.932***	0.352***
2009-10	0.232	6.953**	0.183	0.760**

Source: Self calculated.
Note: *** means significant at one per cent level, ** means significant at five per cent level and * means significant at ten per cent level.

Aggregate Infrastructure Index is positive, significant and increasing between the years 2000-01 and 2009-10.

So, it can be concluded that Weighted Aggregate Index of Economic Growth is translating into Weighted Aggregate Infrastructure Index.

The regression results on impact of 'log Weighted Aggregate Infrastructure Index' on 'log Weighted Aggregate Index of Economic Growth' is given in the Table 5.13.

It is evident from the Table 5.13 that, though the coefficients of log Weighted Aggregate Infrastructure Index (log I_t) is positive and highly significant for both the years 2000-01 and 2009-10, yet it has decreased from 1.086 in 2000-01 to 0.305 in 2009-10 i.e. **Weighted Aggregate Infrastructure Index** elasticity of **Weighted Aggregate Index of Economic Growth** is positive, significant and decreasing between the time points 2000-01 and 2009-10 i.e. Weighted Aggregate Infrastructure Index is not translating into Weighted Aggregate Index of Economic Growth.

So, in the case of district-wise analysis of Gujarat it is found that Weighted Aggregate Index of Economic Growth is translating into Weighted Aggregate Infrastructure Index but not the other way round. It may be the

Table 5.13: The Impact of log Weighted Aggregate Infrastructure Index (log I_t) on log Weighted Aggregate Index of Economic Growth (log E_t) in 2000-01 and 2009-10

Year	*R square*	*F*	*Log (constant)*	*coefficient of (log I_t)*
2000-01	0.382	14.211***	-0.711**	1.086***
2009-10	0.232	6.953**	0.451***	0.305**

Source: Self calculated.
Note: *** means significant at one level, ** means significant at five per cent level and * means significant at ten per cent level.

greater influence of other factors on Weighted Aggregate Index of Economic Growth is the reason behind it.

5.5 District-wise Human Development in the state Gujarat

The initiation of the concept of human development in Gujarat started in 1999 with the formation of Gujarat Social Infrastructure Development Board (GSIDB) under the Chairmanship of the then Chief Minister. As early as in the year 2000 the document 'Vision 2010-Social Sector' was prepared for focused and concentrated development of the social sector. This was followed by preparation of the State Human Development Report (HDR) in 2004.

In this section the district-wise Human Development Index has been calculated for three time points–1991, 2000-01 and 2009-10. The districts are categorised into high, medium and low developed districts with respect to human development indices as well as each component of the human development index used in this study for all the three time points. As there were 19 districts in Gujarat in 1991 and later the districts were bifurcated and the numbers increased to 26 of which 25 districts (except Tapi) are considered in this study for the time points 2000-01 and 2009-10, the performance of the districts with respect to Human Development Index as well as each component of the human development index are compared and the district-wise relationship between Human Development Index and Weighted Aggregate Index of Economic Growth are examined for the time points 2000-01 and 2009-10. The relationship between Human Development Index and Weighted Aggregate Index of Economic Growth has been examined by comparing the category and rank of the districts as well as by cross district regression analysis between these two indicators for the time points 2000-01 and 2009-10.

5.5.1 Measurement of Human Development Index (HDI)

In **Gujarat Human Development Report (2004)**, three components of human development index, namely - **Per Capita Bank Deposit, Educational Attainment Index (Weighted Aggregate Index of Adult Literacy Rate and Percentage of Children Attending School in the age-group of 6-14 years) and Infant Mortality Rate** are used.

As the district-wise data of per capita income or consumption expenditure are not available the data of 'Per Capita Bank Deposit' has been used as an indicator of 'Decent Standard of Living' here.

In the present study also the district-wise Human Development Index has been calculated with **normalised values of the three indicators, namely - Per Capita Bank Deposits; Educational Attainment Index and Infant Mortality Rate.**

Here the **Educational Attainment Index** is the weighted aggregate of two variables, namely: **Literacy Rate for the age group of seven years and above** and **Adjusted Intensity of Formal Education (AIFE)** where 35 per cent of weight has been given to Literacy Rate for the age group of seven years and above and 65 per cent of weight has been given to Adjusted Intensity of Formal Education. The idea behind taking the two indicators of 'Educational Attainment Index' is that 'Literacy Rate for the age group of seven years and above' being an overall ratio alone may not indicate the actual scenario. While Literacy Rate is indicated as a stock variable, AIFE is indicated as a flow variable.

Though, 'Infant Mortality Rate (IMR)' has been considered as an ingredient of HDI here, yet the district-wise data of this indicator for Gujarat is available only for the year 1991 (ref: Gujarat Human Development Report, 2004). So the district-wise estimated value of this indicator for the years 2000-01 and 2009-10 has been used here. Percentage value of district-wise IMR with respect to Gujarat's IMR in 1991 has been calculated and then district-wise IMR in 2000-01 and 2009-10 has been calculated by multiplying these percentage values with Gujarat's 'Infant Mortality Rate' in 2000-01 and 2009-10 respectively. The districts-wise data regarding components of human development index for the three time points are given in Appendix 22 (for 1991), Appendix 23 (for 2000-01), Appendix 24 (for 2009-10).

After normalisation of the indicators (formulae given in Chapter 3) the district-wise Human Development Index (HDI) has been obtained by the arithmetic mean of the three dimension indices.

In this study the maximum and minimum values (for normalisation of the indicators) of all the three indicators have been chosen from the district-wise values of these indicators. Further, for all the three time points- 1991, 2000-01 and 2009-10 the maximum and minimum values are chosen separately as per the given values of that year particularly.

5.5.2 Classification of the Districts with respect to Different Components of Human Development Index

In this section an attempt has been made to categorise the districts into three categories-High, Medium and Low [as per the given formula (given in Chapter-2) based on mean and standard deviation of each component] based on different components of Human Development Index (considered here) on 1991, 2000-01 and 2009-10.

From the Table 5.14 it is evident that, with respect to the indicator **per capita bank deposit index** in 1991, there were six districts– Ahmedabad, Gandhinagar, Kheda, Vadodara, Valsad, Kachchh under high category, four districts– Surat, Rajkot, Junagadh, Jamnagar under medium category and rest of the nine districts (Mahesana, Sabar Kantha, Bhavnagar, Bharuch, Amreli, Surendranagar, Banas Kantha, Panch Mahals, The Dangs) under low category.

In 2000-01 and 2009-10, with respect to the indicator **per capita bank deposit index**, the districts Ahmedabad, Gandhinagar, Vadodara, Kachchh, Navsari, Porbandar, Anand were under high category, the districts Kheda, Surat, Rajkot, Valsad, Bhavnagar, Bharuch, Jamnagar were under medium category and the districts Sabar Kantha, Amreli, Surendranagar, Banas Kantha, Panch Mahals, The Dangs, Patan, Narmada and Dahod were under low category. The district Mahesana which was under low category with respect to this indicator in 2000-01 shifted to medium category in 2009-10. Again, the district Junagadh which was under medium category with respect to this indicator in 2000-01 shifted to low category in 2009-10.

In the case of **educational attainment Index** (1991) the districts were almost equally distributed under high (six districts– Ahmedabad, Gandhinagar, Kheda, Surat, Rajkot, Valsad), medium (seven districts– Vadodara, Mahesana, Sabar Kantha, Junagadh, Bharuch, Amreli, Jamnagar) and low category (six districts– Bhavnagar, Surendranagar, Banas Kantha, Panch Mahals, Kachchh and The Dangs). In 2000-01, with respect to **educational attainment index**, most of the districts were concentrated under high category (nine districts– Ahmedabad, Gandhinagar, Kheda, Surat, Mahesana, Sabar Kantha, Bharuch, Anand and Navsari) and medium category (nine districts– Vadodara, Rajkot, Valsad, Junagadh, Amreli, Panch Mahals, The Dangs, Patan and Porbandar). There were seven districts- Bhavnagar, Jamnagar, Surendranagar, Banas Kantha, Kachchh, Narmada, Dahod under low category with respect to this indicator in 2000-01. In 2009-10, there were eight districts– Gandhinagar, Kheda, Mahesana, Amreli, The Dangs, Anand, Narmada and Navsari under high category, other eight districts– Ahmedabad, Sabar Kantha, Bhavnagar, Bharuch, Jamnagar, Banas Kantha, Panch Mahals and Patan under medium category and the rest of the districts– Surendranagar, Vadodara, Valsad, Rajkot, Dahod, Porbandar, Junagadh, Surat and Kachchh under low category with respect to this indicator. The districts Ahmedabad, Sabar Kantha and Bharuch which were under high category with respect to this indicator in 2000-01 shifted to medium category in 2009-10. The district Surat shifted from high category in 2000-01 to low category in 2009-10 with respect to this indicator. There were two districts Amreli and The Dangs which were under medium category with respect to **educational attainment index** in 2000-01 shifted to high category in 2009-10.

Table 5.14: Categorisation of Districts with respect to Different Components of Human Development Index in 1991, 2000-01 and 2009-10

Year 1991			
Indicators	*High Category Districts*	*Medium Category Districts*	*Low Category Districts*
Per Capita Bank Deposit Index	Ahmedabad, Gandhinagar, Kheda, Vadodara, Valsad, Kachchh.	Surat, Rajkot, Junagadh, Jamnagar.	Mahesana, Sabar Kantha, Bhavnagar, Bharuch, Amreli, Surendranagar, Banas Kantha, Panch Mahals, The Dangs.
Educational Attainment Index	Ahmedabad, Gandhinagar, Kheda, Surat, Rajkot, Valsad.	Vadodara, Mahesana, Sabar Kantha, Junagadh, Bharuch, Amreli, Jamnagar.	Bhavnagar, Surendranagar, Banas Kantha, Panch Mahals, Kachchh, The Dangs.
Infant Mortaliy Rate Index	Ahmedabad, Surat, Rajkot, Valsad, Bhavnagar, Bharuch, Amreli, Jamnagar.	Vadodara, Junagadh,	Gandhinagar, Kheda, Mahesana, Sabar Kantha, Surendranagar, Banas Kantha, Panch Mahals, Kachchh, The Dangs.

(Contd.)

(Contd. Table 5.14)

Indicators	Year 2000-01		
	High Category Districts	*Medium Category Districts*	*Low Category Districts*
Per Capita Bank Deposit Index	Ahmedabad, Gandhinagar, Vadodara, Kachchh, Navsari, Porbandar, Anand.	Kheda, Surat, Rajkot, Valsad, Junagadh, Bhavnagar, Bharuch, Jamnagar.	Mahesana, Sabar Kantha, Amreli, Surendranagar, Banas Kantha, Panch Mahals, The Dangs, Patan, Narmada, Dahod.
Educational Attainment Index	Ahmedabad, Gandhinagar, Kheda, Surat, Mahesana, Sabar Kantha, Bharuch, Anand, Navsari.	Vadodara, Rajkot, Valsad, Junagadh, Amreli, Panch Mahals, The Dangs, Patan, Porbandar.	Bhavnagar, Jamnagar, Surendranagar, Banas Kantha, Kachchh, Narmada, Dahod.
Infant Mortaliy Rate Index	Surat, Rajkot, Valsad, Bhavnagar, Bharuch, Jamnagar, Patan, Anand, Narmada.	Ahmedabad, Gandhinagar, Sabar Kantha, Junagadh, Amreli, Kachchh.	Kheda, Vadodara, Mahesana, Surendranagar, Banas Kantha, Panch Mahals, The Dangs, Porbandar, Dahod, Navsari.

Source: Self calculated.

In 1991, there were eight districts– Ahmedabad, Surat, Rajkot, Valsad, Bhavnagar, Bharuch, Amreli and Jamnagar with high **infant mortality rate index**. The districts with comparatively low **infant mortality rate index** were– Gandhinagar, Kheda, Mahesana, Sabar Kantha, Surendranagar, Banas Kantha, Panch Mahals, Kachchh and The Dangs. There were only two districts– Vadodara and Junagadh under medium category with respect to **infant mortality rate index** in 1991.

In 2000-01 there were nine districts– Surat, Rajkot, Valsad, Bhavnagar, Bharuch, Jamnagar, Patan, Anand and Narmada with high **infant mortality rate index**, six districts- Ahmedabad, Gandhinagar, Sabar Kantha, Junagadh, Amreli and Kachchh with medium **infant mortality rate index** and rest of the districts– Kheda, Vadodara, Mahesana, Surendranagar, Banas Kantha, Panch Mahals, The Dangs, Porbandar, Dahod and Navsari with low **infant mortality rate index**.

In 2009-10, the districts with high **infant mortality rate index** were Ahmedabad, Surat, Rajkot, Valsad, Bhavnagar, Bharuch, Jamnagar, Junagadh, Patan, Anand and Narmada. The districts with medium **infant mortality rate index** were Gandhinagar, Sabar Kantha, Amreli, Kachchh and the districts with low **infant mortality rate index** were Mahesana, Kheda, Surendranagar, Panch Mahals, Vadodara, Porbandar, Banas Kantha, The Dangs, Dahod and Navsari. The districts- Ahmedabad and Junagadh which were under medium category with respect to this indicator in 2000-01 shifted to high category in 2009-10.

5.5.3 District-wise Human Development Index of Gujarat

District-wise scores, categories and ranks with respect to Human Development Index (HDI) for three time points 1991, 2000-01 and 2009-10 are given in the Tables 5.15(a), 5.15(b) and 5.15(c). The categorisation of districts into high, medium and low has been done as per the given formula (given in Chapter-2) based on mean and standard deviation of district-wise human development index scores.

According to the mean and standard deviation of Human Development Index (HDI) in **1991:**

$$\bar{X} + 0.5S = 0.539 \text{ and } \bar{X} - 0.5S = 0.329$$

The districts with Human Development Index greater than or equal to 0.539 are considered as the districts with high Human Development Index in 1991. According to this analysis the districts with high Human Development Index in **1991** were Ahmedabad, Gandhinagar, Surat, Vadodara, Rajkot, Valsad, Bharuch and Jamnagar. The district with medium Human Development Index (with HDI score lower than 0.539 but higher than 0.329) in 1991 were Kheda, Bhavnagar, Junagadh, Amreli and Kachchh. The remaining six districts with HDI scores lower than or equal to 0.329 were categorised as districts with low Human Development Index in 1991. According to this analysis the districts with low Human Development Index were Sabar Kantha, Mahesana, Surendranagar, Panch Mahals, Banas Kantha and The Dangs.

According to the mean and standard deviation of human development index in **2000-01:**

$\bar{X} + 0.5S = 0.514$ and $\bar{X} - 0.5S = 0.332$

The districts with HDI score greater than or equal to 0.514 are categorised as districts with high human development index in 2000-01. The districts Ahmedabad, Surat, Rajkot, Bharuch, Kachchh, Anand and Navsari were with high HDI score in the given time point. The districts with medium Human Development Index (with HDI score less than 0.514 but greater than 0.332) were Gandhinagar, Kheda, Vadodara, Valsad, Bhavnagar, Junagadh, Amreli, Jamnagar, Patan, Porbandar, Narmada and the districts with low Human Development Index (HDI score less than or equal to 0.332) were Mahesana, Sabar Kantha, Surendranagar,

Table 5.15 (a): District-wise Human Development Index Score, Category and Rank in 1991

Districts	*Human Development Index Score 1991*	*Category*	*Rank*
Ahmedabad	0.775	High	1
Gandhinagar	0.727	High	2
Kheda	0.477	Medium	10
Surat	0.576	High	6
Vadodara	0.580	High	5
Mahesana	0.258	Low	14
Sabar Kantha	0.254	Low	15
Rajkot	0.587	High	4
Valsad	0.631	High	3
Bhavnagar	0.478	Medium	9
Junagadh	0.458	Medium	12
Bharuch	0.559	High	7
Amreli	0.365	Medium	13
Jamnagar	0.547	High	8
Surendranagar	0.189	Low	16
Banas Kantha	0.062	Low	19
Panch Mahals	0.147	Low	17
Kachchh	0.471	Medium	11
The Dangs	0.109	Low	18

Source: Self calculated.

Table 5.15 (b): District-wise Human Development Index Score, Category and Rank in 2000-01

Districts	*Human Development Index Score 2000-01*	*Category*	*Rank*
Ahmedabad	0.734	High	2
Gandhinagar	0.500	Medium	8
Kheda	0.334	Medium	18
Surat	0.554	High	6
Vadodara	0.484	Medium	10
Mahesana	0.260	Low	20
Sabar Kantha	0.327	Low	19
Rajkot	0.561	High	5
Valsad	0.477	Medium	12
Bhavnagar	0.469	Medium	14
Junagadh	0.382	Medium	16
Bharuch	0.754	High	1
Amreli	0.340	Medium	17
Jamnagar	0.491	Medium	9
Surendranagar	0.212	Low	22
Banas Kantha	0.001	Low	25
Panch Mahals	0.252	Low	21
Kachchh	0.518	High	7
The Dangs	0.194	Low	23
Patan	0.475	Medium	13
Porbandar	0.479	Medium	11
Anand	0.630	High	3
Narmada	0.406	Medium	15
Dahod	0.132	Low	24
Navsari	0.601	High	4

Source: Self calculated.

Banas Kantha, Panch Mahals, The Dangs and Dahod in 2000-01.

According to the mean and standard deviation of human development index in **2009-10:**

$$\bar{X} + 0.5S = 0.517 \text{ and } \bar{X} - 0.5S = 0.361$$

The districts with high Human Development Index (with HDI score greater than or equal to **0.517**) in 2009-10 were Ahmedabad, Gandhinagar, Bharuch, Amreli, Jamnagar, Anand, Narmada and Navsari. Similarly, the districts with medium Human Development Index (with HDI score lower than **0.517** but higher than **0.361**) were Vadodara, Rajkot, Valsad, Bhavnagar, Junagadh, Kachchh, Patan, Porbandar and the districts with low HDI score (HDI score lower than or equal to **0.361)** were Kheda, Surat, Mahesana, Sabar Kantha, Surendranagar, Banas Kantha, Panch Mahals, The Dangs and Dahod in 2009-10.

Table 5.15 (c): District-wise Human Development Index Score, Category and Rank in 2009-10

Districts	*Human Development Index Score 2009-10*	*Category*	*Rank*
Ahmedabad	0.758	High	1
Gandhinagar	0.612	High	4
Kheda	0.360	Low	17
Surat	0.359	Low	18
Vadodara	0.478	Medium	9
Mahesana	0.348	Low	19
Sabar Kantha	0.326	Low	21
Rajkot	0.471	Medium	12
Valsad	0.469	Medium	13
Bhavnagar	0.473	Medium	11
Junagadh	0.385	Medium	14
Bharuch	0.605	High	5
Amreli	0.535	High	7
Jamnagar	0.532	High	8
Surendranagar	0.243	Low	23
Banas Kantha	0.190	Low	24
Panch Mahals	0.278	Low	22
Kachchh	0.365	Medium	15/16
The Dangs	0.331	Low	20
Patan	0.455	Medium	10
Porbandar	0.365	Medium	15/16
Anand	0.709	High	2
Narmada	0.648	High	3
Dahod	0.141	Low	25
Navsari	0.546	High	6

Source: Self calculated.

It is observed from the above tables that HDI was consistently high in the districts Ahmedabad, Bharuch, Anand, and Navsari on one hand and the districts Mahesana, Sabar Kantha, Surendranagar, Banas Kantha, Dahod, The Dangs and Panch Mahals were always among the bottom liners on the other for the two time points 2000-01 and 2009-10. Though the districts Gandhinagar, Amreli and Narmada and Jamnagar were under medium category of HDI in 2000-01, yet in 2009-10 they managed to shift under high category. Some interesting movements across the districts are noticed over time. For instance, Surat started with an appreciable HDI scenario and it was under high category both in 1991 as well as 2000-01, but its performance declined considerably in 2009-10 and shifted to low category. The category of the districts Rajkot and Kachchh deteriorated and shifted from high to medium category between the years 2000-01 and 2009-10. The category of the district

Kheda also declined and it shifted from medium to low category between the time points 2000-01 and 2009-10.

5.5.4 Comparison of District-wise Performances with respect to Human Development Index Between the time points 2000-01 and 2009-10

To compare the district-wise performances with respect to human development index between the time points 2000-01 and 2009-10, it is required to compare the ranks of the districts with respect to their 'Human Development Index' scores in these two time points. The rank of the districts with respect to 'Human Development Index' for the time points 2000-01 and 2009-10 are given in Table 5.16.

From Table 5.16 it is clear that, whereas fourteen districts improved their ranks with respect to HDI scores between the time points 2000-01 and 2009-10, the ranks of other eleven districts deteriorated. The districts which improved their ranks between the time points 2000-01 and 2009–10 were- Ahmedabad, Gandhinagar, Kheda, Vadodara, Mahesana, Bhavnagar, Junagadh, Amreli, Jamnagar, Banas Kantha, The Dangs, Patan, Anand and Narmada. The rank of these districts were 2, 8, 18, 10, 20, 14, 16, 17, 9, 25, 23,13, 3 and 15 respectively in 2000-01 and improved to 1, 4, 17, 9, 19, 11, 14, 7, 8, 24, 20, 10, 2 and 3 respectively in 2009-10. The districts Amreli (improved its rank from 17th in 2000-01 to seventh in 2009-10) and Narmada (improved its rank from 15th in 2000-01 to third in 2009-10) improved their ranks significantly between these two time points. The districts which deteriorated with respect to their ranks in HDI score between the given time points were- Surat, Sabar Kantha, Rajkot, Valsad, Bharuch, Surendranagar, Panch Mahals, Kachchh, Porbandar, Dahod and Navsari. The rank of these districts were 6, 19, 5, 12, 1, 22, 21, 7, 11, 24 and 4 respectively in 2000-01 and deteriorated to 18, 21, 12, 13, 5, 23, 22, 15/16, 15/16, 25 and 6. The districts Surat (deteriorated its rank from sixth in 2000-01 to 18th in 2009-10), Rajkot (deteriorated its rank from fifth in 2000-01 to 12th in 2009-10) and Kachchh (deteriorated its rank from seventh in 2000-01 to 15th/ 16th in 2009-10) deteriorated their ranks significantly between these two time points.

5.6 District-wise Relationship Between Human Development Index and Weighted Aggregate Index of Economic Growth (with respect to score or category of the districts)

This section of the study is devoted to analyse the inter-relationship between 'Human Development Index' and 'Weighted Aggregate Index of Economic Growth' with respect to the index scores and category of the districts. These two indices are compared for the two time points- 2000-01 and 2009-10 so as to comprehend the relationship between them. Table 5.17 presented the district-wise 'Human Development Index' and

'Weighted Aggregate Index of Economic Growth' scores, their categories and ranks for the given time points.

Comparing the category of the districts between the two time points 2000-01 and 2009-10, it is found that there are some districts which categorically remain same with respect to both of these two indicators in the given time points. The district **Ahmedabad** was under high category,

Table 5.16: Comparison of District-wise Performances with respect to their ranks in Human Development Index Between the two time points- 2000-01 and 2009-10

Districts which improved their ranks (with respect to HDI scores) between 2000-01 and 2009-10		
Name of the Districts	*Rank (with respect to HDI scores) in 2000-01*	*Rank (with respect to HDI scores) in 2009-10*
Ahmedabad	2	1
Gandhinagar	8	4
Kheda	18	17
Vadodara	10	9
Mahesana	20	19
Bhavnagar	14	11
Junagadh	16	14
Amreli	17	7
Jamnagar	9	8
Banas Kantha	25	24
The Dangs	23	20
Patan	13	10
Anand	3	2
Narmada	15	3
Districts with deteriorated ranks (with respect to HDI scores) between 2000-01 and 2009-10		
Name of the Districts	*Rank (with respect to HDI scores) in 2000-01*	*Rank (with respect to HDI scores) in 2009-10*
Surat	6	18
Sabar Kantha	19	21
Rajkot	5	12
Valsad	12	13
Bharuch	1	5
Surendranagar	22	23
Panch Mahals	21	22
Kachchh	7	15/16
Porbandar	11	15/16
Dahod	24	25
Navsari	4	6

Source: Self calculated.

the districts **Bhavnagar and Junagadh** were under medium category and the districts **Surendranagar, Banas Kantha, Dahod, The Dangs and Panch Mahals** were under low category with respect to both of these two indicators in 2000-01 as well as 2009-10. In these districts there is direct and positive relationship between HDI and Weighted Aggregate Index of Economic Growth because good performance of Human Development (HDI) tends to good performance of economic growth (Weighted Aggregate Index of Economic Growth) which in turn promotes further Human Development achievements and medium or low performance of Human Development tends to medium or low performance of economic growth which in turn depress further Human Development achievements.

It is evident from the above table that the district **Gandhinagar** which was under medium category with respect to HDI and high category with respect to Weighted Aggregate Index of Economic Growth in 2000-01, shifted to high category with respect to both of these two indicators in 2009-10. It can be explained that positive influence of high Weighted Aggregate Index of Economic Growth of the district is responsible to shift the district upward from medium to high category with respect to HDI. So, there is direct and positive relationship between these two indicators in this district also.

Though, the district **Vadodara** was under medium category with respect to HDI and high category with respect to Weighted Aggregate Index of Economic Growth in both of the two time points 2000-01 and 2009-10, yet it is found that the HDI score of the district decreased from 0.484 in 2000-01 to 0.478 in 2009-10 and the Weighted Aggregate Index of Economic Growth score also decreased from 4.332 in 2000-01 to 4.181 in 2009-10. So, despite the existence of categorical dissimilarity with respect to these two indicators in this district, there exists direct positive relationship between these two indicators due to their decreasing scores between the two time points.

The district **Mahesana** was under low category with respect to HDI and medium category with respect to Weighted Aggregate Index of Economic Growth both in 2000-01 and 2009-10. As the HDI score of the district increased from 0.260 to 0.348 and Weighted Aggregate Index of Economic Growth score increased from 2.304 to 2.704 between these two time points, it can be concluded that there is direct positive relationship between these two indicators in this district.

The district **Amreli** was under medium category with respect to HDI and low category with respect to Weighted Aggregate Index of Economic Growth in 2000-01. Though, it shifted to high category with respect to HDI, yet it remained low with respect to Weighted Aggregate Index of

Economic Growth in 2009–10. As the scores of both of these two indicators increased significantly between these two time points (HDI score increased from 0.340 to 0.535 and Weighted Aggregate Index of Economic Growth score increased from 0.786 to 1.382) the district achieved direct positive relationship between these two indicators.

The district **Jamnagar** was under medium category with respect to HDI as well as Weighted Aggregate Index of Economic Growth in 2000-01. Though, it shifted to high category with respect to HDI yet remained medium with respect to Weighted Aggregate Index of Economic Growth in 2009-10. Instead of their categorical dissimilarity, the increasing score of these two indicators (HDI score increased from 0.491 to 0.532 and Weighted Aggregate Index of Economic Growth score increased from 1.565 to 1.769) between the two time points 2000-01 and 2009-10, indicates the direct and positive relationship between these two indicators in this district.

The district **Kachchh** was under high category with respect to HDI (score 0.518) and medium category with respect to Weighted Aggregate Index of Economic Growth (Score 1.647) in 2000-01. But in 2009-10, the district's category deteriorated with respect to both of these two indicators and became medium with respect to HDI (score 0.365) and low with respect to Weighted Aggregate Index of Economic Growth (score 1.526) i.e. category and score of both of these two indicators declined in this district between the years 2000-01 and 2009-10. It indicates direct positive relationship between these two indicators in this district.

Though the district **Valsad** was under medium category with respect to HDI and high category with respect to Weighted Aggregate Index of Economic Growth both in 2000-01 and 2009-10 yet the scores of both of these two indicators decreased between these two time points– HDI score decreased from 0.477 to 0.469 and Weighted Aggregate Index of Economic Growth score decreased from 3.662 to 3.216 which indicates direct, positive relationship between these two indicators in this district.

The district **Bharuch** was under high category with respect to HDI and medium category with respect to Weighted Aggregate Index of Economic Growth in both the time points 2000-01 and 2009-10. The HDI score of the district decreased from 0.754 to 0.605 and Weighted Aggregate Index of Economic Growth score decreased from 2.401 to 2.310 between 2000-01 and 2009-10, which indicates direct positive relationship between these two indicators in this district also.

The district **Porbandar** was under medium category with respect to HDI as well as weighted aggregate index of economic growth in 2000-01.

Table 5.17: District-wise Human Development Index and Weighted Aggregate Index of Economic Growth Score, Category and Rank in 2000-01 and 2009-10

Districts	*HDI scores (2000-01) A1*	*Category A1*	*Weighted Aggregate Index Economic Growth Scores (2000-01) (B1)*	*Category B1*	*HDI scores (2009-10) A2*	*Category A2*	*Weighted Aggregate Index Economic Growth Scores (2009-10) (B2)*	*Category B2*
Ahmedabad	0.734	High	7.248	High	0.758	High	6.786	High
Gandhinagar	0.500	Medium	2.865	High	0.612	High	2.940	High
Kheda	0.334	Medium	2.228	Medium	0.360	Low	2.131	Medium
Surat	0.554	High	3.782	High	0.359	Low	4.692	High
Vadodara	0.484	Medium	4.332	High	0.478	Medium	4.181	High
Mahesana	0.260	Low	2.304	Medium	0.348	Low	2.704	Medium
Sabar Kantha	0.327	Low	1.272	Low	0.326	Low	1.766	Medium
Rajkot	0.561	High	2.532	Medium	0.471	Medium	3.313	High
Valsad	0.477	Medium	3.662	High	0.469	Medium	3.216	High
Bhavnagar	0.469	Medium	1.848	Medium	0.473	Medium	1.797	Medium
Junagadh	0.382	Medium	1.442	Medium	0.385	Medium	1.625	Medium
Bharuch	0.754	High	2.401	Medium	0.605	High	2.310	Medium
Amreli	0.340	Medium	0.786	Low	0.535	High	1.382	Low

(Contd.)

(Contd. Table 5.17)

Districts	*HDI scores (2000-01) A1*	*Category A1*	*Weighted Aggregate Index Economic Growth Scores (2000-01) (B1)*	*Category B1*	*HDI scores (2009-10) A2*	*Category A2*	*Weighted Aggregate Index Economic Growth Scores (2009-10) (B2)*	*Category B2*
Jamnagar	0.491	Medium	1.565	Medium	0.532	High	1.769	Medium
Surendranagar	0.212	Low	0.878	Low	0.243	Low	1.396	Low
Banas Kantha	0.001	Low	0.890	Low	0.190	Low	1.538	Low
Panch Mahals	0.252	Low	1.259	Low	0.278	Low	1.415	Low
Kachchh	0.518	High	1.647	Medium	0.365	Medium	1.526	Low
The Dangs	0.194	Low	0.313	Low	0.331	Low	0.720	Low
Patan	0.475	Medium	0.677	Low	0.455	Medium	1.193	Low
Porbandar	0.479	Medium	2.376	Medium	0.365	Medium	1.407	Low
Anand	0.630	High	1.984	Medium	0.709	High	1.767	Medium
Narmada	0.406	Medium	0.492	Low	0.648	High	1.102	Low
Dahod	0.132	Low	0.657	Low	0.141	Low	1.033	Low
Navsari	0.601	High	2.311	Medium	0.546	High	1.851	Medium

Source: Self calculated.

In 2009-10, though the district was under medium category with respect to HDI, yet it shifted to low category with respect to Weighted Aggregate Index of Economic Growth. As the score of both of these two indicators decreased (HDI from 0.479 to 0.365 and Weighted Aggregate Index of Economic Growth from 2.376 to 1.407) significantly between the two time points 2000-01 and 2009-10, it indicates direct positive relationship between these two indicators in this district.

The district **Narmada** was under medium category with respect to HDI and low category with respect to Weighted Aggregate Index of Economic Growth in 2000-01. Though, it shifted to high category with respect to HDI and remained low with respect to Weighted Aggregate Index of Economic Growth in 2009-10, yet the score of both these two indicators increased significantly in this district (HDI score increased from 0.406 to 0.648 and Weighted Aggregate Index of Economic Growth score increased from 0.492 to 1.102) between 2000-01 and 2009-10 which indicates the direct positive relationship between these two indicators in this district.

In the case of **Navsari,** though the district was under high category with respect to HDI and medium with respect to Weighted Aggregate Index of Economic Growth in both the time points 2000-01 and 2009-10, yet the score of these two indicators decreased significantly (HDI score decreased from 0.601 to 0.546 and Weighted Aggregate Index of Economic Growth score decreased from 2.311 to 1.851) between these two time points. It indicates the direct positive relationship between these two indicators in this district.

No such relationship has been found between these two indicators in the districts **Rajkot, Kheda, Sabar Kantha, Patan, Surat and Anand.**

So, it can be concluded that there is direct, positive relationship between Human Development Index and Weighted Aggregate Index of Economic Growth in most of the districts of Gujarat in the given time points.

5.7 Cross Districts Regression Analysis between Human Development Index (HDI) and Weighted Aggregate Index of Economic Growth (WAIEG) in 2000-01 and 2009-10

Cross districts regression analysis (double log) is required to examine the impact of 'Human Development Index' on 'Weighted Aggregate Index of Economic Growth' on one hand and the impact of 'Weighted Aggregate Index of Economic Growth' on 'Human Development Index' on the other for the time points 2000-01 and 2009-10 separately for Gujarat. Simple Ordinary Least Square (OLS) regression analysis (with double log) has been used here.

The **regression results on impact of 'log Weighted Aggregate Index of Economic Growth' on 'log Human Development Index'** is given in the Table 5.18, where the variable 'log Human Development Index (log HDI_t)' has been considered as dependent variable and the variable 'log Weighted Aggregate Index of Economic Growth (log E_t)' has been considered as independent variable.

It is observed from the Table 5.18 that, there is significant positive relationship between these two variables both in 2000-01 and 2009-10. In 2000-01, R-square value was 0.143 i.e.14.3 per cent changes in Human Development Index is explained by changes in Weighted Aggregate Index of Economic Growth. F-value is also significant at 10 per cent level in 2000-01. In 2009-10, the value of R-square became 0.170 i.e. 17.0 per cent changes in 'Human Development Index' is explained by changes in 'Weighted Aggregate Index of Economic Growth'. F-value is significant at 5 per cent level.

It is evident from the table that, though the coefficients of log Weighted Aggregate Index of Economic Growth (log E_t) is positive and highly significant (at 5 per cent level) for both the years 2000-01 and 2009-10, yet it has decreased from 0.656 in 2000-01 to 0.321 in 2009-10 i.e. **Weighted Aggregate Index of Economic Growth** elasticity of **Human Development Index** is positive, significant and decreasing over time (between the years 2000-01 and 2009-10). So, it can be concluded that Weighted Aggregate Index of Economic Growth is not translating into Human Development Index.

The **regression results on impact of 'log Human Development Index (log HDI_t)' on 'log Weighted Aggregate Index of Economic Growth (log E_t)'** is given in the Table 5.19 where the variable 'log Weighted Aggregate Index of Economic Growth (log E_t)' has been considered as dependent variable and the variable 'log Human Development Index (log HDI_t)' has been considered as independent variable.

Table 5.18: The Impact of log Weighted Aggregate Index of Economic Growth (log E_t) on log Human Development Index (log HDI_t) in 2000-01 and 2009-10

Year	*R square*	*F*	*log (constant)*	*Coefficient of (log E_t)*
2000-01	0.143	3.825*	-1.460***	0.656**
2009-10	0.170	4.696**	-1.104***	0.321**

Source: Self calculated.

Note: *** means significant at one per cent level, ** means significant at five per cent level and * means significant at ten per cent level.

Table 5.19 :The Impact of log Human Development Index (log HDI_t) on log Weighted Aggregate Index of Economic Growth (log E_t) in 2000-01 and 2009-10

Year	*R square*	*F*	*Log (constant)*	*Coefficient of (log HDI_t)*
2000-01	0.143	3.825*	0.735***	0.217*
2009-10	0.170	4.696**	1.131***	0.528**

Source: Self calculated.
Note: *** means significant at one per cent level, ** means significant at five per cent level and * means significant at ten per cent level.

It is evident from Table 5.19 that, the coefficients of log Human Development Index (log HDI_t) is positive and significant for both the years 2000-01 and 2009-10. It has increased from 0.217 in 2000-01 to 0.528 in 2009-10. So, **Human Development Index** elasticity of **Weighted Aggregate Index of Economic Growth** is positive, significant and increasing over time (between the years 2000-01 and 2009-10) i.e. Human Development Index is translating into Weighted Aggregate Index of Economic Growth.

It can be concluded that in the case of district-wise analysis of Gujarat Human Development Index is translating into Weighted Aggregate Index of Economic Growth but not the other way round. It may be the comparatively lower expenditure on education and health is the reason behind this.

In this chapter not only the district-wise different facilities related to infrastructure, economic growth and human development and their lacunae are clearly discussed, the inter-relationship between the indicators (WAII and WAIEG as well as HDI and WAIEG) are also analysed. It is found that there is positive, significant relationship between Weighted Aggregate Infrastructure Index (WAII) and Weighted Aggregate Index of Economic Growth (WAIEG) as well as Human Development Index (HDI) and Weighted Aggregate Index of Economic Growth (WAIEG). It is also found that the economic growth (WAIEG) is translating into infrastructure development (WAII) and not the other way round. It may be the increasing effect of other factors on economic growth is the reason behind it. Again, HDI is translating into economic growth (WAIEG) and not the other way round. It may be the comparatively low and less effective investment on education and health is the reason behind it.

6

Trend and Pattern of Public Expenditure on Social and Economic Services in Gujarat

Development of a state both in social and economic fronts depends on the public investment into it. Public investment has great bearing on the growth of the economy. It initiates the process of development in a region. The level and pattern of development of any region, state or country is significantly influenced by the public expenditure pattern.

To analyse the reasons behind Gujarat's high economic growth, comparatively high relative aggregate average economic infrastructure index than relative aggregate average social infrastructure index (as compared to India's average), comparatively low human development, the lopsided economic growth in Gujarat and decreasing impact of weighted aggregate index of economic growth on the human development index (cross district analysis given in Chapter 5), the public investment scenario of the state has been studied based on the public expenditure data of the state for the time period 1991-92 to 2009-10.

To determine the trend and pattern of public expenditure in different social and economic services (as percentage of total public expenditure) both types of expenditure- revenue and capital have been considered. Here total expenditure is the summation of revenue expenditure and capital expenditure where developmental, non- developmental and other expenditure are considered.

In this chapter with the examination of trend and pattern of public expenditure with respect to different social and economic services of Gujarat, the pattern of public expenditure of 15 major states of India in

2009-10 has also been discussed to determine the rank of Gujarat among them.

6.1 Gujarat's Trend and Pattern of Public Expenditure on Different Social and Economic Services

In this section public expenditure of Gujarat on different social services viz. education, sports, arts and culture; health and family welfare; water supply, sanitation, housing and urban development; information and broadcasting; welfare of SCs, STs and OBCs; labour and labour welfare; social welfare and nutrition; others and public expenditure on different economic services viz. agriculture and allied services; rural development; special area programmes; irrigation and flood control; energy; industry and minerals; transport and communication; science, technology and environment; general economic services has been discussed in percentage form (as percentage of total expenditure).

It is evident from the Table 6.1 and Figure 6.1(a) that, Gujarat's social service expenditure (as percentage of total expenditure) decreased from 25.84 per cent in 1991-92 to 24.61 per cent in 1992-93. From 1993-94, it started to increase and became 30.22 per cent in 1995-96. In the time period 1997-98 to 2000-01 it varied between 27.92 per cent and 30.78 per cent and decreased significantly to 19.86 per cent in 2001-02 and 17.91 per cent in 2002-03. From 2003-04 it again started to increase and became 35.89 per cent in 2009-10.

Gujarat's economic service expenditure (as percentage of total expenditure) increased from 39.2 per cent in 1991-92 to 40.24 per cent in 1992-93. Though it decreased to 36.7 per cent in 1993-94, from 1994-95 it again started to increase and became 40.66 per cent in 1995-96. In the time period 1996-97 to 2000-01 it varied between 34.78 per cent and 40.37 per cent. It decreased significantly to 20.16 per cent in 2001-02 and 19.08 per cent in 2002-03. From 2003-04 it again started to increase and became 36.56 per cent in 2008-09. In 2009-10 it decreased to 31.07 per cent.

It is important to note that, in the time period 2001-02 to 2004-05, as Gujarat's non-developmental expenditure was significantly higher than its expenditure on developmental services, the public expenditure on all the developmental services – social as well as economic were lower as compared to other years in the given time period (1991-92 to 2009-10).

It can be concluded that **Gujarat's expenditure on economic services was higher than its expenditure on social services for all the years in the given time period 1991-92 to 2009-10, except for four years- 2003-04, 2004-05, 2007-08 and 2009-10.**

It is observed from the Table 6.1 and Figure 6.1(b)(i) that, the expenditure on education, sports, arts and culture decreased from

Table 6.1: Public Expenditure of Gujarat in Social and Economic Services (as percentage of total expenditure)

Sr. No.	Item	1991-92	1992-93	1993-94	1994-95	1995-96	1996-97
I.	Developmental Expenditure	65.04	64.85	63.64	68.65	70.88	66.59
A	Social Services	25.84	24.61	26.94	29.80	30.22	27.92
i.	Education, Sports, Arts and Culture	13.85	13.18	14.83	16.52	17.45	15.82
ii.	Health and Family welfare	3.66	3.64	3.85	4.36	4.36	4.02
iii.	Water supply, Sanitation, Housing and Urban Development	3.19	3.58	3.56	3.81	3.48	3.48
iv.	Information and Broadcasting	0.16	0.14	0.12	0.13	0.13	0.13
v.	Welfare of SCs, STs and OBCs	1.76	1.94	2.01	2.17	2.09	1.97
vi.	Labour and Labour Welfare	0.53	0.52	0.57	0.62	0.59	0.56
vii.	Social Welfare and Nutrition	2.55	1.48	1.89	2.05	1.99	1.84
viii.	Others	0.13	0.13	0.12	0.14	0.13	0.11

(Contd.)

(Contd. Table 6.1)

Sr. No.	*Item*	*1991-92*	*1992-93*	*1993-94*	*1994-95*	*1995-96*	*1996-97*
B.	Economic Services	39.20	40.24	36.70	38.85	40.66	38.67
i.	Agriculture and Allied Services	4.26	3.97	5.58	4.81	4.55	4.31
ii.	Rural Development	3.69	3.18	3.24	3.24	3.26	2.84
iii.	Special Area Programmes	0.20	0.21	0.18	0.20	0.21	0.18
iv.	Irrigation and Flood Control	11.75	10.81	9.60	13.31	14.94	15.13
v.	Energy	10.60	14.76	11.61	10.69	8.46	9.05
vi.	Industry and Minerals	2.95	2.06	1.33	1.91	3.27	1.59
vii.	Transport and Communication	4.69	4.54	4.39	4.04	4.67	4.16
viii.	Science, Technology and Environment	0.003	0.004	0.008	0.007	0.006	0.008
ix.	General Economic Services	1.04	0.72	0.75	0.65	1.28	1.39
II.	Non-Developmental and Others Expenditure	34.96	35.15	36.36	31.35	29.12	33.41
III.	Total Expenditure (I+II)	100.00	100.00	100.00	100.00	100.00	100.00

Source: Self Calculated on the basis of the data given in Appendix.

Table 6.1: Public Expenditure of Gujarat in Social and Economic services (as percentage of Total expenditure) (*Contd.*)

Sr. No.	Item	1997-98	1998-99	1999-00	2000-01	2001-02	2002-03	2003-04
I.	Developmental Expenditure	69.88	71.00	66.10	62.97	40.02	36.99	40.65
A	Social Services	29.52	30.78	30.69	28.19	19.86	17.91	20.71
i.	Education, Sports, Arts and Culture	15.23	16.31	15.13	11.83	7.55	8.61	9.20
ii.	Health and Family welfare	4.23	4.56	4.22	2.95	1.69	2.05	2.21
iii.	Water supply, Sanitation, Housing and Urban Development	3.83	5.02	5.52	5.50	1.84	2.71	3.87
iv.	Information and Broadcasting	0.11	0.11	0.10	0.09	0.05	0.05	0.07
v.	Welfare of SCs, STs and OBCs	1.96	1.91	1.92	1.41	0.81	0.95	1.27
vi.	Labour and Labour Welfare	0.52	0.50	0.48	0.39	0.23	0.29	0.30
vii.	Social Welfare and Nutrition	3.53	2.26	3.24	5.96	6.38	1.91	2.15
viii.	Others	0.11	0.11	0.09	0.06	1.31	1.33	1.64

(*Contd.*)

(Contd. Table 6.1)

Sr. No.	*Item*	*1997-98*	*1998-99*	*1999-00*	*2000-01*	*2001-02*	*2002-03*	*2003-04*
B.	Economic Services	40.37	40.21	35.41	34.78	20.16	19.08	19.95
i.	Agriculture and Allied Services	4.23	3.99	3.99	2.95	2.37	1.71	2.32
ii.	Rural Development	2.81	3.18	2.51	2.44	0.88	1.37	1.51
iii.	Special Area Programmes	0.15	0.15	0.12	0.09	0.06	0.06	0.07
iv.	Irrigation and Flood Control	15.93	15.05	14.19	9.96	5.40	6.61	4.26
v.	Energy	10.52	10.48	7.61	13.34	8.14	5.46	7.14
vi.	Industry and Minerals	1.24	1.56	1.42	1.38	0.87	0.66	0.51
vii.	Transport and Communication	4.33	4.77	4.19	3.45	1.94	2.57	3.18
viii.	Science, Technology and Environment	0.017	0.016	0.07	0.01	0.01	0.01	0.07
ix.	General Economic Services	1.14	1.02	1.32	1.15	0.49	0.64	0.89
II.	Non-Developmental and Others Expenditure	30.12	29.00	33.90	37.03	59.98	63.01	59.35
III.	Total Expenditure (I+II)	100.00	100.00	100.00	100.00	100.00	100.00	100.00

Source: Self Calculated on the basis of the data given in Appendix.

Table 6.1: Public Expenditure of Gujarat in Social and Economic services (as percentage of Total expenditure) *(Contd.)*

Sr. No.	*Item*	*2004-05*	*2005-06*	*2006-07*	*2007-08*	*2008-09*	*2009-10*
I.	Developmental Expenditure	48.75	62.75	64.46	63.28	69.25	66.96
A	Social Services	24.46	29.47	30.91	32.18	32.69	35.89
i.	Education, Sports, Arts and Culture	10.52	12.58	12.71	13.40	11.69	13.78
ii.	Health and Family welfare	2.55	3.12	2.92	3.22	3.08	3.79
iii.	Water supply, Sanitation, Housing and Urban Development	5.45	5.33	7.64	9.32	12.21	12.21
iv.	Information and Broadcasting	0.06	0.07	0.07	0.10	0.10	0.09
v.	Welfare of SCs, STs and OBCs	1.69	2.00	1.86	1.95	1.88	1.87
vi.	Labour and Labour Welfare	0.32	0.39	0.40	0.46	0.46	0.49
vii.	Social Welfare and Nutrition	2.37	3.49	4.73	2.60	2.76	3.20
viii.	Others	1.51	2.48	0.58	1.13	0.50	0.48

(Contd.)

(Contd. Table 6.1)

Sr. No.	Item	2004-05	2005-06	2006-07	2007-08	2008-09	2009-10
B.	Economic Services	24.28	33.28	33.56	31.10	36.56	31.07
i.	Agriculture and Allied Services	2.76	3.15	3.09	3.82	4.07	4.36
ii.	Rural Development	2.13	2.30	2.45	2.59	2.21	2.29
iii.	Special Area Programmes	0.08	0.08	0.08	0.08	0.07	0.06
iv.	Irrigation and Flood Control	5.63	7.66	11.17	9.12	14.02	7.58
v.	Energy	7.55	12.13	8.68	6.88	7.55	6.17
vi.	Industry and Minerals	1.04	1.00	1.05	1.13	1.38	1.40
vii.	Transport and Communication	3.92	5.65	5.49	6.21	5.84	7.35
viii.	Science, Technology and Environment	0.13	0.13	0.12	0.07	0.04	0.04
ix.	General Economic Services	1.05	1.18	1.44	1.21	1.37	1.82
II.	Non-Developmental and Others Expenditure	51.25	37.25	35.54	36.72	30.75	33.04
III.	Total Expenditure (I+II)	100.00	100.00	100.00	100.00	100.00	100.00

Source: Self Calculated on the basis of the data given in Appendix.

Figure 6.1(a): Percentage of Total Public Expenditure on Social and Economic Services in Gujarat

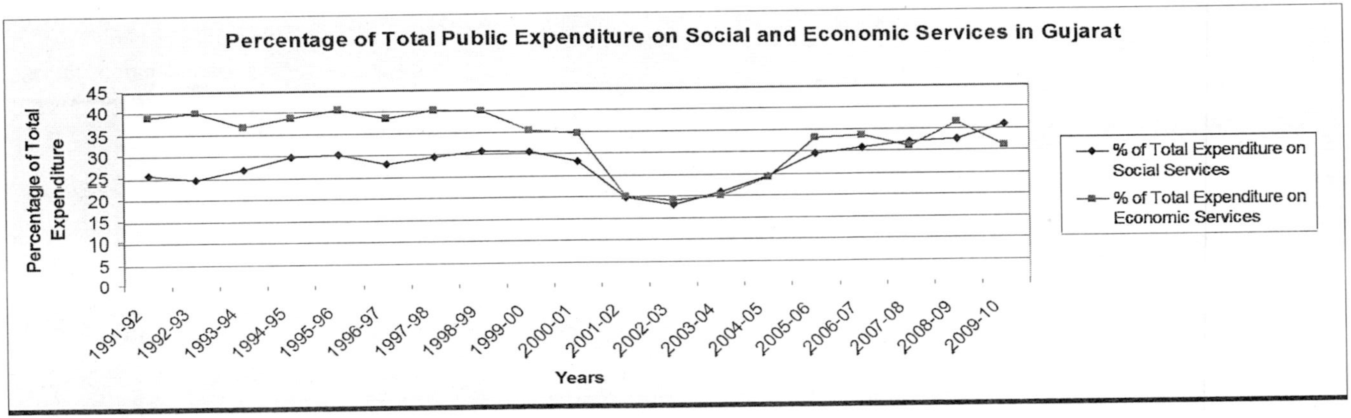

Source: Based on the data given in Table 6.1.

Figure 6.1(b)(i): Percentage of Total Public Expenditure on Selected Social Services in Gujarat

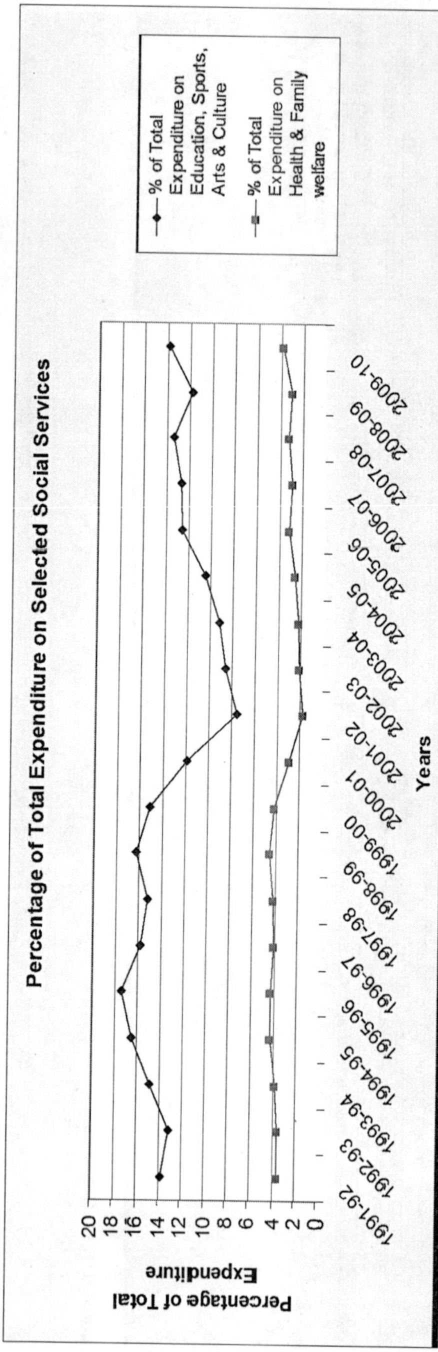

Source: Based on the data given in Table 6.1.

Figure 6.1(b)(ii): Percentage of Total Public Expenditure on Selected Social Services in Gujarat

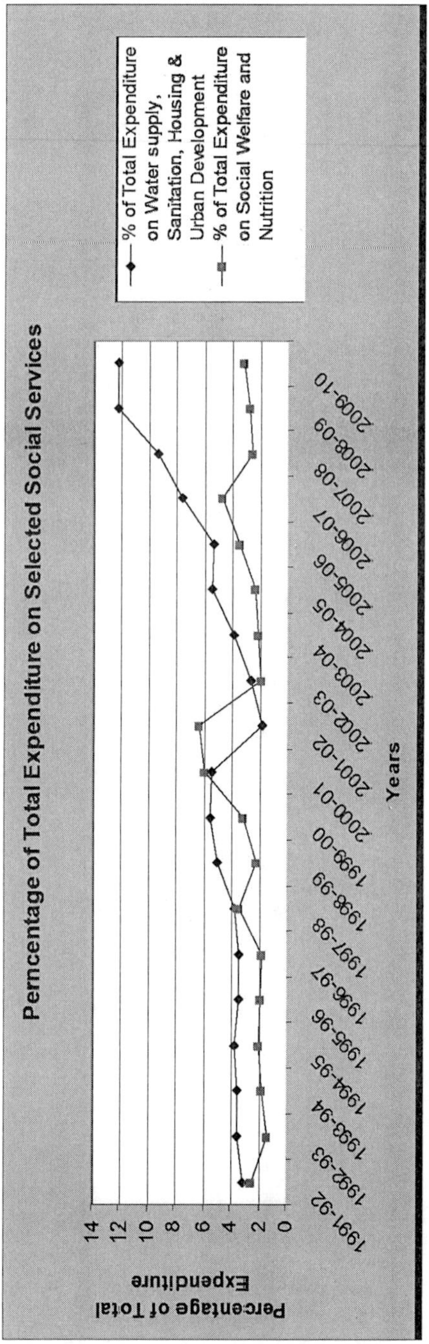

Source: Based on the data given in Table 6.1.

Figure 6.1(c)(i): Percentage of Total Public Expenditure on Selected Economic Services in Gujarat

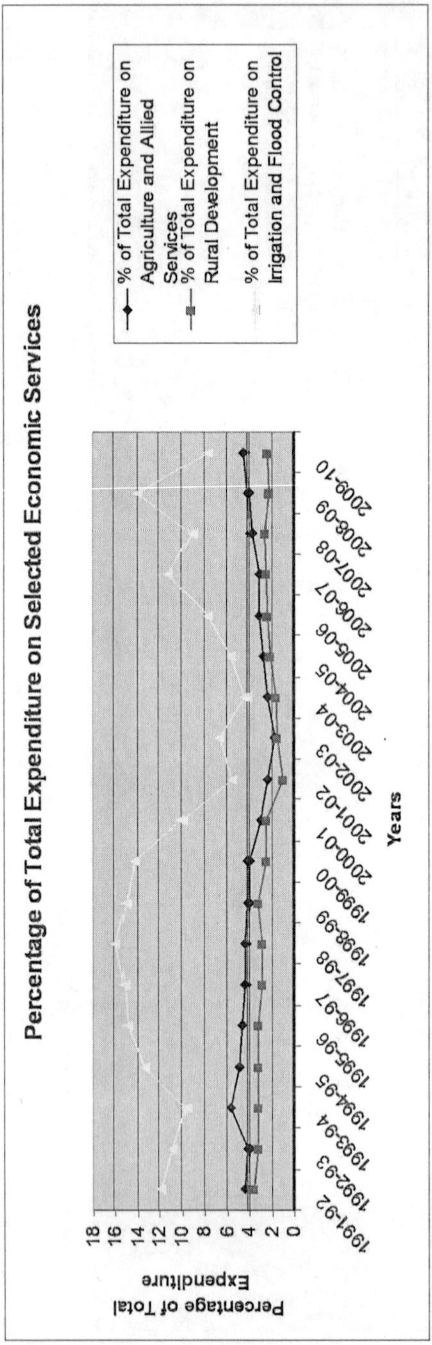

Source: Based on the data given in Table 6.1.

Figure 6.1(c)(ii): Percentage of Total Public Expenditure on Selected Economic Services in Gujarat

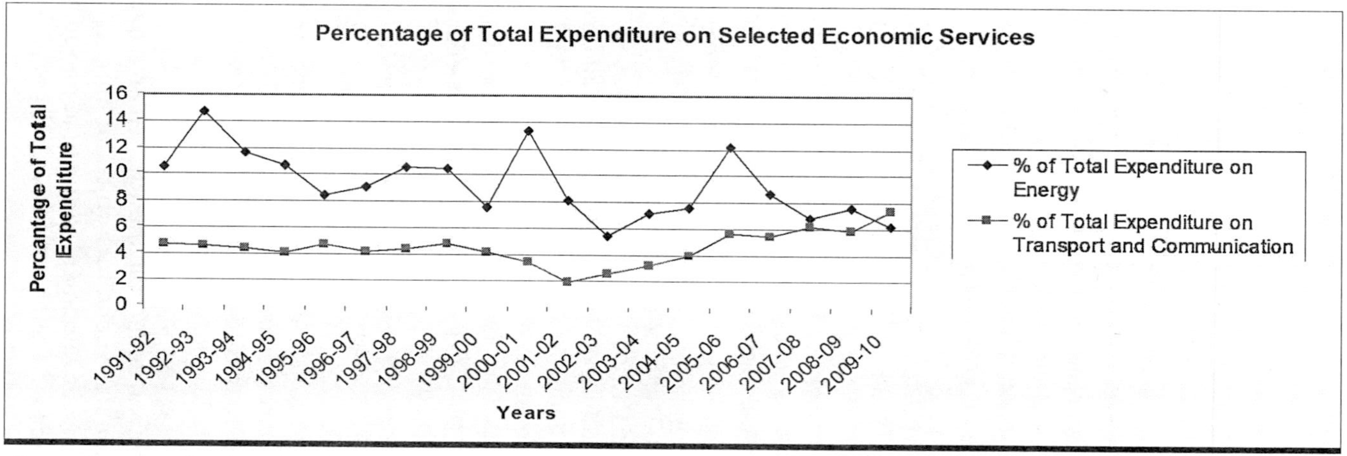

Source: Based on the data given in Table 6.1.

13.85 per cent in 1991-92 to 13.18 per cent in 1992-93. Though it increased significantly to 17.45 per cent in 1995-96, it again decreased to 15.82 per cent in 1996-97 and varied between 15.13 per cent and 16.31 per cent in the time period 1997-98 to 1999-00. It decreased significantly to 11.83 per cent in 2000-01 and varied between 7.55 per cent and 9.20 per cent in the time period 2001-02 to 2003-04. Though it increased from 10.52 per cent in 2004-05 to 13.40 per cent in 2007-08, yet in 2008-09 it again decreased to 11.69 per cent and became 13.78 per cent in 2009-10.

So, it can be concluded that **Gujarat's public expenditure on education, sports, arts and culture recorded a fluctuating trend in the given time period and it declined from 13.85 per cent in 1991-92 to 13.78 per cent in 2009-10.**

Gujarat's expenditure on health and family welfare decreased from 3.66 per cent in 1991-92 to 3.64 per cent in 1992-93.Then it increased to 3.85 per cent in 1993-94 and became 4.36 per cent in 1994-95 as well as 1995-96. In the time period 1996-97 to 1999-00 it varied between 4.02 per cent and 4.56 per cent. It decreased significantly to 2.95 per cent in 2000-01 and 1.69 per cent in 2001-02. In the time period 2002-03 to 2004-05 it varied between 2.05 per cent to 2.55 per cent. Though, it increased to 3.12 per cent in 2005-06, yet it again decreased to 2.92 per cent in 2006-07 and varied between 3.22 per cent and 3.79 per cent in the time period 2007-08 to 2009-10.

So it can be concluded that **Gujarat experienced fluctuating trend in its expenditure on health and family welfare in the time period 1991-92 to 2009-10 and it increased from 3.66 per cent in 1991-92 to 3.79 per cent in 2009-10.**

It is evident from the Table 6.1 and Figure 6.1(b)(ii) that, the expenditure on Water Supply, Sanitation, Housing and Urban Development increased from 3.19 per cent in 1991-92 to 3.81 per cent in 1994-95 and then decreased to 3.48 per cent in 1995-96 as well as in 1996-97. It started to increase from 1997-98 (3.83 per cent) and became 5.52 per cent in 1999-00. In 2000-01, it decreased to 5.50 per cent. In 2001-02, it decreased significantly to 1.84 per cent and varied between 2.71 per cent and 3.87 per cent in the time period 2002-03 to 2003-04. It increased significantly to 5.45 per cent in 2004-05 and decreased to 5.33 per cent in 2005-06. Then, it increased steadily from 7.64 per cent in 2006-07 to 12.21 per cent in 2009-10.

So it can be concluded that **though Gujarat experienced fluctuating trend in its expenditure on Water Supply, Sanitation, Housing and Urban Development in the time period 1991-92 to 2009-10, yet it increased significantly from 3.19 per cent in 1991-92 to 12.21 per cent in 2009-10.**

Gujarat's expenditure on Social Welfare and Nutrition decreased from 2.55 per cent in 1991-92 to 1.48 per cent in 1992-93. It increased to 1.89 per cent in 1993-94 and 2.05 per cent in 1994-95. From 1995-96 (1.99 per cent) it again started to decrease and became 1.84 per cent in 1996-97. In 1997-98, though it increased significantly to 3.53 per cent, yet it again decreased to 2.26 per cent in 1998-99. From 1999-00 (3.24 per cent) it increased steadily and became 6.38 per cent in 2001-02. It decreased significantly to 1.91 per cent in 2002-03 and became 2.15 per cent in 2003-04. Between the years 2004-05 and 2006-07 Gujarat experienced increasing trend with respect to this indicator and it increased from 2.37 per cent in 2004-05 to 4.73 per cent in 2006-07. Though, it decreased to 2.60 per cent in 2007-08, it increased again to 2.76 per cent in 2008-09 and became 3.2 per cent in 2009-10.

So, it can be concluded that **Gujarat's public expenditure on Social Welfare and Nutrition also recorded a fluctuating trend in the given time period 1991-92 to 2009-10 and increased from 2.55 per cent in 1991-92 to 3.2 per cent in 2009-10. It experienced some major hikes in the years 2000-01 (5.96 per cent), 2001-02 (6.38 per cent) and 2006-07 (4.73 per cent).**

It is evident from the Table 6.1 and Figure 6.1(c)(i) that, the expenditure on agriculture and allied services decreased from 4.26 per cent in 1991-92 to 3.97 per cent in 1992-93. Though, it increased to 5.58 per cent in 1993-94, yet it experienced decreasing trend from 1994-95 and decreased from 4.81 per cent in 1994-95 to 1.71 per cent in 2002-03. From 2003-04 (2.32 per cent), it again started to increase and became 3.15 per cent in 2005-06. Though it again decreased to 3.09 per cent in 2006-07, in the time period 2007-08 to 2009-10 it experienced increasing trend- increased from 3.82 per cent in 2007-08 to 4.36 per cent in 2009-10.

So, it can be concluded that, **Gujarat's expenditure on agriculture and allied services recorded fluctuating trend in the given time period. It increased from 4.26 per cent in 1991-92 to 4.36 per cent in 2009-10.**

Gujarat's expenditure on rural development decreased from 3.69 per cent in 1991-92 to 3.18 per cent in 1992-93. Then it increased to 3.24 per cent in 1993-94 as well as 1994-95 and became 3.26 per cent in 1995-96. From 1996-97 (2.84 per cent) it again started to decrease and became 2.81 per cent in 1997-98. Though it increased to 3.18 per cent in 1998-99, from 1999-00 it experienced decreasing trend and decreased from 2.51 per cent in 1999-00 to 0.88 per cent in 2001-02. It again increased to 1.37 per cent in 2002-03 and became 2.59 per cent in 2007-08. In 2008-09, it decreased to 2.21 per cent and became 2.29 per cent in 2009-10.

So, it can be concluded that **Gujarat's public expenditure on rural development also recorded a fluctuating trend in the given time period (1991-92 to 2009-10). It decreased from 3.69 per cent in 1991-92 to 2.29 per cent in 2009-10.**

Gujarat's expenditure on irrigation and flood control decreased from 11.75 per cent in 1991-92 to 10.81 per cent in 1992-93 and became 9.6 per cent in 1993-94. From 1994-95 (13.31 per cent) it again started to increase and became 15.93 per cent in 1997-98. Then, from 1997-98 (15.05 per cent) it started to decrease and became 4.26 per cent in 2003-04. Between the years 2004-05 and 2006-07 it experienced increasing trend and increased from 5.63 per cent in 2004-05 to 11.17 per cent in 2006-07. Though it decreased to 9.12 per cent, in 2007-08, yet in 2008-09 it increased significantly to 14.02 per cent. In 2009-10 it decreased to 7.58 per cent.

So, it can be concluded that **Gujarat experienced highly fluctuating trend with respect to the expenditure on irrigation and flood control in the time period 1991-92 to 2009-10. It decreased from 11.75 per cent in 1991-92 to 7.58 per cent in 2009-10.**

It is evident from the Table 6.1 and Figure 6.1(c)(ii) that, the expenditure on energy increased from 10.6 per cent in 1991-92 to 14.76 per cent in 1992-93. From 1993-94 (11.61 per cent) it started to decrease and became 8.46 per cent in 1995-96. It again started to increase from 1996-97 (9.05 per cent) and became 10.52 per cent in 1997-98. It decreased significantly to 7.61 per cent in 1999-00. Though it again increased to 13.34 per cent in 2000-01, in the year 2001-02 it decreased to 8.14 per cent and then further decreased to 5.46 per cent in 2002-03. From 2003-04 (7.14 per cent) it started to increase and became 12.13 per cent in 2005-06. It decreased to 8.68 per cent in 2006-07 and then further decreased to 6.88 per cent in 2007-08. In 2008-09 it increased to 7.55 per cent and then again decreased to 6.17 per cent in 2009-10.

So, it can be concluded that **Gujarat experienced highly fluctuating trend with respect to the expenditure on Energy in the time period 1991-92 to 2009-10.**

It decreased from 10.6 per cent in 1991-92 to 6.17 per cent in 2009-10.

Gujarat's expenditure on transport and communication decreased from 4.69 per cent in 1991-92 to 4.04 per cent in 1994-95. Though it increased to 4.67 per cent in 1995-96, it again decreased to 4.16 per cent in 1996-97. It increased from 4.33 per cent in 1997-98 to 4.77 per cent in 1998-99. It experienced decreasing trend between the years 1999-00 and 2001-02 and decreased from 4.19 per cent in 1999-00 to 1.94 per cent in 2001-02. In the time period 2002-03 to 2005-06, there was increasing trend of public expenditure on transport and communication in Gujarat and it increased from 2.57 per cent in 2002-03 to 5.65 per cent in 2005-06. Though in 2006-07 it decreased to 5.49 per cent, it increased to 6.21 per cent in 2007-08, then again decreased to 5.84 per cent in 2008-09 and increased again to 7.35 per cent in 2009-10.

So, it can be concluded that **Gujarat experienced highly fluctuating trend with respect to the public expenditure on transport and communication in the time period 1991-92 to 2009-10. It increased from 4.69 per cent in 1991-92 to 7.35 per cent in 2009-10.**

6.2 Public Expenditure of Fifteen Major States of India on Selected Social and Economic Services in 2009-10

In this section the public expenditure of 15 major states of India on Social Services, Education, Sports, Arts and Culture, Health and Family Welfare, Water Supply, Sanitation, Housing and Urban Development, Social Welfare and Nutrition as well as on Economic Services, Agriculture and Allied Activities, Irrigation and Flood Control, Energy, Transport and Communication has been discussed in percentage form (as percentage of total public expenditure).

Here, total expenditure is the summation of total revenue and capital expenditure where developmental (both plan and non-plan), non developmental (both plan and non-plan) expenditure and grants in aids and contributions all are considered.

The main aim of this section is to obtain the rank of Gujarat, among 15 major states with respect to public expenditure (in per cent) in different social and economic services considered here. The data of public expenditures of 15 major states in selected social and economic services are given in the Tables 6.2(a) and 6.2(b).

It is evident from the Table 6.2(a) that, as per 2009-10 data Gujarat obtained fifth rank with respect to developmental expenditure (behind four major states Haryana, Karnataka, Maharashtra and Andhra Pradesh) and fourth rank with respect to expenditure on social services (behind three major states– Rajasthan, West Bengal and Maharashtra). Gujarat obtained 12th rank with respect to public expenditure in education, sports, arts and culture (behind eleven major states- Assam, Bihar, Haryana, Karnataka, Kerala, Maharashtra, Orissa, Rajasthan, Tamil Nadu, Uttar Pradesh and West Bengal) and ninth rank with respect to public expenditure in health and family welfare (behind eight major states– Assam, Uttar Pradesh, Rajasthan, Tamil Nadu, West Bengal, Kerala, Andhra Pradesh and Orissa) among 15 major states of India.

Though, Gujarat obtained first rank with respect to public expenditure on water supply, sanitation, housing and urban development, yet it

Table 6.2 (a): Public Expenditure of 15 Major States in Selected Social Services (as percentage of Total Public Expenditure) in 2009-10

Name of the States	*Developmental Expenditure*	*Expenditure on Social Services*	*Education, Sports, Arts and Culture*	*Health and Family Welfare*	*Water Supply, Sanitation, Housing and Urban Development*	*Social Welfare and Nutrition*
Andhra Pradesh	67.30 (4)	32.69 (11)	9.97 (15)	4.02 (7)	6.33 (6)	6.38 (2)
Assam	55.92 (12)	33.50 (9)	16.39 (7)	5.72 (1)	3.77 (13)	3.14 (12)
Bihar	65.97 (6)	33.44 (10)	18.11 (4)	3.52 (11)	4.45 (9)	5.61 (5)
Gujarat	**66.96 (5)**	**35.89 (4)**	**13.78 (12)**	**3.79 (9)**	**12.21 (1)**	**3.20 (11)**
Haryana	71.53 (1)	34.98 (7)	16.34 (8)	3.37 (12)	7.01 (3)	6.03 (4)
Karnataka	71.35 (2)	35.85 (5)	13.96 (10)	3.57 (10)	6.63 (5)	4.91 (7)
Kerala	49.50 (14)	31.50 (12)	16.66 (6)	4.74 (6)	3.82 (11)	4.90 (8)
Madhya Pradesh	65.77 (7)	28.66 (14)	13.00 (13)	3.32 (14)	3.80 (12)	4.29 (9)

(Contd.)

[Contd. Table 6.2 (a)]

Name of the States	Developmental Expenditure	Expenditure on Social Services	Education, Sports, Arts and Culture	Health and Family Welfare	Water Supply, Sanitation, Housing and Urban Development	Social Welfare and Nutrition
Maharashtra	67.58 (3)	36.57 (3)	19.06 (1)	3.33 (13)	6.68 (4)	2.43 (14)
Orissa	62.81 (9)	34.22 (8)	18.19 (3)	3.83 (8)	3.96 (10)	4.23 (10)
Punjab	44.05 (15)	21.54 (15)	11.90 (14)	3.09 (15)	2.52 (15)	2.59 (13)
Rajasthan	63.01 (8)	39.02 (1)	19.03 (2)	4.83 (3)	10.07 (2)	2.36 (15)
Tamil Nadu	62.45 (10)	35.37 (6)	15.22 (9)	4.77 (4)	5.68 (7)	6.30 (3)
Uttar Pradesh	58.33 (11)	30.51 (13)	13.80 (11)	4.99 (2)	3.64 (14)	5.06 (6)
West Bengal	51.87 (13)	36.63 (2)	17.73 (5)	4.76 (5)	5.44 (8)	6.96 (1)
All States and UTs with Legislature	**63.03**	**33.88**	**15.37**	**4.29**	**6.12**	**4.39**

Source: Calculated on the basis of the data given in CMIE, Public Finance, August 2011.
Note: Ranks of the states are given in brackets.

Table 6.2 (b): Public Expenditure of 15 Major States in Selected Economic Services (as percentage of Total Public Expenditure) in 2009-10

Name of the States	*Expenditure on Economic Services*	*Agriculture and Allied Activities*	*Irrigation and Flood Control*	*Energy*	*Transport and Communication*
Andhra Pradesh	34.61 (4)	2.94 (13)	19.61 (1)	3.84 (10)	3.05 (13)
Assam	22.42 (13)	4.08 (11)	4.32 (10)	0.93 (13)	4.60 (11)
Bihar	32.53 (5)	3.60 (12)	5.25 (8)	4.37 (9)	9.24 (1)
Gujarat	31.07 (6)	4.36 (9)	7.58 (3)	6.17 (6)	7.35 (3)
Haryana	36.55 (2)	6.62 (5)	4.96 (9)	11.70 (2)	8.38 (2)
Karnataka	35.50 (3)	6.90 (4)	6.79 (5)	6.52 (5)	6.03 (6)
Kerala	18 (14)	5.43 (8)	1.59 (15)	0.19 (15)	6.68 (4)
Madhya Pradesh	37.11 (1)	5.80 (7)	5.30 (7)	14.45 (1)	5.03 (9)

(Contd.)

[Contd. Table 6.2 (b)]

Name of the States	Expenditure on Economic Services	Agriculture and Allied Activities	Irrigation and Flood Control	Energy	Transport and Communication
Maharashtra	31.01 (7)	7.01 (3)	8.82 (2)	5.23 (8)	5.52 (8)
Orissa	28.59 (8)	7.52 (1)	7.00 (4)	0.34 (14)	6.14 (5)
Punjab	22.51 (12)	2.56 (15)	5.89 (6)	9.03 (3)	3.17 (12)
Rajasthan	23.99 (11)	4.16 (10)	4.17 (12)	6.74 (4)	2.77 (14)
Tamil Nadu	27.08 (10)	7.30 (2)	2.11 (13)	1.99 (11)	5.53 (7)
Uttar Pradesh	27.82 (9)	5.97 (6)	4.24 (11)	5.77 (7)	4.74 (10)
West Bengal	15.24 (15)	2.87 (14)	1.92 (14)	1.25 (12)	2.66 (15)
All States and UTs with Legislature	**29.15**	**5.53**	**3.97**	**5.31**	**5.81**

Source: Calculated on the basis of the data given in CMIE, Public Finance, August 2011.
Note: Ranks of the states are given in brackets.

obtained 11th rank with respect to public expenditure in social welfare and nutrition (behind ten major states–Andhra Pradesh, Bihar, Haryana, Karnataka, Kerala, Madhya Pradesh, Orissa, Tamil Nadu, Uttar Pradesh and West Bengal). It has been also found from the Table 6.2(a) that, though Gujarat's social service expenditure was higher than the expenditure of 'all states and UTs under legislature,' yet it was lower with respect to education, sports, arts and culture, health and family welfare, social welfare and nutrition.

It is evident from the Table 6.2(b) that, with respect to public expenditure on economic services Gujarat obtained sixth rank (behind five major states- Madhya Pradesh, Haryana, Karnataka, Andhra Pradesh and Bihar). Gujarat obtained ninth rank (behind eight major states–Orissa, Tamil Nadu, Maharashtra, Karnataka, Haryana, Uttar Pradesh, Madhya Pradesh and Kerala) with respect to expenditure on agriculture and allied activities and third rank (behind two major states– Andhra Pradesh and Maharashtra) with respect to expenditure in irrigation and flood control. The state obtained sixth rank with respect to expenditure on energy sector (behind five major states– Madhya Pradesh, Haryana, Punjab, Rajasthan and Karnataka) and third rank with respect to expenditure in transport and communication (behind two states- Bihar and Haryana) among 15 major states of India in 2009-10. It has been also found from the Table 6.2(b) that, Gujarat's percentage of total public expenditure in economic services as well as all the other selected economic services (except in agriculture and allied services) were higher than 'all states and UTs under legislature' in 2009-10.

By comparing Gujarat's position among 15 major states with respect to its expenditure on different social and economic services in 2009-10, it may be concluded that Gujarat's position was not good with respect to its expenditure (as percentage of total public expenditure) on education, sports, arts and culture, health and family welfare, social welfare and nutrition and agriculture and allied services.

7

Summary and Policy Implications

7.1 Summary and Major Findings

In this study an attempt has been made to examine the contributions of Infrastructure and Human Development to accelerate Economic Growth and vice versa in rapidly growing state Gujarat.

'Economic Growth' is the process by which productive capacity of an economy increases over time to bring about rising levels of national income. 'Infrastructure' and 'Human Development' are two essential ingredients which stimulate 'Economic Growth' as well as stimulated by 'Economic Growth'.

Infrastructure is basic physical and organisational structure needed for the operation of a society or enterprise, or the services and facilities necessary for an economy to function. It can be generally defined as the set of interconnected structural elements that provide framework supporting an entire structure of development. Extensive and efficient infrastructure is critical for ensuring the effective functioning of the economy, as it is an important factor determining the location of economic activity and the kinds of activities or sectors that can develop in a particular economy. Infrastructure development, both economic and social is one of the major determinants of economic growth and it contributes to economic growth both by increasing productivity and by providing amenities which enhance the quality of life. In macro-economic literature, a number of studies have found empirical support for a positive impact of infrastructure on aggregate output.

Economic growth is the major concern of any State. It is conventionally measured as the percentage rate of increase in real gross domestic product. More importance is given to the growth of the ratio of GDP to population, which is also called per capita income.

Human development is a crucial ingredient of economic growth. It stimulates as well as stimulated by economic growth. Human Development means to build human capabilities of the people. Though material capital is crucial for economic achievements, yet human capital is no less. In the beginning of 1960's the emphasis was shifted from material capital to human capital.

The present study has examined the crucial issues like infrastructure, economic growth and human development in the state Gujarat. We have found Gujarat, a state with high economic growth on one hand and comparatively low human development on the other. The main thrusts of our study had been to examine, the trend of Infrastructural Components and Economic Growth (Per Capita Net State Domestic Product at factor cost and constant prices) as well as the long run and short run causal relationship between these two components (with the help of time series data analysis) and also Human Development scenario of the state Gujarat with the help of different components related to Human Development. The district-wise cross- section data analysis (for three time points 1991, 2000-01 and 2009-10) has also been done to identify the category of the districts with respect to different components of infrastructure, economic growth and human development as well as weighted aggregate infrastructure index, weighted aggregate index of economic growth and human development index in Gujarat. The relationship between the variables weighted aggregate infrastructure index and weighted aggregate index of economic growth as well as human development index and weighted aggregate index of economic growth at district level in Gujarat has also been analysed in this study. The trend and pattern of public expenditure on social and economic services in the state Gujarat has also been examined in this study to understand the reason behind Gujarat's comparatively low human development instead of its high economic growth and the decreasing impact of weighted aggregate index of economic growth on human development with respect to the result of cross district regression analysis.

The **major findings of the study** are summarised below:

- It has been found that, though there is increasing trend with respect to 'Road Length per 100 sq. km. of area' in the state Gujarat in the time period 1980-81 to 2009-10, yet Gujarat's road length per 100 sq. km. of area is below India's average in the given time period (except in 1999-00). Again, with respect to 'Rail Route Length per 100 sq. km. of area' though the steadily falling trend (due to decline in metre gauge and narrow gauge) has been found in the state Gujarat in the time period 1980-81 to 2009-10, yet its rail route length per 100 sq. km. of area is higher than India's average in the given time period. Further, it has been found that Gujarat's transportation infrastructure stock (with respect to area) is higher than all India's average for the given time period.

We have found from the district-wise analysis of the state Gujarat that, in 1991 the districts were concentrated under medium category with respect to 'Transportation Infrastructure index'. There were seven districts- Ahmedabad, Kheda, Surat, Vadodara, Mahesana, Valsad and Panch Mahals under high category, two districts– Kachchh and The Dangs under low category and rest of the districts (Gandhinagar, Sabar Kantha, Rajkot, Bhavnagar, Junagadh, Bharuch, Amreli, Jamnagar, Surendranagar, Banas Kantha) under medium category with respect to this indicator. For both the time points 2000-01 and 2009-10, most of districts were concentrated under medium category with respect to 'Transportation Infrastructure Index'. In 2000-01, the districts Gandhinagar, Kheda, Surat, Vadodara, Valsad, Anand and Navsari were under high category, the districts Amreli, Jamnagar, Surendranagar, Kachchh, The Dangs and Patan were under low category and the rest of the districts (Ahmedabad, Mahesana, Sabar Kantha, Rajkot, Bhavnagar, Junagadh, Bharuch, Banas Kantha, Panch Mahals, Porbandar, Narmada and Dahod) were under medium category with respect to this indicator. In 2009-10, the districts Ahmedabad, Gandhinagar, Kheda, Surat, Vadodara, Valsad, Anand, Dahod and Navsari were under high category, the districts Amreli, Jamnagar, Surendranagar, Kachchh, The Dangs and Narmada were under low category and the rest of the districts– Mahesana, Sabar Kantha, Rajkot, Bhavnagar, Junagadh, Bharuch, Banas Kantha, Panch Mahals, Patan and Porbandar were under medium category with respect to this indicator. By comparing the district-wise performances with respect to this indicator between the two time points (2000-01 and 2009-10), it has been found that, there were three districts which improved their categories between these two time points– the districts Ahmedabad and Dahod shifted form medium to high category and Patan shifted from low to medium category. The district Narmada is the only exception which deteriorated with respect to its category and shifted from medium to low category with respect to this indicator.

- The 'Communication' infrastructure has been studied with the help of two indicators– Telecommunication and Post Offices. It has been found that, though Gujarat experienced an increasing trend with respect to 'number of telephone connections per hundred people' and it was also higher than India's average in the given time period, yet in the case of 'number of post offices per 100 sq. km. of area', it was lower in Gujarat than India's average in the time period 1983-84 to 2009-10 (except in the year 1986-87). It has also been found that, Gujarat's communication infrastructure stock is higher than India's average in the given time period.

- It has been found that there is an increasing trend of 'per capita electricity consumption' in Gujarat and it is also significantly higher than India's average for the time period 1980-81 to 2009-10.

From the district-wise analysis of the state Gujarat, it has been found that, in 1991 with respect to the indicator 'Percentage of electrified villages to total inhabited villages' most of the districts were found under high category except eight districts of which two districts– Surat and Sabar Kantha were under medium category and other six districts– Vadodara, Junagadh, Bharuch, Banas Kantha, Panch Mahals and Kachchh were under low category. The districts were concentrated under high category in both the time points 2000-01 and 2009-10 with respect to this indicator. In 2000-01, the districts Ahmedabad, Gandhinagar, Kheda, Mahesana, Sabar Kantha, Rajkot, Amreli, Panch Mahals, Surendranagar, The Dangs, Patan, Anand and Navsari were under high category, the districts Surat, Vadodara, Bhavnagar, Junagadh, Bharuch, Banas Kantha, Kachchh and Dahod were under medium category and the rest of the districts (Valsad, Jamnagar, Porbandar and Narmada) were under low category with respect to this indicator. In 2009-10, there were nineteen districts (Ahmedabad, Gandhinagar, Kheda, Surat, Mahesana, Sabar Kantha, Rajkot, Vadodara, Bhavnagar, Junagadh, Bharuch, Amreli, Panch Mahals, Surendranagar, The Dangs, Patan, Anand, Dahod and Navsari) under high category; three districts (Jamnagar, Kachchh and Narmada) under medium category and rest of the three districts (Valsad, Banas Kantha and Porbandar) under low category with respect to the indicator. The districts Surat, Vadodara, Bhavnagar, Junagadh, Bharuch and Dahod which were under medium category in 2000-01 shifted to high category in 2009-10. The districts Jamnagar and Narmada shifted from low to medium category and the district Banas Kantha shifted from medium to low category between the given time points.

- Gujarat has shown an increasing trend with respect to 'numbers of scheduled commercial banks per hundred sq. km. of Area.' But it was higher than India's average only for four years, from 1980-81 to 1983-84 and lower than India's average for the rest of the time period (1984-85 to 2009-10).

It has been observed from the district-wise analysis of the state Gujarat that, with respect to 'Banking Facilities' in the year 1991, there were five districts– Ahmedabad, Kheda, Surat, Vadodara and Valsad under high category, other seven districts– Gandhinagar, Mahesana, Rajkot, Bhavnagar, Junagadh, Amreli and Panch Mahals under medium category and rest of the districts Sabar Kantha, Bharuch, Jamnagar, Surendranagar, Banas Kantha, Kachchh and The Dangs under low

Category. Both in 2000-01 and 2009-10 most of the districts were concentrated under medium and low categories with respect to this indicator. In 2000-01, the districts Ahmedabad, Gandhinagar, Surat, Vadodara, Anand and Navsari were under high category, the districts Kheda, Mahesana, Sabar Kantha, Rajkot, Valsad, Bharuch, Panch Mahals, Porbandar and Dahod were under medium category and rest of the districts Bhavnagar, Junagadh, Amreli, Jamnagar, Surendranagar, The Dangs, Banas Kantha, Kachchh, Patan and Narmada were under low category with respect to this indicator. Similarly, in 2009-10, the districts–Ahmedabad, Gandhinagar, Surat, Vadodara, Anand and Navsari were under high category, the districts Bhavnagar, Amreli, Jamnagar, Surendranagar, The Dangs, Banas Kantha, Kachchh, Patan and Narmada were under low category and the rest of the districts– Kheda, Mahesana, Sabar Kantha, Rajkot, Valsad, Junagadh, Bharuch, Panch Mahals, Porbandar and Dahod were under medium category with respect to this indicator. The district Junagadh was the only district which improved its category and shifted from low category in 2000-01 to medium category in 2009-10 with respect to this indicator.

- Though, there is an increasing trend with respect to 'Gross Irrigated Area as percentage of Gross Cropped Area' in Gujarat, yet it is lower than India's average for the given time period (1980-81 to 2009-10).

In the case of district-wise analysis of the state Gujarat it has been found that, in 1991 most of the districts were under low category with respect to this indicator. There were only six districts– Ahmedabad, Gandhinagar, Kheda, Surat, Mahesana and Banas Kantha under high category, other five districts– Vadodara, Sabar Kantha, Rajkot, Valsad, Bhavnagar under medium category and rest of the districts under low category with respect to this indicator in 1991. Again, in both the time points 2000-01 and 2009-10, most of the districts were concentrated under medium and low category with respect to this indicator. In 2000-01, the districts Gandhinagar, Kheda, Surat, Mahesana, Banas Kantha, Anand and Navsari were under high category, the districts Ahmedabad, Vadodara, Sabar Kantha, Rajkot, Valsad, Bharuch, Kachchh and Patan were under medium category and rest of the districts (Bhavnagar, Junagadh, Amreli, Jamnagar, Surendranagar, The Dangs, Panch Mahals, Porbandar, Narmada and Dahod) under low category with respect to this indicator. In 2009-10, the districts Gandhinagar, Kheda, Surat, Mahesana, Banas Kantha, Anand and Navsari were under high category, the districts Amreli Jamnagar, Surendranagar, Kachchh, Patan, The Dangs, Panch Mahals, Porbandar and Dahod were under low category and rest of the districts (Ahmedabad, Vadodara, Sabar Kantha, Rajkot, Valsad, Bhavnagar, Junagadh, Bharuch and Narmada) were under medium category with respect to the indicator 'Gross Irrigated Area as percentage of Gross Cropped Area'. After comparing the performances of the districts with respect to this indicator between the two time points (2000-01 and 2009-10), it has been found that, the districts Bhavnagar, Junagadh and Narmada improved their categories and shifted from low to medium category. There were two medium category districts – Kachchh and Patan, which deteriorated with respect to their categories and shifted to low category between this two time points.

- It has been found from the district-wise analysis of the state Gujarat that, with respect to the indicator 'Percentage of villages have clean drinking water to total inhabited villages' most of the districts were under high category in 1991. There were only three districts– Surat, Jamnagar and Panch Mahals under medium category and four districts– Sabar Kantha, Banas Kantha, Kachchh and The Dangs under low category with respect to this indicator. Though, most of the districts were concentrated under high and medium category with respect to this indicator in 2000-01, yet most of them shifted from medium category to high category in 2009-10. In 2000-01, the districts Gandhinagar, Kheda, Surat, Rajkot, Valsad, Anand and Navsari were under high category, the districts Ahmedabad, Vadodara, Mahesana, Sabar Kantha, Bhavnagar, Bharuch, Amreli, Banas Kantha, Panch Mahals, Dahod, Patan were under medium category and rest of the districts Junagadh, Jamnagar, Surendranagar, Kachchh, Porbandar, The Dangs and Narmada under medium category with respect to this indicator. In 2009-10, the districts Ahmedabad, Gandhinagar, Kheda, Surat, Mahesana, Sabar Kantha, Rajkot, Vadodara, Valsad, Bhavnagar, Junagadh, Bharuch, Amreli, Panch Mahals, Jamnagar, Surendranagar, The Dangs, Patan, Porbandar, Anand, Narmada, Dahod, Navsari were under high category, the district Banas Kantha was under medium category and the district Kachchh was under low category with respect to this indicator. After comparing the district-wise performances with respect to this indicator between the time points 2000-01 and 2009-10, it has been found that, the districts Ahmedabad, Vadodara, Mahesana, Sabar Kantha, Bhavnagar, Bharuch, Amreli, Panch Mahals, Dahod and Patan shifted from medium category to high category and the districts Junagadh, Jamnagar, Surendranagar, Porbandar, Narmada and The Dangs shifted from low to high category between the time points 2000-01 and 2009-10.
- In the case of 'Education', two indicators have been considered in this study– 'Numbers of schools per hundred sq. km of area' and 'Numbers of teachers per hundred pupils.' It has been found that, though there is increasing trend of the state Gujarat with respect to 'number of

schools per hundred sq. km. of area', yet it is lower than India's average in the given time period (1980-81 to 2009-10). Again, in the case of 'Numbers of teachers per hundred pupils' the state shows increasing trend in the given time period. It was higher than India's average for twenty one years (from 1983-84 to 1986-87, 1988-89 to 1996-97 and from 2002-03 to 2009-10) and lower than India's average for rest of the nine years. It has also found that the educational infrastructure stock of the state Gujarat is lower than India's average in the given time period.

In the case of district-wise analysis of the state Gujarat it has been found that, in 1991 with respect to 'Educational Facilities', there were six districts (Ahmedabad, Kheda, Vadodara, Sabar Kantha, Valsad, Panch Mahals) under high category, eight districts (Bhavnagar, Amreli, Jamnagar, Bharuch, The Dangs, Surendranagar, Banas Kantha, Kachchh) under low category and the remaining five districts (Gandhinagar, Surat, Mahesana, Rajkot, Junagadh) under medium category. Though, most of the districts were found either under high category and low category with respect to this indicator in 2000-01, yet in 2009-10 most of the districts were found under low category. In 2000-01, the districts Ahmedabad, Gandhinagar, Kheda, Surat, Vadodara, Mahesana, Sabar Kantha, Valsad, Panch Mahals, Anand, Dahod and Navsari were under high category, the districts Bhavnagar, Bharuch, Amreli, Jamnagar, Surendranagar, The Dangs, Banas Kantha, Kachchh, Patan, Porbandar and Narmada were under low category and remaining two districts– Junagadh and Rajkot under medium category with respect to this indicator. In 2009-10, there were eight districts (Ahmedabad, Gandhinagar, Kheda, Surat, Vadodara, Panch Mahals, Anand and Dahod) under high category, six districts (Mahesana, Sabar Kantha, Valsad, Navsari, Junagadh and Rajkot) under medium category and rest of the districts (Bhavnagar, Bharuch, Amreli, Jamnagar, Surendranagar, The Dangs, Banas Kantha, Kachchh, Patan, Porbandar and Narmada) under low category with respect to this indicator. There were four districts- Mahesana, Sabar Kantha, Valsad and Navsari which shifted from high category (2000-01) to medium category (2009-10) with respect to this indicator.

- There are two indicators namely– 'Number of medical institutions per hundred sq. km. of area' and 'Number of beds in medical institutions per hundred people', which have been considered to represent the health infrastructure in the state Gujarat. It has been found that, with respect to the indicator 'Numbers of medical institutions per hundred sq. km. of area', the state Gujarat has not only shown a decreasing trend, it is also lower than India's average in the given time period (1980-81 to 2009-10). Decrease in number of PHCs, CHCs and urban government hospitals in

Gujarat are some major reasons behind its decreasing trend with respect to this indicator. Though, the trend of 'Numbers of beds in medical institutions per hundred people' is decreasing, yet it is higher than India's average for all the years in the given time period (except in 2009-10). It has been found that, Gujarat's health infrastructure stock (composite index of these two indicators) was higher than India's average for the time period 1980-81 to 2006-07 and lower than India's average for rest of the time period (2007-08 to 2009-10).

In the case of district-wise analysis of the state Gujarat it has been found that, in 1991 with respect to 'Health Facilities', there were five districts– (Ahmedabad, Kheda, Surat, Vadodara and Valsad) under high category, other five districts (Gandhinagar, Banas Kantha, Panch Mahals, Kachchh and The Dangs) under low category and rest of the nine districts (Mahesana, Sabar Kantha, Rajkot, Bhavnagar, Junagadh, Bharuch, Amreli, Jamnagar, Surendranagar) under medium category. Most of the districts were found under low category in both the time points 2000-01 and 2009-10. In 2000-01, there were nine districts (Ahmedabad, Gandhinagar, Kheda, Vadodara, Mahesana, Valsad, Panch Mahals, Anand and Navsari) under high category, five districts (Surat, Sabar Kantha, Junagadh, Bharuch and Narmada) under medium category and rest of the districts (Rajkot, Bhavnagar, Amreli, Jamnagar, Surendranagar, The Dangs, Banas Kantha, Kachchh, Patan, Porbandar and Dahod) under low category with respect to this indicator. In 2009-10, the districts Gandhinagar, Kheda, Surat, Mahesana, Valsad, Panch Mahals, Anand, Navsari and Dahod were under high category, the districts Bhavnagar, Bharuch, Amreli, Jamnagar, Surendranagar, The Dangs, Banas Kantha, Kachchh, Patan, Rajkot and Porbandar were under low category and the rest of the districts (Ahmedabad, Vadodara, Sabar Kantha, Junagadh, and Narmada) were under medium category with respect to this indicator. After comparing the district-wise performances with respect to this indicator between the two time points 2000-01 and 2009-10, it has been found that, the districts Ahmedabad and Vadodara shifted from high to medium category and the district Bharuch shifted from medium to low category between. The districts Dahod (under low category in 2000-01) and Surat (under medium category in 2000-01) improved their health facilities and shifted to high category in 2009-10.

- It has been found from this study that, though Gujarat's economic infrastructure stock was higher than India's average for all the years in the given time period (1980-81 to 2009-10), yet its social infrastructure stock was higher than India's average for the time period 1983-84 to 2004-05 and lower than India's average for the rest of the years considered in this study. Gujarat's aggregate average infrastructure stock is also higher than India's average for all the years in the given time period (1980-81 to 2009-10).

In the case of district-wise analysis of the state Gujarat it has been found that, in 1991 with respect to the 'weighted aggregate infrastructure index' the districts Ahmedabad, Kheda, Surat, Vadodara, Mahesana and Valsad were under high category, the districts Gandhinagar, Sabar Kantha, Rajkot Bhavnagar, Panch Mahals and Junagadh were under medium category and rest of the districts (Bharuch, Amreli, Jamnagar, Surendranagar, Banas Kantha, Kachchh and The Dangs) were under low category. In 2000-01, the districts Ahmedabad, Gandhinagar, Kheda, Surat, Vadodara, Mahesana, Anand and Navsari were under high category, the districts Sabar Kantha, Rajkot, Valsad, Bharuch, Panch Mahals and Dahod were under medium category and rest of the districts (Bhavnagar, Junagadh, Amreli, Jamnagar, Surendranagar, Banas Kantha, Kachchh, The Dangs, Patan, Porbandar and Narmada) were under low category with respect to this indicator. In 2009-10, the districts Ahmedabad, Gandhinagar, Kheda, Surat, Vadodara, Valsad, Anand and Navsari were under high category, the districts Mahesana, Sabar Kantha, Rajkot, Junagadh, Banas Kantha, Panch Mahals and Dahod were under medium category and the districts Bhavnagar, Bharuch, Amreli, Jamnagar, Surendranagar, Kachchh, The Dangs, Patan, Porbandar and Narmada were under low category with respect to this indicator. After comparing the performances of the districts with respect to weighted aggregate infrastructure index between the two time points 2000-01 and 2009-10, it has been found that the districts– Surat, Valsad, Dahod, Junagadh, Narmada and Bhavnagar improved their ranks and the districts Anand, Navsari, Ahmedabad, Kheda, Mahesana, Sabarkantha, Bharuch, Patan and Porbandar deteriorated with respect to their ranks between these two time points. Further, the district Valsad shifted from medium category to high category, the districts Junagadh and Banas Kantha shifted from low to medium category between these two time points. The districts Mahesana (shifted fron high to medium category) and Bharuch (shifted from medium to low category) degraded with respect to their categories between the given time points (2000-01 and 2009-10).

- In this study, the state Gujarat has been compared with fifteen major states of India with respect to their infrastructure index (2009-10). It has been found that, the state Gujarat obtains second rank with respect to Weighted Aggregate Economic Infrastructure Index as well as Weighted Aggregate Infrastructure Index (only after Haryana). The comparatively better economic infrastructure due to Gujarat's improved transportation, communication, electricity infrastructure is the reason behind it. Again, the state obtains fourth rank with respect to Weighted Aggregate Social Infrastructure Index (after Kerala, Karnataka and Tamil Nadu). The comparatively low education infrastructure and health infrastructure (with respect to number of medical institutions per 100 sq. km. of area) are the reasons behind it.

- It has been found that the trend of per capita NSDP (at factor cost and constant prices) is increasing in the state Gujarat for the time period 1980-81 to 2009-10. It has been also found that, Gujarat's economic growth is higher than India's average economic growth in the given time period except for the years 1987-88 and 1991-92.

In the case of district-wise analysis of the state Gujarat it has been found that, with respect to **'Weighted Aggregate Index of Economic Growth'** (1991), the districts Ahmedabad, Gandhinagar, Surat, Vadodara, Rajkot, Valsad and Kachchh were under high category, the districts Kheda, Mahesana, Bhavnagar, Junagadh and Jamnagar were under medium category and the rest of the districts (Sabar Kantha, Bharuch Amreli, Surendranagar, Banas Kantha, Panch Mahals and The Dangs) were under low category. In 2000-01, the districts Ahmedabad, Vadodara, Surat, Valsad and Gandhinagar were under high category, the districts Kheda, Mahesana, Rajkot, Bhavnagar, Junagadh, Bharuch, Jamnagar, Kachchh, Porbandar, Anand and Navsari were under medium category and the districts Sabar Kantha, Amreli, Surendranagar, Banas Kantha, Panch Mahals, The Dangs, Patan, Narmada and Dahod were under low category with respect to this indicator. Similarly, in 2009-10, the districts Ahmedabad, Gandhinagar, Surat, Vadodara, Rajkot and Valsad were under high category, the districts Kheda, Mahesana, Sabar Kantha, Bhavnagar, Junagadh, Bharuch, Jamnagar, Anand and Navsari were under medium category and the rest of the districts (Amreli, Surendranagar, Banas Kantha, Panch Mahals, Kachchh, The Dangs, Patan, Porbandar, Narmada and Dahod) were under low category with respect to this indicator. After comparing the performances of the districts with respect to 'Weighted Aggregate Index of Economic Growth' between the two time points 2000-01 and 2009-10, it has been found that the districts– Surat, Rajkot, Mahesana, Kheda, Bhavnagar, Jamnagar, Junagadh, Sabar Kantha, Banas Kantha and Narmada improved their ranks and the districts Vadodara, Valsad, Gandhinagar, Bharuch, Porbandar, Navasari, Anand, Kachchh and Dahod deteriorated with respect to their ranks between the given time points. The district Porbandar was one of the districts whose rank has diminished severely between these two time points. It obtained eighth rank in 2000-01 and deteriorated to 19th in 2009-10. There are some districts which improved their categories with respect to this indicator between the two time points– the district Rajkot which was under medium category in 2000-01 shifted to high category in 2009-10 and the district Sabar Kantha which was under low category in 2000-01 shifted to medium category in 2009-10 with respect to this indicator. Again, there were two districts– Kachchh and Porbandar which deteriorated with respect to their categories and shifted from medium to low category between 2000-01 and 2009-10 with respect to this indicator.

- In Gujarat, as the district-wise data of per capita income or expenditure is not available, nine indicators of economic growth related to banking, agriculture and industry has been considered to calculate weighted aggregate index of economic growth.

It has been found that, with respect to **'Weighted Composite Banking Index'** in 1991, there were five districts- Ahmedabad, Gandhinagar, Vadodara, Valsad and Kachchh under high category, other five districts– Kheda, Surat, Rajkot, Junagarh, Jamnagar were under medium category and rest of the nine districts Mahesana, Sabar Kantha, Bhavnagar, Bharuch, Amreli, Surendranagar, Banas Kantha, Panch Mahals and The Dangs under low category. In 2000-01, the districts Ahmedabad, Vadodara, Surat, Valsad, Porbandar, Kachchh were under high category, the districts Gandhinagar, Rajkot, Bhavnagar, Jamnagar, Bharuch, Anand and Navsari were under medium category and rest of the districts (Kheda, Sabar Kantha, Mahesana, Junagadh, Amreli, Surendranagar, Banas Kantha, Panch Mahals, The Dangs, Patan, Narmada, Dahod) were under low category with respect to this indicator. Similarly, in 2009-10, the districts Ahmedabad, Gandhinagar, Surat, Vadodara, Rajkot were under high category, the districts Mahesana, Sabar Kantha, Valsad, Bhavnagar, Bharuch, Amreli, Jamnagar, Surendranagar, Banas Kantha, Panch Mahals, Patan, Porbandar, Anand, Navsari were under medium category and rest of the districts (Kheda, Junagadh, Panch Mahals, The Dangs, Narmada and Dahod) were under low category with respect to this indicator. After comparing the district-wise performances with respect to this indicator between the two time points (2000-01 and 2009-10), it has been found that, the districts Gandhinagar and Rajkot shifted from medium to high category, the districts Mahesana, Sabar Kantha, Surendranagar, Banas Kantha, Panch Mahals, Patan shifted from low to medium category. The district Porbandar deteriorated with respect to its category between these two time points and shifted from high category to medium category.

Further, with respect to **'Weighted composite agricultural index'**, it has been found that, in 1991 there were eight districts– Ahmedabad, Gandhinagar, Kheda, Surat, Vadodara, Mahesana, Valsad, Panch Mahals under high category, five districts– Sabar Kantha, Bhavnagar, Junagadh,

The Dangs and Kachchh under medium category and rest of the districts Rajkot, Bharuch, Amreli, Jamnagar, Surendranagar, Banas Kantha under low category. Most of the districts were concentrated under high and low category in 2000-01 and high and medium category in 2009-10 with respect to this indicator. In 2000-01, the districts Ahmedabad, Gandhinagar, Kheda, Surat, Mahesana, Valsad, Junagadh, Anand and Navsari were under high category, the districts Vadodara, Sabar Kantha, Panch Mahals, Porbandar and Dahod were under medium category and rest of the districts (Rajkot, Bhavnagar, Bharuch, Amreli, Jamnagar, Surendranagar, Banas Kantha, Kachchh, The Dangs, Patan and Narmada) under low category with respect to this indicator. In 2009-10, the districts Ahmedabad, Gandhinagar, Kheda, Surat, Rajkot, Junagadh, Anand, Dahod, Navsari were under high category, the districts Vadodara, Mahesana, Sabar Kantha, Valsad, Bhavnagar, Jamnagar, Banas Kantha, Panch Mahals, Porbandar, Narmada were under medium category and rest of the districts– Bharuch, Amreli, Kachchh, Surendranagar, The Dangs, Patan were under low category with respect to 'Weighted composite agricultural index'. After comparing the district-wise performances between the two time points (2000-01 and 2009-10), it has been found that, the district Rajkot improved its category and shifted from low to high category. The district Dahod shifted from medium to high, the other four districts Bhavnagar, Jamnagar, Banas Kantha and Narmada shifted from low to medium category between these two time points with respect to this indicator. There were only two districts– Mahesana and Valsad, which deteriorated with respect to their categories and shifted from high to medium category.

In 1991, there were four districts– Ahmedabad, Surat, Rajkot and Valsad were under high category, eight districts– Gandhinagar, Kheda, Vadodara, Mahesana, Bhavnagar, Bharuch, Jamnagar, Surendranagar under medium category and rest of the districts– Sabar Kantha, Junagadh, Amreli, Banas Kantha, Panch Mahals, Kachchh, The Dangs under low category with respect to **'Weighted Composite Industrial Index'**. In 2000-01, there were six districts (Ahmedabad, Kheda, Surat, Mahesana, Rajkot, Valsad) under high category, ten districts (Gandhinagar, Vadodara, Sabar Kantha, Bhavnagar, Junagadh, Bharuch, Amreli, Jamnagar, Surendranagar, Panch Mahals) under medium category and rest of the districts (Banas Kantha, Kachchh, The Dangs, Patan, Porbandar, Anand, Dahod, Navsari and Narmada) under low category with respect to this indicator. Though most of the districts were concentrated under medium and low category with respect to 'Weighted composite industrial index' in 2000-01, yet in 2009-10, the districts were equally distributed under high (nine districts– Ahmedabad, Kheda, Surat, Mahesana, Rajkot,

Valsad, Bhavnagar, Junagadh, Bharuch) and low (nine districts–Amreli, Banas Kantha, Kachchh, The Dangs, Patan, Porbandar, Anand, Narmada, Dahod) categories. The rest of the districts- Gandhinagar, Vadodara, Sabar Kantha, Jamnagar, Surendranagar, Panch Mahals and Navsari were under medium category with respect to this indicator. After comparing the district-wise performances with respect to this indicator between this two time points (2000-01 and 2009-10), it has been found that, there were four districts which improved their categories – Bhavnagar, Junagadh and Bharuch (shifted from medium to high category) and Navsari (shifted from low to medium category) between these two time points. The district Amreli deteriorated with respect to its category and shifted from medium (2000-01) to low category (2009-10).

- It has been found from time series analysis of the state Gujarat for the time period (1980-81 to 2009-10) that there is long run as well as short run bi-directional positive and significant causal relationship between log Weighted Aggregate Infrastructure Index and Economic Growth (log Per Capita NSDP at factor cost and constant prices) in the state Gujarat.
- The Human Development in the state Gujarat has been examined with the help of different relevant indicators related to human development and the state's position in India as well as between fifteen major states of India with respect to these components of human development. It has been found from the analysis that Gujarat is an economically growing state with Rs 48511 (third rank) Per Capita NSDP at factor cost and constant prices in 2009-10. The state has obtained fifth rank with respect to rural Monthly Per Capita Consumption Expenditure (MPCE) Rs1065.4 and seventh rank with respect to urban MPCE Rs 1914.7 (at current prices) among 15 major states. As per 2009-10 data there is 23 per cent below poverty line population in the state Gujarat against India's 29.8 per cent and the state has obtained sixth rank (in ascending order) among 15 major states of India. Gujarat has obtained first rank with lowest urban unemployment (18) and fifth rank with respect to rural unemployment (8) among 15 major states of India in 2009-10. As per 2007-08 data, Gujarat has obtained 14th rank (in ascending order) with 3.26 per cent of working children as compared to India's 1.92 per cent among 15 major states of India. Gujarat has attained 79.31 per cent literacy rate (as per 2011 census data). There is strong discrimination between male and female literacy rate in the state also. As per Census 2011 data, there are 87.23 per cent of male literates against 70.73 per cent of female literates in Gujarat. As per 2009-10 data, though the state Gujarat's gross enrollment ratio (GER) is high in primary classes (with 120.42 GER the state ranked third among 15 major states), yet it decreases to 86.51 in upper primary classes and the state has obtained seventh rank among 15 major states

of India. It may be high drop out rate in primary classes 25.66 in 2009-10 (Gujarat obtained tenth rank (in ascending order) among 15 major states) is a major reason behind it. In upper primary classes also the drop out rate of the state was very high 39.70 (ranked eighth among 15 major states) in 2009-10. The state has obtained ninth rank with pupil-teacher ratio 32 in primary classes and 33 in upper primary classes in 2009-10.

The state Gujarat has obtained sixth rank (in descending order) with 75.7 per cent of pucca houses among 15 major states of India in 2009. In 2009, with 93.4 per cent of households with electricity connection, Gujarat has obtained seventh rank among 15 major states of India. A large proportion of households (42.65 per cent) in Gujarat are without latrine facility (i.e. use either public latrine or in open) and the state has obtained sixth rank (in ascending order) among 15 major states. With 90.3 **per cent** (in 2011) of households have improved source of drinking water facility, the state Gujarat has obtained eighth rank (in descending order) among 15 major states of India.

Gujarat's Infant Mortality Rate (IMR) was 44 in 2010. The state has obtained seventh rank among 15 major states of India with respect to this indicator. The state Gujarat has obtained sixth rank among 15 major states of India with Life Expectancy at Birth (LEB) 69.1 in the time period 2006–10. Gujarat's Under Five Mortality Rate (U5MR) was 61 in 2009. The state has obtained ninth rank (in ascending order) among 15 major states of India with respect to this indicator. It is also a major concern that the state Gujarat has 69.7 per cent of Anaemic children against India's 69.5 per cent (in 2005-06). The state has obtained eighth rank among 15 major states of India with respect to this indicator. As per 2005-06 data, both in Gujarat and India 55.3 per cent of women were anaemic and the state has obtained eighth rank among 15 major states of India with respect to this indicator. Gujarat has also significantly high Maternal Mortality Rate (MMR) 148 (in 2007-09) and it has obtained sixth rank among 15 major states of India. Gujarat's 36.3 per cent of women are with B.M.I. less than 18.5 and the state has obtained ninth rank among 15 major states of India in 2005-06.

Again, with 38.77 per cent of malnourished children (0-5 years), Gujarat has obtained eighth rank and with 4.56 per cent of severely malnourished children Gujarat has obtained 14th rank among 15 major states [the state was only better than the state Bihar (25.94 per cent) with respect to severely malnourished children] in 2011. There were 56.6 per cent of children with complete vaccination in Gujarat (against India's 61 per cent) in 2009. The state has obtained 11th rank (in descending order) among 15 major states of India with respect to this indicator. The total fertility rate (TFR) of the state Gujarat in the time period 2008–10 was 2.5 (against India's 2.6) and ranked tenth (in ascending order) among 15 major states of India. As per Census 2011 it has been found that, Gujarat's sex ratio is very low 918 (against India's average 940) and the state has obtained 11th rank (in descending order) among 15 major states of India.

In Human Development Index, the state Gujarat obtained sixth rank in 1991 and has remained stagnant for the time points 1999-00 and 2007-08. Human Development Index is a composite index consist Health Index, Income Index and Education Index. Between the time points 1999-00 and 2007-08, whereas in health index Gujarat has improved its rank from eighth to sixth, in income index its rank has remained same i.e. fourth and in education index the state's rank has deteriorated from sixth to eighth. In this section 15 major states of India have been distributed into Virtuous Cycle, Lopsided Economic Growth, Lopsided Human Development and Vicious Cycle with respect to their categories in HDI and Economic Growth (per capita net state domestic product at factor cost and constant prices). It has been found that Gujarat was under Lopsided Economic Growth for all the three time points 1991, 1999-00 and 2007-08 with high Economic Growth but medium Human Development Index. It means Gujarat's Economic Growth is not transforming into Human Development and it may be due to comparatively low expenditure on health and education in Gujarat.

From district-wise analysis of the state Gujarat it has been found that, in 1991, the districts Ahmedabad, Gandhinagar, Surat, Vadodara, Rajkot, Valsad, Bharuch and Jamnagar were under high category, the districts Kheda, Bhavnagar, Junagadh, Amreli and Kachchh were under medium category and the remaining six districts (Sabar Kantha, Mahesana, Surendranagar, Panch Mahals, Banas Kantha and The Dangs) were under low category with respect to Human Development Index. In 2000-01, the districts Ahmedabad, Surat, Rajkot, Bharuch, Kachchh, Anand and Navsari were under high category, the districts Gandhinagar, Kheda, Vadodara, Valsad, Bhavnagar, Junagadh, Amreli, Jamnagar, Patan, Porbandar, Narmada were under medium category and the districts Mahesana, Sabar Kantha, Surendranagar, Banas Kantha, Panch Mahals, The Dangs and Dahod were under low category with respect to Human Development Index. Similarly, in 2009-10, with respect to HDI, the districts under high category were Ahmedabad, Gandhinagar, Bharuch, Amreli, Jamnagar, Anand, Narmada and Navsari, the districts under medium category were Vadodara, Rajkot, Valsad, Bhavnagar, Junagadh, Kachchh, Patan, Porbandar and the districts under low category were Kheda, Surat, Mahesana, Sabar Kantha, Surendranagar, Banas Kantha, Panch Mahals, The Dangs and Dahod.

By comparing the district-wise HDI between the two time points– 2000-01 and 2009-10, it has been found that HDI was consistently high for the districts Ahmedabad, Bharuch, Anand, and Navsari on one hand and the districts Mahesana, Sabar Kantha, Surendranagar, Banas Kantha, Dahod, The Dangs and Panch Mahals were always among the bottom liners on the other. Though the districts Gandhinagar, Jamnagar, Amreli and Narmada were under medium category of HDI in 2000-01, yet in 2009-10 they managed to shift under high category. Some interesting movements across the districts have been noticed over time. For instance, Surat started with an appreciable HDI scenario and it was under high category both in 1991 as well as 2000-01, but its performance declined considerably in 2009-10 and shifted to low category. The category of the districts Rajkot and Kachchh deteriorated and shifted from high to medium category between the years 2000-01 and 2009-10. The category of the district Kheda also declined and it shifted from medium to low category between the time points 2000-01 and 2009-10. By comparing the ranks of the districts with respect to HDI between these two time points (2000-01 and 2009-10), it has been found that, some districts which improved their ranks were- Ahmedabad, Gandhinagar, Kheda, Vadodara, Mahesana, Bhavnagar, Junagadh, Amreli, Jamnagar, Banas Kantha, The Dangs, Patan, Anand and Narmada. Again, the districts which deteriorated with respect to their ranks in HDI score between the given time points were– Surat, Sabar Kantha, Rajkot, Valsad, Bharuch, Surendranagar, Panch Mahals, Kachchh, Porbandar, Dahod and Navsari.

- District-wise Human Development Indices have been calculated with normalised values of the three indicators, namely, Per Capita Bank Deposits; Educational Attainment Index and Infant Mortality Rate. It has been found that with respect to the indicator 'Per capita bank deposit index' in 1991, there were six districts– Ahmedabad, Gandhinagar, Kheda, Vadodara, Valsad, Kachchh under high category, four districts– Surat, Rajkot, Junagadh, Jamnagar under medium category and rest of the nine districts (Mahesana, Sabar Kantha, Bhavnagar, Bharuch, Amreli, Surendranagar, Banas Kantha, Panch Mahals and The Dangs) were under low category. It has been observed that, in 2000-01 and 2009-10 the districts Ahmedabad, Gandhinagar, Vadodara, Kachchh, Navsari, Porbandar, Anand were under high category, the districts Kheda, Surat, Rajkot, Valsad, Bhavnagar, Bharuch, Jamnagar were under medium category and the districts Sabar Kantha, Amreli, Surendranagar, Banas Kantha, Panch Mahals, The Dangs, Patan, Narmada and Dahod were under low category with respect to this indicator. The district Mahesana which was under low category with respect to this indicator in 2000-01 shifted to medium category in 2009-10. Again, the district Junagadh which was under medium category with respect to this indicator in 2000-01 shifted to low category in 2009-10.

In the case of 'Educational Attainment Index' (1991), it has been found that the districts were almost equally distributed under high (six districts– Ahmedabad, Gandhinagar, Kheda, Surat, Rajkot, Valsad), medium (seven districts– Vadodara, Mahesana, Sabar Kantha, Junagadh, Bharuch, Amreli, Jamnagar) and low category (six districts– Bhavnagar, Surendranagar, Banas Kantha, Panch Mahals, Kachchh and The Dangs) categories. In 2000-01, most of the districts were concentrated under high and medium category with respect to this indicator. The districts Ahmedabad, Gandhinagar, Kheda, Surat, Mahesana, Sabar Kantha, Bharuch, Anand and Navsari were under high category, the districts Vadodara, Rajkot, Valsad, Junagadh, Amreli, Panch Mahals, The Dangs, Patan, Porbandar were under medium category and rest of the districts (Bhavnagar, Jamnagar, Surendranagar, Banas Kantha, Kachchh, Narmada and Dahod) were under low category with respect to educational attainment index in 2000-01. In 2009-10, there were eight districts– Gandhinagar, Kheda, Mahesana, The Dangs, Amreli, Anand, Narmada and Navsari under high category, the other eight districts– Ahmedabad, Sabar Kantha, Bhavnagar, Bharuch, Jamnagar, Banas Kantha, Panch Mahals and Patan under medium category and the rest of the districts Surat, Vadodara, Surendranagar, Rajkot, Valsad, Kachchh, Porbandar, Junagadh, Dahod under low category with respect to 'Educational Attainment Index'. After comparing the district-wise performances with respect to this indicator, it has been found that, the districts Ahmedabad, Sabar Kantha and Bharuch which were under high category with respect to this indicator in 2000-01 shifted to medium category in 2009-10. The district Surat shifted from high category in 2000-01 to low category in 2009-10. There were two districts Amreli and The Dangs which were under medium category with respect to educational attainment index in 2000-01 shifted to high category in 2009-10.

Further, with respect to 'Infant Mortality Rate index' in 1991, there were eight districts– Ahmedabad, Surat, Rajkot, Valsad, Bhavnagar, Bharuch, Amreli and Jamnagar under high category, other nine districts – Gandhinagar, Kheda, Mahesana, Sabar Kantha, Surendranagar, Banas Kantha, Panch Mahals, Kachchh and The Dangs under low category and rest of the districts– Vadodara and Junagadh under medium category. In 2000-01, there were nine districts- Surat, Rajkot, Valsad, Bhavnagar, Bharuch, Jamnagar, Patan, Anand and Narmada under high cayegory, six districts- Ahmedabad, Gandhinagar, Sabar Kantha, Junagadh, Amreli and Kachchh under medium category and rest of the districts- Kheda, Vadodara, Mahesana, Surendranagar, Banas Kantha, Panch Mahals,

The Dangs, Porbandar, Dahod and Navsari under low category with respect to this indicator. In 2009-10, the districts Ahmedabad, Surat, Rajkot, Valsad, Bhavnagar, Junagadh, Bharuch, Patan, Anand, Narmada and Jamnagar were under high category, the districts Gandhinagar, Sabar Kantha, Amreli and Kachchh were under medium category and the districts Kheda, Vadodara, Mahesana, Surendranagar, Banas Kantha, Panch Mahals, The Dangs, Porbandar, Dahod and Navsari were under low category with respect to 'Infant Mortality Rate index'. After comparing the district-wise performances with respect to this indicator, it has been found that, the districts– Ahmedabad and Junagadh which were under medium category with respect to this indicator in 2000-01 shifted to high category in 2009-10.

- It has been found from the district-wise analysis (to examine the relationship between 'Weighted Aggregate Infrastructure Index' and 'Weighted Aggregate Index of Economic Growth' in Gujarat by comparing the score or category of the districts with respect to these two indicators between the two time points– 2000-01 and 2009-10) that the districts Ahmedabad, Gandhinagar, Surat, Vadodara, Mahesana, Sabar Kantha, Valsad, Kachchh, Porbandar, Anand, Navsari, Junagadh, Amreli, Surendranagar, The Dangs, Narmada, Patan, Dahod, Kheda, Bharuch, Bhavnagar have positive relationship between these two indicators. According to this analysis there were four districts– Panch Mahals, Jamnagar, Banas Kantha and Rajkot which have no link between these two indicators, neither category-wise nor change in the direction of aggregate score-wise.

Further, it has been observed from the cross district regression analysis between 'log Weighted Aggregate Infrastructure Index' and 'log Weighted Aggregate Index of Economic Growth' that there is significant positive relationship between these two variables both in 2000-01 and 2009-10. Though, the impact of 'log Weighted Aggregate Index of Economic Growth' on 'log Weighted Aggregate Infrastructure Index' is positive, significant and increasing (increased from 0.352 in 2000-01 to 0.760 in 2009-10) over time (between 2000-01 and 2009-10), yet the impact of 'log Weighted Aggregate Infrastructure Index' on 'log Weighted Aggregate Index of Economic Growth' is positive and significant and decreasing over time (decreased from 1.086 in 2000-01 to 0.305 in 2009-10). So, Weighted Aggregate Index of Economic Growth is translating into Weighted Aggregate Infrastructure Index but not the other way round. It may be the comparatively greater influence of other factor on economic growth is the reason behind it.

- It has been found from the district-wise analysis [to examine the relationship between 'Human Development Index (HDI)' and 'Weighted

Aggregate Index of Economic Growth' in Gujarat by comparing the score or category of the districts with respect to these two indicators between the two time points 2000-01 and 2009-10] that except the districts Rajkot, Kheda, Sabar Kantha, Patan, Surat and Anand all the other nineteen districts have achieved the direct positive relationship between these two indicators.

It has been observed from the cross district regression analysis between 'log Human Development Index' and 'log Weighted Aggregate Index of Economic Growth' that there is significant, positive relationship between these two variables in both the time points 2000-01 and 2009-10. The impact of log Human Development Index on log Weighted Aggregate Index of Economic Growth is positive, significant and increasing between the time points 2000-01 and 2009-10 (co-efficient of log Human Development Index has increased from 0.217 in 2000-01 to 0.528 in 2009-10). So, Human Development Index is translating into Weighted Aggregate Index of Economic Growth. It has also been found that Weighted Aggregate Index of Economic Growth elasticity of Human Development Index is positive, significant and decreasing (decreased from 0.656 to 0.321) between the years 2000-01 and 2009-10 i.e. Weighted Aggregate Index of Economic Growth is not translating into Human Development Index. It may be the comparatively lower expenditure on education and health is the reason behind this.

- It has been found from the analysis of trend and pattern of public expenditure on social and economic services in Gujarat for the time period 1991-92 to 2009-10 that, the state Gujarat experienced comparatively high social service expenditure (as compared to economic service expenditure) only four years- 2003-04, 2004-05, 2007-08 and 2009-10 in the given time period. In 2009-10 the state Gujarat, with high social service expenditure (as compared to its economic service expenditure) has obtained fourth rank among 15 major states of India. Gujarat has experienced fluctuating trend with respect to expenditure on education, sports, arts, culture- varied between 7.55 per cent and 17.45 per cent (of total public expenditure) in the time period 1991-92 to 2009-10. It has been decreased from 13.85 per cent in 1991-92 to 13.78 per cent in 2009-10. The state Gujarat has obtained 12th rank among 15 major states with respect to expenditure on education, sports, arts, culture (as percentage of total public expenditure) in 2009-10. Gujarat's expenditure on education, sports, arts, culture (as percentage of total expenditure) has not only been decreased between the years 1991-92 and 2009-10, it was also lower than eleven major states in India in 2009-10.

It has been found that, Gujarat's expenditure on health, family welfare varied between 1.69 per cent and 4.56 per cent (of total public expenditure) in the given time period (1991-92 to 2009-10). It has increased from 3.66 per cent in 1991-92 to 3.79 per cent in 2009-10. Gujarat has obtained ninth rank among 15 major states of India with respect to its expenditure on health and family welfare (as percentage of total public expenditure) in 2009-10. So Gujarat's expenditure on health, family welfare (as percentage of total expenditure) was lower than eight major states in India in 2009-10.

It has been found that Gujarat experienced highly fluctuating trend varied between 1.84 per cent and 12.21 per cent in the given time period (1991-92 to 2009-10) with respect to the percentage of total public expenditure on water supply, sanitation, housing and urban development. It has increased from 3.19 per cent in 1991-92 to 12.21 per cent in 2009-10. Gujarat has obtained first rank among 15 major states with highest expenditure on water supply, sanitation, housing and urban development (as percentage of total public expenditure) in 2009-10. So Gujarat's expenditure on water supply, sanitation, housing and urban development (as percentage of total expenditure) has not only been increased significantly between the years 1991-92 and 2009-10, it was also highest among fifteen major states in India in 2009-10.

It has been found that, Gujarat's expenditure on social welfare and nutrition varied between 1.48 per cent and 5.96 per cent in the time period 1991-92 to 2009-10. Though, it has increased from 2.55 per cent in 1991-92 to 3.20 per cent (as percentage of total public expenditure) in 2009-10, yet the state Gujarat has obtained 11th rank among 15 major states of India with comparatively low expenditure on social welfare and nutrition (as percentage of total expenditure) in 2009-10.

Gujarat's expenditure on economic services (as percentage of total public expenditure) was significantly higher than its social service expenditure for all the years in the time period 1991-92 to 2009-10, except in– 2003-04, 2004-05, 2007-08 and 2009-10. In 2009-10 the state Gujarat obtained sixth rank among 15 major states with comparatively lower expenditure on economic services (31.07 per cent) than social services (35.89 per cent).

Gujarat's expenditure on agriculture and allied services (as percentage of total public expenditure) varied between 1.71 per cent and 5.48 per cent in the time period 1991-92 to 2009-10. It has increased from 4.26 per cent in 1991-92 to 4.36 per cent in 2009-10. Gujarat has obtained ninth rank among 15 major states with respect to this indicator in 2009-10. So Gujarat's expenditure on agriculture and allied services (as percentage of total expenditure) was lower than eight major states in India in 2009-10.

Gujarat's expenditure on irrigation and flood control (as percentage of total public expenditure) was highly fluctuating– varied between 4.26 per cent and 15.93 per cent in the time period 1991-92 to 2009-10. It has decreased from 11.75 per cent in 1991-92 to 7.58 per cent in 2009-10 and the state Gujarat obtained third rank among 15 major states of India with respect to this indicator in 2009-10.

Gujarat has experienced highly fluctuating trend with respect to the expenditure on energy (as percentage of total public expenditure) also. It varied between 5.46 per cent and 14.76 per cent in the time period 1991-92 to 2009-10. It has decreased from 10.6 per cent in 1991-92 to 6.17 per cent in 2009-10 and the state Gujarat has obtained sixth rank among 15 major states of India with respect to this indicator.

It has been found that, Gujarat's expenditure on transport and communication (as percentage of total public expenditure) varied between 1.94 per cent and 7.35 per cent in the time period 1991-92 to 2009-10. It has increased from 4.69 per cent in 1991-92 to 7.35 per cent in 2009-10 and the state Gujarat has obtained third rank among 15 major states of India with respect to this indicator in 2009-10.

So, after comparing Gujarat's position among 15 major states with respect to its expenditure on different social and economic services in 2009-10, it has been concluded that Gujarat's position was not good with respect to its expenditure (as percentage of total public expenditure) on education, sports, arts and culture, health and family welfare, social welfare and nutrition and agriculture and allied services.

7.2 Policy Implications

1. It has been found that Gujarat's Road length per 100 sq. km. of area, Gross Irrigated area as percentage of gross cropped area, Number of post offices per 100 sq. km. of area, Number of scheduled commercial banks per 100 sq. km. of area, Number of schools per 100 sq. km. of area and Number of medical institutions for 100 sq. km. of area are below India's average for the time period 1980-81 to 2009-10. Though, Gujarat obtained second rank with respect to its 'Weighted Aggregate Economic aggregate Infrastructure Index' and 'Weighted Aggregate Infrastructure Index' (only after Haryana), yet it obtained fourth rank with respect to 'Weighted Aggregate Social Infrastructure Index' (after three states– Kerala, Karnataka and Tamil Nadu). So, investment programme needs to be chalked out by Gujarat government to increase its infrastructure facilities with respect to these indicators.

2. Though Gujarat's literacy rate increased to 79.31 per cent as per Census 2011 data yet the state's gender disparity in literacy rate is high- the male and female literacy rate in Gujarat are 87.23 per cent and

70.73 per cent respectively. Again, the state's sex ratio is 918 which is lower than India's average (940). Percentage of child labour is also high in the state. Though the state's enrollment ratio in primary section is very high yet it is comparatively low in high and higher secondary classes because of its high drop out rate. To improve the state's education scenario, with child education, female and adult education is also required. It is a well-known fact that only an educated person can understand the requirement of education for his or her children. As the prosperity of future generation mostly depends on women, women education and empowerment need to be given more importance. The educated parents can also understand the requirement of female child and also have the knowledge about the requirement of family planning. This will not only improve sex ratio in Gujarat but also decrease the percentage increment in population.

Keeping in view the disadvantageous position of Gujarat population on the front of education and sex ratio, it is suggested that a comprehensive education policy should be evolved to take care of these hurdles in attaining still faster growth rate in the state.

3. Though there is impressive decline in infant mortality rate (IMR), under five mortality rate (U5MR) and maternal mortality rate (MMR) in Gujarat over the period under study, yet the figures turn unattractive when compared with the respective rates achieved by the state Kerala (the state with lowest IMR, U5MR and MMR among 15 major states of India). As compared to Kerala, the state Gujarat has almost 3.42 times high IMR (2011), 4.36 times high U5MR (2009) and 1.83 times high MMR (2007-09). So, there is urgent need to improve the health facilities to obtain IMR, U5MR and MMR comparable with Kerala. It is also found from the study that prevalence of calorie undernourishment (per cent), prevalence of under-weight children is high in Gujarat. The percentage of anaemic children and women, percentage of women with Body-Mass Index <18.5 are also high in Gujarat. So policy-makers need to increase attention to nutrition and availability of quality food to needy people. As per 2009 data, Gujarat's percentage of completely immunised children (12 to 23 months) is significantly lower than India's average and the state obtains 11th rank with respect to this indicator among 15 major states. So, Gujarat needs to invest more to increase its percentage of completely immunised children.

4. Though Gujarat's position vis-à-vis fifteen major states of India is encouraging with respect to toilet facility, yet nearly two-fifth of population is not having the latrine facilities within their premises. So, policy- makers need to increase attention to increase toilet facilities in the state. The possible help either in the form of subsidy or loan or both should be extended to all beneficiaries who want to have toilets in their homes irrespective of income groups. Interest-free bank loans should be provided to all beneficiaries who want to have toilets in their houses. The programme of construction of toilets in rural areas is linked to making people aware of sanitation standards and the adverse health impact of unsanitary conditions which require house-to-house contacts and follow-up. This can only be done effectively by the well-coordinated efforts of NGOs and government. The role of NGOs is, thus, very crucial in the implementation of the sanitation programme.

5. Both in 1999-00 as well as 2007-08, the state Gujarat has obtained sixth rank in HDI among 15 major states of India. With respect to the ingredients of HDI, though Gujarat obtained fourth rank with respect to its income index for both of the two time points– 1999-00 and 2007-08, the state obtained eighth rank with respect to education index and sixth rank with respect to health index in 2007-08. It may be the comparatively low health index and education index are the major reasons behind Gujarat's sixth rank with respect to HDI score among 15 major states. So increasing, effective public investment is required to make Gujarat's social infrastructure (education and health) stronger and to improve human development.

6. Glaring disparities on the basis of district-wise availability of infrastructure facilities, economic growth and human development were noticed in this study. It is suggested to evolve a development policy to target to remove the drawbacks in various districts. For this, district-wise public investment programme has to be chalked out. It is found that the public expenditure in Gujarat on social as well as economic services registered a fluctuating pattern showing that there has not been a consistent policy of public investment in the state. It is suggested that a long run policy, keeping in view the emerging requirements, should be chalked out in the state in order to achieve steady growth in respective sector.

7. It has been found that Gujarat's public expenditure (as percentage of total public expenditure) was comparatively low on education, sports, arts and culture, health and family welfare, social security, welfare and nutrition and agriculture and allied services. The state obtained 12th, 9th, 11th and 9th among 15 major states with respect to these indicators. So Gujarat needs more investment in these sectors to improve its human development as well as agricultural upliftment. The Gujarat government may explore the possibilities of attracting private investment in these sectors to plug the gap between required and actual investment (generally public investment).

8. It has been found that, Kerala obtained first rank among 15 major states with respect to weighted aggregate index of social infrastructure index in 2009-10. The state Kerala obtained first rank with highest MPCE (both in rural and urban), literacy rate (in overall as well as with respect to male and female), Sex ratio and human development index. Again, it has been also found that Kerala has lowest score with respect to poverty ratio, percentage of population have no latrine within premises use, infant mortality rate, under five mortality rate, percentage of working children, percentage of anaemic children (0-5 years), percentage of anaemic women, maternal mortality rate, percentage of women with B.M.I.<18.5, total fertility rate. Kerala was under virtuous cycle with high economic growth as well as high human development index for the two time points (1999-00 and 2007-08). So, Kerala can be considered as model state for social and human development. The state Gujarat can follow different related policies of the state Kerala (which are suitable for the state) to achieve high human development and still higher economic growth.

Appendices

Appendix 1 : Relative Index of Transportation, Communication, Education and Health of Gujarat (with respect to India)

Year	*Relative Index of Transportation*	*Relative Index of Communication*	*Relative Index of Education*	*Relative Index of Health*
1980-81	112.14	143.39	81.26	109.75
1981-82	116.10	147.18	82.56	111.62
1982-83	117.16	149.84	84.62	112.24
1983-84	117.29	150.48	87.44	119.63
1984-85	116.21	150.63	87.44	121.14
1985-86	115.28	149.77	86.48	127.75
1986-87	114.41	149.70	86.02	126.53
1987-88	113.04	142.66	86.19	121.09
1988-89	105.70	142.97	89.62	127.06
1989-90	106.39	143.01	90.08	123.92
1990-91	108.50	139.09	88.73	121.10
1991-92	108.51	136.70	89.12	137.53
1992-93	107.87	135.63	91.78	154.37
1993-94	108.06	133.38	94.31	150.75
1994-95	107.28	131.18	92.36	157.20

(Contd.)

(Contd.Appendix -1)

Year	Relative Index of Transportation	Relative Index of Communication	Relative Index of Education	Relative Index of Health
1995-96	104.30	127.85	89.58	156.74
1996-97	103.40	123.95	89.30	149.22
1997-98	105.84	123.02	82.90	148.66
1998-99	104.89	122.18	82.38	145.99
1999-00	121.06	123.82	82.08	144.68
2000-01	120.61	125.02	82.16	144.62
2001-02	120.26	123.14	81.68	145.61
2002-03	116.85	124.90	84.28	145.49
2003-04	115.76	120.21	83.52	136.80
2004-05	110.32	119.55	84.91	118.82
2005-06	110.17	115.06	88.83	108.88
2006-07	110.54	114.69	89.43	101.47
2007-08	110.40	112.65	85.88	94.56
2008-09	109.14	110.33	83.32	90.85
2009-10	107.93	105.70	88.58	87.44

Source: Self calculated.

Appendix 2: Relative Aggregate Average Economic Infrastructure Index, Relative Aggregate Average Social Infrastructure Index and Relative Aggregate Average Infrastructure Index in Gujarat (with respect to India)

Year	*Relative Aggregate Average Economic Infrastructure Index*	*Relative Aggregate Average Social Infrastructure Index*	*Relative Aggregate Average Infrastructure Index*
1980-81	124.76	95.51	114.12
1981-82	127.15	97.09	116.22
1982-83	126.60	98.43	116.36
1983-84	128.02	103.54	119.12
1984-85	125.52	104.29	117.80
1985-86	125.60	107.12	118.88
1986-87	123.80	106.28	117.43
1987-88	123.36	103.64	116.19
1988-89	119.80	108.34	115.63
1989-90	120.58	107.00	115.64
1990-91	120.23	104.92	114.66
1991-92	124.49	113.33	120.43
1992-93	124.07	123.08	123.71
1993-94	123.50	122.53	123.15
1994-95	122.24	124.78	123.16

(Contd.)

(Contd.Appendix -2)

Year	*Relative Aggregate Average Economic Infrastructure Index*	*Relative Aggregate Average Social Infrastructure Index*	*Relative Aggregate Average Infrastructure Index*
1995-96	122.11	123.16	122.49
1996-97	120.72	119.26	120.19
1997-98	123.89	115.78	120.94
1998-99	123.96	114.18	120.41
1999-00	132.65	113.38	125.64
2000-01	132.36	113.39	125.46
2001-02	131.34	113.64	124.91
2002-03	129.70	114.88	124.31
2003-04	126.87	110.16	120.79
2004-05	136.65	101.87	124.00
2005-06	133.43	98.85	120.86
2006-07	131.24	95.45	118.23
2007-08	129.37	90.22	115.13
2008-09	128.67	87.08	113.55
2009-10	128.34	88.01	113.68

Source: Self calculated.

Appendix 3 : Per Capita NSDP at Factor Cost and Constant Prices (base:1999-00) in Gujarat, India and Relative Index

YEAR	GUJARAT	INDIA	Relative Index
1980-81	9157	8594	106.55
1981-82	9837	8910	110.40
1982-83	9478	8940	106.02
1983-84	11059	9464	116.85
1984-85	10823	9609	112.63
1985-86	10318	9782	105.48
1986-87	10743	9979	107.66
1987-88	9374	10083	92.97
1988-89	12919	10916	118.35
1989-90	12480	11342	110.03
1990-91	12466	11724	106.33
1991-92	11239	11600	96.89
1992-93	14590	11989	121.69
1993-94	13896	12379	112.25
1994-95	16667	12909	129.11

(Contd.)

(Contd.Appendix -3)

YEAR	*GUJARAT*	*INDIA*	*Relative Index*
1995-96	16601	13582	122.23
1996-97	17932	14400	124.53
1997-98	18767	14700	127.67
1998-99	19484	15372	126.75
1999-00	18864	16035	117.64
2000-01	17227	16393	105.09
2001-02	18200	16963	107.29
2002-03	19509	17278	112.91
2003-04	22387	18482	121.13
2004-05	23346	19525	119.57
2005-06	26268	21055	124.76
2006-07	28335	22769	124.45
2007-08	31780	24426	130.11
2008-09	33547	25630	130.89
2009-10	36665	27101	135.29

Source: Central Statistical Organisation.
(Relative Index is Self Calculated)

Appendix 4: District-wise Data Regarding Components of Human Development Index in Gujarat (1991)

Districts	*Per Capita Bank Deposit Index*	*Educational Attainment Index*	*Infant Mortality Rate Index*
Ahmedabad	0.921	0.745	0.659
Gandhinagar	1.000	1.000	0.182
Kheda	0.550	0.586	0.295
Surat	0.526	0.567	0.636
Vadodara	0.735	0.483	0.523
Mahesana	0.115	0.524	0.136
Sabar Kantha	0.018	0.472	0.273
Rajkot	0.413	0.576	0.773
Valsad	0.608	0.579	0.705
Bhavnagar	0.202	0.324	0.909
Junagadh	0.310	0.473	0.591
Bharuch	0.169	0.508	1.000
Amreli	0.075	0.383	0.636
Jamnagar	0.431	0.413	0.795
Surendranagar	0.078	0.308	0.182
Banas Kantha	0.005	0.000	0.182
Panch Mahals	0.015	0.221	0.205
Kachchh	0.933	0.276	0.205
The Dangs	0.000	0.326	0.000

Source: Self calculated.

Note: For normalisation of the indicators, as the maximum and minimum values of all the three indicators have been chosen from the district-wise values of these indicators in the given time point, the district with maximum value with respect to any indicator get the index value 1.000 and the district with minimum value with respect to any indicator get the index value 0.000.

Appendix 5 : District-wise Data Regarding Components of Human Development Index in Gujarat (2000-01)

Districts	*Per Capita Bank Deposit Index*	*Educational Attainment Index*	*Infant Mortality Rate Index*
Ahmedabad	0.840	0.660	0.703
Gandhinagar	0.490	0.550	0.459
Kheda	0.238	0.520	0.243
Surat	0.321	0.530	0.811
Vadodara	0.694	0.380	0.378
Mahesana	0.081	0.700	0.000
Sabar Kantha	0.039	0.510	0.432
Rajkot	0.374	0.390	0.919
Valsad	0.265	0.300	0.865
Bhavnagar	0.238	0.250	0.919
Junagadh	0.163	0.280	0.703
Bharuch	0.262	1.000	1.000

(Contd.)

(Contd. Appendix -5)

Districts	*Per Capita Bank Deposit Index*	*Educational Attainment Index*	*Infant Mortality Rate Index*
Amreli	0.086	0.340	0.595
Jamnagar	0.368	0.160	0.946
Surendranagar	0.076	0.180	0.378
Banas Kantha	0.000	0.000	0.000
Panch Mahals	0.037	0.340	0.378
Kachchh	1.000	0.150	0.405
The Dangs	0.013	0.380	0.189
Patan	0.093	0.360	0.973
Porbandar	0.768	0.290	0.378
Anand	0.636	0.550	0.703
Narmada	0.002	0.270	0.946
Dohad	0.003	0.150	0.243
Navsari	0.833	0.590	0.378

Source: Self calculated.

Appendix 6: District-wise Data Regarding Components of Human Development Index in Gujarat (2009-10)

Districts	*Per Capita Bank Deposit Index*	*Educational Attainment Index*	*Infant Mortality Rate Index*
Ahmedabad	1.000	0.570	0.704
Gandhinagar	0.701	0.690	0.444
Kheda	0.179	0.680	0.222
Surat	0.300	0.000	0.778
Vadodara	0.723	0.340	0.370
Mahesana	0.185	0.860	0.000
Sabar Kantha	0.051	0.520	0.407
Rajkot	0.325	0.200	0.889
Valsad	0.255	0.300	0.852
Bhavnagar	0.170	0.360	0.889
Junagadh	0.131	0.320	0.704
Bharuch	0.295	0.520	1.000
Amreli	0.081	0.930	0.593

(Contd.)

(Contd. Appendix -6)

Districts	*Per Capita Bank Deposit Index*	*Educational Attainment Index*	*Infant Mortality Rate Index*
Jamnagar	0.289	0.380	0.926
Surendranagar	0.079	0.280	0.370
Banas Kantha	0.009	0.560	0.000
Panch Mahals	0.041	0.460	0.333
Kachchh	0.649	0.040	0.407
The Dangs	0.017	0.790	0.185
Patan	0.055	0.420	0.889
Porbandar	0.505	0.220	0.370
Anand	0.532	0.890	0.704
Narmada	0.017	1.000	0.926
Dohad	0.000	0.200	0.222
Navsari	0.568	0.700	0.370

Source: Self calculated.

Appendix 7: District-wise Weighted Composite Index of Different Components of Infrastructure in Gujarat (1991)

Districts of Gujarat	*Weighted Composite Index of Transportation*	*Weighted Index of Irrigation*	*Weighted Index of Drinking Water*	*Weighted Index of Electricity*
Ahmedabad	0.049	0.748	0.36485	0.1721
Gandhinagar	-0.243	0.859	0.36485	0.1721
Kheda	0.035	0.710	0.36485	0.1718
Surat	0.012	0.557	0.36456	0.1701
Vadodara	-0.007	0.410	0.36485	0.1664
Mahesana	-0.056	0.654	0.36485	0.1721
Sabar Kantha	-0.177	0.461	0.36380	0.1711
Rajkot	-0.137	0.279	0.36485	0.1721
Valsad	-0.006	0.413	0.36485	0.1719
Bhavnagar	-0.175	0.269	0.36485	0.1718
Junagadh	-0.149	0.248	0.36485	0.1608
Bharuch	-0.259	0.192	0.36485	0.1638

(Contd.)

(Contd. Appendix -7)

Districts of Gujarat	*Weighted Composite Index of Transportation*	*Weighted Index of Irrigation*	*Weighted Index of Drinking Water*	*Weighted Index of Electricity*
Amreli	-0.260	0.166	0.36485	0.1716
Jamnagar	-0.271	0.223	0.36434	0.1716
Surendranagar	-0.342	0.180	0.36485	0.1714
Banas Kantha	-0.222	0.448	0.36369	0.1670
Panch Mahals	-0.062	0.239	0.36467	0.1643
Kachchh	-0.687	0.216	0.36361	0.1661
The Dangs	-1.115	0.007	0.36369	0.1721
MAXIMUM VALUES	-0.08	0.500	0.36480	0.17128
MINIMUM VALUES	-0.35	0.267	0.36432	0.16771

Source: Self calculated.

Appendix 7: District-wise Weighted Composite Index of Different Components of Infrastructure in Gujarat (1991) Contd.

Districts of Gujarat	*Weighted Composite Index of Banking Facilities*	*Weighted Composite Index of Educational Facilities*	*Weighted Composite Index of Health Facilities*
Ahmedabad	1.3632	1.465	0.9987
Gandhinagar	0.4592	0.868	0.4882
Kheda	0.9403	1.531	1.1341
Surat	0.8378	1.066	1.9452
Vadodara	0.8512	1.152	0.9554
Mahesana	0.5030	1.084	0.9315
Sabar Kantha	0.3389	1.267	0.6225
Rajkot	0.4985	0.800	0.6201
Valsad	1.0350	1.161	1.0508
Bhavnagar	0.3756	0.665	0.7224
Junagadh	0.4387	0.841	0.8568
Bharuch	0.3349	0.725	0.5886

(Contd.)

(Contd. Appendix -7)

Districts of Gujarat	*Weighted Composite Index of Banking Facilities*	*Weighted Composite Index of Educational Facilities*	*Weighted Composite Index of Health Facilities*
Amreli	0.3619	0.677	0.6349
Jamnagar	0.2765	0.584	0.5328
Surendranagar	0.2344	0.577	0.9247
Banas Kantha	0.2429	0.665	0.4005
Panch Mahals	0.4270	1.336	0.3294
Kachchh	0.1158	0.428	0.4179
The Dangs	0.2395	0.630	-0.0087
MAXIMUM VALUES	0.68453	1.08599	0.94927
MINIMUM VALUES	0.35489	0.75857	0.53975

Source: Self calculated.

Appendix 8: District-wise Weighted Composite Index of Different Components Related to Economic Growth in Gujarat (1991)

Districts of Gujarat	*Weighted Composite Banking Index*	*Weighted Composite Agricultural Index*	*Weighted Composite Industrial Index*
Ahmedabad	2.72	0.34	2.65
Gandhinagar	3.18	0.45	0.50
Kheda	1.73	0.34	0.64
Surat	1.67	0.36	1.84
Vadodara	2.27	0.31	0.77
Mahesana	0.71	0.32	0.56
Sabar Kantha	0.43	0.20	0.36
Rajkot	1.39	0.16	1.50
Valsad	1.86	0.41	1.12
Bhavnagar	0.89	0.19	0.57
Junagadh	1.13	0.29	0.29
Bharuch	0.83	0.14	0.58

(Contd.)

(Contd. Appendix -8)

Districts of Gujarat	*Weighted Composite Banking Index*	*Weighted Composite Agricultural Index*	*Weighted Composite Industrial Index*
Amreli	0.52	0.08	0.28
Jamnagar	1.44	0.06	0.70
Surendranagar	0.56	-0.005	0.50
Banas Kantha	0.39	0.09	0.19
Panch Mahals	0.41	0.40	0.22
Kachchh	2.58	0.23	0.22
The Dangs	0.34	0.23	0.01
MAXIMUM VALUES	1.76	0.31	1.04
MINIMUM VALUES	0.88	0.18	0.38

Source: Self calculated.

Appendix 9: District-wise Weighted Composite Index of Different Components of Infrastructure in Gujarat (2000-01)

Districts of Gujarat	*Weighted Composite Index of Transportation*	*Weighted Index of Irrigation*	*Weighted Index of Drinking Water*	*Weighted Index of Electricity*
Ahmedabad	0.309489196	0.410331	0.431336	0.366093
Gandhinagar	0.646534096	0.849357	0.445135	0.366093
Kheda	0.389309738	0.64002	0.439348	0.366093
Surat	0.384603451	0.680219	0.441129	0.365361
Vadodara	0.363356271	0.521573	0.434007	0.362432
Mahesana	0.312480066	0.749366	0.436677	0.366093
Sabar Kantha	0.300914397	0.458747	0.438903	0.366093
Rajkot	0.194196638	0.301238	0.439348	0.366093
Valsad	0.366076209	0.34169	0.441129	0.345592
Bhavnagar	0.18180549	0.263441	0.434897	0.365727
Junagadh	0.207698733	0.243721	0.403292	0.357307
Bharuch	0.15450302	0.330692	0.430445	0.365361
Amreli	0.140732165	0.176344	0.433561	0.366093
Jamnagar	0.021417839	0.130077	0.41086	0.349253

(Contd.)

(Contd. Appendix -9)

Districts of Gujarat	*Weighted Composite Index of Transportation*	*Weighted Index of Irrigation*	*Weighted Index of Drinking Water*	*Weighted Index of Electricity*
Surendranagar	0.047422208	0.2441	0.399286	0.366093
Banas Kantha	0.172305121	0.57239	0.420653	0.360601
Panch Mahals	0.328215159	0.180136	0.436677	0.366093
Kachchh	-0.271028958	0.341437	0.398841	0.356574
The Dangs	-0.068298077	0.0067	0.436677	0.366093
Patan	0.139878367	0.413239	0.438903	0.366093
Porbandar	0.161523287	0.175838	0.322723	0.311911
Anand	0.452003281	0.949602	0.445135	0.366093
Narmada	0.142291483	0.211233	0.413085	0.351449
Dohad	0.32891134	0.060804	0.438903	0.365727
Navsari	0.52591058	0.723705	0.4438	0.366093
MAXIMUM VALUES	0.33360976	0.525316	0.439104	0.366549
MINIMUM VALUES	0.14097032	0.272764	0.413276	0.354771

Source: Self calculated.

Appendix 9: District-wise Weighted Composite Index of Different Components of Infrastructure in Gujarat (2000-01) Contd.

Districts of Gujarat	*Weighted Composite Index of Banking Facilities*	*Weighted Composite Index of Educational Facilities*	*Weighted Composite Index of Health Facilities*
Ahmedabad	1.2713431	1.625867	0.5173284
Gandhinagar	0.76454582	1.828787	0.9516237
Kheda	0.65982696	1.532018	0.5251376
Surat	0.81369217	1.230875	0.4329339
Vadodara	0.85166632	1.226413	0.5048555
Mahesana	0.51578745	1.491405	0.5582050
Sabar Kantha	0.36843469	1.27424	0.3433700
Rajkot	0.44711485	0.805196	0.1317925
Valsad	0.69277207	1.088591	0.5372678
Bhavnagar	0.27298346	0.639556	0.0974120
Junagadh	0.29004546	0.849821	0.2019071
Bharuch	0.48253584	0.77457	0.2016727
Amreli	0.20663956	0.62987	0.1425094
Jamnagar	0.33711609	0.517524	-0.0352399
Surendranagar	0.19625677	0.53914	0.0282399

(Contd.)

(Contd. Appendix -9)

Districts of Gujarat	Weighted Composite Index of Banking Facilities	Weighted Composite Index of Educational Facilities	Weighted Composite Index of Health Facilities
Banas Kantha	0.19628931	0.70141	0.1416179
Panch Mahals	0.37105196	1.310935	0.5484429
Kachchh	0.29972234	0.324285	-0.0727000
The Dangs	0.12467866	0.584872	0.0772782
Patan	0.3406065	0.584219	0.1208178
Porbandar	0.49208709	0.722407	0.1518384
Anand	1.15332907	1.468939	0.6673853
Narmada	0.23004201	0.766429	0.2686426
Dohad	0.35913817	1.469776	-0.0106093
Navsari	1.35329418	1.302605	0.7675168
MAXIMUM VALUES	0.6950275	1.222298	0.4482709
MINIMUM VALUES	0.3522525	0.800882	0.1756688

Source: Self calculated.

Appendix 10: District-wise Weighted Composite Index of Different Components Related to Economic Growth in Gujarat (2000-01)

Districts of Gujarat	*Weighted Composite Banking Index*	*Weighted Composite Agricultural Index*	*Weighted Composite Industrial Index*
Ahmedabad	4.086683346	0.409285058	2.75193004
Gandhinagar	1.574114339	0.749095549	0.541976296
Kheda	0.644910945	0.446995285	1.1358365
Surat	1.342327716	0.598341924	1.841438176
Vadodara	3.271134597	0.258512291	0.802710013
Mahesana	0.611036326	0.436478641	1.256722306
Sabar Kantha	0.571574751	0.23985168	0.460473634
Rajkot	1.155501612	0.076107157	1.300815105
Valsad	1.186028761	0.512148527	1.963611079
Bhavnagar	1.206256002	0.050117269	0.59147507
Junagadh	0.670761234	0.395815607	0.375042219
Bharuch	1.393895517	0.001472302	1.005827583
Amreli	0.66537997	-0.218736939	0.339749557
Jamnagar	0.998964712	-0.007637257	0.574104712

(Contd.)

(Contd. Appendix -10)

Districts of Gujarat	Weighted Composite Banking Index	Weighted Composite Agricultural Index	Weighted Composite Industrial Index
Surendranagar	0.641659559	-0.247144065	0.483159777
Banas Kantha	0.526780178	0.096408287	0.266495415
Panch Mahals	0.518776346	0.256551224	0.483507119
Kachchh	1.678829392	-0.260720945	0.229339628
The Dangs	0.296991904	0.003433917	0.012415104
Patan	0.626422287	-0.027067786	0.077653496
Porbandar	2.010639844	0.300602052	0.065216662
Anand	1.258257721	0.612327468	0.113683772
Narmada	0.368904348	0.052672556	0.070004067
Dohad	0.338008075	0.277834219	0.040898912
Navsari	1.36716482	0.730748486	0.21293155
MAXIMUM VALUES	1.607241809	0.37555618	1.02732493
MINIMUM VALUES	0.713638535	0.08392322	0.332436493

Source: Self calculated.

Appendix 11: District-wise Weighted Composite Index of Different Components of Infrastructure in Gujarat (2009-10)

Districts of Gujarat	*Weighted Composite Index of Transportation*	*Weighted Index of Irrigation*	*Weighted Index of Drinking Water*	*Weighted Index of Electricity*
Ahmedabad	0.31201188	0.396794	0.323279642	0.064851
Gandhinagar	0.64427463	0.597598	0.323279642	0.064851
Kheda	0.37051592	0.59541	0.323279642	0.064851
Surat	0.38611507	0.503365	0.323279642	0.064851
Vadodara	0.34878947	0.375183	0.323279642	0.064851
Mahesana	0.29315238	0.532676	0.323279642	0.064851
Sabar Kantha	0.22804344	0.370983	0.323279642	0.064851
Rajkot	0.14230405	0.349284	0.323279642	0.064851
Valsad	0.42937125	0.399594	0.323279642	0.061998
Bhavnagar	0.10466927	0.356459	0.323279642	0.064851
Junagadh	0.14148896	0.369233	0.323279642	0.064851
Bharuch	0.06035919	0.32181	0.323279642	0.064851
Amreli	0.02400328	0.212353	0.323279642	0.064851
Jamnagar	-0.0881985	0.252689	0.322342131	0.064759

(Contd.)

(Contd. Appendix -11)

Districts of Gujarat	*Weighted Composite Index of Transportation*	*Weighted Index of Irrigation*	*Weighted Index of Drinking Water*	*Weighted Index of Electricity*
Surendranagar	-0.0820712	0.230115	0.323279642	0.064851
Banas Kantha	0.08779124	0.451829	0.320693405	0.062245
Panch Mahals	0.29249189	0.185142	0.323279642	0.064851
Kachchh	-0.5130864	0.235277	0.280962337	0.063241
The Dangs	-0.3547194	0.004637	0.323279642	0.064851
Patan	0.04480214	0.270538	0.323279642	0.064851
Porbandar	0.08600647	0.225827	0.323279642	0.058626
Anand	0.45924857	0.735229	0.323279642	0.064851
Narmada	0.01880356	0.342372	0.323279642	0.063554
Dohad	0.30921532	0.215153	0.323279642	0.064851
Navsari	0.55701756	0.537401	0.323279642	0.064851
MAXIMUM VALUES	0.3044304	0.442886	0.325671747	0.064981
MINIMUM VALUES	0.0397616	0.28247	0.317220253	0.063547

Source: Self calculated.

Appendix 11: District-wise Weighted Composite Index of Different Components of Infrastructure in Gujarat (2009-10) (Contd.)

Districts of Gujarat	*Weighted Composite Index of Banking Facilities*	*Weighted Composite Index of Educational Facilities*	*Weighted Composite Index of Health Facilities*
Ahmedabad	0.995521	1.327297204	0.3551322
Gandhinagar	0.59224	1.656777507	0.9310524
Kheda	0.386083	1.248213149	0.5449444
Surat	0.981444	1.859270452	0.6574678
Vadodara	0.599937	1.092643199	0.4165378
Mahesana	0.377224	0.891417123	0.5128572
Sabar Kantha	0.201443	1.060193773	0.3442479
Rajkot	0.29202	0.742737532	0.1359167
Valsad	0.44672	1.070100956	0.6021447
Bhavnagar	0.188903	0.51380137	0.1335737
Junagadh	0.207321	0.772425059	0.2502191
Bharuch	0.240366	0.517512513	0.1759404
Amreli	0.149677	0.398699025	0.1319143
Jamnagar	0.128976	0.316751835	-0.0877220

(Contd.)

(Contd. Appendix -11)

Districts of Gujarat	Weighted Composite Index of Banking Facilities	Weighted Composite Index of Educational Facilities	Weighted Composite Index of Health Facilities
Surendranagar	0.112279	0.308948854	0.0256528
Banas Kantha	0.103221	0.576184849	0.2220230
Panch Mahals	0.203583	1.302127472	0.5541390
Kachchh	0.049505	0.083958076	-0.0929007
The Dangs	0.047094	0.507642011	0.0824619
Patan	0.134821	0.461216126	0.1334260
Porbandar	0.250472	0.550003925	-0.0848603
Anand	0.686651	1.319682964	0.6853590
Narmada	0.113788	0.586223156	0.2628035
Dohad	0.212816	1.252933049	0.7060680
Navsari	0.766197	1.076440635	0.7813664
MAXIMUM VALUES	0.477769	1.086962389	0.4806525
MINIMUM VALUES	0.199695	0.632493756	0.18972873

Source: Self calculated.

Appendix 12: District-wise Weighted Composite Index of Different Components Related to Economic Growth in Gujarat (2009-10)

Districts of Gujarat	*Weighted Composite Banking Index*	*Weighted Composite Agricultural Index*	*Weighted Composite Industrial Index*
Ahmedabad	4.094177737	0.568126201	2.123244307
Gandhinagar	1.727249132	0.562132799	0.650995231
Kheda	0.570043073	0.556557067	1.004226276
Surat	1.613470573	0.560381257	2.517784285
Vadodara	2.97159112	0.44559059	0.764115584
Mahesana	1.089290904	0.489588246	1.125214271
Sabar Kantha	0.84479643	0.453390817	0.467805266
Rajkot	1.653856704	0.514628912	1.144223333
Valsad	1.105297195	0.482974183	1.627955734
Bhavnagar	0.812035552	0.471962412	0.512789421
Junagadh	0.682709418	0.567813079	0.374852943
Bharuch	0.939664291	0.3007017	1.069559643
Amreli	0.762796257	0.263966307	0.354942895
Jamnagar	0.760044247	0.392583627	0.616731735

(Contd.)

(Contd. Appendix -12)

Districts of Gujarat	*Weighted Composite Banking Index*	*Weighted Composite Agricultural Index*	*Weighted Composite Industrial Index*
Surendranagar	0.749038055	0.140911758	0.506019083
Banas Kantha	0.899328773	0.365258148	0.273725321
Panch Mahals	0.538016936	0.440799734	0.435850816
Kachchh	1.118570091	0.169060131	0.238035597
The Dangs	0.444285835	0.25356818	0.022496827
Patan	0.723094101	0.275398582	0.194942076
Porbandar	0.873355943	0.378656457	0.155385585
Anand	0.885619768	0.660579748	0.22033211
Narmada	0.586484124	0.361287753	0.154244042
Dohad	0.428461618	0.513522043	0.091070866
Navsari	0.871970979	0.522810269	0.456695667
MAXIMUM VALUES	1.520642207	0.495986794	1.000198803
MINIMUM VALUES	0.698977702	0.360993206	0.36806031

Source: Self calculated.

Appendix 13: Total Public Expenditure (Revenue+Capital) Pattern in Gujarat (Rs. in crore)

Sr. No.	*Item*	*1991-92*	*1992-93*	*1993-94*	*1994-95*
I.	Developmental Expenditure	5063.36	5634.48	5917.63	6530.72
A	Social Services	2011.65	2138	2505.14	2834.49
i.	Education, Sports, Arts and Culture	1078.41	1145.45	1378.65	1571.74
ii.	Health and Family Welfare	285.18	316.36	357.92	414.57
iii.	Water Supply, Sanitation, Housing and Urban Development	248.45	311.02	330.68	362.6
iv.	Information and Broadcasting	12.16	11.88	11.54	12.68
v.	Welfare of SCs, STs and OBCs	137.22	168.91	186.51	206.06
vi.	Labour and Labour Welfare	41.52	44.8	53.17	58.51
vii.	Social Welfare and Nutrition	198.57	128.69	175.35	195.44
viii.	Others	10.14	10.89	11.32	12.89

(Contd.)

(Contd. Appendix -13)

Sr. No.	Item	1991-92	1992-93	1993-94	1994-95
B.	Economic Services	3051.71	3496.48	3412.49	3696.23
i.	Agriculture and Allied Services	331.89	344.93	518.56	457.94
ii.	Rural Development	287.27	275.95	301.5	307.91
iii.	Special Area Programmes	15.46	17.95	16.61	19.41
iv.	Irrigation and Flood Control	915.1	939.12	892.63	1266.11
v.	Energy	825.46	1282.15	1079.8	1016.75
vi.	Industry and Minerals	229.6	179.38	124	181.38
vii.	Transport and Communication	365.16	394.21	408.64	384.45
viii.	Science, Technology and Environment	0.23	0.33	0.77	0.70
ix.	General Economic Services	81.18	62.46	69.98	61.58
II.	Non-Developmental and Others Expenditure	2722.12	3053.74	3380.51	2981.77
III.	Total Expenditure (I+II)	7785.48	8688.22	9298.14	9512.49

Source: Statistical Abstract of Gujarat States and Socio-Economic Review, Gujarat State (for different years).

Appendix 13: Total Public Expenditure (Revenue+Capital) Pattern in Gujarat (Rs. in crore) (Contd.)

Sr. No.	*Item*	*1995-96*	*1996-97*	*1997-98*	*1998-99*	*1999-00*
I.	Developmental Expenditure	7662.8	8673.85	10570.53	13671.02	14905.62
A	Social Services	3266.86	3637.09	4464.61	5927.85	6920.88
i.	Education, Sports, Arts and Culture	1886.96	2061.03	2303.55	3141.15	3412.01
ii.	Health and Family welfare	470.89	523.02	639.75	877.17	951.21
iii.	Water supply, Sanitation, Housing and Urban Development	375.76	453.22	578.8	967.05	1244.44
iv.	Information and Broadcasting	13.81	17.14	17.37	21.22	22.24
v.	Welfare of SCs, STs and OBCs	225.6	255.99	296.36	367.61	431.85
vi.	Labour and Labour Welfare	63.85	72.42	78.2	97.19	108.29
vii.	Social Welfare and Nutrition	215.53	239.47	533.66	434.94	731.62
viii	Others	14.46	14.8	16.92	21.52	19.22

(Contd.)

(Contd. Appendix -13)

Sr. No.	*Item*	*1995-96*	*1996-97*	*1997-98*	*1998-99*	*1999-00*
B.	Economic Services	4395.94	5036.76	6105.92	7743.17	7984.74
i.	Agriculture and Allied Services	492.18	561.49	639.46	768.47	899.71
ii.	Rural Development	352.45	370.11	425.77	612.61	565.08
iii.	Special Area Programmes	22.99	23.9	22.29	28	26.24
iv.	Irrigation and Flood Control	1615.39	1970.26	2409.8	2897.62	3199.80
v.	Energy	914.99	1179.42	1591.83	2017.29	1716.91
vi.	Industry and Minerals	353.8	207.76	188.1	300.41	319.22
vii.	Transport and Communication	505.38	541.64	654.42	918.93	944.20
viii.	Science, Technology and Environment	0.68	1.1	2.56	3.1	15.19
ix.	General Economic Services	138.08	181.08	171.69	196.74	298.39
II.	Non-Developmental and Others Expenditure	3147.78	4352.05	4555.84	5584.97	7644.52
III.	Total Expenditure (I+II)	10810.58	13025.9	15126.37	19255.99	22550.14

Source: Statistical Abstract of Gujarat States and Socio-Economic Review, Gujarat State (for different years).

Appendix 13: Total Public Expenditure (Revenue+Capital) Pattern in Gujarat (Rs. in crore) (Contd.)

Sr. No.	Item	2000-01	2001-02	2002-03	2003-04	2004-05
I.	Developmental Expenditure	19610.98	17295.5	15608.49	16321.09	18538.98
A	Social Services	8779.58	8583.01	7557.73	8312.5	9303.61
i.	Education, Sports, Arts and Culture	3684.77	3263.55	3634.36	3692.65	4001.94
ii.	Health and Family welfare	918.92	728.77	863.54	886.68	971.07
iii.	Water supply, Sanitation, Housing and Urban Development	1712.83	796.03	1141.73	1552.99	2072.22
iv.	Information and Broadcasting	29.5	19.9	22.16	27.67	22.93
v.	Welfare of SCs, STs and OBCs	438.04	348	402.55	511.67	642.60
vi.	Labour and Labour Welfare	121.21	100.54	122.68	120.58	120.18
vii.	Social Welfare and Nutrition	1854.83	2758	807.49	861.51	899.75
viii.	Others	19.48	568.22	563.22	658.75	572.92

(Contd.)

(Contd. Appendix -13)

Sr. No.	Item	2000-01	2001-02	2002-03	2003-04	2004-05
B.	Economic Services	10831.4	8712.49	8050.76	8008.59	9235.37
i.	Agriculture and Allied Services	917.59	1024.31	719.7	929.77	1049.34
ii.	Rural Development	760.73	379.14	578.91	606.3	808.18
iii.	Special Area Programmes	29.35	24.57	25.54	29.16	31.91
iv.	Irrigation and Flood Control	3100.6	2335.3	2787.42	1710.48	2140.84
v.	Energy	4155.06	3516.82	2301.65	2866.91	2871.84
vi.	Industry and Minerals	430.44	376.85	277.65	204.99	395.85
vii.	Transport and Communication	1076.02	838.39	1085.82	1275.63	1489.50
viii.	Science, Technology and Environment	4.22	3.31	3.7	28.37	50.45
ix.	General Economic Services	357.39	213.8	270.37	356.98	397.46
II.	Non-Developmental and Others Expenditure	11533.26	25918.45	26584.02	23825.68	19490.16
III.	Total Expenditure (I+II)	31144.24	43213.95	42192.51	40146.77	38029.14

Source: Statistical Abstract of Gujarat States and Socio-Economic Review, Gujarat State (for different years).

Appendix 13: Total Public Expenditure (Revenue+Capital) Pattern in Gujarat (Rs. in crore) (Contd.):

Sr. No.	*Item*	*2005-06*	*2006-07*	*2007-08*	*2008-09*	*2009-10*
I.	Developmental Expenditure	21495.35	25283.67	27022.62	35952.96	40418.40
A	Social Services	10094.93	12121.83	13741.85	16972.15	21664.94
i.	Education, Sports, Arts and Culture	4309.30	4986.20	5722.83	6069.66	8315.49
ii.	Health and Family welfare	1069.33	1146.11	1374.27	1601.45	2285.06
iii.	Water supply, Sanitation, Housing and Urban Development	1826.47	2994.73	3979.79	6339.31	7369.86
iv.	Information and Broadcasting	24.86	29.07	43.67	50.83	52.55
v.	Welfare of SCs, STs and OBCs	686.50	728.43	833.06	975.84	1131.50
vi.	Labour and Labour Welfare	133.99	157.64	195.59	238.31	293.21
vii.	Social Welfare and Nutrition	1194.03	1853.69	1108.44	1435.15	1928.56
viii.	Others	850.45	225.96	484.20	261.3	288.71

(Contd.)

(Contd. Appendix -13)

Sr. No.	Item	2005-06	2006-07	2007-08	2008-09	2009-10
B.	Economic Services	11400.42	13161.84	13280.77	18980.81	18753.56
i.	Agriculture and Allied Services	1078.54	1210.11	1630.97	2115.04	2631.8
ii.	Rural Development	787.21	959.48	1104.93	1146.92	1382.19
iii.	Special Area Programmes	29.06	30.14	32.96	35.97	38.70
iv.	Irrigation and Flood Control	2623.81	4380.08	3895.93	7281.37	4573.31
v.	Energy	4156.61	3405.26	2937.10	3920.51	3725.05
vi.	Industry and Minerals	341.72	411.40	480.81	718.06	847.87
vii.	Transport and Communication	1933.86	2154.17	2651.76	3030.25	4435.10
viii.	Science, Technology and Environment	45.65	45.24	29.58	19.47	21.69
ix.	General Economic Services	403.96	565.96	516.73	713.22	1097.75
II.	Non-Developmental and Others Expenditure	12761.42	13938.45	15680.96	15966.92	19939.28
III.	Total Expenditure (I+II)	34256.77	39222.12	42703.58	51919.88	60357.68

Source: Statistical Abstract of Gujarat States and Socio-Economic Review, Gujarat State (for different years).

Bibliography

Antle, John M. 1983. **Infrastructure and Aggregate Agricultural Productivity: International Evidence**. Economic Development and Cultural Change 31(3), April, pp. 609-19.

Anas, Alex. Lee, Kyu Sik and Murray, Michael. May, 1996. **Infrastructure bottlenecks, Private provision and Industrial productivity–A study of Indonesian and Thai Cities**. Policy Research Working Paper 1603. The World Bank. Operations Evaluation Department. Infrastructure and Energy Division. pp. 1-23.

Source: elibrary.worldbank.org/docserver/download/1603.pdf

Aqeel, Anjum. and Butt, Mohamad Sabihuddin. December, 2001. **The relationship between energy consumption and economic growth in Pakistan**. Asia Pacific Development Journal. Vol. 8, No. 2. pp. 101-110.

Arrow, J. Kenneth. June 1962. **The Economic Implications of Learning by Doing. Review of Economic Studies**. Vol. 29. pp. 155-173.

Barro, Robert J. and Salai-i-Martin, Xavier. 2004. **Economic Growth**. Second Edition. MIT Press, Cambridge, MA, U.S.A. ISBN-978-81-203-2551-7. pp. 239-284.

Bhagat, L.N. 1986. **Interregional disparities in agricultural infrastructure: A case study of Bihar**. Indian Journal of Agricultural Economics. Vol. XXXVIII, No. 1, January–March 1986. pp. 56-62.

Bihari, Swarnalekha.1974. **Human resources for economic development with reference to India**. Department of Economics, Banaras Hindu University. pp. 7-20, 115-120.

Source: dspace.vidyanidhi.org.in:8080/dspace/handle/2009/111.

Boopen Seetanah. 2006. **Transport Infrastructure and Economic Growth: Evidence from Africa Using Dynamic Panel Estimates**. The Empirical Economic Letters, 5(1): January, 2006. ISSN 1681 8997.

Brooks, Douglas H. and Stone, Susan F. 2010. **Infrastructure and Trade Facilitation in Asian APEC**. Asian Development Review, Vol. 27, No. 1, pp.135-159.

Source:www2.adb.org/Documents/periodicals/ADR/ADR-VoL27-1-Brooks-stone.pdf.

Calderon, Cesar and Serven, Luis. Sept, 2004. **The effects of infrastructure development on growth and income distribution**. Policy Research Working Paper Series 3400, September 2004. The World Bank. pp. 1-26.

Canning, David and Pedroni, Peter. November, 2004. **The Effect of Infrastructure on Long Run Economic Growth**.

Source:http://web.williams.edu/Economics/wp/pedronii nfra structure.pdf

Centre For Monitoring Indian Economy Pvt. Ltd. (CMIE), Mumbai. October 2000. **Profiles of Districts**.

Centre For Monitoring Indian Economy Pvt. Ltd. (CMIE), Mumbai. August 2011. **Public Finance**.

Dhungel, Kamal Raj. 2008. **A Causal Relationship between Energy Consumption and Economic Growth**. Asia-Pacific Journal (June, 2008). Volume 15, No. 1. pp. 137-148

Dholakia, Ravidra H. 2002. **Economic Reforms and Development Strategy in Gujarat**.

Source: iimahd.iimahd.ernet.in/assets/snippets/workingpaperpdf/2002-12- 02RavindraHDholakia.pdf

Duraisamy, P. and Mahal, Ajay. 2005. **Health, Poverty and Economic Growth in India.** Published in the book **'Financing and Delivery of Health Care Services in India.'** National Commission on Macroeconomics and Health, Ministry of Health and Family Welfare, Government of India, New Delhi. pp. 3-17

Elberts, Randall W. 2009. **Understanding the Contribution of Highway** Investment on National Economic Growth: Comments on Mamuneas's **Study**. W.E. Upjohn Institute for Employment Research.

Source: http://research.upjohn.org/reports/115

Felloni, Fabrizio. Wahl, Thomas. and Wandschneider, Philips. 2001. **Evidence of the Effect of Infrastructure on Agricultural Production**

and Productivity: Implications for China. Pullman: Washington State University. pp. 103-117.

Source: Downloaded from http://www.google.co.in/

Goel, Deepika. 2002. **Impact of Infrastructure on Productivity: Case of Indian Registered Manufacturing**. Working Paper No. 106. Centre for Development Economics. July, 2002.

Source: http://www.cdedse.org/pdf/work106.pdf

Ghosh, Madhusudan. 2006. **Economic Growth and Human Development in Indian states**. Economic and Political Weekly. Vol.41, No. 30, July 29 –August 4, 2006, pp. 3321-3329.

Gujarati, D.N. (2007). **Basic Econometrics**. McGraw-Hill International. New York. Fourth Edition. pp. 792-830.

Hirchman, Albert O. 1961. **The Strategy of Economic Development**. Yale University Press. New Haven. pp. 83-84.

Harbison, Federic. and Myres, Charles A. 1964. **Education, Manpower and Economic Growth: Strategies of Human Resource Development**. McGraw-Hill Book Co. Reviewed by Peterson, Richard A. 1965. American Journal of Sociology. Vol. 70. No. 4. pp. 513-514.

Iqbal, Javed. and Khurran, Nadeem. 2006. **Exploring causal relationship among Social, Real, Monetary and Infrastructure Development in Pakistan**. Pakistan Economic and Social Review, Volume XLIV. No.1(Summer 2006). pp. 39-56.

India Human Development Report, 2011. Institute of Applied Manpower Research, Planning Commission, Government of India. Oxford University Press.

India Today (March 11, 2013). **Budget 2013 cover story**. pp. 38-39.

Jahan, Selim. 2000. **Measuring Human Development: Evolution of the Human Development Index**. pp. 2 to 4.

Source: http://hdr.undp.org/en/media/Jahan_HDI.pdf

Jatain, Satyawan.2007. **Inter-Regional Disparities in the Economic Development of Haryana (1967-2000): An Empirical Study**.

A Thesis- Doctor of Philosophy. Punjab University. Chandigarh.

JBICI Research Paper No. 31. **Impact Assessment of Irrigation Infrastructure Development on Poverty Alleviation: A case study from Pakistan**.

Source: www.jbic.go.jp/en/research/report/research- aper/pdf/rp31_e02.pdf.

Kindleberger, C.P. 1965. **Economic Development**. pp. 2/e,3.

Kuznets, Simon. (March,1955). **Economic Growth and Income Inequality**. American Economic Review 45. pp. 1-28.

Kaur, Parminder. 1991. **Education and Human Resource Development in Rural Punjab : A study of Bathinda District**. A Dissertation- Master of Philosophy. Punjabi University, Patiala.

Koutsoyiannis, A. 2001. **Theory of Econometrics.** Palgrave. pp. 424-436.

Lucas, Robert E. Jr. 1988. **On the Mechanics of Economic Development. Journal of Monetary Economics**. Vol. 22. pp. 3-42.

Lutkepohl, Helmut. Kratzig, Markus. 2004. **Applied Time Series Econometrics**. Cambridge University Press. pp. 87-157.

Myrskylä, Mikko. Kohler, Hans-Peter and Billari, Francesco C. 2000. **Advances in Development Reverse Fertility Declines**. pp. 1-2.

Source: *fugu.ccpr.ucla.edu/.../**Kohler-advances**%20in% 20 **development**.pdfý*

Mohanty, Amar Kumar. Nayak, Narayan Chandra and Chatterjee, Bani. 2009. **Infrastructure development across districts of Orissa. The Indian Economic Journal,** Part IV, Vol. LXXXIX. pp. 619-640.

Mukherjee, Sacchidananda. Chakraborty, Debashis. 2010. **Is there any relationship between Economic Growth and Human Development? Evidence from Indian States**. MPRA Paper No. 22997.

Source: http://mpra.ub.uni-muenchen.de/22997/

Majumder, Rajarshi. November, 2007. **Infrastructure and Regional Development in India**. MRPA Paper No. 4814. Downloaded on 24.10.2010 from http://mpra.ub.uni-muenchen.de/4814/

Mody, Ashoka. 1997. **Infrastructure Development.** Planning Commission. Chapter II, p. 54.

Source: planningcommission.nic.in/plans/stateplan/sdr.../sdr_orich2.doc

Nair, P. R. Gopinathan. 1976. **Education and Economic Development in Kerala**. pp. 1-23 and 159-168.

Source: dspace.vidyanidhi.org.in:8080/dspace/handle/2009/111.

National Human Development Report, 2001. Planning Commission,Government of India. March 2002.

Pradhan, Rudra Prakash.2009. **Education and Economic Growth in India: Using Error Correction Modelling**. International Research

Journal of Finance and Economics. Issue (25) 2009. EuroJournals Publishing, Inc. pp. 140-147.

Prakash, H. May, 2003. **Evaluation of Institutional Base for Infrastructure in Industrial Development of Karnataka. Mysore University**. pp. 1-5 and 165-180. *Source:* dspace.vidyanidhi.org.in:8080/dspace/handle/2009/111

Planning Commission (Secretariat for Infrastructure), 2008. **Definition of Infrastructure**. pp. 1-3. *Source*: http://infrastructure. gov.in/pdf/doi.pdf.

PricewaterhouseCoopers. November, 2008. **Infrastructure in India- A Vast Land of Construction Opportunity.** p. 4.

Source: www.pwc.in/en_IN/in/assets/pdfs/infrastructure_in_ india.pdf

Pillai, Vijayamohan N. 2008. **Infrastructure, Growth and Human Development in Kerala**. Centre for development studies, Prasanth Nagar, Ulloor, Trivandrum, Kerala, India. pp. 1-52.

Source: http://mpra.ub.uni-muenchen.de/7017/

Romer, Paul M. 1986. **Increasing Returns and Long Run Growth. Journal of Political Economy**. Vol. 94. pp. 1002-1037.

Ramirez, Alejandro. Ranis, Gustav and Stewart, Frances (2000), **Economic Growth and Human Development**. QEH Working Paper Series- QEHWPS18. pp. 2-15.

Source: economics.ouls.ox.ac.uk/12332/qehwps18.pdf.

Rossini, Peter. Kupke, Valerie. January, 2012. **Granger Causality Test for the Relationship between House and Land Prices**.

Source: Downloaded on 24.4.2011 from http://www.prres.net/papers/Rossini_Granger_ Causality_test_ relationship_House_and_land_prices.pdf

SAI India. **Infrastructure Development in the Post Crisis Period- Role of SAI Government Audit on Investment in Infrastructure of the Country**. p. 1.

Source: Downloaded on 5.4.2013 from portal2.tcu.gov.br.

Singhal, Divya. 2003. **Human Development in Rajasthan– The Education Challenge**. Maharshi Dayanand and Saraswati University, Ajmer. pp. 1-6, 31-51, 207-212.

Source: dspace.vidyanidhi.org.in:8080/dspace/handle/2009/111

Sultana, Baseerath. 2005. **A Critical Study of Infrastructure Development in Karnataka with special reference to Mysore District**. Mysore University. pp. 1-9, 46-56, 257.

Source: dspace.vidyanidhi.org.in:8080/dspace/handle/2009/111

Seeta Prabhu, K. Sarker, P.C. 1992. **Identification of Levels of Development- Case of Maharashtra**. Economic and Political Weekly 27(36). pp. 1927-1937.

Suryanarayana, M.H. Aggrwal, Ankush. Seeta Prabhu, K. 2011. **Inequality Adjusted Human Development Index for India's States**. UNDP, New Delhi, India.

Source: Downloaded from http://www.undp.org/content/dam/india/docs/inequality_adjusted_human_development_index_for_ indias_state1.pdf

Surekha, S. 2006. **Infrastructure and Economic Development with special reference to Transport and Communication in Karnataka**. Department of Studies in Economics and Co-operation, University of Mysore, Manasagonggotri, Mysore- 570006. pp. 1-28 and 258-275.

Source: dspace.vidyanidhi.org.in:8080/dspace/handle/2009/111

Thaker, Hrima H. and Shiyani, R.L. 2009. **Socio-Economic Development in Gujarat: Rosy Picture with Concerns**. Journal of Rural Development, NIRD, Hyderabad. October-December 2009, Vol. 28, No.(4). pp. 515-528.

Tiwari, A.K. 2000. **Infrastructure and Economic Development in Himachal Pradesh**. Indus Publishing Company, New Delhi. ISBN 81-7387-105-1.

UNDP(1990). **Human Development Report**. p.10.

Venu, Menon Sudha. 2008. **Drivers of Economic Growth in Gujarat**.

Source:mpra.ub.uni-muenchen.de/9233/2/MPRA_ Paper_9233. pdf.

Villanneva, Delano.1994. **Openness, Human Development and Fiscal Policy: Effects on Economic Growth and Speed of Adjustment**. Staff-Papers– International Monetary Fund, Vol. 41, No. 1, March 1994, pp. 1-29.

Source: http://www.jstor.org/stable/3867483.

Wauschkuhn, Markus. 2001. **Telecommunications and Economic Development in China**.

Source: www.iwim.uni_bremen.da/publikationen/pdf/c016.pdf.

World Bank. 1994. **World Development Report 1994: Infrastructure for Development**. Oxford University Press. New York. pp. 1-2, 14-15.

World Bank. 2001. **Privatisation and Basic Infrastructure Services for the Urban Poor**. A policy Research paper. pp. 1-20.

Source: http://go.worldbank.org/WBPB326SCO

Index